Operating Systems
with Linux

John O'Gorman

palgrave

To Meg

First published 2001 by
PALGRAVE
Houndmills, Basingstoke, Hampshire RG21 6XS and
175 Fifth Avenue, New York, NY 10010
Companies and representatives throughout the world

PALGRAVE is the new global academic imprint of
St. Martin's Press LLC Scholarly and Reference Division and
Palgrave Publishers Ltd (formerly Macmillan Press Ltd).

ISBN-10: 0-333-94745-2
ISBN-13: 978-0-333-94745-6

This book is printed on paper suitable for recycling and made
from fully managed and sustained forrest sources. Logging,
pulping and manufacturing processes are expected to conform
to the environmental regulations of the country of origin.

A catalogue record for this book is available from
the British Library

Printed and bound in Great Britain by
Biddles Ltd., King's Lynn, Norfolk

Contents

Preface   ix

1 Introduction   1
1.1   What is an operating system?   1
1.2   What does an operating system do?   2
1.3   Interfaces to operating systems   5
1.4   Historical development of operating systems   6
1.5   Types of operating system   11
1.6   Design of operating systems   15
1.7   Summary   18
1.8   Discussion questions   20

2 Interfaces to an operating system   23
2.1   The system service interface   23
2.2   Interface with the hardware   29
2.3   Summary   35
2.4   Discussion questions   36

3 Process manager   39
3.1   The concept of a process   39
3.2   Use of processes   40
3.3   Processors and processes   41
3.4   Processes and threads   42
3.5   Representing processes   45
3.6   Process creation   48
3.7   Thread creation and termination   51
3.8   Process life cycle   53
3.9   Context switching   57
3.10   Scheduling   59
3.11   Null process   63
3.12   Process termination   64

3.13	Summary	65
3.14	Discussion questions	66

4 Concurrency **69**
4.1	Process interaction	69
4.2	Software solutions for mutual exclusion	73
4.3	Software solutions for two processes	74
4.4	Software solutions for many processes	79
4.5	Summary	84
4.6	Discussion questions	84

5 Low level IPC mechanisms **87**
5.1	The Unix signal mechanism	87
5.2	Implementation of signals	89
5.3	Hardware mechanisms	93
5.4	Semaphores	95
5.5	Applications of semaphores	96
5.6	Producers and consumers	100
5.7	Readers and writers	103
5.8	Implementation of semaphores	111
5.9	System V semaphores	113
5.10	POSIX semaphores	117
5.11	Limitations of semaphores	118
5.12	Sequencers and eventcounts	118
5.13	Summary	122
5.14	Discussion questions	123

6 Higher level mechanisms for IPC **127**
6.1	Data passing mechanisms	127
6.2	Message queues	129
6.3	System V message queues	130
6.4	POSIX message queues	133
6.5	Conditional critical regions	133
6.6	Monitors	136
6.7	Examples using monitors	139
6.8	Active objects	143
6.9	Path expressions	144
6.10	Summary	145
6.11	Discussion questions	146

7 Deadlock **149**
7.1	Terminology and tools	149
7.2	Deadlock prevention	151
7.3	Deadlock avoidance	152
7.4	Deadlock detection and recovery	159

| | 7.5 | Summary | 164 |
| | 7.6 | Discussion questions | 165 |

8	**Memory manager**		**167**
	8.1	Objectives of a memory manager	167
	8.2	Virtual memory	172
	8.3	Base and length registers	173
	8.4	Segmentation	177
	8.5	Cache memory	181
	8.6	Paging	184
	8.7	Architecture independent memory model	190
	8.8	System services for memory management	194
	8.9	Page replacement	196
	8.10	Paged segmentation	201
	8.11	Fetch policies	203
	8.12	Summary	205
	8.13	Discussion questions	206

9	**Input and output**		**209**
	9.1	Design objectives	209
	9.2	Uniform treatment of devices and files	211
	9.3	Directory name space	212
	9.4	Inodes	218
	9.5	Opening files	225
	9.6	File sharing	234
	9.7	File input and output	235
	9.8	Synchronous and asynchronous I/O	237
	9.9	Locks	241
	9.10	Buffering	244
	9.11	Close	247
	9.12	Summary	248
	9.13	Discussion questions	249

10	**Regular file systems**		**253**
	10.1	The file manager	253
	10.2	File system types	254
	10.3	Disk organisation	255
	10.4	An Ext2 partition	260
	10.5	Mounting a file system	268
	10.6	Ext2 file operations	273
	10.7	Ext2 inode operations	276
	10.8	Summary	279
	10.9	Discussion questions	280

11 Special files   **283**
    11.1   Device drivers   283
    11.2   Configuring the kernel   284
    11.3   Operations on devices   286
    11.4   STREAMS   291
    11.5   Terminal I/O   296
    11.6   Summary   299
    11.7   Discussion questions   300

12 IPC files   **301**
    12.1   Unix pipes   301
    12.2   The socket mechanism   304
    12.3   Interprocess communication using sockets   306
    12.4   Unix domain sockets   312
    12.5   Summary   317
    12.6   Discussion questions   318

13 Distributed systems   **321**
    13.1   Features of distributed systems   322
    13.2   Transparency   323
    13.3   System architecture   324
    13.4   Client/server systems   329
    13.5   Naming   330
    13.6   Distributed operating systems   335
    13.7   Environments for distributed computing   338
    13.8   Summary   342
    13.9   Discussion questions   343

14 Communication   **345**
    14.1   Sockets for networking   345
    14.2   IP sockets   347
    14.3   Network interrupt handler   351
    14.4   Extended transport interface   354
    14.5   Remote procedure call   354
    14.6   RPC programming   359
    14.7   Low level RPC programming   366
    14.8   Summary   367
    14.9   Discussion questions   369

15 Concurrency in distributed systems   **371**
    15.1   Event ordering   371
    15.2   Distributed mutual exclusion   375
    15.3   Atomic transactions   379
    15.4   Concurrency control   382
    15.5   Distributed deadlocks   385

15.6	Distributed shared memory	387
15.7	Summary	390
15.8	Discussion questions	392

16 Distributed file systems — **395**

16.1	Introduction	395
16.2	Caching	398
16.3	Replication	399
16.4	DCE distributed file service	401
16.5	Sun network file system	403
16.6	The mount protocol	404
16.7	The NFS daemons	409
16.8	NFS protocols	411
16.9	NFS version 3	413
16.10	Caching with NFS	415
16.11	File locking with NFS	415
16.12	Summary	417
16.13	Discussion questions	418

17 Fault tolerance and security — **421**

17.1	Fault tolerance	421
17.2	Faults in file systems	422
17.3	Faults in distributed systems	424
17.4	Security	425
17.5	Protection mechanisms	427
17.6	Access matrix	429
17.7	Security in distributed systems	430
17.8	Kerberos	434
17.9	Summary	438
17.10	Discussion questions	439

A Further reading — **441**

A.1	Introduction	441
A.2	Interfaces to an operating system	442
A.3	Process manager	442
A.4	Concurrency	442
A.5	Low level IPC mechanisms	443
A.6	Higher level mechanisms for IPC	443
A.7	Deadlock	443
A.8	Memory manager	443
A.9	Input and output	444
A.10	Regular file systems	444
A.11	Special files	444
A.12	IPC files	445
A.13	Distributed systems	445

A.14   Communication   445
A.15   Concurrency in distributed systems   445
A.16   Distributed file systems   446
A.17   Fault tolerance and security   446
A.18   Bibliography   446

Index   **448**

Preface

This book takes an approach to teaching operating systems that is new in several important ways. The approach taken is one that

- Presents the basic theory of operating system design and implementation in some depth.

- Exposes the student to the internals of operating systems through the presentation of how they are actually implemented; throughout the text, the theory is illustrated with one running example using Linux.

- Gives a practical introduction to related system services, using the POSIX interface.

No textbook currently available blends the three elements outlined above. Hence the uniqueness of this present book.

Motivation

I will begin to argue the motivation for a new approach to teaching operating systems by considering why students study operating systems at all. Or maybe even more to the point, why do academics teach it?

There are a number of very good reasons why a study of operating systems should be part of a computer systems course.

- There is a certain minimum knowledge of *how* an operating system does what it does that is required by anyone who is going to be seriously involved in computer systems. This is what distinguishes a professional from someone who merely uses a computer.

- From time to time, decisions have to be made about the selection of an operating system. To make an informed decision on this, it is necessary to understand something about the strengths and weaknesses of contending systems. And this requires a knowledge not just of the terminology used by salespeople, but understanding exactly what the claims and counter-claims actually mean.

- All operating systems are tunable. There are a large number of parameters which can affect their performance. They normally come with these set to default values. Performance can be improved by adjusting values to suit the special circumstances of a particular site.

  But this certainly needs some knowledge of what an operating system is doing. It is just as easy to degrade performance, by making the wrong adjustments. A knowledge of how such tunable parameters affect performance requires some insight into the internals of an operating system.

- At some time or another, every programmer has been faced with a requirement which their particular programming language cannot meet. But the operating system is just waiting there, ready to be of assistance. Even if one does not study systems programming in any great depth, it is important to know that there are such things as system services available, and have some idea of the sort of services they offer.

- Finally, operating systems are some of the largest pieces of software that have yet been written. Many of the ideas and techniques used by system designers can be applied, and are of general use, over the whole field of software development. It is an excellent exercise to analyse the structure of an operating system; to identify the sort of problems that designers are faced with; to see what options are available to solve these problems; to understand the tradeoffs involved in different options; to see which solutions were adopted—and why.

  In general, the study of operating systems is largely concerned with learning the lessons of others. So an operating systems course could and should provide a good background for other courses on software design and development. Students should come out of such a course with knowledge and experience which will be of lasting use in their future careers as software engineers.

A new approach

The reasons just cited as to why operating systems are part of the curriculum have led me to develop an approach to the teaching of this subject, which has three components.

1. Obviously students must be presented with the basic concepts of operating systems, which have developed over the past 50 years. So the theory of operating system design and implementation, as covered by all of the major textbooks, will certainly be investigated in some depth. All courses I am aware of cover this. But many or most of them do not go beyond it.

2. As well as the theory, students should have some degree of exposure to the internals of operating systems.They should see how the mechanisms and algorithms they are learning about are actually implemented in practice. For example, rather than just saying that a process control block contains

such and such information, and maybe drawing a block diagram of it, students are presented with how it is actually declared in C. This ties in with their developing experience of writing programs, and makes it more immediate, more real.

I have found that if this is to be attempted with any hope of success, it is necessary to restrict discussion to one particular system. This goes against the accepted wisdom, that students should be exposed to as many systems as possible, so that they get as broad a view as possible. But in my experience, if students investigate one system sufficiently deeply, they can easily convert to another if and when they have to. They know what they are looking for. It is just a question of 'how is that done here?'

Throughout the book, the theory will be illustrated by one running example. The system chosen is Linux, as implemented on a PC. This system is in widespread use in teaching institutions, and its source code is readily and freely available.

3. There should be a practical, programming aspect to the course. As each particular topic is being examined in theory, and in its practical implementation, students should be introduced to the related system services.

I consider it essential that students at least know that there is such a system interface, and what it can do. But it is also very important that they have practical experience of how to get system services to work for a programmer. This part cannot be taught theoretically—there must be practical work.

While this practical experience is only relevant to the one system under study, students also know that this is possible on all systems—they have only to read the manual. For system services, I use the POSIX interface. It is hard to quibble with that choice.

In this context I put considerable emphasis on error checking. System programming is different from application programming, when it can normally be seen from the screen whether the program worked correctly or not. When a system service is called, for example to change some attribute of the operating system, there is no visible indication of whether the operation was successful or not. So return values must be assiduously checked. A student who is well versed in this is at an advantage in an applications area requiring robust programming.

There are no programs in this book. I believe in giving students the concepts, and the building blocks (system services), and letting them get on from there themselves. The appendix contains dozens of references to the relevant sections of specialist books on systems programming, which contain all the programs one could ever need.

Need for this textbook

At present there is no textbook suitable for a course such as outlined above. An instructor would need to draw material from three textbooks. One of the books on general operating system theory would be needed for the fundamentals. Then, for the internals of the system of choice, a specialist book on the design and implementation of that system would be needed. Finally, for the practical element, students would require one of the textbooks on systems programming.

There is need of a textbook which draws all of these together. Hence the present book, which integrates these three streams into one text. In any of these three areas, the specialist books cover the material more thoroughly. This book has the one, but significant, advantage that it covers all three.

Target audience

The target audience would be students whose lecturers want to combine three elements in an operating systems course: theory, Linux internals, and the POSIX system service interface. It has it all between one set of covers.

It should be attractive to an instructor who is already facing the challenge of drawing material from many sources. But I hope that by providing the material in a convenient format, it will also encourage others to take up this new approach to the teaching of operating systems.

It is aimed particularly at operating systems modules in specialist computer systems or computer science courses; or at computer science majors in general science courses; also possibly at students in specialist postgraduate courses. But it is not aimed directly at computer systems minors, taking 8–12 week courses in operating systems.

Some may be disappointed to find that there is no treatment of system management, or shell programming. This is because, in my experience at least, graduates of the sort of course this book is aimed at do not make careers in system management. Such positions tend to be filled from sub-degree courses, and there are many excellent textbooks available which cover Linux shell programming and system management.

While intended as an academic textbook, it may also be of interest in the non-academic field: for example, to users of Linux who wish to know more.

Required background

This book is not for an absolute beginner. It is assumed that a reader would already have some knowledge of how a computer system works, for example would have completed a module in computer organisation, or computer architecture, or an introduction to computing. The later chapters on distributed systems assume an introductory knowledge of computer networks. For the practical work, an elementary knowledge of C programming is required.

For better or worse, Linux is the system of choice underlying the whole text. I assume that readers would have access to a computer running Linux, and would have some familiarity with one of the Linux shells. In the best Unix tradition, so much source material is also available on a Linux machine. There is a wealth of information in the manual pages, and the source files. The book will be constantly referring readers back to these sources.

Discussion questions

Each chapter has its own set of discussion questions.These are generally intended to lead a student to a deeper appreciation of the material. Some require further reading of manual pages or the recommended reference material. Others require further thought about material already covered. They can be used as the basis for discussion in tutorial groups, or to motivate private study.

Further reading

While this text covers all of the fundamentals, because of its size this coverage is necessarily limited. As it sets out to cover a broader area than traditional texts, it does not treat any specific topic as deeply as these do. It does, however, provide pointers to other material. But unlike most other textbooks, it does not attempt to provide exhaustive references to the secondary, and even less the primary, literature in the subject. I doubt if many students ever make much use of these references.

Instead, it takes a two-stage approach. A reading list of about a dozen volumes is assumed. These cover the three main areas. Between them they contain all of the background reading that might ever be needed for such a course. It is expected that all of these would be available to a student, either in a library reference collection, or on short-term loan. One title from each of the three areas would cover most of the material. The wider choice is to ensure that no matter how much variation there is in the availability of textbooks, a student should always have access to the core material.

For anybody who wishes to go even further into a particular topic, the reading lists in these books will provide anything they desire.

Instructor's manual

The approach proposed in this preface, and taken in the book, is a novel one. In order to encourage lecturers to adopt this approach to teaching operating systems, a separate instructor's manual is also available. This parallels the main text chapter by chapter, and provides assistance in the following areas.

The operating system theory is reinforced by further reading, over and above that given in the main text. This will facilitate lecturers who wish to put more emphasis on algorithms, or who wish to take a more mathematical approach to the subject.

As support for the systems programming part of the course, there are copious references to actual programs as given in standard books on that subject. Many such books also provide these programs on disk. There is no lack of suggestions for project work. This material is in the instructor's manual, rather than in the main text, to facilitate those lecturers who prefer to get their students to work things out for themselves.

Finally, there are comments on each of the discussion questions. These are not solutions, as the questions are not looking for hard fact answers. The questions are intended to form the basis of discussion, for example at tutorials; so the comments indicate a direction in which the discussion might be steered.

Overview

Chapter 2 deals with the interfaces to an operating system. This material is not usually dealt with so early on in a course. But having introduced an operating system as one layer of software in a computer system, it is fitting to get the interfaces out of the way before plunging into the internals of that layer. As the system service interface is an important element of the approach, a general introduction to it should be given at this point.

The second section of Chapter 2, the interface with the hardware, is traditionally dealt with in conjunction with I/O. I think it fits in more neatly here, when dealing with interfaces in general.

Chapter 3 introduces processes and threads, and the data structures used to represent them in Linux. Then it examines process creation, the creation and termination of threads within processes, process state, scheduling, and the termination of processes. This is all traditional material; what is extra here is the explanation of how all of these elements are implemented within the Linux kernel, and the system services which control it from the outside.

The next four chapters deal with concurrency. I firmly believe that for general computer systems students concurrency is best taught in the context of operating systems. It is a logical implication of the process concept. But when at the same time students are given practical work creating processes and threads, using semaphores and message passing mechanisms—then concurrency is no longer a theoretical idea. They see concurrency in action on their own screens. And they find their own programs becoming indeterminate—a shock to everything they have learnt about programming up to this!

Chapter 4 introduces the problem, and looks at software solutions. This is not strictly operating systems. But working through algorithms, seeing where they are wrong, and correcting them, is extremely useful both for getting a feel for concurrency, and for algorithms in general.

Chapter 5 looks at various low level mechanisms available for interprocess communication, signals, semaphores, and eventcounts. The mechanisms available in Unix are examined, from the point of view both of the interface, and of the implementation.

Chapter 6 looks at higher level mechanisms such as message queues, conditional critical regions, monitors, and path expressions. Again, it could be argued that some of this is not operating systems. But it is dealt with in many of the standard textbooks. And I think it is good for a student to be aware of all of the possibilities, from signals at one end to path expressions at the other. The treatment of concurrency is rounded off by Chapter 7, on deadlock.

Chapter 8 is traditional memory management, with the addition of material specific to Linux, and the POSIX interface. Chapter 9 deals with generic, high-level aspects of I/O in Linux, emphasising the role of file descriptors, inodes, and the virtual file system. It also covers synchronous and asynchronous I/O, locks, and buffering.

The next three chapters look at different low-level aspects of I/O. Regular file systems, and in particular Ext2, are dealt with in Chapter 10. This includes both the static layout on disk, and the dynamic aspects of mounting and accessing a file system.

Devices are the subject of Chapter 11. An introduction to STREAMS is included here, even though this is not part of Linux. Some interprocess communication mechanisms, such as pipes and Unix domain sockets, are fully integrated into the I/O system. For this reason they are given a chapter of their own at this point (Chapter 12).

Chapter 13 presents a more or less traditional introduction to distributed systems. Chapter 14 goes on to examine how two machines can actually communicate. This extends the treatment of Unix domain sockets, already seen in Chapter 12, to the IP domain. Then it moves up a step, and examines RPC.

Once the RPC mechanism is available, Chapter 15 goes on to look at how it can be used to develop distributed services, such as distributed concurrency and deadlock control, and shared memory. At present the most developed area is distributed file systems, so Chapter 16 concentrates on that, using NFS as the running example. The final chapter deals with protection and security. This material has been left until now, so that it can include security in distributed systems.

John O'Gorman
University of Limerick

Fault masking

With a group of servers, while some may fail, others continue to provide service.

An operation could be performed on three or more different servers, and majority voting used to identify a failed server, and to mask the fault. Non-functioning servers can also be detected and masked in this way.

At one extreme, all requests could be performed by all servers. Another possibility is to designate one server as the primary, and all the others as backups. The primary is used for all the work, as long as it performs correctly. If it fails, then one of the backup servers takes over. The backup machine could periodically check that the primary is alive and working. But it could just be slow, and seem to be dead.

It is necessary to keep the backup machines up to date. The primary could do this, at fixed intervals. Another possibility is that the secondary could snoop on the network and log all requests, so that when it takes over it can get up to speed by repeating all transactions. Yet another possibility is a dual ported disk, attached to both the primary and one of the backup servers. But as this is a single point of failure, such a disk would need to be replicated.

Recovery

When the failed element has been repaired, it is necessary to notify all the sites in the system, possibly reconfigure logical rings, and even change the coordinator again. Local tables, for example tables of available resources, machine loads, etc., may need to be updated.

In order for a system to be able to recover after a crash, all data that has actually been committed must have been permanently saved. This means at least to disk, and possibly even copies on multiple disks. So each server has a recovery manager, which maintains sufficient state in stable storage to be able to recover from all foreseen faults. While an individual server is recovering, the distributed system as a whole can continue, if there is sufficient replication of resources. If proper consistency controls are in place, then all non-faulty servers should be in the same state, and can vote a majority.

The recovery manager maintains its own recovery file. This is a history of all transactions performed by the server. In practice it is organised as a full copy of all the data items managed by that particular server, made some time in the recent past. This is followed by a history of all changes made to the data since then. At fixed intervals a new recovery file is created, starting with a full copy. The whole procedure is reminiscent of incremental backup.

17.4 Security

It is hardly necessary to argue the need for security in computer systems today. Obviously, confidential information needs to be protected both for commercial reasons, and for personal privacy.

While we think immediately of protecting data, it is also very important to protect programs, to ensure that they cannot be altered or replaced. If not, an intruder could substitute a different version, which would be able to perform all sorts of illegal operations.

Threats to security

Threats to security come at different levels.

- Disclosure of data to unauthorised third parties. Leakage happens when confidential information is accidentally made available to an unauthorised agent. Stealing is when such an agent·takes positive action to access the information.

- Denial of service, so that even though the data is still there, a user can no longer access it.

- Corruption of data, through its being overwritten either intentionally or inadvertently. This can result from hardware or software failure, and can be partial or total. Tampering is when data in the system is changed, in such a way that it still appears to be valid. Vandalism is when data is changed so as to be meaningless.

- Corruption or infiltration of the process which implements security. Remember that it is always the operating system which implements any protection scheme. If the operating system is not properly protected itself, then an intruder could alter it, and thus negate even the strictest protection regime.

Security policy

A security policy is a statement of the rules and practices that regulate how a computer system manages, protects, and distributes sensitive information.

Certain operations are restricted to designated users. The security policy decides whether a given subject (user, process, etc.) can be permitted to gain access to a specific object (resource, data, file, etc.).

Each process has a set of privileges for which the user is authorised, and which give rights to access certain objects, through operating system functions. These privileges are acquired when a user logs on to the system, and are normally inherited by each new process that the user creates. The ideal is to use the fewest privileges for the shortest time.

A computer system should have sufficient hardware and software to enforce a security policy, and offer adequate protection from threats. Such a security policy is implemented by the trusted computing base of a system, which includes the kernel, and code running in the process which enforces the security policy, and which oversees and monitors interactions between subjects and objects.

Orange book model

A classification of computer systems has been developed, based on the strictness of the security policy they implement. It is known as the orange book model. Systems are classified from D up to A1, as follows.

- D: Failed to meet any higher requirements.

- C1: Users can protect private information and keep others from accidentally reading or destroying data.

- C2: Users are individually accountable for their actions. It is possible to record every command a user issues, and identify it with that user.

- B1: There is at least an informal statement of the security policy in use. This must provide the ability to identify data uniquely, both internally and when it is exported. It must also enforce access control over at least selected subjects and objects.

- B2: A clearly defined and documented formal security policy is in place. Access controls must extend to all subjects and objects.

- B3: The portion of the system that runs in kernel mode must be small enough to be subjected to rigorous analysis and test.

- A1: The security policy model must be formally verified.

17.5   Protection mechanisms

Once there is more than one user, or even more than one process, on a machine, it becomes necessary to provide some protection. We need to control the access which processes have to different resources. We have already introduced mechanisms for protection at different places in the operating system. When dealing with memory management, we have seen how a virtual memory checks protection at every memory reference. The input/output manager also implements protection checks each time a file is opened. In a system such as Unix, where peripheral devices are allocated through the file system, the standard file protections also apply to such hardware devices.

But there is a growing need to implement protection mechanisms on a system-wide basis, rather than in an *ad hoc* manner here and there in the operating system. Of course, any worthwhile scheme must allow legitimate sharing, while preventing unauthorised interference.

Protection can be implemented in many different ways, from an all or nothing level, down to a very fine granularity. Generally there is a tradeoff between the granularity of the protection, and the overhead of implementing it.

Physical exclusion

If the system can only be accessed from specific terminals in a designated area, then traditional security methods such as locks or identity checks can be used to control access to those terminals. This level of protection is normally only used in the highest security areas.

Exclusion of unauthorised users

The traditional approach to this is to issue each user with an account name and a password. The problems with passwords are well known. Many systems will not allow a user to set a password which is easily cracked. Obviously for any password based system to work, the password file itself must be inaccessible. It is a common practice that only encrypted versions of passwords are stored, and the encryption algorithm cannot be reversed.

Protection after access

The next level of protection, after access, is the division into user and kernel mode. We have seen how CPUs can only execute privileged instructions when in kernel mode. We have also seen the use of hardware memory protection mechanisms. The combination of these two mechanisms means that information in system space is protected against access by ordinary users. Information on backing store is also protected, because it can only be accessed indirectly by system services, which can validate requests.

This is a common method of protection on multiuser systems. But it is unsatisfactory, because it is all or nothing. A process executing in kernel mode has all privileges, whether it needs them or not.

Protection at the segment level

When dealing with the memory manager, we have seen that each segment can be given different protection. This is noted in the respective descriptor in the segment table. It is possible for two processes to reference the same physical segment through different descriptors with different protection bits set.

All resources, both hardware devices and pseudo devices such as disk files, are represented by data structures in memory. So as long as we can protect these data structures, we can protect the devices and other resources they represent. All protection is then performed by segment protection, implemented by the memory management hardware.

This is certainly an improvement, but it still has the weakness that access rights remain unchanged during the lifetime of a process. A process may need access to a particular segment just once, for example at initialisation. But it retains that right, even though unneeded. This is a potential security hole.

Protection for current activity only

So we introduce the idea of need-to-know, or access rights for the current activity only.

For example, consider two processes performing two way communication through a shared buffer. Access privileges for the buffer segment should be dependent on whether a process is currently engaged in reading or writing. So we need mechanisms for granting and rescinding privileges while a process is running.

Protection domains

This leads on to the notion of protection domains, also known as protection spheres, contexts, or regions. The idea here is to extend the simple two domains—user and kernel—to an arbitrary number. Each domain defines a different set of privileges or capabilities. A process runs in a domain with those capabilities which just allow it to conduct legitimate business. Then if transitions between domains are strictly controlled by the operating system, we have the tightest possible security. Transitions to domains of greater privilege should be vetted with particular care.

17.6 Access matrix

The most general way of tracking who can access what, and how, in a system, is to use an access matrix.

The rows of the matrix represent processes, also known as subjects, or domains. This is the 'who' part. The columns represent the resources, or objects. This is the 'what'. The entries in the array represent the 'how' part.

Figure 17.1 shows an example of a simple access matrix. Entry $[i, j]$ defines the set of operations that a process, executing in domain D_i, can invoke on object O_j.

	File1	File2	File3	CDdrive	Printer
Domain1	Read		Read		
Domain2				Read	Print
Domain3		Read	Execute		
Domain4	Read/Write		Read/Write		

Figure 17.1: Example access matrix

An access matrix for even a small system can grow quite large. Most of the entries will be empty. Such a sparse matrix is very wasteful of space. So they are rarely implemented as actual matrices. Other methods are used, purely to pack the relevant data in more concisely. We will now go on to consider some of these.

No matter how it is implemented, the information in the access matrix should not be accessible to user level processes. It itself is a protected object, maintained by the operating system, accessed by the user only indirectly.

Global table

Each entry in such a table is a set of ordered triples of the form <Domain, Object, RightsSet>. For example, the information from the first row of Figure 17.1 would be encapsulated as <Domain1, File1, Read>, <Domain1, File3, Read>.

If the triple corresponding to a particular operation exists, then that operation is valid. Otherwise it is invalid.

Even though it does not take up as much space as a full access matrix, such a table is usually large. Also, if a particular object can be accessed by every subject, then it must have a separate entry for each domain. This tends to inflate the size of the table.

Capability lists

One way of slicing the access matrix is to have a separate list for each domain. This would consist of the couples <Object, RightsSet>. As such a list specifies what a subject operating in that domain can do, not surprisingly it is known as a capability list. The capability list for Domain1 in Figure 17.1 would be <File1, Read>, <File3, Read>.

Access control lists

Another way of compacting an access matrix is to store each column in the matrix as a separate access list of ordered pairs <Domain, RightsSet>. With this scheme, each object has its own access control list. For example, the access list for File1 in Figure 17.1 would be <Domain1, Read>, <Domain4, Read/Write>.

If there are any default access rights, these could be put at the head of the list, e.g. <AllDomains, RightsSet>. So the defaults would be checked first, before going on to scan the remainder of the list.

A proposed extension to the Ext2 file system would include such access control lists. The links for this already exist in the on disk ext2_inode, but it is not yet implemented in the standard kernel.

17.7 Security in distributed systems

Data passing over communications lines is particularly vulnerable to attack. Eavesdropping on the line is the simplest way of stealing data. Masquerading as a legitimate source of request messages is another way of obtaining unauthorised information. Or valid messages can be intercepted and tampered with, causing servers to perform unauthorised actions. Another technique is to store copies of messages, and replay them at a later time. For example, authorisation to an ATM to issue money could be replayed later, in the hope of effecting a second issue. So a system must assume all messages are untrustworthy, until proven otherwise. This extends to mutual suspicion between clients and servers, hence the need for some form of authentication protocol.

Servers themselves are always in danger of being infiltrated. The best known method is still password cracking. Viruses and worms are other ways to get control of a server. A trojan horse is an unauthorised security loophole, deliberately written in by a programmer.

There are two aspects to security in a distributed system, authentication of the different machines and users in the system, and the protection of messages passing between them.

Authentication

This involves the set of techniques whereby a computer can identify a remote user, or vice versa.

One way authentication

The classic mechanism has been passwords; an improvement would be non-forgeable identifiers, such as fingerprints or voice patterns. These are of less value in a distributed system, as it is relatively easy to substitute a stored copy.

Two way authentication

It is not sufficient for a machine to authenticate a user; the user must also be able to authenticate the machine. It is important to know that it is the legitimate server, and not a fake. A common method is to have one trusted authentication machine in the system. Each user can agree an authentication key with this authentication server. But this means that the server is involved in all transactions, and so can become a bottleneck.

Cryptography

The aim of cryptography is to conceal private information from unauthorised eyes. The sender uses a rule to transform from plaintext to ciphertext; the recipient uses an inverse rule. An improvement on a rule is a function, with a key as a parameter. This relies on the secure distribution and storage of keys.

Cryptography using keys also involves authentication: possession of the appropriate encryption or decryption key can be used to authenticate the sender or receiver. Modern systems are moving towards authentication servers, that authenticate users and issue keys. Of course this is putting all of the eggs in one basket. If this server is compromised, all security is broken. It is now accepted that such security systems need to be rigidly designed, using formal methods.

Secret key encryption

The key is issued in two forms. One is used to encrypt messages. Another, that can be sent securely to the recipient, is used to decrypt them. But secure distribution of such keys is a problem.

One possibility is to use an authentication server to distribute them. Each user has a secret key, known only to that user, and the authentication server. This server maintains a table of <name, secret key> pairs, which is used to authenticate clients.

Suppose, for example, a client A wishes to communicate secretly with B. It first authenticates itself to the server by sending a message encrypted with its secret key. This message asks for a key to communicate with its destination B. This is the first of the sequence of messages illustrated in Figure 17.2.

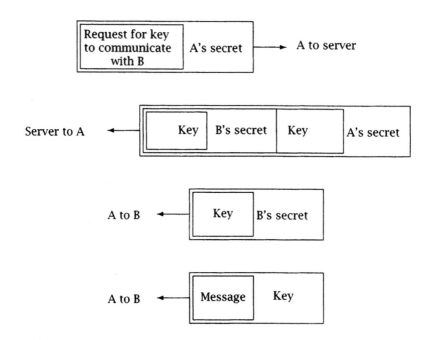

Figure 17.2: Sequence of messages with secret keys

The server uses A's secret key to decrypt this message, so proving that it must have come from A. It then generates a one-off key for this communication between A and B, and sends this key, as well as a copy of this key encrypted with B's secret key, back to A. This whole message is encrypted with A's secret key, so A can decrypt it. This is the second message in Figure 17.2.

A then sends the encrypted version of the one-off key to B. This is the third message in Figure 17.2. As the server originally encrypted this with B's secret key, B is able to decrypt it, and extract the one-off key. A never learns B's secret key.

Then A encrypts its message, using the one-off key, and sends this encrypted message to B. This is the final message in Figure 17.2. B uses the one-off key to decrypt it, thus proving that it must have come from A.

The data encryption standard (DES) is currently the most widely used method for such secret key encryption. With this, 64 bits of plaintext and a 56 bit key produce 64 bits of cyphertext.

Public key encryption

Each participant has two keys, one private, one public, such that either can be used to decrypt a message encrypted with the other. Algorithms have been developed for the generation and use of such key pairs.

Anyone can encrypt a message with the public key, but only the recipient can decrypt it, using the private key. Note that messages are always encrypted with the key of the recipient. However, there must be some way to ensure that the public key is authentic.

Digital signatures

Handwritten signatures are widely used, despite problems with them. With the growth in the number of computer documents, there is a need for third party ability to authenticate such documents, to verify both authorship and ownership. Again, either secret or public keys can be used for this.

Secret keys

This requires the use of an authentication server. The source process sends the message encrypted with its secret key to such a server, which verifies the sender. The server adds a certificate of authenticity, and encrypts the message with the secret key of the destination. The receiver then has the assurance of the server that the message is authentic: see Figure 17.3.

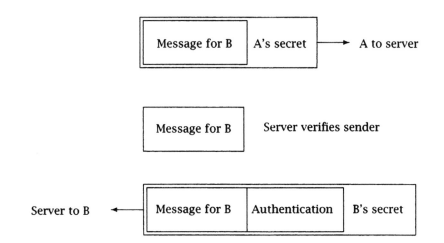

Figure 17.3: Digital signature with secret key

Public keys

The document is encrypted using the private key. Anyone can decrypt it using the public key, but only the originator could have encrypted it. So its authenticity is guaranteed. If the sender wants to ensure that only one particular person can decrypt it, then after it is encrypted with the private key of the sender, that encrypted document is further encrypted with the public key of the recipient. Figure 17.4 shows the message as it actually passes over the network.

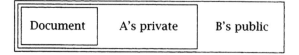

Figure 17.4: Encryption for both security and authentication

Security is guaranteed: only the recipient can unwrap the first layer of encoding, using his private key. Using the public key of the sender to unwrap the inner layer of encoding guarantees the authenticity of the document.

17.8   Kerberos

Kerberos, named after the mythical three-headed guard dog, is an authentication mechanism which was developed specifically for distributed systems. It assumes a system made up of very many untrustworthy workstations, several servers such as file servers, print servers, etc., and one registry server which is absolutely trustworthy. Physical access to this machine will be restricted.

The registry server manages the security database, a sort of successor to the password file in Unix. It consists of two servers, the authentication server, and the ticket granting server. Kerberos assumes its messages may be intercepted, copied, and retransmitted; it guarantees that none of its messages are of any value to an interloper.

The sequence from logging in to when the first authenticated RPC can be sent has three phases. The client first gets an authentication ticket and key for itself from the authentication server. It then uses these to communicate with the ticket granting server, so that it can get a ticket to communicate with an ordinary server, e.g. file, print, etc. After that, it can use that server until the ticket expires. See Figure 17.5.

Initial authentication

The first stage in the Kerberos system is logging on, and identifying yourself. This is only done once, as with a standard Unix system. It is built into the standard logon procedure, and is transparent to the user. But behind the scenes there is quite a lot extra going on. The various steps are as follows.

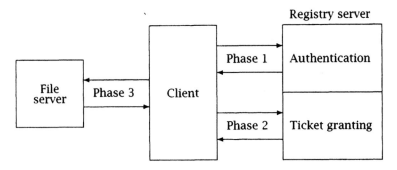

Figure 17.5: Three phases in the Kerberos system

1. The user types in the username, as usual. A message is then sent to the authentication server. This contains two names, the username, and the name of the ticket granting server. As all names are in the public domain, there is nothing to be gained from intercepting this message, so it is sent un-encrypted.

2. The authentication server looks up the encrypted password for the user, and that for the ticket granting server. These encrypted passwords will now be used as secret keys for communication with the user and the server.

3. It then constructs a ticket which will authenticate that user to the ticket granting server. All Kerberos tickets have six fields:

   - login name of the user
   - name of the server it is a ticket for, in this case the ticket granting service
   - network address of the user's workstation
   - session key for communication with the server it is a ticket for—this is just a random number
   - timestamp, to guard against intercepted message replaying, and reuse of old messages
   - expiry time, typically 8 hours, to limit user's access to the system.

   Tickets are always encrypted when passing over the network, as they contain sensitive information, such as the session key. Even the user cannot decrypt a ticket, as that would make it possible to alter the timestamp. As this particular ticket is intended for the ticket granting server, it is encrypted with the secret key of that server.

4. Next a message, consisting of a copy of the session key, and this encrypted ticket, is encrypted with the user's secret key, and sent back to the machine at which the user is attempting to log on.

5. Only when this message arrives is the user prompted for a password. This is encrypted, to generate the user's secret key, and the password is then

removed from memory. Note that the password never travels on the net-work.

6. The user's secret key (the encrypted password) is then used to decrypt the message from the authentication server. The logon program now has an encrypted ticket, and a session key. These two items of information are saved for the duration of the logon session.

The messages passed in this phase are illustrated in Figure 17.6.

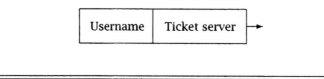

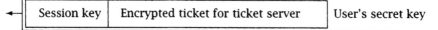

Figure 17.6: Initial exchange of messages with authentication server

Requesting a ticket for a server

Before using any server on the system, the user must first obtain a ticket for that server. The ticket can be reused any number of times, until it expires.

For the purposes of the example here, we will assume that the user is requesting service from a file server. But the procedure is the same, no matter what service is being requested.

1. The user sends a message to the ticket granting server, asking for a ticket for the file server, and a key to encrypt communication with that server. This message has three fields.

    • The encrypted ticket received at logon. This will authenticate the user to the ticket granting server.

    • An authenticator, constructed by the user. It consists of the username, network address, and time. This is encrypted using the session key received at logon. It will be used to check that the user is really the owner of the ticket, and has not stolen it.

    • The name (in clear) of the file server for which it wants a ticket.

    This whole message is not encrypted any further, as the two secret parts of it are already encrypted. Such a message is illustrated in Figure 17.7.

2. The ticket granting server can decrypt the ticket, because it was encrypted with its own secret key. This gives it the session key, with which it can decrypt the authenticator. Now it can check if

    • the ticket is still valid—not time expired

Encrypted ticket for ticket server	Authenticator	Session key	File server name

Figure 17.7: Authenticating a user to a file server

- the logon name in the ticket is the same as the name in the authenticator
- the network address in the ticket is the same as the address in the authenticator
- the time in the authenticator is recent, i.e. within a few seconds. This is to prevent an intruder capturing a valid message, and replaying it at a later time.

3. It now creates a new ticket. Like all Kerberos tickets, this has six fields. The second field is the name of the file server, and the fourth field is a new session key, generated at random. This ticket is encrypted, using the private key of the file server. It gets this key from its own database.

4. Then it sends a message back to the requesting user, consisting of the new session key, and the encrypted ticket. This whole message is encrypted with the original session key. The user has a copy of this stored since logon. The format of such a message is illustrated in Figure 17.8.

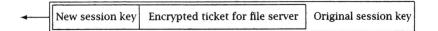

New session key	Encrypted ticket for file server	Original session key

Figure 17.8: Authenticating a user to a file server

5. When the user decrypts this message, it has a key for encrypting messages to the file server, and a ticket for the file server.

These steps are only required the *first* time it wants to use a particular server.

Requesting service

Now that the user has got a session key for communicating with the file server, it carries out the following procedure on each read or write.

1. The user builds a new authenticator, and encrypts it with the session key provided for communicating with the file server.

2. It sends a message to the file server, consisting of the ticket, the encrypted authenticator, and the particular service it is requesting. There is no need to encrypt this message, as the two secret parts of it are already encrypted. A sample message is shown in Figure 17.9.

| Encrypted ticket for file server | Authenticator | Session key | Request |

Figure 17.9: Requesting service of a file server

3. The file server decrypts the ticket, using its own secret key. This gives it the session key.

4. It uses this session key to decrypt the authenticator. It can then perform the same checks as described for the ticket granting server, and decide whether to carry out the request, or not.

While the same ticket and session key can be used for repeated requests to the same server, a new authenticator must be used each time. This is because authenticators are timestamped, and quickly go stale.

ONC with kerberos

Once Kerberos is installed, the ONC RPC mechanism will use it transparently. We have seen that the default authentication is AUTH_NONE. We also saw how to install Unix style authentication, by changing one field (cl_auth) in the handle returned by clnt_create(). Kerberos authentication can be installed in a similar way, and after that it is transparent to the client. The server will only accept a request with a Kerberos ticket. Because of the heavy overhead involved in this, it is possible to implement NFS security in such a way that authentication is done once only, at mount time.

17.9 Summary

1. Faults can be of different types, hardware or software, transient, intermittent, or permanent. A fault tolerant system first tries to detect a fault; then it either masks the fault or fails gracefully.

2. Users must have confidence that their files will be there when required. Disks do fail, so operating systems have procedures built into them to recover from such failures. The simplest method is frequent backups.

3. Distributed systems are particularly prone to faults. The first step is to detect them. Then a system can try to mask them in some way, such as reconfiguring the system to work around the faulty element. It must also be able to recover when the fault is repaired.

4. Threats to security do not just come from malicious outsiders, but can also result from faults within the system itself. They can range from disclosure of information, through denial of service and corruption of data, to losing control of the process which implements security.

Modern computer systems are expected to have a formal description of just how secure they are. The orange book model ranks them from D up to A1.

5. Protection has already been implemented at different places in the operating system. The trend now is to draw all of this together into one protection or security manager. Protection mechanisms can range from physical exclusion, through exclusion of unauthorised users, then protection after access, to fine grained protection domains.

6. The most general way of tracking who can access what, and how, in a system, is to use an access matrix. This can be implemented as a global table, capability lists, or access control lists.

7. Distributed systems are very open to security threats. There are two aspects to this: authentication of servers and clients, and protection of messages passing between them. There is also a need for authentication of machine readable documents.

8. Kerberos is an authentication mechanism designed for distributed systems. It has one absolutely trusted registry server, which does all authentication. It is designed in such a way that all messages containing information that might be of use to an interloper are encrypted.

17.10 Discussion questions

1. Investigate how error correcting codes can be used to recreate corrupted data.

2. Repeating the operation will sometimes clear a transient fault on a disk read. Should the same approach be taken to write faults?

3. Incremental backups only copy those files which have not changed since the last backup. Which feature of the Ext2 file system facilitates this?

4. Investigate the so-called 'Byzantine generals problem'.

5. Discuss the advantages and disadvantages of carrying out access checks only when a file is opened, as opposed to doing it at every read or write.

6. When a password is typed at the keyboard, even though not echoed on the screen, it is still stored somewhere in memory. Would it be possible to find this part of memory, and thus discover another user's password?

7. Suggest ways in which the system could enforce protection on two processes performing two way communication through a shared buffer, so that a process has read access only when it should be reading, and write access only when it should be writing.

8. If a particular security domain had read access to every object, then a capability list for that domain would have to have an entry for every object. Can you suggest some way of abbreviating this?

9. Suggest a safeguard against attempts to intercept and store messages on a network, and replaying them later.

10. Does the use of an authentication server really solve the problem of authentication, or does it just open up the possibility of one really huge hole in security?

11. With reference to the sequence of messages in Figure 17.2, could an imposter masquerade as B, and be able to decrypt the message?

12. With public key encryption, how can you be sure that the public key you are using is really that of your intended recipient, and not that of an imposter, who intercepts the message, and decrypts it?

13. Using the private key to encrypt a document guarantees that only the claimed originator could have encrypted it. But it also means that anyone can read it. Is it possible to have both a digital signature, and an encrypted document?

14. What is the purpose of an authenticator in the Kerberos system?

Further reading A

As this text sets out to cover a broader area than traditional books on operating systems, it does not treat any specific topic as deeply. This appendix provides pointers to other material. But unlike most other textbooks, it does not attempt to provide exhaustive references to the secondary, and even less the primary, literature in the subject.

Instead, it takes a two stage approach. A reading list of about a dozen volumes is assumed, as listed in Section A.18. These cover the three main areas. Between them they contain all of the background reading that might be needed for a course such as covered in this book.

For anybody who wishes to go even further into a particular topic, the reading lists in these books will provide anything they desire.

A.1 Introduction

All books on operating systems cover this introductory material. For example, Silberschatz Chapter 1; Nutt Sections 1.1, 3.2; Tanenbaum and Woodhull Section 1.1; Stallings Chapter 2; Tanenbaum (1992) Chapter 1.

The historical introduction is also covered in Tanenbaum and Woodhull Section 1.2; Stallings Section 2.2.

The history of Unix is introduced in Silberschatz Section 20.1; Stallings Sections 2.6, 2.7; Tanenbaum (1992) Section 7.1.

The history of Linux is outlined in Silberschatz Section 21.1; Card Section 1.1; and Maxwell Chapter 1. Silberschatz deals with the different types of operating systems in Chapter 1, as does Nutt in Section 1.2.

Material on operating system design can be found in Silberschatz Sections 3.1, 3.5, 3.8; Nutt Section 3.1; Tanenbaum and Woodhull Section 1.5; with Unix specific material in Silberschatz Section 20.2; Nutt Section 18.3; Tanenbaum (1992) Section 7.2; and Linux specific material in Silberschatz Section 21.2; Card Chapter 2, and Section 12.2; Beck Section 1.1; and Maxwell Chapter 3.

A.2   Interfaces to an operating system

For more on the system service interface see Silberschatz Sections 2.6, 3.2,
3.3, 20.3; Nutt Section 3.3; Tanenbaum and Woodhull Sections 3.1, 3.2; Haviland Section 1.3. Robbins and Robbins Appendix A, and Gray Chapter 1 are a
good introduction to system programming in Unix, and Gray introduces manual pages in Appendix A. Haviland also covers errno and perror() in Section
2.4, and Appendix A. The system service interface to Linux is discussed in Beck
Section 3.3; Card Section 2.4; and Maxwell Chapter 5.

The interface with the hardware is covered in Silberschatz Section 12.2;
Nutt Section 5.1; Stallings Section 1.7; Tanenbaum and Woodhull Section 3.1;
Tanenbaum (1992) Section 5.1. For polling, see Silberschatz Section 12.2, or
Nutt Section 5.1. Interrupt handling is described in Silberschatz Section 12.2;
Nutt Section 4.5; and Stallings Section 1.4. Silberschatz covers direct memory
access in Section 12.2, as does Nutt in Section 5.1.

A.3   Process manager

General background on process management can be found in Silberschatz Section 4.1; Nutt Chapter 6; Tanenbaum and Woodhull Section 2.1; Stallings Chapter 3; Tanenbaum (1992) Section 2.1. Material specific to Unix is in Silberschatz
Section 20.5; and Tanenbaum (1992) Section 7.3.

The internals of process management is dealt with in Tanenbaum and
Woodhull Sections 2.5, 2.6 (for MINIX); Silberschatz Section 21.4; Beck Sections
3.1, 3.1; Card Chapter 4; and Maxwell Chapter 7 (for Linux).

For more on process creation see Silberschatz Section 4.3, or Nutt Section
2.3. The fork/wait/exec group of system calls are described in Robbins and
Robbins Chapter 2; Grey Chapter 3; and Haviland Chapter 5.

For more information on threads see Silberschatz Chapter 5; Nutt Section
2.4; Stallings Section 4.1; Tanenbaum (1992) Section 12.1; Tanenbaum (1995)
Section 4.1; for threads programming see Robbins and Robbins Chapter 9.

Scheduling is dealt with in Silberschatz Section 4.2 and Chapter 6; Nutt
Chapter 7; Tanenbaum and Woodhull Section 2.4; Stallings Chapters 9, 10;
Tanenbaum (1992) Section 2.4. The Linux scheduling subsystem is described
in Silberschatz Section 21.5; Beck Section 3.2; Card Section 4.6; and Maxwell
Chapter 7.

A.4   Concurrency

Further material on interprocess communication is available in Silberschatz
Sections 4.4, 4.5; Nutt Sections 8.1, 8.2; Tanenbaum and Woodhull Section 2.2;
Stallings Section 5.1; Tanenbaum (1992) Sections 2.2.1-2.2.4. The software
algorithms presented in this chapter are also presented in Silberschatz Sections
7.1-7.3; Nutt Section 8.1; and Stallings Section 5.2.

A.5 Low level IPC mechanisms

An introduction to the concept of a signal in Unix can be found in Silberschatz Section 20.3. For the implementation of signals in Linux, see Silberschatz Section 21.9; Card Chapter 5; Beck Section 3.2; or Maxwell Chapter 6. Signal programming is covered in Robbins and Robbins Chapter 5; Gray Chapter 4; and Haviland Chapter 6. Robbins and Robbins Section 10.4 specifically deals with signal handling in a multi-threaded environment.

For more on hardware locks see Silberschatz Section 7.4; or Stallings Section 5.3.

All textbooks cover semaphores. See Silberschatz Sections 7.5, 7.6; Nutt Section 8.3; Tanenbaum and Woodhull Section 2.2; Stallings Sections 5.4, 5.7; Tanenbaum (1992) Section 2.2. System V semaphores are described in Beck Section 5.5; Card Chapter 11; and Maxwell Chapter 9. Programming with semaphores is covered in Robbins and Robbins Chapter 8, and Sections 10.1, 10.2; Haviland Section 3.3, and in Gray Chapter 7.

More information on sequencers and eventcounts can be found in Nutt Section 9.4; or Tanenbaum (1992) Section 2.2.

A.6 Higher level mechanisms for IPC

The theory on message queues can be found in Nutt Section 9.3; Tanenbaum and Woodhull Section 2.2; Stallings Section 5.6; and Tanenbaum (1992) Section 2.2. System V message queues are described in Beck Section 5.5; Card Chapter 11, especially Sections 11.2 and 11.5; and Maxwell Chapter 9. Gray Chapter 6 and Haviland Section 8.3 cover the programming aspects.

Monitors are described in Silberschatz Section 7.7; Nutt Section 9.2; Tanenbaum and Woodhull Section 2.2; Stallings Section 5.5; and Tanenbaum (1992) Section 2.2. Robbins and Robbins Section 10.3 covers programming with condition variables.

A.7 Deadlock

For further reading on deadlock, see Silberschatz Chapter 8; Nutt Chapter 10; Tanenbaum and Woodhull Section 3.3; Stallings Chapter 6; and Tanenbaum (1992) Chapter 6.

A.8 Memory manager

The hardware aspects of memory management are dealt with by Silberschatz Sections 2.3, 2.4; Nutt Section 4.3; and Stallings Sections 1.5, 1.6. Silberschatz has a section on protection, 2.5.

All textbooks devote a chapter to memory management software: Silberschatz Chapter 9; Nutt Chapter 11; Tanenbaum and Woodhull Chapter 11;

Stallings Chapter 7; Tanenbaum (1992) Chapter 3. For further information on the concept of virtual memory, see Silberschatz Chapter 10 and Section 20.6; Nutt Chapter 12; Stallings Chapter 8; and Tanenbaum (1992) Section 7.3. More specific information on Linux can be found in Silberschatz 21.4; Beck Chapter 4; Card Chapter 8; and Maxwell Chapter 8.

Gray Chapter 8 and Haviland Section 8.3 deal with programming for shared memory.

A.9   Input and output

General background on input and output can be found in Silberschatz Section 11.1; and Tanenbaum (1992) Section 4.1. Directories are covered in Silberschatz Section 11.3; Nutt Section 13.5, 13.6; Tanenbaum and Woodhull Sections 5.1, 5.2; Stallings Section 12.3; Tanenbaum Section 4.2; and Haviland Section 1.1.

Unix specific information is introduced in Silberschatz Sections 20.7, 20.8; Stallings Sections 11.8 and 12.7; and Tanenbaum (1992) Section 7.3. For Linux, see Silberschatz Section 21.7; Beck Sections 6.1, 6.2; and Card Chapter 6. Nutt covers the opening and closing of files in Section 13.2, and devotes Section 5.2 to buffering. Locking is dealt with in Beck Section 5.2; and Haviland, Section 8.2.

Haviland covers I/O programming is Chapter 4.

A.10   Regular file systems

File organisation is covered by Silberschatz Chapter 11; Tanenbaum and Woodhull Section 5.3; Stallings Section 12.2; Tanenbaum (1992) Section 4.3; Card Chapter 6; and Beck Sections 6.1, 6.2. Disk organisation is described in Silberschatz Chapter 13; Nutt Section 5.4; and Stallings Section 12.6.

Unix specific information is introduced in Silberschatz Section 20.7; and (for MINIX) in Tanenbaum and Woodhull Sections 5.6–5.7. The Ext2 file system is described in Silberschatz 21.7; Card Section 6.6; and Beck Section 6.4. Robbins and Robbins covers file related system services in Chapter 3. Haviland deals with Unix file systems, and especially caching, in Section 4.5.

A.11   Special files

General background on devices can be found in Silberschatz Chapter 12; Nutt Chapter 5; Stallings Section 11.1; Tanenbaum (1992) Chapter 5; as well as in Card Chapter 7. Nutt Section 4.4 introduces device hardware. Device drivers are covered in Nutt Section 5.3; and Beck Chapter 7. Further information on terminals can be found in Tanenbaum and Woodhull Section 3.9; and Card Chapter 9. Haviland covers the programming of device files in Section 4.6, and terminal I/O in Chapter 9.

A.12 IPC files

Beck introduces pipes in Section 5.3. Card devotes Chapter 10 to communication with pipes. For pipe programming, see Gray Chapter 5, and Haviland Chapter 7.

A general introduction to sockets can be found in Silberschatz Sections 15.1 and 20.9; or Beck Section 8.2. Haviland covers socket programming in Chapter 10, as does Gray in Chapter 10.

A.13 Distributed systems

For a general introduction to distributed systems, and the design issues involved, see Silberschatz Chapter 14; Nutt Section 17.1; Tanenbaum (1992) Chapter 9; and Tanenbaum (1995) Chapter 1. Tanenbaum deals with system models in (1992) Section 12.2 and (1995) Section 4.2; and processor allocation in (1992) Section 12.3 and (1995) Section 4.3. Stallings covers process migration in Section 14.1. Silberschatz deals with network operating systems in Section 14.1. Distributed operating systems are introduced by Silberschatz in Section 14.1; also Nutt Sections 18.7, 18.8. Finally Silberschatz deals with CORBA in Section 15.4; and Tanenbaum (1995) introduces DCE in Chapter 10.

A.14 Communication

A general introduction to communication in distributed systems can be found in Silberschatz Chapter 14; Nutt Chapter 15; and Stallings Section 13.1.

Client/server architecture is dealt with in Nutt Section 15.6; Stallings Section 13.4; Tanenbaum (1992) Section 10.2; and Tanenbaum (1995) Section 2.3.

Sockets are introduced by Silberschatz Sections 15.1 and 20.9. For networking in Linux, see Silberschatz Section 21.10, but especially Beck Chapter 8. Socket programming is covered by Robbins and Robbins Section 12.4, and Gray Chapter 10. Robbins and Robbins mention the transport layer interface in Section 12.5.

For an overview of RPC see Silberschatz Section 15.2; Nutt Section 17.3; Stallings Section 13.6; Tanenbaum (1992) Section 10.3; and Tanenbaum (1995) Section 2.4. RPC programming is covered by Robbins and Robbins Chapter 14, and Gray Chapter 9. Gray gives syntax diagrams for the ONC RPC language in Appendix C.

A.15 Concurrency in distributed systems

Silberschatz deals with distributed concurrency in Chapter 16; Nutt in Section 17.1; Stallings in Section 14.3; Tanenbaum (1992) in Chapter 11; and Tanenbaum (1995) in Chapter 3.

Silberschatz deals specifically with distributed deadlocks in Section 16.3, as does Stallings in Section 14.4, and Tanenbaum (1995) in Section 3.5.

For further reading on distributed shared memory, see Nutt Section 17.4, or Tanenbaum (1995) Chapter 6.

A.16 Distributed file systems

For a general introduction to distributed file systems, see Silberschatz Chapter 17; Nutt Chapter 16; Tanenbaum (1992) Chapter 13; and Tanenbaum (1995) Chapter 5. Material specific to ONC NFS can be found in Silberschatz Section 17.6. NFS programming is covered by Robbins and Robbins Section 14.8.

A.17 Fault tolerance and security

Fault tolerance is covered by Tanenbaum (1995) Section 4.5. Protection mechanisms are dealt with in Silberschatz Chapter 18; Nutt Section 14.1; Tanenbaum and Woodhull Section 5.5; and Tanenbaum (1992) Section 4.5. For further information on security, see Silberschatz Chapter 19; Nutt Sections 14.2–14.5; Tanenbaum and Woodhull Section 5.4; Stallings Chapter 15; and Tanenbaum (1992) Section 4.4.

A.18 Bibliography

These are the books which have been referenced in this chapter. They cover the three main areas of operating systems theory, Linux internals, and system programming. It is expected that all of these books would be available to a student, either in a library reference collection, or on short-term loan. One title from each of the three areas would cover most of the material. The wider choice is to ensure that no matter how much variation there is in the availability of textbooks, a student should always have access to the core material.

Operating systems theory

Nutt, G. (2000) *Operating Systems a Modern Perspective*, 2nd edn. Reading, MA: Addison-Wesley.

Silberschatz, A. et al. (2000) *Applied Operating System Concepts*. New York: Wiley.

Stallings, W. (1998) *Operating Systems*, 3rd edn. Upper Saddle River, NJ: Prentice Hall.

Tanenbaum, A. (1992) *Modern Operating Systems*. Englewood Cliffs, NJ: Prentice Hall.

Tanenbaum, A. (1995) *Distributed Operating Systems.* Englewood Cliffs, NJ: Prentice Hall.

Tanenbaum, A. and Woodhull, A. (1997) *Operating Systems: Design and Implementation*, 2nd edn. Upper Saddle River, NJ: Prentice Hall.

Linux internals

Beck, M., et al. (1998) *Linux Kernel Internals*, 2nd edn. Harlow, Essex: Addison-Wesley.

Card, R., et al. (1997) *The Linux Kernel Book.* Chichester: Wiley.

Maxwell, S. (1999) *Linux Core Kernel Commentary.* Scottsdale, AZ: The Coriolis Group.

System programming

Gray, J. (1997) *Interprocess Communications in Unix.* Upper Saddle River, NJ: Prentice Hall.

Haviland, K., et al. (1999) *Unix System Programming*, 2nd edn. Harlow, Essex: Addison-Wesley.

Robbins, K. and Robbins, S. (1996) *Practical UNIX Programming.* Upper Saddle River, NJ: Prentice Hall.

Index

abort(), 26
absolute pathname, 214
accept(), 310, 349
access control list, 430
access matrix, 429-430
access permissions, 221
access time, 222
access(), 222
active objects, 143
acyclic graph directory, 215-217
address format, 305
address map, 172, 173, 203
address modification, 173
address space, 172
aio_read(), 239
aio_write(), 239
allocation strategies, 260
Amoeba, 337
anticipatory fetch policies,
    204-205
application program, 2, 5
associative memory, 181, 182
asynchronous event, 41
asynchronous I/O, 237-241
asynchronous operation, 329
atomic transactions, 379-382
atomic updates, 71-72
authentication, 357, 431
    mechanism, 434
    one way, 431
    server, 431-434
    ticket, 434
    two way, 431

authenticator, 436-438
authunix_parms structure, 364
automounter, 407

backing store, 168
backups, 423
banker's algorithm, 155-159
    example, 157-159
base register, 173-177
    protection, 174-175
    relocation, 173-174
batch monitor, 8
batch system, 7, 12, 59
Bell laboratories, 10
Berkeley Internet name domain,
    334
bind(), 309, 349
binding, 357
bitmapped display, 9
block allocation, 268
block bitmap, 263, 268
block device, 285
block group, 260
block group descriptor, 262-263
block size, 222
blocking I/O, 237-238
boot block, 256
bootstrap program, 256
bounded buffer, 120-121, 140
BSD, 11
buddy system, 176
buffer, 70, 100-102, 128
buffer cache, 246-247, 275

buffer_head structure, 246
buffering, 244-247
    algorithm, 245
    motivation, 245
busy waiting, 112
byzantine failure, 424

cache, 169, 181-184, 398-399, 402
    addressing, 181-182
    consistency, 398, 399
    invalidation, 94
    manager, 402
    timing, 183
call back, 416
call by reference, 356
call_body structure, 367
callrpc(), 366
canonical mode, 297
capability list, 430
cascading aborts, 383
cascading mounts, 405
CDFS, 255
character device, 285
chdir(), 214
checksum, 352, 422
chmod(), 221, 244
Chorus, 337
chown(), 222
ciphertext, 431
client authentication, 364
client crash, 359
client process, 395
client stub, 362
client/server, 329-330
clnt_create(), 363, 364, 438
clnt_destroy(), 363
clnt_pcreateerror(), 363
clnt_perrno(), 366
clnt_perror(), 363
clock skew, 371, 415
clone(), 48, 49, 92, 229
close(), 220, 244, 247, 276, 296,
        311, 403
closedir(), 215
Clouds, 337
cluster, 257

command interpreter, 5, 6
commit, 380-385, 414
communication, 3, 345
compatibility, 5
computational speedup, 326
computational state, 39
concurrency, xiv, 3, 8-9, 69-83
    distributed systems, 371-385
concurrency control, 382-385
    locking, 382-385
        implementation, 383-385
        strict two phase, 383
        two phase, 382-383
    optimistic, 385
condition variable, 137-139
conditional critical regions,
        133-136
    example, 134-136
    outline, 134
connect(), 310, 315, 349
content addressable memory, 181
context switching, 57-59
contiguous allocation, 257-258
control register, 287, 289
cooked mode, 297
cookie, 414
cookie verifier, 414
coordinator, 375, 377, 380, 381,
        386, 387
CORBA, 338-339
    object request broker,
        338-339
    overview, 338
corruption of data, 426
corruption of security process, 426
creat(), 225
critical section, 73, 375, 376, 378
cryptography, 431-433
    public key, 433
    secret key, 432-433
cycle stealing, 35

data abstraction, 137
data block, 267-268
data cache, 184
data encryption standard, 433

data token, 402
DCE, 340-342
    directory service, 341
    diskless support, 342
    distributed file service, 342,
        401-402
    remote procedure call, 341
    security service, 341
    threads, 341
    time service, 341, 371-372
DCOM, 339-340
deadlock, 103, 118, 149-164, 196,
        376, 378
    avoidance, 152-159
        distributed systems,
            385-386
        safety algorithm, 157
    conditions, 151
    detection, 159-163
        distributed systems,
            386-387
        example, 161-163
    distributed, 385-387
    prevention, 151-152
        distributed systems, 385
    recovery, 163-164
        distributed systems, 387
default directory, 214
delayed-write caching, 398
denial of service, 426
dentry structure, 226
DES, 433
deserialising, 362
detaching a thread, 53
device driver, 212, 254, 283-284,
        291
    dynamic loading, 284
    dynamic unloading, 284
device number, 221
device register, 29
device structure, 346
device switch, 285
device_struct structure, 285, 286
digital signature, 433-434
direct memory access, 34-35
directory

file, 214, 215, 224, 232
    namespace, 212-218
    removing entry, 218
    service, 401
    tree, 214, 248, 269, 279
dirent structure, 214
dirty bit, 196
dirty page, 389
disclosure of data, 426
disk block allocation, 257-260
    contiguous, 257-258
    file map, 259
    indexed, 259-260
    links, 258
disk label, 256
disk organisation, 255-260
distributed computing, 329
distributed computing
        environment, 340-342
    directory service, 341
    diskless support, 342
    file service, 342
    RPC, 341, 356
    security service, 341
    threads, 341
    time service, 341
distributed file system, 395-417
    transparency, 396
distributed mutual exclusion
    centralised algorithm,
        375-377
    distributed algorithm,
        377-379
distributed operating system,
        335-337
    Amoeba, 337
    Chorus, 337
    Clouds, 337
    Mach, 335-337
        interprocess
            communication, 336-337
        messages, 336
        ports, 336
distributed shared memory,
        387-390
    caching, 389-390

granularity, 389
implementation, 388
ring based, 390
runtime support, 388-389
distributed system, 10, 12, 14,
    321-342
concurrency, 371-385
deadlock avoidance, 385-386
deadlock detection, 386-387
  centralised algorithm,
    386-387
  distributed algorithm, 387
deadlock prevention, 385
economy, 322
fault, 424-425
incremental growth, 323
naming, 330-335
performance, 323
reliability, 322
resource sharing, 322
security, 430-438
transparency, 323-324
  access, 323
  concurrency, 324
  failure, 324
  location, 324
  migration, 324
  performance, 324
  replication, 324
  scaling, 324
distributed transaction, 380-382
DNS, 330, 331
domain name, 331
double indirect block, 264
driver process, 284
dup(), 229
dup2(), 229
duplicate request cache, 415
dynamic relocation, 171

eavesdropping, 430
Eisenberg and McGuire algorithm,
    79-82
elections, 376-377
  bully algorithm, 376
  ring algorithm, 377

Episode file system, 342, 401
errno, 24-26
error checking, xi
error correcting code, 422
ethernet, 295, 351-352
ethhdr structure, 351
event ordering, 371-375
eventcount, 118-122
  ADVANCE, 119
  AWAIT, 119
  READ, 119
exchange instruction, 94
exclusion of unauthorised users,
    428
exec(), 51, 92, 229, 244
exit(), 64
Ext2, 255
  directory, 267
  partition, 260-268
ext2_dir_entry structure, 267
ext2_group_desc structure, 262
ext2_inode structure, 264, 430
ext2_inode_info structure, 273,
    276, 278
ext2_sb_info structure, 272
ext2_super_block structure,
    261-262
extended transport interface, 354
extent, 257
external data representation, 362
external pager, 389

failure, 424
fault
    detecting, 211, 422
    distributed system, 424-425
    file system, 422-424
    masking, 425
    recovery, 422-425
    tolerance, 322, 421-425
fault handling, 4
fchdir(), 214
fcntl(), 239, 242, 416
fetch on demand, 204
fetch policies, 203-205
FIFO, 303-304

file access, 227–228
file descriptor, 228–229, 291, 293,
        296, 301, 308, 354
file handle, 406, 411–414
file manager, 17, 253–254
    objectives, 254
    overview, 253–254
file map, 259
file operations
    devices, 286–291
        ioctl, 290
        lseek, 286
        mmap, 290–291
        open, 291
        poll, 290
        read, 286–289
        readdir, 290
        release, 291
        write, 289–290
    Ext2, 273–276
        mmap, 275
        open, 276
        read, 274
        readdir, 275
        release, 276
        write, 275
file sharing, 234–235
file structure, 230, 231, 233, 234,
        236, 239, 243, 247, 286,
        291, 293, 296, 301, 304,
        308, 311, 312
file system, 3, 253–278
    distributed, 395–417
    fault, 422–424
    mounting, 268–273, 330
    types, 254–255
file type, 221
file_lock structure, 242–244
file_operations structure, 231, 237,
        241, 285, 290, 291, 295
file_system_type structure, 255,
        407
files_struct structure, 48, 228
filter routine, 362
fingerprint, 431

fork(), 48–50, 65, 92, 229, 234,
        244, 293, 301, 302
formatting, 255
fragment, 266–267, 274
free space management
    contiguous, 257–258
    indexed, 260
    links, 258
free(), 167
fstat(), 222
fstatfs(), 270
fsync(), 247
ftp, 330, 395
ftruncate(), 196
function call, 354

general graph directory, 217
general purpose system, 12–13
getcwd(), 214
getgid(), 47
gethostbyaddr(), 334
gethostbyname(), 334
getmsg(), 296
getpeername(), 310
getpid(), 47, 51
getpmsg(), 296
getppid(), 47, 51, 65
getsockopt(), 347
getuid(), 47
global namespace, 396
global table, 430
gossip message, 400
graphical user interface, 5, 6, 9
growing phase, 382

happened before relationship,
        373–375, 377, 387
hard link, 215–216, 221, 411
hard mount, 407
hardware fault, 421
hardware interface, 29–35
hash structure, 219, 246
header, 350
    ethernet, 351
    IP, 352
    TCP, 353

UDP, 352
heavyweight process, 43

I/O channel, 8
I/O procedure, 235-237, 254
I/O processor, 8
I/O subsystem, 211
idempotent, 357, 358
idle workstation, 327
inconsistent retrieval, 382
incremental backup, 423
index block, 259, 264
indexed allocation, 259-260
indirect block, 264
inetd port monitor, 365
infiltration of security process, 426
inode structure, 277, 278
inode bitmap, 263
inode operations Ext2, 276-278
    bmap, 278
    create, 276
    followlink, 278
    link, 277
    lookup, 276
    mkdir, 277
    mknod, 277
    readlink, 278
    readpage, 278
    rename, 278
    rmdir, 277
    symlink, 277
    unlink, 277
    writepage, 278
inode structure, 218, 234, 235,
        237, 244, 247, 264, 270,
        272-274, 276-278, 286,
        291, 293, 296, 301, 304,
        307, 311, 315, 412, 415
inode table, 264-267
inode_operations structure, 223,
        237, 276
inodes, 218-225
    operations on, 222-224,
        276-278
input/output, 3, 7, 17, 209-247
    design objectives, 209-211

character code
    independence, 210
    device independence, 210
    efficiency, 209-210
    error handling, 210-211
    protection, 210
    sharing, 210
    manager, 235
    request block, 284
instruction cache, 184
interactive computing, 9
interactive system, 12-13
interface, 5-6
    definition, 361
    specification, 360-361
        example, 361
    with hardware, 29-35
intermittent fault, 421
Internet, 330-332, 334, 335, 342,
        343
    domain, 346
    domain name system, 334
    protocol, 346
    protocol address, 331
interprocess communication,
        87-122, 225
interrupt, 8
    clock, 34
    distinguishing, 32-33
    handler, 351, 352
    inhibition, 93
    mechanism, 31-34
    priority, 33-34
    priority level, 34
    service routine, 283, 287, 289
ioctl(), 294, 296
IORB, 284
IP packet, 352
ipc_perm structure, 113
iphdr structure, 352
isastream(), 293
isatty(), 297

job control language, 8
jobstep, 164

Kerberos, 434-438
    initial authentication, 434-436
    requesting a ticket, 436-437
    requesting service, 437-438
    ticket, 435
kernel mode, 26, 55, 56, 428
kernel thread, 44
kill(), 88, 89

Lamport's algorithm, 82-83
layered design, 15
lchown(), 222
length register, 173-177
    protection, 174-175
    relocation, 173-174
library functions, 90
lightweight process, 43
limit register, 173-177
    protection, 174-175
    relocation, 173-174
link(), 216
linked allocation, 258
Linux, xi, xii, 5, 11, 18, 88
    directory, 214
    internals, xii
    page faults, 194
    page frames, 185-186
    page replacement, 199
    page table, 187-188
    POSIX semaphores, 117
    scheduling, 61-63
listen(), 310
load balancing, 326
lock bit, 196
lock manager, 383, 402, 416
locking algorithm, 384
locks, 241-244
    advisory, 242
    implementation, 242-244
    mandatory, 244
logging on, 3
logical address, 171, 172, 177
logical block size, 255
lost messages, 358
lost update, 382
lseek(), 232

lstat(), 222

Mach, 335-337
    interprocess communication,
        336-337
    messages, 336
    ports, 336
mail server, 332
malloc(), 167
masking a fault, 422
master server, 334
memory
    compaction, 171, 176-177
    dual ported, 29-30
    extension, 4
    leaks, 363-364
    mapping, 194-195
memory management, 4, 16,
        167-196
    objectives, 167-172
        address mapping, 169-171
        allocation, 167-168
        extension, 171-172
        multi level storage, 168-169
        protection, 171
        sharing, 171
message passing, 127-133
    asynchronous, 128
    synchronous, 129
message priority, 129
message queue, 129-133
    POSIX, 133
    System V, 130-133
        evaluation, 133
        implementation, 130-131
        interface, 131-132
microcomputer, 10
microkernel, 17-18
minicomputer, 10
mkdir(), 214
mknod(), 215, 286, 303
mlock(), 195
mm_struct structure, 191
mmap(), 194, 195, 275, 290, 389
modified bit, 196
modify time, 222

modular design, 16-17
monitor, 136-143
    evaluation, 142-143
    outline, 137
mount protocol, 404-408
    client, 407
    server, 406
mount(), 269, 270, 404, 408
mounting a file system, 268-273
mounting remote directories, 405
mprotect(), 195
mq_close(), 133
mq_open(), 133
mq_receive(), 133
mq_send(), 133
mq_unlink(), 133
msg structure, 130
msgbuf structure, 132
msgctl(), 132
msgget(), 131
msghdr structure, 311, 312
msgrcv(), 132
msgsnd(), 132
msqid_ds structure, 130
msync(), 195
multi-threading, 43
multi-user, 9, 13
multilevel priority queue, 60-61
multiplexing I/O, 239-241
multiprocessor scheduling, 63
munlock(), 195
munmap(), 195
mutual exclusion, 73-83, 97, 120, 287
    distributed, 375-379
        ring algorithm, 379
    many processes, 79-83
    using a guard, 74-75
    using flags and turns, 77-79
    using turns, 75
    using two flags, 76
    using two guards, 76

name cache, 227
name server, 330, 332, 357
name translation, 226-227

named pipes, 303-304
naming schemes, 396-398
network, 321
    device, 291
    file system, 225, 255, 330
    format, 362
    interface card, 346
    interrupt handler, 351-353
    lock manager, 403
    management, 17
    operating system, 10, 12-14, 330, 342
networking, 9
NFS, 403-417
    caching, 415
        client, 415
        server, 415
    daemons, 404, 409-410
        client, 409-410
        server, 409
    locking, 415-417
    protocols, 404, 411-414
        version 2, 411-413
        version 3, 413-414
    semantics, 403
    transparency, 403-404
nfs_inode_info structure, 409, 412, 415
nfs_sb_info structure, 407
non-blocking I/O, 238-239
non-canonical mode, 297
non-forgeable identifier, 431
nowait I/O, 238-239
null process, 63-64

ONC, 359, 438
one phase commit, 380
one way authentication, 431
open file list, 230-231
Open Group, 11
open network computing, 359
open systems, 10
open(), 225, 228, 232, 234, 236, 238, 244, 276, 291, 293, 301, 303, 403, 409
opendir(), 215

opening files, 225-233
OpenVMS, 236
operating system, 1-5
    design, xii, 15-18
    history, 6-11
    internals, x, xii
    parameters, x
    study of, ix-x
    theory, xii
orange book, 427
OS/2, 236

packet_type structure, 352
page frame, 184
page cache, 186, 275
page descriptor, 184, 189
page fault, 189, 204
page frame, 186
page replacement, 196-198
page size, 184-185
page structure, 185, 274, 278
page table, 184, 189
paged segmentation, 201-203
paging, 184-190
    address mapping, 188-189
    evaluation, 189-190
paper tape, 7
parallelism, 326
partition, 256
partitioning computation, 323
password cracking, 431
password file, 334
path expressions, 144-145
pathconf(), 301
pause(), 92
permanent fault, 421
perror(), 26, 229, 363
physical address, 172
physical address space, 171
physical block size, 255
physical exclusion, 428
pidhash, 45-46
pipe(), 301, 302
pipe_inode_info structure, 302
pipelines, 144
pipes, 301-304

evaluation, 304
implementation, 302-303
named, 303-304
placement policies, 175
    best fit, 175
    first fit, 175
    worst fit, 175
plaintext, 431
pointers to blocks, 264-265
poll(), 240-241, 290, 304
pollfd structure, 240
polling, 31
portmapper, 360
POSIX, xi, xii, 11, 87, 194
    condition variable, 139
    message queue, 133
    semaphore, 117-118
        named, 117-118
        unnamed, 117
    shared memory, 196
    thread, 44
presence bit, 180
primary server, 332
printf(), 238
priority, 59-61
    calculating, 62-63
    inversion, 111, 118
procedure call, 354
process, 39
    competition, 70-72
    concept, 39-40
    control block, 45-48
    cooperation, 69-70
    creation, 48-51
        implementation, 48-49
        shell exercise, 49
        system service exercise,
          49-51
    descriptor, 45
    interaction, 69-73
    life cycle, 53-56
    management, 16, 39-65
    migration, 326-327
    pipeline, 69
    representation, 45-48
    state, 53-54, 69

termination, 64-65, 163
use of, 40-41
process control system, 14
processor, 41
processor allocation, 326
processor pool, 328
producer/consumer problem,
    70-71, 100-103, 120-121
program, 39
programmable interrupt
    controller, 33
protection
    after access, 428
    at segment level, 428
    bits, 179, 184
    domains, 429
    for current activity only, 429
    mechanisms, 427-429
proto structure, 313, 315, 316,
    348, 350, 351
proto_ops structure, 307, 310-312
protocol, 305
    IP domain, 345-353
    Unix domain, 305
pseudo terminal, 298
pthread, 44
pthread library, 49
pthread_cancel(), 53
pthread_cond_destroy(), 139
pthread_cond_init(), 139
pthread_cond_signal(), 139
pthread_cond_wait(), 139
pthread_create(), 51
pthread_detach(), 53
pthread_exit(), 53
pthread_join(), 52, 53
pthread_mutex_destroy(), 139
pthread_mutex_init(), 139
pthread_mutex_lock(), 139
pthread_mutex_unlock(), 139
public key, 434
punched cards, 7
putmsg(), 296
putpmsg(), 296

raw mode, 297

read(), 235, 237-240, 296, 301,
    304, 312, 317, 351, 419
read/write interlock, 399
readdir(), 215
readers/writers, 103-111, 141
reading list, xiii, 441
reading replicated files, 399
readv(), 236
real-time system, 59
recent transaction list, 358
recovery file, 425
recovery manager, 425
recvfrom(), 312
recvmsg(), 312
redundancy, 322, 422
reference string, 197
refusing work, 327
region, 190
registration service, 357
registry server, 434
relative pathname, 214
relocating loader, 170
remote procedure call, 329,
    354-367
replacement algorithm
    FIFO, 198
    LRU, 198
    NRU, 198-199
    OPTimal, 197
replica manager, 399
replication, 399-401
    network partitions, 400-401
reply_body structure, 367
request structure, 288, 289
resolving a name, 333-334
resource
    allocation graph, 149-151,
        154, 159
    instance, 149
    management, 4-5, 99
    preemption, 164
    sharing, 4-5
    type, 149
response time, 59
Ritchie, Dennis, 10
rmdir(), 214

rollback, 164
root directory, 257, 268
root inode, 272, 273
root server, 333
RPC, 354-367, 395
    language, 360
    parameter, 354, 356
    program generator, 362
    programming, 359-367
        low level, 366-367
rpc_msg structure, 366
rpcbind, 360
rpcgen, 362, 364

safe state, 153-154
satellite computer, 7, 8
scanf(), 238
sched_get_priority_max(), 62
sched_get_priority_min(), 62
sched_getparam(), 62
sched_getscheduler(), 62
sched_setparam(), 62
sched_setscheduler(), 62
scheduling, 4, 8-9, 59-63
    Linux, 61-63
    multiprocessor, 63
    policy, 62
search path, 213
second chance, 198
second extended file system, 225,
        260-278
secondary server, 332
secret key, 433
security, 3, 227-228, 260, 274,
        325, 425-438
    distributed systems, 430-438
    features, 423
    policy, 426-427
    threats to, 426
segment descriptor, 177
segment fault, 180
segment removal, 180-181
segment table, 177
segmentation, 177-184
    extending memory, 179-180
    implementation, 177-178

protection and sharing, 179
select(), 240-241, 304
sem structure, 114
sem_close(), 118
sem_destroy(), 117
sem_getval(), 117
sem_init(), 117
sem_open(), 117
sem_post(), 117
sem_queue structure, 115
sem_trywait(), 117, 118
sem_unlink(), 118
sem_wait(), 117
semaphore, 95-118
    applications of, 96-111
    definition, 95
    implementation, 111-116
    limitations of, 118
    mutual exclusion, 97
    operations, 96
    POSIX, 117-118
    producer/consumer, 100-103
    reader/writer, 103-111
    resource management, 99
    SIGNAL, 96
    synchronisation, 98-99
    System V, 113-116
    WAIT, 96
sembuf structure, 116
semctl(), 116
semget(), 116
semid_ds structure, 113
semop(), 116
send(), 311
sendmsg(), 312
sendto(), 312
sequencer, 118-122
    TICKET, 119
serial equivalence, 382
serialising, 362
server, 321
    crash, 358
    process, 395
    stub, 362
session key, 435-438
setgid(), 47

setsockopt(), 347
setuid(), 47
shared library, 190
shared memory
    architecture, 72
    distributed, 387-390
        caching, 389-390
        granularity, 389
        implementation, 388
        ring based, 390
        runtime support, 388-389
    POSIX, 196
    System V, 195
shm_open(), 196
shm_unlink(), 196
shmat(), 195
shmctl(), 195
shmdt(), 195
shmget(), 195
shrinking phase, 382
shutdown(), 311
sigaction structure, 92
sigaction(), 92
sigaddset(), 90
sigdelset(), 90
sigemptyset(), 90
sigfillset(), 90
sigismember(), 90
signal, 87-92, 239
    asynchronous, 88-89
    blocking, 90
    default action, 91
    delivery, 91-92
    generation, 89-90
    handler, 91-92, 239
    implementation, 89-92
    pending, 89
    synchronous, 88
    use of, 92
signal_struct structure, 91
sigpending(), 90
sigprocmask(), 90
sigsuspend(), 92
sigwait(), 92
silent failure, 424
single level directory, 213

single resource allocator, 139-140
single user system, 12-13
sk_buff structure, 315-319, 350,
        351
slave server, 334
sleep(), 240
sock structure, 312, 314, 315, 317,
        347-349, 352, 353
sockaddr_in structure, 348
sockaddr_un structure, 314
socket
    accepting connections, 310
    addressing, 305
    binding, 309
    closing a connection, 311
    connecting, 309-311
    creating, 306-309
    I/O subsystem, 308-309
    IP domain, 345-353
        accepting connections, 349
        binding, 348-349
        connecting, 349-350
        creating, 347-348
        receiving data, 351
        requesting a connection,
            349-350
        sending data, 350-351
    mechanism, 304-306
    pairs, 310
    receiving data, 312
    requesting connections, 310
    sending data, 311-312
    system services, 311-312
    TCP, 349
    Unix domain, 312-317
        accepting connections, 315
        binding, 314-315
        connecting, 315-316
        creating, 312-314
        receiving data, 317
        sending data, 316-317
socket structure, 307, 310, 311,
        315, 348, 349, 368
socket(), 301, 306, 310
socketpair(), 310
sockets, 304-317, 345-353

soft mount, 407
software fault, 421
software instruction set, 23
software interrupts, 89
special files, 283-298
spinlock, 95
spooling, 8
stack, 354
standard network format, 356
stat structure, 222
stat(), 222
stateful service, 395-396
stateless service, 395-396, 412
statfs(), 270
static relocation, 170
status manager, 416-417
status register, 30-31
strategy routine, 288
STREAMS, 291-296
    adding modules, 294
    closing, 296
    message processing, 295-296
    multiplexing, 294-295
    opening, 293
    removing modules, 294
    system services, 296
stub, 355
subroutine, 355
Sun network file system, 403-417
Sun network information system,
        334-335
Sun RPC, 359
super block, 260-262
super_block structure, 270
super_operations structure, 271
SVR4, 11
swap space, 168, 180
swapping, 9
symbolic link, 216-217, 265, 411
symlink(), 216
sync(), 247
synchronisation, 70, 98-99,
        119-120, 239
synchronous I/O, 237-241
synchronous operation, 329
sysfs(), 255

system load, 327
system management, 4
system programming, xii
system service, x-xii, 5, 6
    errors, 24-26
    interface, 23-29
    kernel function, 27-29
    library function, 27
    mode change, 27
    programming interface, 24-26
    return value, 24, 50
    sockets, 311-312
    STREAMS, 296
System V
    message queue, 130-133
        evaluation, 133
        implementation, 130-131
        interface, 131-132
    semaphore, 113-116
        indivisibility, 116
        operations, 116
        table, 113-116
    shared memory, 195
system-wide cache, 398

t_accept(), 354
t_bind(), 354
t_close(), 354
t_connect(), 354
t_listen(), 354
t_open(), 354
t_rcv(), 354
t_snd(), 354
t_unbind(), 354
tag, 182
tampering, 430
tape reader, 7
task_struct structure, 46-48, 53,
        54, 57, 60-62, 64, 89-92,
        191, 214, 228, 241, 243,
        244, 250
tcdrain(), 297
tcflush(), 297
tcgetattr(), 297
TCP, 346
tcphdr structure, 353

tcsetattr(), 297
telnet, 298, 299, 326, 330
terminal I/O, 296-298
termios structure, 297
test and set instruction, 93-94
Thompson, Ken, 10
thread, 42-44, 329
    creation, 51-52
    example, 43-44
    implementation, 44
    kernel, 44
    library, 44
    POSIX, 44
    termination, 52-53
thread safe, 44
thread_struct structure, 57, 58
threats to security, 426
ticket granting server, 434
time redundancy, 422
time service
    DCE, 371-372
    Internet time protocol, 372
    network time protocol, 372
    time synchronisation protocol,
        372
    Unix, 372
time slice, 60
timeout, 358, 379
timer interrupt, 199
timesharing, 9, 13
timestamp, 374, 378, 412
TLI, 354
token, 379, 390
token manager, 402
token ring, 295
total backup, 423
transaction
    ACID properties, 380
    distributed, 380-382
    id, 410
    model, 379-380
transient fault, 421
transitions between states, 55
translation look-aside buffer, 181
transmission control protocol, 346
transport level interface, 354

tree-structured directory, 213-215
triple indirect block, 264
trojan horse, 431
truncate(), 196
trusted computing base, 426
ttyname(), 297
two level caching, 398
two level directory, 213
two part naming scheme, 397
two phase commit, 381-382
two way authentication, 431

UDP, 346
udphdr structure, 352
UFS, 255
umask(), 221
umount(), 269, 273, 408
universal time, 371
Unix
    buffer cache, 246-247
    files, 211
    history of, 10-11
    signals, 87-92
    time service, 372
unlink(), 218
unlocking algorithm, 384
user authentication, 410
user datagram protocol, 346
user mode, 26, 55-56, 428
utime(), 222
utimes(), 222

valid bit, 180, 184
VDU terminal, 9
virtual machine, 3, 15, 23
virtual memory, 9, 172-173
vm_area_struct structure, 191,
    275, 291
vm_operations_struct structure,
    193
voice pattern, 431
volatile environment, 58

wait I/O, 237-238
wait(), 64, 65
wait-for graph, 160, 386

wait_queue structure, 54, 241, 243
WIMP interface, 9
working set
    implementation, 201
    model, 199–201
    window, 200
workstation, 321, 324–325, 434
    diskless, 325
    stand-alone, 324–325
write(), 235, 237–239, 290, 296,
        301, 304, 311, 409
write-on-close caching, 398
write-through caching, 390, 398
writev(), 236
writing replicated files, 400
    available copies, 400
    primary copy, 400
    quorum based, 400
    read one/write all, 400

X terminal, 328
XDR, 362
XTI, 354

zombie, 65

Introduction 1

Operating systems have been enjoying a high profile lately. Both OS/2 and Microsoft Windows have been advertised on prime time television. Daily newspapers have carried articles promoting Linux. Operating system vendors have been charged with attempts to monopolise the market. Some journalists have been so carried away as to write of operating system wars. As a result of all of this, most owners of personal computers are aware that something called an operating system is part of their machine.

The term 'operating system' is certainly in common use. At least it is one of the buzzwords regularly presented to us. As with so many of these words, such as 'digital' or 'microwave', we use them with little or no understanding of what they really mean—they are just labels. Not many people understand exactly what an operating system is, and certainly not how it works. To be fair, most people probably do not need such an understanding. But for those who do, this book sets out to provide it.

1.1 What is an operating system?

An operating system is part of the software of a computer. It is a program, a set of instructions for the computer. More than that, it is in fact the most fundamental piece of software running on any computer. Figure 1.1 shows in a very simplified way the basic components of a computer system. But while simple, it is important for understanding just where an operating system fits in. So let us consider the various layers in this figure.

Nowadays, a significant proportion of the population will have used a computer at some time or other. Many people have used a spreadsheet, or a word processor, maybe even an accounting package. These are all applications written by others. It is assumed that most readers of this book will also have written applications of their own, in a programming language such as C.

Figure 1.1 shows the application program interacting with the operating system. You may be wondering about just how this happens when you write a program. Indeed even an experienced programmer may have some doubt that it happens at all. Yet it does, and the details of this interaction will be a significant theme in this book.

user
⇕
application program
⇕
operating system
⇕
hardware

Figure 1.1: Overview of a computer system

The operating system is itself a program, which is written, compiled, tested and debugged just like any other program. It is certainly larger than anything the average student has written so far. This program is run whenever a computer is switched on. It is almost always done automatically, no special command is required. So users may not be aware that it happens every time they switch on a machine. It stays running until the machine is switched off.

But that still leaves the question: why do we need it? The answer is that a 'raw' machine, bare hardware, is very inhospitable. It needs programming in its own binary machine code. Remember—we are dealing with digital computers. Everything is represented by numbers. English text, pictures, programs, whether in C or assembler—all are represented in the machine by numbers in binary format. Programming at this level is definitely not user-friendly.

Another problem with a raw machine is that every make and model of peripheral device needs to be handled differently. So when programming for the bare hardware, input routines have to be written specifically for the actual model of keyboard in use. Then if that program were to be moved to another machine, with even a slightly different model of keyboard, the input part of it would have to be changed. Computers would not have made much progress if things had stayed at that level. Very simply, operating systems were invented to solve these—and other—problems.

Most people who use computers, even those who spend their lives designing computer systems, never see a 'raw' machine. The average user stays at the top level of the diagram, and uses application programs written by others. Even application programmers see and use a (hopefully) user-friendly interface provided by the operating system. If, as a programmer, you were never aware of the operating system, and assumed your programs interacted directly with the hardware, then that is a tribute to how seamlessly the operating system integrates itself into the whole system.

1.2   What does an operating system do?

Now that we have established how and why an operating system fits into a computer system, we can start to discuss what it actually does. An operating system has been likened to a government: it does no productive work itself, but provides an environment which helps others to do productive work.

Ease of use

An operating system helps a user to develop and run programs by providing a convenient environment. Remember that in the context of an operating system, the user is a programmer. In the jargon that has come into use, it provides a virtual machine, instead of the real machine. It does this by supplying simple functions which can be called to carry out the most commonly required operations, particularly in the following areas.

- It deals with logging on to the system, identifying the user, typically with a password, including the ability to change a password. It also provides facilities for logging off.

- After this, it allows users to start programs: sometimes one at a time, sometimes more than one at the same time. All users are familiar with this facility, having launched programs by clicking on icons, or by typing a program name. This may have been thought of as part of the computer system, and not specifically of the operating system. Most systems also have some way of stopping a program in an emergency.

  Another aspect, that may not be so familiar, is the ability to allow programs to communicate among themselves. The pipe facility (|) in Unix uses the operating system for this purpose.

- Concurrency. Larger machines tend to have many users doing different things on them at the same time. Even on smaller personal computers, the trend is towards one user having many applications running at the same time. The operating system arranges that all of this runs smoothly.

- Input and output. As indicated earlier, operating systems cover up the differences between alternative makes and models of devices. So, for example, a programmer can use a `scanf()` statement, and be sure that it will work with all keyboards.

- File systems. Every computer user takes filing systems for granted. Information is saved in a file. It can be a word processor document, a program, a spreadsheet—the user thinks up a name for it, and it is saved somewhere. Next time it is required, as long as the name can be remembered, that data is there ready for use, just as it was left. This includes creating, listing, copying, moving, and deleting files.

  All of that work is done by the operating system.

- Communication with other machines. The operating system hides all of the complexity involved in this, encapsulating it all in a simple function call. It also covers up differences between machines, so that any model of computer can communicate seamlessly with any other.

- Security. The operating system must ensure that unauthorised users do not access the system, and that even authorised users do not exceed their authorisation.

- Error handling and recovery. Things will go wrong sometimes. The operating system is responsible for detecting errors, and dealing with them. Its main aim is not to let the error crash the running program, and certainly not to let it affect other jobs.

- Particularly on larger multi-user systems such as Unix, there will be facilities for system management. These would include things such as adding and deleting users, assigning passwords and quotas, formatting new disks, adding new peripherals, or backing up whole file systems.

    An operating system will be able to monitor and report on the status of the computer. This will vary from such items as file space on a disk, through load on the CPU, to abnormal conditions such as printer off line or out of paper.

    Typically these facilities are not available to an ordinary user—they require special privilege.

Management and sharing of resources

The operating system may be viewed as a manager, responsible for resources such as the CPU, memory, disks, and printers. By having a suitable mix of work in the machine at any one time, the best possible use can be made of all resources.

- The most important resource is the CPU, and the management of this is called scheduling.

- Memory management. This involves keeping track of which parts of memory are in use, and which are free. It also keeps track of which programs the memory in use has been allocated to, and provides mechanisms by which programs can ask for more memory, or give back memory they no longer need.

    Another aspect of memory management is extending memory. This means that the operating system pretends to have very much more memory available than has actually been installed in the machine, and allocates this pretend memory to running programs— and it works!

- Another service that operating systems provide in this area are techniques to overlap input and output with processing. While one program is taking input from the keyboard, another can be writing to a file, while a third is doing some processing. This means that the overall efficiency of the machine is improved.

- Larger machines tend to have many users doing different things on them at the same time. As there is only one memory, and one CPU, it is easy for them to interfere with one another. The operating system sees to it that each separate program is protected from all others.

    Yet sometimes programs do want to interact, to share. So the operating system must be able to allow that, too. This seems contradictory, and would drive a human controller neurotic.

System compatibility

An operating system can hide some differences in hardware between machines. For example, the dozens of different makes and models of PC all run Windows, or Linux. So all application programs run on any of them, despite the differences between them. In fact, when a program will not run on a particular machine, it is almost always because the programmer jumped over the operating system, and contacted the hardware directly. Programmers do this sometimes to make things run faster (games, for example), but at the cost of compatibility.

Referring to Figure 1.1 again, the operating system can be slightly different at the bottom, to suit different hardware, but strictly identical on all machines at the top.

Finally, coming back to our government analogy, it is important that the operating system does all of this efficiently and economically. Resource use by the system, in terms of CPU time, memory, use of the disk, must be reasonable.

1.3 Interfaces to operating systems

The discussion so far could be summed up: an operating system is software, which makes the hardware more useful, more user-friendly. This description may not sit comfortably on many people, who have been using operating systems such as Windows NT, or Unix. It is not what they have known. Unix is very often equated with 'the shell prompt'. The first thing that strikes people about Windows would probably be 'icons you click on'.

There are two common applications with which computer users are very familiar: graphical user interfaces, abbreviated to GUI, such as Windows; and command interpreters, such as one of the Unix shells. The Bash shell, which produces the bash# prompt, is an example.

To see where these fit in, it is essential to understand that they are all only *applications*. They sit on top of, and use, the operating system, just like any other application, just like any other user written program. They are not strictly part of the operating system. True, they always come with it, and it would not be as useful without them. Just as the operating system makes the hardware more user-friendly, so these make the operating system itself more user-friendly.

Any particular operating system can have more than one of these interfaces. For example, Unix can have the C shell, or the Bourne shell, or the Bash shell. There is no reason why one could not be written as a student project—it is only another program.

In Figure 1.2—a slightly different version of Figure 1.1—these user interfaces, indeed all application programs, call system services. These are the *real* interface to the operating system. 'System services' is the name used to describe the set of functions provided by an operating system to enable a user to request service from it. Typically there would be hundreds of these functions. As well as the more obvious ones such as handling disks and other peripherals,

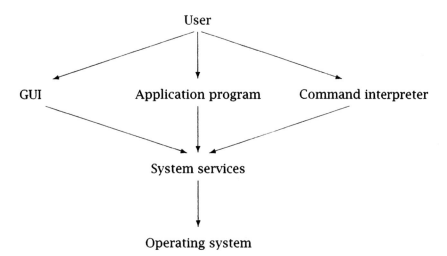

Figure 1.2: Interfaces to an operating system

there will also be services which allow values inside the operating system itself to be queried and set.

Compilers for high-level languages use these system services all the time. For example, output commands such as printf() are translated by the C compiler to calls on the appropriate system service for the underlying operating system.

This book will be dealing with the lower half of Figure 1.2, with the system services and the operating system itself. We will not be dealing with command interpreters, application programs, or GUIs.

1.4   Historical development of operating systems

Operating systems did not just appear fully formed on the computer scene. As with anything else, a knowledge of where we have come from always helps in the understanding of where we are at. So we will look at how operating systems have developed over the past fifty years, to where they are today.

Late 40s—bare hardware

In the beginning, there was only hardware. There was no operating system. The programmer was also the user, and in many cases the designer and builder as well. The programmer did everything an operating system does today.

Programs and data were entered in binary by means of switches on the front of the machine. Each switch represented one bit. Output was by means of lights, with each light representing one bit.

Productivity was very low, both in terms of human users and of the hardware. Only very small programs were feasible, and certainly only one at a time.

Early 50s—punched cards

The very first program run on the machine after it was powered up, called the bootstrap program, was still entered on the switches. But this program instructed the machine how to read from paper tape or from punched cards. Any other program could be punched on paper tape or on cards, and then loaded automatically.

Now that larger programs could be loaded relatively easily, the way was open for the development of high-level languages, and programs that translated from these high-level languages into machine code (compilers).

But we were still in the era of one program at a time. Also there were many manual operations involved in running a computer. And the programmer was still very much the operator.

Late 50s—human interface

This period saw the introduction of specialist operators, who were not programmers themselves, but who tended the machine, fed the programmers' punched cards to the machine, and delivered back the output in the form of cards or printout. The programmer no longer interacted directly with the machine. The operators acted as a *human* interface between the programmer and the hardware.

Attempts were made to reduce the number of manual operations involved, by sequencing jobs of the same kind together. For example, instead of treating jobs on a first come first served basis, the operators would wait until they had three or four COBOL compilations ready to be run, and then process them all together. So the COBOL compiler was loaded only once, instead of three or four times. We would describe this as the beginnings of working in batches. Such batch working certainly made the operators more efficient. But from a programmer's point of view, it was not the most user-friendly of systems. They had lost their direct contact with the machine, and frequently their jobs had to wait in a queue.

Input and output has always been a bottleneck in computing. Card readers could handle about 20 cards per second, even though the CPU could handle data far faster than that. When magnetic tape began to be used with computers, its first application was to ease that bottleneck. Tape readers could handle data equivalent to about 300 cards per second. So for a while, satellite computers were built and used. These were single-purpose machines which copied data from cards to tape at slow speed. Then the tape was rewound, transferred to the main computer, and the data copied from tape to memory, at high speed. When a computation was finished, the results were output to tape at high speed. Then later they were transferred from tape to a printer, at the slow speed of the printer. This was a first attempt to match the speed of a device with the speed of the CPU. The next logical step was multiple satellites, all serving the main computer either on the input or output side. We have here the first hint of more than one thing being done at the same time.

Early 60s—concurrency

Human intervention was another source of delay in the system. Loading cards, mounting and carrying tapes, starting and stopping devices— all of this slowed things down. To get the full advantage from batching, ideally a whole batch of jobs should be processed automatically.

So instead of giving verbal commands to a human operator, the programmer punched instructions on special control cards, which were inserted at the appropriate places before and after the program cards and the data cards. These commands were written in specially developed job control languages, or JCLs. The other side of the coin was the development of the batch monitor. This was a program which read, interpreted, and executed the command cards. Such command interpreters are still with us today, in the form of the Unix shells, or batch files in Microsoft Windows. So here we have the beginning of operating systems as we know them today.

Channels and interrupts A landmark hardware development in the early 60s was the I/O channel. This was a hardware controller that supervised I/O devices; previously such work had been done by the CPU. So as well as the CPU, we now also had peripheral processing units, or PPUs, sometimes known as I/O processors. Once started, such a channel runs independently of the CPU. This allows I/O to be overlapped with computing.

Another hardware development that went along with the channel was the invention of the interrupt mechanism. This allowed the channel to inform the CPU when it had finished.

Most programs spend some of their time doing computation, some doing I/O. When a program is computing, the devices are idle. When it is doing I/O, the CPU is idle. An ideal would be to assign some work to the processor, and the channels, when they would otherwise be idle. This means that more than one program would be running at the one time.

As there was typically only one CPU, only one program could be computing. But as there were several or many devices, more than one program could be doing I/O. As I/O is slow, and computing is fast, such a scheme could begin to match up the disparity in speed between the two.

The new random access devices which were becoming available, drums first, then disks, replaced tapes on the satellite computers. Unlike tapes, these did not need to be rewound. So the card reader could be writing the end of a file to a disk, while the CPU was reading the beginning of the same file from the disk. As there was no longer any need to physically transport tapes from machine to machine, there was a corresponding increase in efficiency. Effectively, the satellite computers became part of the mainframe machine. This mode of operation was known as simultaneous peripheral operation on line, which led to the acronym SPOOL.

Scheduling As the spooling devices were random access, jobs did not have to be executed in the order in which they were submitted, or read from cards. It was now possible to schedule jobs, according to some priority scheme.

This was first implemented with multi-stream batch systems, where there were a number of different job queues, each with a different priority. One might be for small, short jobs such as compiling a single program, another for long production jobs such as the company payroll. All of this led to developments in scheduling, getting the best use of resources, and protection.

Late 60s—interactive computing

All of the developments described to date were still used in batch mode. Now we have the first attempts to provide interactive use at a reasonable cost. The basic idea was to timeshare the computer. As the name implies, each user gets a share of the computer's time, but each user's turn comes around so fast that the system gives the impression that each has a machine of their own. The operating system, which replaced the human operator, had to ensure that all of this worked.

Punched tape and cards were not appropriate for interactive computing. Mechanical tele-typewriters were used for a while, but eventually VDU terminals were developed, and have become almost universal. While these were originally character based, modern workstations now have bitmapped displays, which allow us to use high quality colour graphics.

70s—virtual memory

Computer users found that programs were growing in size, and required more memory than users could afford. The initial solution was to break programs up into smaller subprograms, each of which would fit in the available memory at any one time. These were then swapped in and out as required—a complicated and time-consuming task, known as overlaying.

Eventually operating systems were adapted to cater for this problem as well, and began to provide large virtual, or pretend memory. This allowed larger programs to run, at no extra financial cost, but it slowed machines down. So effectively we were trading speed against cost.

With timesharing, and multi-user systems of all sorts, the issue of protecting one program from another became more and more important. Once again, the responsibility for managing this was placed on the operating system.

80s—graphical interfaces

One of the significant developments of the 80s was the graphical user interface or GUI. As the keyboard had previously replaced the punched card, so now the WIMP (window, icon, mouse, pull-down menu) interface began to supplement, if not replace, the keyboard.

Another significant development was networking. The ability to link machines together led to demands on operating systems to control this communication. There was a certain fusing of the fields of operating systems and computer networks. There was also development in the standardisation of protocols, the rules and regulations, for communication between computers.

90s—distributed systems

Networking has grown from merely connecting machines, to providing shared resources such as file systems or printers. Network operating systems were developed to control this (Windows for Workgroups, Novell, etc.). Now things have got to a stage where we have groups of machines acting as one, collaborating on some task. We talk about distributed systems, and of course they call for distributed operating systems to control this sort of interaction.

Another feature of operating systems in the 90s has been the move to open systems. Previously, operating systems had been developed specifically for particular hardware platforms, e.g. VMS for the VAX, MSDOS for the PC. Now there is a move to build generic operating systems, which would run on any hardware, e.g. OpenVMS on the VAX or Alpha; NT on the PC or Alpha; Unix on almost anything.

Minicomputers and micros

The foregoing sections have given an outline of the mainstream history of operating systems. But there were two other waves of computer development, which overlapped this.

Minicomputers began in the early 60s. At that time computers cost millions of pounds; the earliest minicomputers only cost tens of thousands. Of course there was a catch: they were as primitive as the machines of the 40s. But the price meant that they could be bought as departmental machines, in universities or commercial companies. So there was a significant market for them. They improved much more rapidly than the mainstream machines, as all of the development work had been done. By the late 70s their operating systems had all of the facilities of mainframes.

The third wave of microcomputers began in the mid 70s. This repeated the path taken by minicomputers 15 years earlier. Now primitive machines could be produced for a few thousand pounds, aimed at the personal market. They improved even more rapidly. By now they have caught up with their big brothers in almost everything.

History of Unix

As the Linux version of Unix will be used as a running example throughout this book, it is appropriate to look briefly at the history of its development.

The first Unix system was developed at Bell Laboratories by Ken Thompson on a PDP-7 minicomputer in 1969. It was a small, general purpose, timesharing system, built solely for internal use in Bell Labs. It was successful, and in 1970 it was moved to a PDP-11. A quotation from the *Programmer's Manual* in 1972 is interesting with hindsight: 'The number of Unix installations has grown to 10, with more expected.'

Dennis Ritchie designed the C language, and in 1973 Ritchie and Thompson rewrote Unix in C. This was very unusual at that time. It was taken for granted that an operating system had to be written in assembler, that the sort

of manipulations required could not be programmed in a high-level language. But once it was written in a language like C, moving it to a different architecture was relatively simple. It did not have to be rewritten in assembler—it merely had to be recompiled on the new machine. This was a very important factor, explaining why Unix came to be found on so many different computers.

Bell Labs were not allowed to sell operating systems, so from 1974 onwards Unix was licensed to universities 'for educational purposes.' But following a change in the legal situation, by 1978 Version 7 was on sale commercially. By 1982, Bell Labs were marketing System III. The next commercial version was System V, in 1984. It is currently at System V Release 4, or SVR4.

When Unix was originally licensed to universities, they were also given the source code. And of course many or all of them thought they could improve on it. Thus different versions began to proliferate. The most significant of these was a derivative of Version 7, developed by the University of California at Berkeley. This is known as the Berkeley Software Distribution, abbreviated to BSD. It is currently at 4.4 BSD, but is not being developed further.

Linux is an unusual version of Unix for a number of reasons. It was a totally new development, not based on any of the standard versions. Also, from its beginning in 1991, both the source code and compiled versions have been made freely available. Probably for this reason, it has become very popular.

The existence of so many versions of Unix, each slightly different, even at their system services interface, made life very difficult for companies developing software to run on Unix. They effectively had to develop a different version of their software for each version of Unix. So attempts are currently underway to establish a standard interface. The main thrust of this is POSIX—an acronym for Portable Operating System Interface. This is being encouraged by the IEEE.

Note that POSIX is not an operating system—it is a standard for operating system designers. And it is not limited to Unix type systems; it is being promoted as a standard interface to all operating systems. OpenVMS, OS/2, and Windows NT are examples of non-Unix operating systems which are POSIX compliant.

The Unix trademark is now owned by the Open Group, formed in 1996. They publish a range of technical standards, some of which overlap with POSIX.

1.5 Types of operating system

From the overview given in the previous section, it is not surprising that many different types of operating system have grown up over the 50-year history of computing. This diversity is due to attempts by designers to meet particular requirements, to write specialist systems dedicated to specific purposes. We must be aware of the different possibilities, at least in outline, before we bury our heads in Unix. This will help us to see just where it fits into the overall picture.

The most important distinction that has arisen historically is between *batch* and *interactive* systems. Then there is the combination of these in the *general purpose* system. Of late, *network* and *distributed* systems have become important. There are also some very specialised systems, which we will not study. It will suffice to mention them in passing.

Batch systems

These were the earliest systems developed, so we will look at them first.

In such a system, the program, the data, and the commands to manipulate the program and data, are all submitted together to the computer in the form of a 'job'. There is little or no interaction between users and an executing program. Obviously this is not very suitable for program development, even though it was once used for this.

There is still a use for batch systems, even today. In any situation where the data is all available beforehand, and there is no need for interaction with a running program, a batch system is quite adequate. One classic example of this is payroll processing, where all of the information on hours worked, rates of pay, tax allowances, etc., is available beforehand, and the computer can be allowed to run off on its own, printing pay slips. Another example is printing account statements, such as bank or credit card statements. There is no need for any operator interaction once the job has been started.

The advantage of a batch environment, or a 'job shop', is that it can provide a wide variety of different devices and software, which would not be cost effective for an individual user to purchase.

Interactive

This is the most common mode of computing today, using keyboard, mouse, and screen. It is what most people think of when they say computing. For a programmer, it is a significant improvement on batch systems: it is possible to intervene directly while a program is being developed, or as it is running.

Single user Some systems provide interactive computing on a single user basis. Examples would be Windows NT and OS/2. Linux is most frequently used in single user mode.

The traditional argument against such an arrangement was the cost of a CPU, and its gross underutilisation. This argument is no longer valid. It is now economical to provide a CPU which might be used for less than an hour in total in a whole day. But it is still not cost effective to supply the wide variety of I/O devices and utility programs, most of which the user will need only rarely.

The present state of the art is a single user machine which is multitasking. It does more than one thing at the same time for the one user. The motivation behind this is to improve productivity. But it brings up the whole question of protection. One job must not have free access to files, data, or programs belonging to another. On the other hand there may be times when you want

one job to share with another—so the protection has to be selective. A large proportion of operating system code is involved with dealing with this.

Terminology in this area is very confusing (and confused). Different companies and authors use the same words with different meanings, and different words to mean the same thing. In general, we can take process to mean the same as task, so multiprocessing is the same as multitasking. But be warned that this is not universally true. Some authors reserve the term multiprocessing for computers with more than one CPU.

Multi user Other systems provide interactive computing on a multi-access or multi-user basis. We will take that to mean simultaneous access to a computer system through two or more terminals. The motivation behind this is the sharing of resources and information, for the following reasons.

- Cost. This refers particularly to peripheral devices, such as printers.

- It can be useful, even essential, to share programs and data.

- It removes some redundancy. If many users are running the same program, such as an editor, which happens frequently, there is need only to have one copy of the editor code in memory, instead of five or ten copies. As an editor could be half a Megabyte or more in size, this can result in quite a significant saving.

On the other hand, such simultaneous access can lead to problems:

- Allocating resources to different users, especially doing so in a fair way.

- When two or more users are sharing data, problems arise if they try to change it at the same time.

Multi-user systems are commonly implemented by means of timesharing. Each user is given the illusion of having their own machine. The primary objective of such an operating system is good terminal response time. When a key is pressed, the corresponding character should be seen on the screen almost immediately.

General purpose

In practice, a given environment may want a bit of everything. For example, a timesharing system may support interactive users, but also include a batch monitor. Unix is certainly interactive, but it will also process shell scripts, which are basically batch files.

Network operating systems

It is common practice today to share resources such as printers and databases across a network. Network operating systems handle the underlying processes required for such sharing. They are also responsible for links with systems

outside the local network. They must have facilities for ensuring the security of data, and also the ability to monitor traffic and faults on the network.

A further development in this area is the integration of a network operating system with the general purpose operating system already found on desktop workstations. Windows NT Server is an example, and Unix can also be configured this way.

Distributed systems

This is the most recent development in operating systems, meeting the requirements of a multi-user system in a new way. Basically it consists of a group of machines acting together as one.

When a user starts a program, it may actually run on the local machine. But if that computer is heavily loaded, and the operating system knows that another machine is idle, then the job may be transferred to that idle machine. Or for example, if a program is run on one machine, to process data that is held on another machine, the operating system will decide which is most efficient— to bring the data to the program, or to send the program to the data.

All this migration of data or of programs from one machine to another is totally under the control of the distributed operating system, and the user is not aware of it.

Process control

Examples of situations in which specialist process control operating systems would be used are chemical plants, life support systems, fly-by-wire aeroplanes. Such systems have the following features:

- rapid response to external events—a fast processor and I/O channels
- reliability—typically it must be failsafe; that is if anything goes wrong, the system it is controlling will be left in a safe state
- minimum of operator involvement required.

Specialist systems

Specially designed operating systems would be in order when the computer system is dedicated to processing large volumes of data, which are maintained in an organised way. There may also be frequent changes to the data. Examples would be airline seat reservation systems, or banking systems, where it is important that the data be up to date. The operating system must mask the organisation and structure of the data from the user, and optimise for fast response to requests.

Each user should have the impression that they are the only one. Such systems must also be able to handle situations where two or more users are changing the same data at the same time, e.g. two travel agents booking the last seat on a plane.

1.6 Design of operating systems

An operating system is a large—very large—piece of software. As with any software, ideally it should be designed and built in layers, with each layer dependent on the one beneath. At the bottom, the facilities provided by the hardware; at the top, the system services interface.

For example, at the hardware level, complicated setting and testing of bits in registers may be needed to get a character to a printer. The lowest software layer provides a function to do this, which hides all the details of hardware, not to mention the complication of different models of hardware.

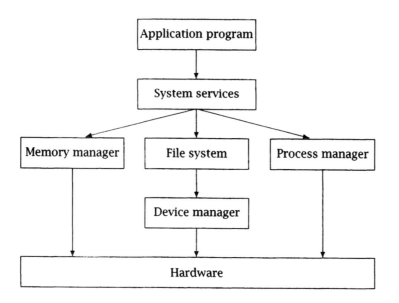

Figure 1.3: Layered structure

Each layer can be considered as providing a virtual machine, a successively more user-friendly interface. The top layer is the virtual machine as seen by the user. An outline example is given in Figure 1.3. Sometimes instead of this vertical picture, the layered structure is envisaged as a series of concentric circles, surrounding the hardware.

Most early operating systems were not built this way. They were designed at a time when the theoretical basis of operating system construction was not well understood. Nor were methods of managing large software projects well understood either, which contributed to poor design and implementation.

There were also frequent additions of patches to repair bugs, or provide extra functionality, often at the request of users. None of this contributed to clean design. Frequently there were large amounts of spaghetti code, as illustrated in Figure 1.4, which made it extremely difficult to debug and maintain.

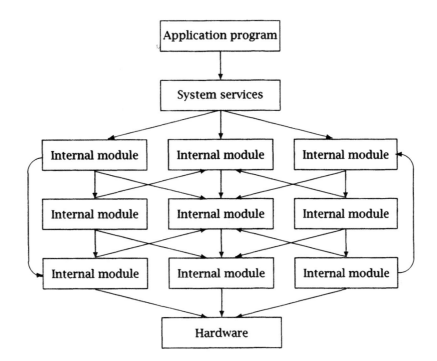

Figure 1.4: Poorly designed system

An operating system should be able to grow in an organised way. It should be possible to make additions to one part of the system, without knock-on problems somewhere else. It should also be possible to correct errors when they are discovered, without causing others. This typically happens when values in variables in one part of a program can be changed unexpectedly by code somewhere else in the system. All of this implies modularity. It also demands that the code be well documented.

Modular design

To design, build, and maintain large software systems requires a high-level view of how the system is structured, and how its different components work together. So we will start with a top-level break down of an operating system.

Earlier in this chapter we viewed an operating system as a single module, providing an abstract machine, which is easier to use than the real machine. Such a system has two interfaces; one 'upwards', the system services interface; one 'downwards', the interface to the hardware.

On the next level down, an operating system can be decomposed into a collection of modules. These would include:

- Process Management
- Memory Management

- I/O Management
- File Storage, which uses I/O, and adds protection and security
- Network Management.

Such an operating system is illustrated in Figure 1.5. The remainder of the book will look at each of these modules, one by one.

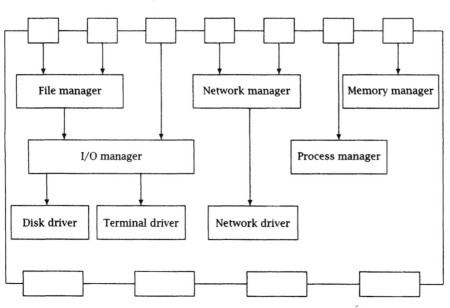

Figure 1.5: Modular operating system

Microkernel

Operating systems have tended to grow larger and more complex. A relatively new proposal is to restructure the operating system into two layers. The lower layer is the microkernel, which provides the absolutely minimum facilities. For example, at the hardware level, the microkernel provides a function to deal with the setting and testing of bits in registers, needed to get a character in or out of the computer.

Above this microkernel is a layer which provides optional extra services, as well as implementing all of the functions which are part of a particular system service interface. This is sometimes called an emulation layer, as it tries to make itself look like some particular operating system from the outside. The microkernel provides its own private interface, which is used by any emulation layer built above it.

It could even be possible to emulate more than one system service interface at the same time. Figure 1.6 shows a microkernel with both a POSIX interface, and a Microsoft Win32 application programming interface layered above it. Sometimes these are referred to as different 'personalities'. The NT operating system is built like this.

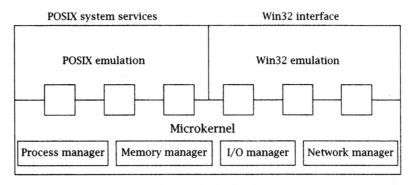

Figure 1.6: Microkernel with two personalities

Linux

Linux is built as a very traditional monolithic kernel. So its structure is best described by Figure 1.5. It is not really a good example of how to design an operating system. The main explanation for this lies in its history. It was not designed from the ground up—it would be more accurate to say that it evolved.

It was originally written for the relatively slow 386 architecture, so performance was far more important than well-structured design. This is particularly obvious in time-critical sections of the kernel. In such places the C code becomes very cryptic and difficult to read. Frequently it drops into assembler. And always it shows the influence of the 386 architecture, on which it was originally developed.

However, it is still a good system to use as a basis for a course on operating systems. The wide availability of the source code outweighs any of the disadvantages mentioned here.

1.7 Summary

1. An operating system is a program which sits between the raw hardware and applications. It provides a user-friendly interface to applications programmers, hiding the complexity and diversity of the hardware.

2. It provides an environment which makes it easier for applications programmers to do productive work:

- supplies simple functions that carry out the most commonly required operations
- manages and shares the resources of the computer system, such as CPU, memory, disks, and printers
- hides some differences in the hardware.

It does all of this as efficiently and economically as possible.

3. Most users are familiar with graphical user interfaces and command interpreters. These are just applications, which sit on top of the operating system, and make it more user friendly. Like all applications, they in turn make use of system services. These are the real interface to an operating system.

4. The earliest computers had no operating systems, with the programmer interacting directly with the hardware. The first operating systems were no more than loaders. Satellite computers, with their control programs, as introduced in the 50s, were a first attempt to overcome the disparity between the speed of a device and the speed of the CPU.

In the 60s, verbal commands to operators were replaced with machine readable commands, written in job control languages. On the I/O front, the introduction of the I/O channel and the interrupt was a landmark. This overlapping of I/O and computation led to concurrency, which in turn led to developments in scheduling, resource optimisation, and protection.

In the late 60s, timesharing led to the development of VDU terminals.

The 70s was the era of virtual memory. Then in the 80s, networking and the GUI were the development areas. Distributed systems and open systems were at the forefront of operating systems research in the 90s.

The first minicomputers were produced in the early 60s, by the late 70s their operating systems had all the facilities of mainframes. Microcomputers, beginning from the mid 70s, have now caught up with their big brothers in almost everything.

The first Unix system was developed in 1969. In 1973, it was rewritten in C, thus making it portable. The downside of this is the large number of slightly different versions that resulted. At present efforts are underway to standardise it, mainly involving POSIX and the Open Group.

5. Many different types of operating system have been developed, to meet particular requirements. The most important distinction that has arisen historically is between batch and interactive systems. In a batch system, the program and data are submitted together in the form of a 'job'.

Interactive systems are where the user is involved in a dialogue with the computer, using keyboard, mouse, screen. Some systems, such as Windows NT and OS/2, provide interactive computing on a single user basis; others do so on a multi-user or multi-access basis.

Both of these are frequently combined in general purpose systems. There are also specialist systems for controlling networks, and distributed

operating systems for controlling groups of machines acting together as one.

6. Earlier operating systems were not designed and built in accordance with modern standards for software development, and tended to contain large amounts of spaghetti code. It is now accepted that such large pieces of software should be designed and built in a modular fashion. The top-level decomposition of an operating system would include modules to manage processes, memory, I/O, communications, and file systems.

   A more recent design trend isolates the absolutely necessary features in a microkernel. Other services can then be layered on top of this. Finally, different system service interfaces can make it look like different operating systems, or 'personalities'.

   Linux is not particularly well designed. Its strength as an example system is that it is freely available.

1.8 Discussion questions

1. Do you find the arguments for studying operating systems, as given in the Preface, to be convincing? Why? Or do you think operating system courses should be abolished? Can you think of any other reasons why they should be part of a computer systems course?

2. An operating system is an extra layer of software in a computer, extra instructions to be executed, which slows an application program down. Discuss the advantages and disadvantages of removing operating systems altogether.

3. Many of the things an operating system does seem to be relevant to large, multi-user systems—overlapping input and output, communicating with other machines, providing virtual memory. Is such an operating system really needed on a single user, personal, computer?

4. Is Windows NT an operating system? Or a GUI? Or both?

5. Early computer systems got on without operating systems. What has changed, that we need them today?

6. Some of the landmark developments in computer systems have been high-level languages, the interrupt mechanism, interactive computing, VDUs, GUIs, networking. Which one would you consider most important, and why?

7. Linux was originally developed for the Intel 386 hardware. What other machines is it available on at present?

8. What might be the next big breakthrough in operating systems?

9. It is still a common practice for system managers to run batch programs on Unix systems. Investigate the sort of 'jobs' these would be carrying out.

10. Learning to program in a batch environment, in which the compiler might run only a few times a day, would seem to make a difficult task almost impossible. Yet some argue that the discipline involved in getting it right first time produced better programmers. Discuss.

11. What use is a multitasking operating system on a single user machine? Surely the one user can only do one thing at a time?

12. As hardware costs continue to fall, and networks develop, do you think there is any future for multi-user machines?

13. Distributed systems certainly seem to have great advantages. List some aspects which might make you slow to move from stand-alone systems.

14. Can you find any book or article which gives an overview of Linux along the lines of Figure 1.5? If not, what does this say about the design of Linux?

Interfaces to an operating system 2

We have seen that an operating system is one of several layers of software between the hardware and the user. Where each of these layers meet, there must be some way of passing instructions and information from one layer to the other, in both directions. This is called the interface.

Before going on to consider the internals of the system, we will first of all examine this interface.

An operating system has two interfaces. One is with the application programs which use it. This is known as the system call or system service interface. The other is with the hardware. As they are quite different, we will treat them separately.

2.1 The system service interface

System services are the functions which the operating system offers to perform on behalf of application programs. Many programmers, because they never use system services directly, are unaware that they even exist. But all programs use them, even if indirectly. Compilers are aware of the system services available on the machine they are generating code for, and include calls to these functions in the code they generate. For example, a Unix compiler will translate any request for input or output in a high-level language to one of the two most common system services, read() or write().

Just like any functions you have written yourself, they are passed parameters, they perform some operations, and return a value. The difference is that these functions have been written by the operating system designers, and are available in a library for your use. They can run into hundreds. Just as the set of assembly language instructions defines what you can do with a particular CPU, so the set of system services defines what you can do with any particular operating system. They are sometimes called 'the software instruction set'.

As explained in the previous chapter, an operating system makes the raw hardware look different to the programmer, more user friendly. It presents a virtual machine to the user, and the set of system services defines what this virtual machine can do.

For Unix, they are traditionally described in Section 2 of the manual. The shell command man 2 intro will give an overview.

System services from the outside

The programming interface is relatively simple. System services are all described fully in the on-line manual pages. Anything that is said here is only a summary. The manual pages specify the header files required for each system service. These must always be included. The manual pages also give the order, type and meaning of each parameter, as well as explaining what aspect of the function each parameter controls. They also give the type and meaning of the value returned by the function. The programmer calls the function with the appropriate parameter values. The linker looks for the function in the standard C library, and binds it into the executable program.

Return value

System services are written and called as C functions. This means that they return a value. In most cases, these functions are of type int. But there are a growing number of exceptions, including a few declared as void, and the manual page should always be checked.

This return value is not just to be discarded. System programming is different from application programming, when it can normally be seen from the screen whether the program worked correctly or not. When a system service is called, for example to change some attribute of the operating system or write to a disk, there is no visible indication of whether the operation was successful or not. The only indication is the value returned.

The specific meaning of this value in each case is defined in the appropriate manual page. But in most cases, if the call did not work for some reason or other, the return value is -1. If the call did work, some other value is returned. This success value should be checked, to see that it is correct. It is not sufficient just to check that a call did not fail. It may have succeeded, but not done what was intended.

Errors

Normally a program should not continue after a system call fails—presumably it was called for some purpose, which has not now been achieved. But the reason why it failed is probably more important.

When a system call fails, the appropriate C function also passes back a value indicating the reason it failed. The mechanism it uses for this is an extern variable of type int, called errno. This is declared in the include file /usr/include/errno.h.

From here on we will use the standard C shorthand to refer to such files in the /usr/include directory, and just say <errno.h>.

For portability it is better to rely on this declaration, rather than declaring errno yourself in your program. The linker will identify it with the variable declared in the programs in the C library. So the system service will put a value into that variable, and your program is able to read that value. The situation is illustrated in Figure 2.1. The shell command man errno will give more information.

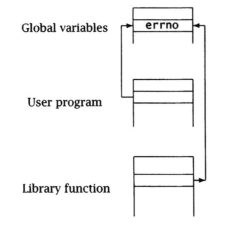

Figure 2.1: Memory layout for global variables

It is important to note that the value in errno is valid only if the library function returned -1. If the call was successful, and it returned any other value, then errno can still be accessed, but its value is undefined. In fact, the system does not change the value in errno after a successful call. This means it always contains the value relating to the last unsuccessful call, no matter how far back in the program that was.

So errno gives a number indicating why the system call failed. But it's not much use knowing, for example, that error 17 has occurred. We need to find out which error has been given the number 17. How? Back to the manual pages.

Each manual page gives a list and an explanation of all the possible errors that can happen for that particular system call. But, they are not identified there by number, rather by literal constants, such as EAGAIN or EBADPARM. The last piece of the jigsaw puzzle is to connect the int returned in errno with the constant explained on the manual page.

This missing piece is the header file <errno.h>, in which each of these literal constants is defined. So if this file is included in the program, then each of the possible values of errno can be tested using the literal constants, and an appropriate message printed, as illustrated in Figure 2.2. This must be done for every system call. And some of these have many possible errors. So it looks as if system programs are going to become rather long.

```
#include <errno.h>

ret_val = sysservice();
if (ret_val == -1) switch(errno)
            {case EAGAIN:    printf("one message");
                             break;
             case EBADPARM: printf("another message");
            };
```

Figure 2.2: Checking error values

The C library contains a useful function for just this situation, perror().
When called, it prints an appropriate message corresponding to the current
value in errno. The manual page for perror() will give more information.

Note that you can add your own message to the one perror() prints, if
you wish. This is because perror() cannot know which system call caused
errno to be set. It may not be very useful just to be told that such and such an
error has occurred. But if the extra information 'at such a point in the program'
is included, then just the correct amount of debugging information is printed
on the screen.

One word of warning about perror(). It should only be called immediately after a system call has returned -1. If called from anywhere else in a
program, it will still interpret the (spurious) value in errno, and print a spurious error message, causing unnecessary confusion.

When a system call fails, it is normally good practice to terminate a program at that stage. Something has gone wrong. There is no point in continuing
on, and maybe just compounding the error. So a call to perror() should always be followed by a call to abort(), which will display helpful debugging
information.

System services from the inside

Now let us look a little more closely at these functions. First of all we need
to take a detour into the CPU. All modern CPUs operate in at least two different modes. In one of these, called user mode, the CPU can only execute
a subset of its instructions—the more common ones, like add, subtract, load
and store, etc. In the other mode, called kernel mode, the CPU can execute
all of its instructions, including extra privileged instructions. These typically
access special registers which control protection on the machine. Normally the
machine runs in user mode. When it wants to do something special, it has to
change into kernel mode.

Obviously this changing between modes is very dependent on the underlying hardware. While Linux is hardware independent, it is most frequently
found on IBM compatible PCs, with Intel CPUs. So the description here will be
based on that architecture. Linux is also implemented on other architectures,
which have their own ways of carrying out such mode changes. The relevant

technical reference manuals will have to be consulted for each one. Note that this is the only major section in the book where the treatment is Intel specific.

Library function

Each system service is known to the programmer by name, and is called by name, such as read() or write(). This is understandable for the programmer side of the interface. But internally, the operating system identifies each service by number. The numbers corresponding to each one can be found in <asm/unistd.h>.

The actual C library function which the application calls does very little work. It puts the appropriate system call number into the EAX register, puts the parameters into registers beginning with EBX, and then executes a special machine instruction, which causes a software interrupt. On the PC, this instruction is INT. There are 256 possible software interrupts; the one reserved for entry to the Linux kernel is INT 0x80.

Mode change

The 386 has a special register, IDTR, which points to an interrupt descriptor table (IDT) in memory. There is one entry in this table for each of the 256 possible interrupts. When the INT 0x80 instruction is executed by the C library function, the CPU goes to the appropriate entry in the interrupt descriptor table, and reads the 8 byte descriptor stored there. Reading this descriptor has two effects on the CPU. First of all, it changes the processor to execute in kernel mode. But it also causes it to read its next instruction from a different place in memory—a sort of implied jump. It transfers control to a common system call handler in the kernel, known as system_call(), from the architecture specific assembly language file entry.S.

Kernel function

This does some housekeeping to make sure that it does not overwrite any information the user program may have in the CPU registers. It then uses the system call number (in the EAX register) to index into a system dispatch table, sys_call_table, also declared in entry.S, to find the address of the kernel code which executes that particular system service.

There are two tables involved here, which may lead to some confusion. Only one entry in the first table, the interrupt descriptor table, is relevant to a system service, that is entry 0x80. This contains the address of the system_call() routine. The second table, sys_call_table, has one entry for each possible system service; each entry contains the address of the operating system function which carries out that system service. The system_call() routine uses the value in the EAX register to index into this table, and to find the address of the appropriate code. See Figure 2.3.

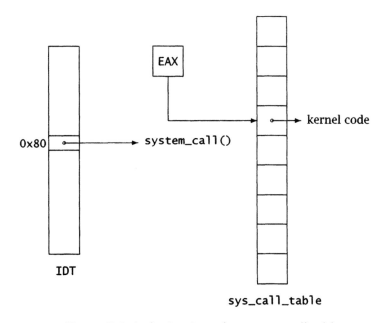

Figure 2.3: Indexing into the system call table

When the kernel code is finished, it uses another special machine instruction, IRET, to change the mode back to user. Like all functions, it then returns to its caller, which in the present case was system_call(). This restores any register values it may have saved, and returns an appropriate value to the C library function. This in turn arranges that any data to be returned to the user is in the expected format.

For example, one of the parameters to the read() system service is a pointer to an area of memory. The C function will move the data that has just been read to that area. It will also determine what value the C function itself is to return. If the call failed, it would put an appropriate value into errno, and return −1.

Finally it returns control to its caller, the application program. Figure 2.4 illustrates the whole procedure.

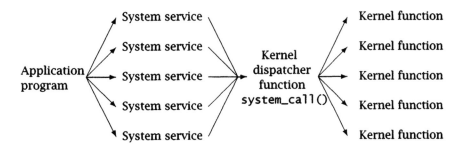

Figure 2.4: Calling a system service

2.2 Interface with the hardware

As might be expected, the interface between the operating system and the hardware does not—cannot—use the call/return mechanism used with interfaces between two layers of software. This interface between the software and the hardware is unique. It is also very much dependent on the particular hardware involved. Here we will generalise as much as possible.

Simple interface

Any computer has a certain amount of memory. This memory has certain characteristics. First of all, each byte of it has a unique id-number, known as its address. Memory is normally installed so that addresses are consecutive, though this is not absolutely necessary. Another characteristic of memory is that when we write some value to a particular byte, we expect that same value to be there when we read from that byte in the future. We expect it to remember that value—hence the name memory.

Transferring data

Memory may be visualised as dead-ended. When a CPU puts a value into a particular byte along the data bus, the only way that value can be read is along the same data bus, in the opposite direction. This is illustrated in Figure 2.5.

Data bus (8 bits)

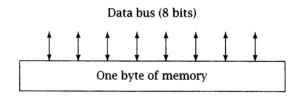

One byte of memory

Figure 2.5: Computer memory

It is possible to build memory so that it is dual ported. This means that there are two paths into and out of a particular byte. In such a situation, if a value is put into a particular byte, there is no guarantee that it will be there at a later time. It may have been removed on the other path, or rewritten over the other path.

This is the mechanism that is used to get bytes of information in and out of a computer. One particular location in the address space is chosen for a particular device, and instead of ordinary memory, it is implemented with this dual ported memory, more frequently referred to as a device register. One side of it is connected to the data bus of the computer, as usual.

The other side is connected directly to the device. This is illustrated in Figure 2.6. Now the device can put data into that register, and the program can retrieve that data, as if reading it from memory. Conversely, the program

can put data into the register, just as if writing to memory. The device can then read that data directly.

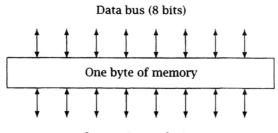

Data bus (8 bits)

One byte of memory

Connection to device

Figure 2.6: Dual-ported memory

To look at it another way, memory can be visualised as a set of pigeon holes, as used for sorting letters. If they are solidly backed up against a wall, then anything put in from the front will have to stay there until taken out from the front. If the door of the room is locked, we have a closed system. We can move items from one pigeon hole to another, or to the desk (the CPU). But we cannot get new items into the room, or get items out of the room.

Now if a hole is knocked through the wall behind one of these pigeon holes, into the next room, we have our way in and out. When we put letters into that particular slot, we expect someone in the next room to take them, and do something with them. Likewise we know that new letters from the outside world will appear here from time to time. We might even become more sophisticated, and have two such slots, one for in and the other for out.

Synchronisation

Coming back to the computer, we have a problem with synchronisation. When a key is pressed on a keyboard, the keyboard hardware puts the value of the code corresponding to that key in the appropriate register. If the program does not remove that value before the next key is pressed, the previous value will be overwritten and lost. Another possibility is that after a program has taken a value from the register, it may come back to take the next value before another key has been pressed. In this case it will get a second copy of the previous value, which is not what we want either.

So there must be some way for the device to tell the program that it has put in a value, and for the program to tell the device that it has taken one out, and that the register is ready for the next one.

The simplest way to do this is to use another register. The first one is known as the data register, the second as the status register. Individual bits in this status register have particular meanings. For example, for an input device, bit 7 set might mean 'there is a byte in the register', so bit 7 clear would mean 'a byte has been read from the register'. With such a scheme, the device

would check status bit 7 every time before it put a byte into the data register, and afterwards it would also set bit 7 of the status register. The program would first check status bit 7, and only if it were set would it remove the data byte. Then it would clear status bit 7. With more sophisticated hardware, just reading the data byte would automatically clear this bit.

Multiple devices

It is common for device registers to be implemented as separate electronic components, not physically part of main memory. Such registers still have their unique addresses, and are connected to the internal buses of the computer, as shown in Figure 2.7.

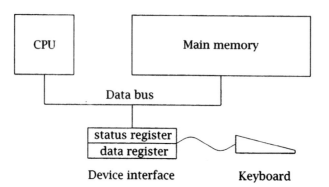

Figure 2.7: Keyboard interface with computer

More complex devices would have more complex interfaces. A disk drive, for example, might have three registers to specify the surface, track, and sector for the operation, along with bits in the status register to specify whether the operation was a read or a write— as well as the synchronisation bits and the data register.

On a realistic computer, there would be many such sets of registers. The CPU would periodically have to check the appropriate status bits for each one. This is called polling. It is simple, but wasteful of CPU cycles.

Interrupt mechanism

Because polling is wasteful, another mechanism has been developed. A special signal line, called an interrupt line, connects the CPU with all of the devices. By putting an electrical pulse on this line, any device can get the attention of the CPU. Such a configuration is shown in Figure 2.8.

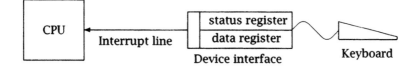

Figure 2.8: Interface using interrupt line

Simple mechanism

With this mechanism, the CPU can be busy processing, and ignore the devices. When any device has data to deliver, it goes through the same procedure as before, but now it also puts an electrical pulse on the interrupt line. When the CPU receives this signal, it stops what it is doing and runs the polling routine. We still have polling, but now only when some device has data to transfer. We poll to find out which one.

The polling routine finds which device interrupted, and takes the byte of input data from it. The CPU then returns to whatever it was doing before the interrupt occurred.

How does the CPU get back to exactly where it was before the interrupt occurred? Presumably the CPU was executing an application program, unconnected with the source of the interrupt. When the device signalled, the CPU finished the instruction it was executing, but did not go on to the next one. Instead, it saved the address of this next instruction, which on the Intel architecture it got from the EIP register. It then jumped to the polling routine, by fetching its address into the EIP register from a predefined location.

When the polling routine terminates, the CPU restores the saved value of the EIP registers, thus setting the machine up just as it was before the interrupt occurred. All architectures have an IRET machine instruction, or something similar. This restores the value to the EIP, thus setting the machine up exactly as it was before the interrupt. So the first instruction executed after the interrupt is the one that was about to be executed just before the interrupt occurred.

Distinguishing between interrupts

Interrupts are very frequent occurrences. There may be dozens every second on a heavily loaded machine. The need to poll many devices each time, to find the one that has actually interrupted, is an unacceptable overhead. Hardware designers have developed the interrupt mechanism so as to put more of the identification into hardware, and thus make it faster. Such development has taken two paths: one typified by the Intel series of CPUs, where there is only one interrupt line; the other involves the introduction of many interrupt lines, as found in most modern architectures.

Single Interrupt Line The Intel 8088 was designed at a time when the number of transistors that could be integrated onto one chip was quite limited. The designers had space in the CPU to implement only one interrupt line. For compatibility reasons, all of the successor CPUs still have only one line.

This means that the CPU only knows that *some* device has interrupted—it has to poll to find out which one. But the designers automated the polling, which enables it to be done sufficiently quickly.

With this architecture, when a device interrupts, the CPU saves the EIP register, as usual. It then puts a signal on another line, the acknowledge line. All of the devices are connected to this. The interrupting device hears the acknowledgement, and in turn puts an 8 bit number on the data bus, which the CPU reads. This number is then used to index into the interrupt descriptor table, which we saw in Section 2.1. The address from the appropriate entry is loaded into the EIP register, causing the CPU to take its next instruction from that address. These addresses each point to a handler program, or a driver, for a specific device.

So when, for example, device number 7 puts a 7 on the data bus, the CPU begins to execute driver 7, which has been tailor made for that device.

When the handler finishes, control returns to the next instruction in the interrupted program, as usual.

Multiple Interrupt Lines Another possibility at the hardware level is to have more than one interrupt line—8, 16, or 32. Then depending on which line the interrupt is signalled, the CPU jumps to one of 32 handlers. While a different line could be attached to each device, it is more common to devote one line to each type of device. So for example, when a terminal interrupts, the CPU jumps to a terminal handler, which then polls to determine which particular terminal requires service.

Priority among interrupts

One final point is to consider what happens when two devices interrupt at the same time. In practice, all possible sources of interrupts are arranged in priority order. While dealing with an interrupt of a particular priority, the CPU will not allow itself to be interrupted by another interrupt of the same, or lower, priority.

On machines with a single interrupt line, the prioritisation is not done by the CPU, but by another chip called a programmable interrupt controller or PIC. See Figure 2.9.

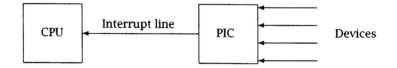

Figure 2.9: Interrupt arbitration by controller

The devices are physically connected to the PIC, which in turn is connected to the CPU via the single interrupt line. At boot time, the PIC is programmed with information about the interrupt priority level (IPL) of each device, and which interrupt number it is to request for each device. If two devices interrupt at precisely the same moment, the PIC decides on the order in which they are to be serviced. It interrupts the CPU to service the first, waits until it is finished, and then interrupts for service for the second. If a device with a higher priority interrupts while the CPU is servicing an interrupt with a lower priority, then the PIC will signal the CPU to service the new interrupt.

On machines with many interrupt lines, all of this arbitration is done by the CPU itself. Each line has a different priority. This is not set up at boot time, but is a feature of the CPU design. The priority of a device depends on the interrupt line to which it is attached. This is decided either by the designer of the computer, or when the device is installed. It is not easily changed.

Clock interrupt handling

One unique device that deserves special mention is the system clock. This continually interrupts the CPU, typically 100 times per second. The clock interrupt has the second highest priority of all. Only the power failure interrupt has higher priority, for obvious reasons.

Each time the clock interrupts, its handler performs operations which will be discussed in context throughout the book. Here it is sufficient to be aware that it exists.

Direct memory access

All of the foregoing discussion, even with the most sophisticated interrupt mechanism, presupposed that data is transferred one byte at a time through a register. This is ideal for a byte at a time device, such as a keyboard. To speed things up for other devices, such as disk drives or printers, the register could be made wider: 16 bits, 32 bits, even 64 bits. But this is not really a solution for fast devices. Disk drives want to transfer blocks of 8kB at a time; network devices want to transfer 10Mbits per second. In such cases it would be intolerable to have to interrupt after every few bytes.

So a totally different solution has been developed. The status register of our previous example has been retained, and even extended. The interrupt mechanism is also retained. Some extra processing ability is added to the device electronics. Then the data register is removed, and the data bus connected directly to the device. As well as this, the address bus of the computer is also connected directly to the device. This arrangement is known as a direct memory access (DMA) controller, and is illustrated in Figure 2.10.

Let us now examine how an 8kB block of data is written to a disk drive using DMA. The CPU sets up the various bits in the status register as before. But now the block of data to be written is not in a register—it is in the memory of the computer. So there are two extra registers in the device: one for the

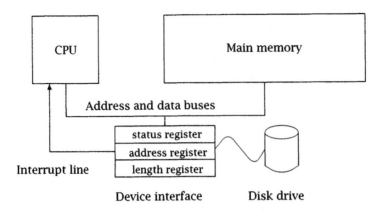

Figure 2.10: Direct memory access

address in memory where the block is to be found, and another for its length. Once this has been done, the CPU is finished, and goes on to do some other work. The DMA processor now moves the data from main memory, sharing the address and data buses with the CPU. While the CPU is fetching an instruction from memory, the DMA controller stays idle. When the CPU is executing that instruction, and not using the bus, or memory, the DMA controller sneaks in and moves a byte from memory to the device. This is sometimes called 'cycle stealing'. When the required number of bytes have been transferred, it interrupts the CPU to let it know.

2.3 Summary

1. Systems services are the functions which the operating system offers to perform on behalf of applications programs. They are documented in Section 2 of the Unix manual.

   They are written and called as C functions. The value returned must always be checked, as it is the only indication of how successful the operation was. If it did not work, the reason for failure is available in `errno`.

   Internally, each system service is only a C wrapper which switches the CPU into kernel mode, and calls the kernel `system_call()` function. This transfers control to the specific kernel function; afterwards it switches back to user mode, and returns to the caller.

2. The interface between the operating system and the hardware is implemented by means of dual-ported memory known as device registers. Data can be moved in or out through such registers, one byte at a time.

   To avoid the CPU wasting time repeatedly checking to see if there is new data available, an interrupt mechanism can be added. The interrupt from the clock device, which occurs at regular intervals, is used by the operating system to regulate itself.

Finally, peripheral processing units known as DMA controllers can be used to handle all the work of moving data between memory and a device, leaving the CPU free for more productive processing.

2.4 Discussion questions

1. Programs written in C are easily portable across machines of different architectures. Explain how the compiler arranges that the printf() function has an identical effect on two different machines, with two different architectures.

2. Investigate the system services available on a non-POSIX style operating system, such as NT or OpenVMS.

3. It is a common misconception that the header file associated with a system service contains the code for that system service. Examine one such header file and see what it actually does contain.

4. Check the manual page for the read() system service. Describe all of the checks you would have to perform on the value returned by this function, to be sure that you had covered every possibility.

5. Investigate the strerror() library function. Can you suggest any use for this?

6. All system services call a special machine instruction, which causes the CPU to change to kernel mode. It seems that you could write your own assembler program, using this instruction, and hence take over the machine yourself. Investigate the special instruction on the hardware you are using, and find out why it is not as easy as it seems.

7. Investigate the format of an entry in the interrupt table for the Intel architecture.

8. Many computer architectures assign I/O ports to addresses in ordinary memory, as described in Section 2.2. Others, such as Intel, have a special I/O address space, separate from the memory address space. Investigate how a program can distinguish between the same address (for example 0x100) in both of these address spaces.

9. If a system did not have an interrupt mechanism, then it would use polling to check the status registers of devices. Does it have to poll continually, or could it just run the polling routine at intervals?

10. When a device interrupts, the EIP value of the running program is stored automatically, and the EIP value of the interrupt handler loaded into the hardware registers. But the general purpose registers presumably still contain values belonging to the running program.

    The interrupt handler cannot run without using some general purpose registers. How can it do this without overwriting values belonging to the running program?

11. Interrupt routines can be called from a running program, using the INT instruction. What would happen if a programmer called an interrupt number for which there was no handler? How could the operating system deal with this?

12. Suggest a priority order in which all of the devices attached to a PC could be arranged.

13. Linux does the most urgent processing required for an interrupt immediately. Less urgent processing is delayed, so that if other interrupts occur, they too can be dealt with immediately. Investigate how 'bottom halves' are used in Linux to delay such less urgent processing.

14. List some of the functions you think might be carried out by the clock interrupt handler.

Process manager 3

At the end of Chapter 1, the modules which go to make up an operating system were identified. We now turn to the first of these, the process manager.

3.1 The concept of a process

There are a number of key words and ideas in this area.

A **program** is a sequence of instructions. It is effectively an algorithm translated into some programming language. On its own, a program does nothing. It is inert.

As a first cut, a **process** can be described as 'a program in action'. When the instructions that make up a program are actually being carried out, there is a process. Another way of putting this might be 'a sequence of actions, which result from executing the instructions specified in a program'. This gives the idea that a process is something active. The relationship between a program and a process is similar to the relationship between a recipe for baking a cake, and the actual process in the kitchen, from the ingredients, through the mixing, and the baking, right up to the eating.

A very formal definition would be 'a sequence of states, resulting from the action of a set of instructions on the states as they develop'. At first sight this does not seem to be the same thing at all. It seems to be a static concept, not something dynamic, as presented in the previous paragraph. So it is necessary to explain what is meant by a computational state, in this context. It is like a photograph of the internals of the computer, taken at a particular instant. It includes the values in the CPU registers, the value in each byte of memory, the value in each of the special registers associated with hardware devices.

At any given time, the computer is in a particular state. Then an instruction is executed. This changes at least one value somewhere in the machine, and moves it to a (very slightly) different state. This is true even if it is a no operation instruction NOP—at least the program counter has been changed to point to the next instruction.

Consider the very small assembler program given in Figure 3.1. We are only interested in the program counter (EIP), one CPU register (EAX), and one

memory location (total). Obviously there are many other elements which go to make up the full state of the machine, but only those shown are relevant to the example.

```
1: MOV EAX, 7     ; load the value 7 into register EAX
2: INC EAX        ; increment register EAX
3: MOV total, EAX; store the value from register EAX to total
```

Figure 3.1: Program to illustrate change of state

The sequence of states corresponding to the execution of this program is shown in Figure 3.2.

	EIP	EAX	total
Initial state	1	0	0
State after 1st instruction	2	7	0
State after 2nd instruction	3	8	0
State after 3rd instruction	4	8	8

Figure 3.2: States as program executes

So the definition is saying that a process consists of all of these states, from the initial state to the final one. It is similar to a movie, which is made up of hundreds of thousands of still pictures. When we view all of them in the correct order, we have the movie. This idea of a process as a sequence of states will be important when we come to consider several processes running on the one machine at the same time.

There is not a 1 to 1 correspondence between a program and a process, and a consideration of this may help to pin these ideas down.

One process may involve more than one program. Most operating systems allow a program to issue an instruction to run another program. So in some states a process may be executing instructions from program A, and then later states may be executing instructions from program B.

It is also possible for one program to be involved in more than one process, at the same time. Sharing program code is common on multitasking systems. For example, if a number of programmers are using the editor at the same time, only one copy of the editor program will be loaded into memory. They will each be reading instructions from the same copy. Of course, there will be a separate copy of the editor data for each process—presumably each user is editing his or her own file.

3.2 Use of processes

A brief look at how processes might be used in the implementation of a computer system may help to clarify some of the ideas presented in the previous section.

With some systems each user is allocated one process. This is created when the user logs on, and every program the user activates is run as part of this process. On other systems, a new process may be created for every command the user issues, and every program run. This latter is the Unix style.

There could be several processes going to make up the operating system. The process manager is itself a process. It would have the highest priority, and when needed it would get access to the processor before any other process. Then the memory manager, and the file manager, would each consist of one or more processes.

Each source of asynchronous events is given a process of its own. Such an asynchronous event is anything that can happen independently of the running program, and so at unpredictable times. This generally results in a process being dedicated to each hardware device.

For example, there would be a process created for the network device, which would spend most of its time inactive, asleep. But when a message arrives over the network, this operating system process is there waiting to respond. It is woken up (by an interrupt), deals with the network device, passes the message on to the appropriate user process, and goes to sleep again. The user process cannot be expected to do this. It cannot know in advance when a message is going to arrive. And it cannot just sit there waiting for a message—it has to get on with its own processing.

Unix has traditionally taken a different approach from the one outlined above. It has very few system processes. Most of the Unix code, even kernel code, is executed as part of the current user's process. It is said to execute in the context of the user's process. But as seen in the previous chapter, while executing kernel code the process has extra privileges—it has access to any internal data structures it requires in the operating system, and it can execute privileged instructions on the CPU. The ps -ax command can be used to get a listing of all processes, including system processes.

3.3 Processors and processes

A processor is the agent which runs a process, by executing the instructions contained in its associated program. Typically, there are far fewer processors than processes. In fact, in most cases there is only one processor. So processes get their share of time on the processor. This would only be when they are in a position to do some work—a process is never given processor time while it is waiting for keyboard input, for example.

Consider the situation outlined in Figure 3.3, where the solid lines represent CPU execution, and the dashed lines represent the operation of some peripheral device.

Process A is executing on the (one) processor. It sends a request to read data from drive 1. The disk drive begins the read operation, but this will take some time, as the head has to move, and the correct sector has to be under the head before it can read.

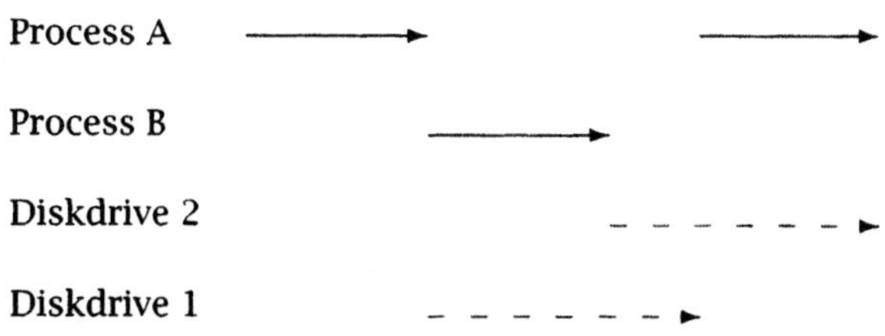

Process A   ———————→   ———————→

Process B   ———————→

Diskdrive 2   – – – – – – ►

Diskdrive 1   – – – – – – ►

Figure 3.3: Overlap of processor and devices

In the meantime, process A cannot continue. So the operating system gives the processor to process B. This process executes some instructions, then it sends a request to read data from drive 2. While waiting for this data, process B cannot execute any further instructions.

Now if these are the only two processes on the machine, the CPU is idle. Note that the two drives can be operating at the same time, as they are separate physical devices. Also one process can be operating on the CPU while the drives are working. But there can be no overlap of processes. Only one can be active at any given time, because there is only one CPU.

Eventually, drive 1 delivers the required information. The operating system copies the data from drive 1 into the memory space of process A, and restarts that process at the next instruction after the request for data. It proceeds on from there.

Some time later, drive 2 signals that it has copied the information it was requested to read. At this stage, the operating system can allow process A to continue. Or, as B has been idle for quite some time, it might seem fair to give B some processor time now. The resolution of this question is left until we consider scheduling in Section 3.10.

3.4 Processes and threads

We have seen in the previous section that sometimes a process is running on the processor, building up state. At other times it is idle, for one reason or another. The overhead involved in moving from running to idle can be considerable. It happens frequently that a process begins running and almost immediately stops to wait for some input to become available. The operating system has to save the whole state of the process. There is a similar overhead involved when a process begins running again. All of the saved state has to be restored, and the machine set up exactly as it was when the process last ran. And this overhead is on the increase, as the number and size of CPU registers grows, and as operating systems become more complex, so requiring ever more state to be remembered.

This has led to a distinction being made between the unit of resource allocation, and the unit of execution. Traditionally, these have been the same. One process involved one path of execution through one program, using one

block of allocated resources, especially memory. Now the trend is to have one unit of resource allocation, one executable program, with many paths of execution through it at the same time. The terminology that is evolving tends to refer to the old system as heavyweight processes, or just processes. The new style are called lightweight processes, or threads, but there is no consistency.

A thread has access to all of the resources assigned to the process. It can be defined as a single, sequential flow of control within a program. A process begins life with a single thread; but it can then go on to create further threads of control within itself.

Now that one process can have many threads of control, if one thread is blocked, another can execute. It is not necessary to save and restore the full state of the machine for this, as it is using the same memory, program, files, devices—it is just jumping to another location in the program code. But each thread must maintain some state information of its own, for example the program counter, stack pointer, general purpose registers. This is so that when it regains control, it may continue from the point it was at before it lost control.

The example we used earlier, of baking a cake, can be extended to baking several cakes. We still have only one process. There is only one set of resources. There is only one recipe. But while one cake is in the oven, we may be mixing the ingredients for another. We are following the recipe at two different places at the same time. Instead of idly waiting for the first cake to be baked, we are using that time productively.

Example

A file server is a good example of the usefulness of multi-threading. If there is only one thread, then it can only handle one request at a time. And as it will spend quite a proportion of its time waiting for the disk drive, the total amount of work it does for its clients will be nothing near its capacity. Figure 3.4 illustrates this under use of resources. The CPU is idle some of the time, and drive 2 is idle all the time.

Process A   ────────▶   ────────▶

Diskdrive 2

Diskdrive 1   ─ ─ ─ ─ ─ ─ ▶

Figure 3.4: An underutilised system

However, if there are many threads of control in the server process, while some are blocked waiting for the disk drive, another can be processing a request from a new client. In this way the server is limited only by the capacity of the disk drive to provide information. Figure 3.5 illustrates this situation, with the CPU fully occupied, and both disk drives in fairly constant use.

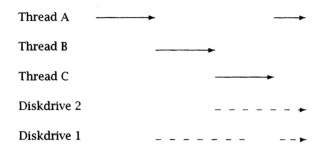

Figure 3.5: High utilisation of CPU and disk drives

A common way to implement this is to create a new thread for each request. When the request is fully serviced, the thread is destroyed. There might
be one dispatcher thread, which accepts incoming requests, and creates worker
threads to carry them out. Or instead, there could be a fixed number of worker
threads, each of which reads and deals with its own requests.

Implementation

Sometimes a threads package is implemented as a set of library routines, running entirely at user level. This saves on the overhead of involving the kernel each time control changes from one thread to another. The kernel gives
control of the CPU to a process. The program that process is executing calls
library functions which divide up the time among a number of threads. This
approach has the serious drawback that if one thread calls a system service
such as read(), and it has to wait for a key to be pressed, the kernel will block
the whole process, and give the CPU to another. The kernel just does not know
about threads. It might be viewed as a cheap way to implement threads on top
of an existing system.

The other possibility is for threads to be implemented in the kernel itself, which then handles all the switching between threads. Linux has such
a threads package. The interface to it is the pthread library of routines, an
implementation of the POSIX 1003.1c standard of 1995. However, Linux has a
unique way of providing threads within the kernel. It really creates a new process. But it specifies that the original and new processes are to share the same
memory, program, and open files. To the user, these new processes appear,
and are manipulated, as POSIX threads.

Some routines from the C libraries do not port very well to multi-threaded
environments. They expect to be the only thread of execution in a process, and
so may adjust links in tables without taking any precautions. When there is
more than one thread of control in a process, such assumptions are not valid.
As all threads have access to all the data structures in the memory space of
the process, there is always the possibility of two or more threads interfering
with one another's work. Because of this, libraries have to be rewritten to be
thread safe.

3.5 Representing processes

As with all software systems, an operating system uses data structures to represent the objects it is dealing with. We will examine many such structures in the course of our study; all will be declared as C structs.

For each process known to it, the operating system maintains a data structure known as a process descriptor or a process control block. This contains all of the information which it needs to control the process.

Before we get into the details of how Linux implements process control blocks, there are some design points to consider. All of this can be implemented statically, in fixed size tables. This has the advantage that the information relating to a particular process can be found immediately by indexing into this table. The downside is that there can be a lot of wasted space, if there are only a few processes running, and space has been allocated for hundreds; furthermore, there is a maximum number of processes that can be running at one time.

Another possibility is to allocate space dynamically, only for as long as required; this is usually done using a linked list. This means that there is never too much or too little space allocated for process control blocks. The drawback is that you cannot index into such a list—you have to search it sequentially. This has to be done frequently, so it represents a significant overhead.

Process control blocks in Linux

Linux actually uses both systems. The structures themselves are allocated dynamically, when a new process is created, and kept on a doubly linked list. But to avoid the overhead of frequently searching this list, the structures are also maintained as a hash list. The hash table at the root of this list is set up statically at boot time. This is illustrated in Figure 3.6.

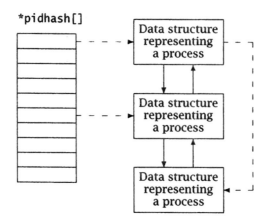

Figure 3.6: How the system keeps track of processes

The hash list is defined as `struct task_struct *pidhash[]`, in the file `<fork.c>`. Each element of the list is merely a pointer to a linked list of process control blocks, as indicated by the dashed lines in Figure 3.6.

The task_struct structure in Linux

The structure which is used in Linux to represent a process is `task_struct`, and is defined in `<sched.h>`. One `task_struct` is allocated per active process. It contains all of the data needed to keep track of the process, whether it is running or not. The operating system guarantees to keep this information in memory at all times.

This is probably the single most important data structure in the Linux kernel, so we will examine it in detail. The most relevant fields in `task_struct` are shown in Figure 3.7. There is a sense in which this is a sort of table of contents for the remainder of the book.

```
struct task_struct{
        volatile long          state;
        long                   counter, priority;
        struct task_struct     *next_task, *prev_task;
        struct task_struct     *next_run, *prev_run;
        int                    exit_code, exit_signal;
        int                    pid;
        struct task_struct     *p_opptr, *p_cptr;
        struct wait_queue      *wait_chldexit;
        struct task_struct     *pidhash_next;
        unsigned long          policy;
        struct tms             times;
        unsigned long          start_time;
        unsigned short         uid, gid;
        struct thread_struct   tss;
        struct files_struct    *files;
        struct mm_struct       *mm;
        struct signal_struct   *sig;
        sigset_t               signal, blocked;
};
```

Figure 3.7: Data structure representing a process

- The values in the `state` field will be discussed in detail in Section 3.8.

- The `counter` field contains the amount of CPU time (measured in Linux's own unit of 'ticks') remaining to this process. The `priority` field contains the priority of the process. Their use by the scheduler will be discussed in Section 3.10.

- The `next_task` and `prev_task` fields are the backward and forward pointers which hold the whole linked list of structures together. The list is headed by the global variable `init_task`.

- The next_run and prev_run fields are the backwards and forwards pointers which hold the structure on the run queue. This will be discussed in Section 3.8.

- The information to be returned to the parent when this process terminates is in exit_code. This will be discussed in Section 3.12. If the process was terminated by a signal, then the exit_signal field contains the number of that signal. Signals will be discussed in Chapter 5.

- Each process is given its own unique process identification number (pid) when it is created. This number is maintained in the pid field. This is the unique identifier which is hashed into the list of Figure 3.6, to find the task_struct corresponding to a particular process. The getpid() system service returns the pid of the current process, while getppid() returns that of the parent process.

- There are a number of pointers to the structures representing other processes, which are related to this one. The process which actually created it is pointed to by p_opptr. Its most recently created child process is pointed to by p_cptr.

- When a process is waiting for a child to terminate, it waits on a struct wait_queue pointed to from the wait_chldexit field. This is discussed in Section 3.12.

- As we have seen, these task_struct structures are maintained on a hash list, which is threaded through the pidhash_next field.

- The policy field determines the scheduling policy associated with this process. The significance of this field is discussed in Section 3.10.

- The time the process has spent in user mode and in kernel (system) mode is kept in times.

- The time when the process was created is kept in start_time.

- There are a number of identifiers associated with the process. The operating system uses these ids to determine whether or not to grant a process access to specific system resources. The id of the user who created the process is in uid. The system service getuid() returns this value, while setuid() allows a process with the appropriate privileges to change its uid.

- There is a corresponding group identifier gid associated with the process, which identifies the group to which the owner belongs. The system service getgid() returns this value. The gid can be changed using setgid().

- The tss field contains a copy of the processor registers, saved when the process is not running. This is sometimes known as the volatile environment. It contains all the information that needs to be saved when a process loses control of a processor. While it is architecture specific, it would include the values in all of the registers, especially the program counter (EIP)

and the program status word or flags register, EFLAGS. It is described in detail in Section 3.9.

- The `files_struct` which `files` points to contains information about the I/O streams which this process has open. This will be dealt with in Chapter 9, which will open up the whole second half of the book.

- The `mm` field points to a structure containing control information used for memory management, and will be followed up in Chapter 8.

- The `sig` field is a pointer to the array of signal handlers declared in this process, and its relevance will be explained in Section 5.2.

- There are two bitmaps for dealing with signals. The first, `signal`, identifies those signals which are pending to the process; the second, `blocked`, identifies signals which the process has currently masked. These will be discussed in detail in Section 5.2.

3.6 Process creation

All operating systems have some way of creating new processes. With most of them, the name of an executable program is required as a parameter to the relevant system service. The process control block representing the new process is then linked onto the process structure, where it is indistinguishable from the others already there, and competes with them for a share of CPU time.

In Unix the system service which creates a new process is `fork()`. This creates an exact copy of the running process. So immediately after the call to `fork()` there are two processes, each executing the same program. Each of them is at exactly the same point in the program—the next instruction after the `fork()`, and both will continue on from there. This is not very useful. Normally, one of them then asks the operating system to run another program, so the end result is one process executing one program, and the second process executing the other.

Implementation

When the `fork()` system service is called, the Linux kernel first checks if the user has the required permissions to create a new process. If so, then it allocates memory for a new `task_struct`. It is linked with the already existing structures, through the `next_task` and `prev_task` fields. It is assigned a new pid, and this is used to hash the structure into the `pidhash[]` table. All of the other fields are copied from its parent's `task_struct`. The new process has its own copies of all of these—but it begins life with its parent's values.

Linux also has a non-standard system service, `clone()`. This is similar to `fork()`, but it has a number of parameters, specifying which resources are to be shared with its parent. Depending on the parameters passed to `clone()`,

it can share memory (including program), file systems (root and current directory), open files, signal handlers, id number. The `fork()` system service is actually implemented internally by a call to `clone()`.

In Linux, the `pthread` library creates new threads by a call to `clone()`. This effectively creates a new process, identical to its parent in everything except the volatile environment, the `tss` field.

Shell exercise

The following simple exercise gives a feel for creating a second process. It is assumed that readers are familiar with one of the Unix shells. Remember from what was said in Chapter 1 that the shell command interpreter is just another program. When a command is entered, for example `ls`, the shell creates a new process to run the corresponding program, and blocks itself until that child process terminates. Then it wakes up again, prints its prompt, and waits for the next input.

In Unix it is legal to put an & after a shell command, for example `ls` &. In this case the shell creates a new process to run the `ls` program as before, but now it does not block itself. It just goes around its internal loop, prints its prompt again, and waits for input. Almost always this new prompt is mixed in with the output from the `ls` program, and it seems that there was no prompt after the list of files. But a careful examination will show that it is there somewhere. This is evidence that two things are going on at the same time.

Another example is to type `sleep 100` & at the prompt. This creates a process which runs the sleep program, and tells it to sleep for 100 seconds. So now there is a second process in existence, even if it is doing nothing. The system should have responded with something like [1] 234. The number in this example is the unique identifier for the new process, and will vary each time. Of course the shell is still active in this case, and will put up its prompt.

If the `ps` command, which lists the processes in the system, is run at this stage, it should show that there are two processes belonging to the current user.

The `kill` command sends a signal to terminate a process. It takes two parameters, the number of the signal to send, and the id number of the process to be terminated. With the previous example, the command `kill SIGKILL 234` sends the SIGKILL signal to process number 234, which should terminate the sleeping process. After this, the `ps` command should show that there is only the one process running.

System service exercise

We now go on to look at how a new process is created from within a running program. As this is the first exercise in system programming, the reader is referred to the introduction to system programming given in Section 2.1.

The first system service we will use is `fork()`. There are no parameters to this system service. Remember what it does. It creates a new process, running

a duplicate copy of the existing program. Both processes continue execution at the next instruction after the fork(). The three-line example in Figure 3.8 illustrates this.

```
printf ("Before the fork\n");
fork ();
printf ("After the fork\n");
```

Figure 3.8: Program to illustrate fork()

Before running this program, work out what output would be expected on the screen, and why. Then try the program. Were the results as expected? Normally the duplication of the second message would be considered an error. After all, the program only gave instructions to print it once. But of course after the fork(), there are two copies of the program running, and each prints the message once.

Return values

The example in Figure 3.8 did not consider the possible return values from fork(). If for some reason the fork() does not work, then it will return -1. So the value in errno must be checked. According to the manual page there are only two possibilities. EAGAIN means that the maximum number of processes allowed to a user by the system administrator has been exceeded. There is not much that can be done about that. ENOMEM means that there is not enough memory available to create the new process. This is a very unusual situation. The program should print an appropriate error message and terminate.

Parent and child

Remember that fork() will return a value in both processes. The value returned in the child process will always be 0. This is the magic key to deciding whether the program is executing in the parent or child process. If fork() returns a positive number, not only is it in the parent process, but that number is the id-number of the child process.

So now it is possible to write a program which, after the fork, checks for these three possible return values. If the value is -1, it does error handling. If it is 0, then it prints a message saying that it is the child. Any other number, and it prints a message saying it is the parent. This checking can be done either with nested ifs, or with a switch statement.

The next step is to get the parent to print odd numbers, and the child to print even numbers. It may be necessary to print the first thousand or so numbers, because the parent gets a good start on the child, but eventually the output from the two processes will begin to appear interspersed on the screen. It is actually possible to see each process getting its share of time on the processor.

Two other system services can be tried out at this stage. Both the parent and the child can call `getpid()`, which returns the pid of the process which calls it. The parent of course already knows the pid of the child, which was returned by `fork()`. The child can get the pid of the parent by calling `getppid()`. The values returned by these calls can be used by the processes to print information about themselves.

Running a new program

One or other, or both, of the processes can be directed to run a different program, by using the `exec()` system call. This deallocates the memory used by the old program, allocates memory for and loads in the new program file, and sets the state of the CPU registers to begin execution of the new program.

This is an unusual system service, in that it cannot be called directly. There are several functions in the C library which a programmer can use. Each of these passes the request on to `exec()`. The reason for this extra complication is that the new program to be run may require parameters to be passed to it. These can be passed as a list, or as an array. Then the full pathname for the new executable can be given, or the program can be searched for in the PATH directories. Finally the new program can inherit the environment of its parent, or it can be passed a new environment of its own. All of these possibilities are catered for by the different library functions.

3.7 Thread creation and termination

The interface used for manipulating threads is the POSIX `pthread` library of functions. All thread functions return 0 if successful, otherwise an error code. Note that they return the error code; `errno` is not used. Hence `perror()` cannot be used either.

Thread creation

A new thread is created by the `pthread_create()` function. At the library level, each thread has an identifier of type `pthread_t`. A variable of this type must be declared in the program, and its address passed as a parameter to `pthread_create()`.

The second parameter specifies the attributes the new thread will have. A NULL value here means that the new thread will have the default attributes.

The third parameter specifies where the new thread will begin execution. As the new thread belongs to the same process, it must execute code from within the same program. But it cannot start just anywhere. Each thread starts at the beginning of some function, known as its start routine, and terminates when it comes to the end of that function. It may, of course, call other functions, even nested sub-functions.

So this third parameter is the address of the start routine—in C this is its name, without the usual (). Remember you are not calling the function, you are passing its address to the thread creator. The difference between calling a function, and creating a thread to execute a function, is illustrated in the upper and lower parts of Figure 3.9.

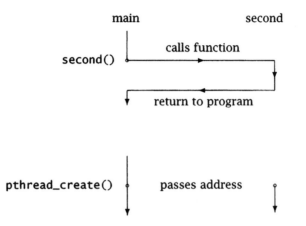

Figure 3.9: Function call and thread creation

With a function call, the main program is suspended until the function has completed; it then resumes at the instruction after the function call. When a new thread is created to execute a function, the main program is not held up; both continue in parallel.

The difference can be illustrated with an extension of an example we have seen before. If you run low on flour while baking, you can stop what you are doing, and go to the shop to buy some. Then, when you return, you can take up exactly where you stopped. The other possibility is that you can send someone else to the shop (in good time), while you continue with what you have.

The start function for a thread must always be declared in such a way that it takes one argument, a pointer to void, and also returns a pointer to void.

To pass parameters to the function called in the new thread, there is a fourth argument, another pointer to void. The thread creator arranges that this pointer is passed to the thread's start routine.

Each thread has its own stack, so it has its own private copy of any local variables declared in the function. Another thread executing the same function will have a different copy of these variables.

A thread exists until it both terminates and has been detached.

Thread termination

A thread can terminate in one of three different ways.

- It comes to the end of its start routine. The return value of the function is saved, to be returned to the caller of a pthread_join().

- Alternatively, a thread can call `pthread_exit()` anywhere in its code, giving it a return value, a pointer to void. The pointer in `pthread_exit()` must point to data that exists after the thread exits—so that data must be declared as `static`.

- Some other thread calls `pthread_cancel()`, which is a request to terminate as soon as possible.

But in all cases the data structure representing the thread remains in the system until it has been detached.

Detaching a thread

A thread can be detached in two ways.

- Some other thread calls `pthread_detach()`. If the target thread has already terminated, then all of its data structures are removed from the system at this stage. If not, then it is marked for deletion when it does terminate.

- Some other thread calls `pthread_join()`, which allows a return value to be passed back. The caller is then blocked until the thread terminates.

3.8 Process life cycle

Each process has a life cycle of its own, during which it may be in one of five different states. The state a process is in at any particular time is recorded in the `state` field of its `task_struct` structure.

States

It may be in the TASK_RUNNING state. This means that it is ready and able to do some work. Typically there would be many processes in this state, linked together on a run queue, through the `next_run` and `prev_run` fields of the `task_struct`. But on a single processor machine, only one of them can be using the CPU at any one time. On a multiprocessor of course, as many processes can be actually executing as there are CPUs.

A process may, for some reason or other, be unable to use the CPU, even if offered it. In general, a process in this state is waiting for some event. This may be a physical resource, such as a printer or a modem, or it may be waiting for an event such as a key to be pressed, or as in Section 3.3, waiting for requested data to be delivered from a disk.

The mechanism for waiting on an event is always invoked by the process itself; one process cannot force another to wait for an event. A process must specify to the kernel which event it is waiting for.

In Linux, waiting processes are kept on wait queues, one per event. For example, a process waiting for keyboard input would be linked from a pointer in the data structure representing the keyboard. When a key is pressed, the interrupt handler finds the `task_struct` representing the waiting process, changes its state to TASK_RUNNING, and moves it to the run queue.

To allow more than one process to wait on the same event, a link data structure `wait_queue`, is used, see Figure 3.10, from `<linux/wait.h>`.

```
struct wait_queue{
        struct task_struct *task;
        struct wait_queue   *next;
};
```

Figure 3.10: An entry in a wait queue

The situation where three processes are waiting for a particular resource is illustrated in Figure 3.11.

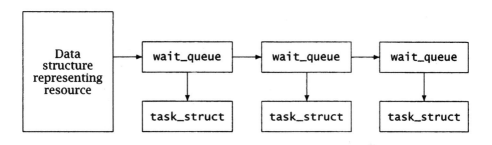

Figure 3.11: Three processes waiting for a resource

Sometimes the delay is likely to last a long time, such as waiting for a key to be pressed, or a message to come in over the network. With long-term waiting like this, some other event may occur in the system which affects this process, possibly causing it to stop waiting. An example would be the user pressing a break key. It must be possible to wake the process up from such a wait. So it is said to be waiting interruptibly, and is in the TASK_INTERRUPTIBLE state.

If the delay is likely to be short, such as waiting for a request for a read on a file to complete, then the process is not allowed to be interrupted. The reasoning behind this is that it is going to wake up in a short time, anyway, and it can then attend to whatever event has occurred. Such a process is in the TASK_UNINTERRUPTIBLE state.

After a process has been terminated, but while its `task_struct` is still in the system, it is in the TASK_ZOMBIE state.

Finally, a process can be halted, not at its own request, but by some other process. Typically this is when a process is being debugged, and it is being stepped through its execution one instruction at a time. Such a process is in the TASK_STOPPED state.

Transitions

The possible transitions between the states are shown in Figure 3.12, which for completeness, also shows where processes enter and leave the system.

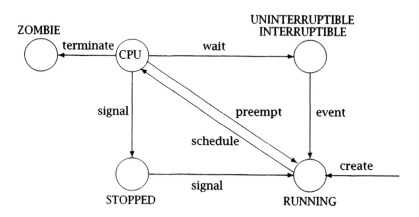

Figure 3.12: Process states and transitions

When a new process is created, it always begins in the TASK_RUNNING state, on the run queue. Eventually it will be given a time slice on the CPU. When this transition takes place is the responsibility of the scheduler.

A process may stop using the CPU for four reasons.

- It may do so voluntarily, while it is waiting for a resource, and so it moves either to the TASK_INTERRUPTIBLE or the TASK_UNINTERRUPTIBLE state.

- It may decide to terminate itself, so it moves to the TASK_ZOMBIE state.

- The operating system may take the processor from it, even though it has further instructions to execute. This is called preemption. The operating system does this when a process has used up its share of time, or when the CPU is needed to handle some more urgent work. In either case, when a process is preempted, it moves back to the run queue.

- Finally, a process moves to the TASK_STOPPED state when it is stopped by a signal from its parent, or some other process. A subsequent signal moves it to the run queue.

A process leaves the TASK_INTERRUPTIBLE or the TASK_UNINTERRUPTIBLE state when the event it is waiting for occurs. The only way it can move is to the TASK_RUNNING state, where it will take its turn and eventually move back to the CPU.

Transitions between user and kernel mode

As explained in the previous chapter, all modern CPUs have two modes of operation. In kernel mode, the CPU can execute all of its instruction set, including

some very specialised instructions, called the privileged instruction set. This would include instructions to set and change protection, to halt the processor, and even the instruction to change between user and kernel mode.

In user mode, the processor can execute most of its instruction set, certainly all of the instructions in normal application programs, but it cannot execute any privileged instructions.

This dual mode of operation introduces extra complications into the state transitions we have just examined. Only one process can still be running at the one time, but now it can be running in either user mode or in kernel mode.

An expanded version of the right-hand side of the diagram is given in Figure 3.13.

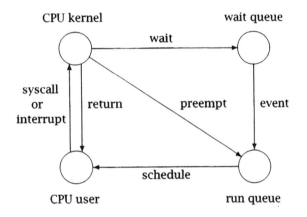

Figure 3.13: Running in user or kernel mode

A process is always scheduled from the run queue on to the CPU in user mode. There are two occasions when it moves from user mode to kernel mode. The first is when an interrupt occurs. Referring back to the example in Section 3.3, process A is running in user mode when drive 2 interrupts. The hardware interrupt mechanism automatically suspends process A, changes the CPU to kernel mode, and runs the appropriate code to service the disk. When this code is finished, the return from interrupt instruction sets the CPU back to user mode, and returns to executing code in process A.

The other occasion when a change from user mode to kernel mode occurs is when the running process makes a call to a system service. But this introduces an unusual feature. The system service software causes an interrupt—a software interrupt this time. While this is different in origin from the more normal hardware interrupt, its effect is the same. So calls to system services are just special cases of an interrupt causing a transfer to kernel mode.

The wait transition results from a system call, so the process will always be running in kernel mode when this occurs. Preemption typically occurs when a timer interrupts, so the process will also be in kernel mode when it is preempted.

3.9 Context switching

This is the name given to the whole procedure of re-allocating a processor from one process to another. As we have seen in the last section, a process loses control of the processor for one of four reasons. Either it terminates, it moves onto a wait queue to wait for a resource to become available, it is stopped by a signal, or a timer interrupts to tell it that it has used up its time slice. It is absolutely essential that the current state of the machine be saved, when a process loses control of the CPU. This state includes the values in the general purpose registers, stack pointer, memory management registers, and most especially the processor status register and the program counter. When eventually some time in the future the process now being switched out becomes eligible to run again, it will then be possible to set up the machine exactly as it was after the last instruction was executed. So the next instruction will operate on the correct state, and the process (sequence of states) will continue properly.

This state, or volatile environment, is saved in the architecture specific `struct thread_struct`. This is the `tss` field of the `task_struct`. For the PC specific version, see Figure 3.14, from `<asm/processor.h>`. This contains a field for each of the hardware registers. The CR3 register holds a pointer to the data structures concerned with memory management. Next there is a copy of the instruction pointer (EIP) and status register (EFLAGS), then the four general purpose registers, then four pointer and index registers, finally six segment registers.

```
struct thread_struct{
        unsigned long   cr3;
        unsigned long   eip;
        unsigned long   eflags;
        unsigned long   eax,ebx,ecx,edx;
        unsigned long   esp;
        unsigned long   ebp;
        unsigned long   esi;
        unsigned long   edi;
        unsigned short  ss;
        unsigned short  cs;
        unsigned short  ds;
        unsigned short  es;
        unsigned short  fs;
        unsigned short  gs;
};
```

Figure 3.14: The volatile environment of a process

With the general purpose registers, pointers, and segment registers, values are copied directly from the hardware registers to the `thread_struct`. But this cannot be done in the case of the EIP and EFLAGS registers. These now contain

values corresponding to the context switcher, which is the currently running program. To find the values corresponding to the process being switched out, we have to remember that a context switch will always have been initiated by an interrupt. The interrupt mechanism will have saved the EIP and FLAGS of the running process on the stack. And so the context switcher pops these values from the stack to the thread_struct.

The movement of data involved in this first half of context switching is shown in Figure 3.15. The dashed lines represent data saved by the interrupt mechanism; the solid lines represent work done by the context switcher.

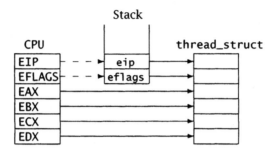

Figure 3.15: Data saved by context switcher

Presumably the state of the new process is available in its thread_struct. This was saved there when it was context switched out, some time previously. This state is now copied from the thread_struct to the appropriate registers.

The whole sequence of operations involved in context switching from ProcessA to ProcessB is shown in Figure 3.16, with time running down the page.

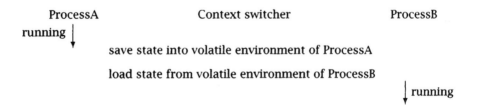

Figure 3.16: Context switching

The order in which the various items of information are copied to the registers from the thread_struct is not important, except that it is essential that the value of the EIP be the last item moved. Remember that there must be some program giving instructions for all of this moving. It is in fact the context switcher. While it is running, the EIP is pointing to context switcher code. If the EIP were the first register restored, then the next instruction would not be taken from context switcher code, but from wherever the EIP is now pointing—into the middle of the new program. So the program would be started up, without most of its state. This would lead to chaos.

There is considerable overhead in this context switching. There may be dozens of 32-bit (or even 64-bit) registers to move, in two directions. Because it is an operation that is done so frequently, speed is important. Modern machines tend to have special instructions to do this, rather than expecting the operating system designers to write code for it.

3.10 Scheduling

The previous section examined how a process is set up to run on a processor. Scheduling determines *which* process will be next. The main objective of the scheduler is to see that the CPU is shared among all contending processes as fairly as possible. But fairness can mean different things in different situations.

In an interactive system, the scheduler tries to make the *response time* as short as possible. A typical target would be 50–150ms. Users can find it quite off-putting if the response time varies wildly, say from 10–1000ms. If one keystroke is echoed immediately, and the next is not echoed for a second, a user is inclined to press the key again, with all the consequent errors.

A batch system will not be concerned with response time, but with maximising the use of expensive peripherals. Many different scheduling algorithms have been developed for such systems, such as first-come first-served (FIFO), and shortest-job-first (SJF). In this section we concentrate on the algorithms implemented in Linux. See the further reading section at the end of the chapter for references to others.

In real-time systems, the scheduler will have to be able to guarantee that response time will never exceed a certain maximum. For example, a multimedia system handling video and audio must have access to the processor at predefined intervals.

One very simple scheduling policy would be static, fixed priority ordering. This would be suitable in a process control situation. The function and duration of all processes would be known in advance, at design time. So a decision can be made once and for all on who goes next.

For example, a process controlling a sensor may be run, followed by a process which does some calculations on the input data, followed by a process which controls a valve. Then the sensor process again.

Priority

This simple sort of scheduling will not work in an interactive system. There is no way to predict in advance how many processes will be running, or how long they will want to run for. They could be scheduled on a first-come first-served basis. But this way some long-running, though unimportant processes could monopolise the system, while urgent processes languish on a queue.

So a common practice is to order all of the runnable or ready processes by some priority criterion. There could be any number of priorities, typically 8, 16, or 32. The simplest way to think about it is that this priority reflects the

importance of the owner of the process, and is allocated when it is created.
The descriptors of all runnable processes are linked into a queue, ordered by
decreasing priority. This is an extra set of links, threaded through each process
control block. It is known as the run queue. The highest priority (most eligible)
process is at the head, then the next, and so on. All the other processes, which
are not runnable, are linked together (through the same fields) on another
queue, known as the wait queue. The situation is illustrated in Figure 3.17.

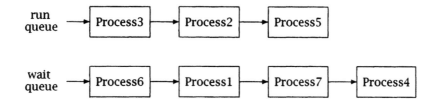

Figure 3.17: Processes on the ready and wait queues

When the CPU finishes with one process, the one at the head of the queue is
chosen to run next. A question arises as to where to put the current or running
process. It could be at the head of the queue. Another possibility is that it could
be taken off the queue altogether, and pointed to directly from some location
in the kernel. Linux for example keeps a pointer to the `task_struct` of the
running process in the global variable `current`.

This scheme allows a high priority process to stay ahead of a lower priority
one in the queue. But once such a low priority process does eventually get
to run on the CPU, there is nothing to stop it monopolising the system, and
holding up higher priority processes which later become runnable.

So a further extension to the priority mechanism is required. Now when a
process is scheduled onto the CPU, it is not given unlimited use of it. Instead
it gets a certain time slice on the processor. This is called the quantum. Each
time the hardware timer interrupts, the scheduler decrements the quantum.
When it gets to zero, it is time to context switch. If a process is still runnable
when its time is up, the context switcher moves it back to its appropriate place
in the queue.

The size of the time slice can have an effect on performance. If it is too
large, interactive processes will find themselves spending long periods of time
waiting for the CPU. Timesharing will become very obvious to the user. On the
other hand, as the time slice is decreased, the overhead of context switching
grows. So if the time slice is too small, the machine could spend most of its
time context switching, instead of doing productive work.

Multilevel priority queues

Some systems use separate queues for each priority. Each queue is organised
as a set of links through the process control blocks, and within each queue a
process is given a quantum on the CPU, then moved to the tail of the queue.

The scheduler will only select a process from a queue when all higher priority queues are empty.

A system can allow for the possibility of the priority changing over time. For example, consider a system with two priorities, high and low, as illustrated in Figure 3.18. Interactive processes would be given high priority—they need to be able to respond quickly to external events, such as a key being pressed. Processes which are making intensive use of the CPU and have no interaction with the terminal, such as compilations, can be given low priority. Nobody is going to get upset it it takes a second or two longer.

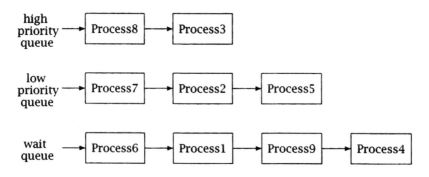

Figure 3.18: Two different priority queues

When a process is created, it is initially put on the high-priority queue. If it uses its full timeslice, this implies that it is compute bound. So when it is context switched out, it is moved to the tail of the low-priority queue. On the other hand, if the process gives up the processor to wait for an I/O event, it can be assumed that it is interactive, and it is moved to the wait queue, but with high priority. Then when the event it is waiting for occurs, it is moved to the high-priority queue. This queue is allocated the processor sooner, but is expected to keep it for a shorter time. It is always offered the processor before the low-priority queue.

The situation described can be generalised to any number of priorities. Typically, different queues would have different time slices. I/O bound processes would have high priority, hence receive rapid service. But they would have short time slices, because it is unlikely that they will do much processing before giving up the processor and waiting for more I/O.

On the other hand, CPU bound processes have lower priorities, hence they have to wait longer between turns on the CPU. But they would have longer time slices, so when they do get the processor, they can make significant use of it.

Scheduling in Linux

Linux has 64 priorities, ranging from 0 (the lowest) to 63. Each new interactive process is assigned a base priority of 12. This static priority is contained in the `priority` field of the `task_struct`. Linux has only one run queue, linked

through the `next_run` and `prev_run` fields of the `task_struct`. Each time the scheduler is called, it searches this to find the most eligible process.

Scheduling policies

By default, the system is timesharing. All runnable processes have equal access to the CPU. But there are other possibilities, which we will look at briefly before concentrating on timesharing. The policy in use is recorded in the `policy` field of `struct task_struct`.

SCHED_RR This is fixed priority. An RR (for round robin) process is given its priority when it is created, and it does not change throughout its lifetime. Such a process runs until one of these three events occurs.

- It blocks itself, in which case it moves to the wait queue.
- It is preempted because a higher priority process has become runnable. In this case, it stays on the run queue.
- It uses up its quantum, in which case it also remains on the run queue. When, and how, it is allocated a new quantum will be described shortly.

SCHED_FIFO This is also fixed priority, but it has no quantum. It runs until it blocks or is preempted.

These two specialised policies are used by real-time applications, and by some system processes within the kernel.

SCHED_OTHER This is the normal timesharing policy. It adjusts process priorities to favour interactive ones over compute-intensive ones.

The policy in force for any process can be examined and changed by using the `sched_getscheduler()` and `sched_setscheduler()` functions, respectively. The static priority associated with a process can be examined and changed using the `sched_getparam()` and `sched_setparam()` system services, respectively.

The maximum and minimum static priority which can be allocated under any particular policy can be found using `sched_get_priority_max()` and `sched_get_priority_min()`.

Calculating priority

In Unix, priority has always been related to the amount of CPU time the process used, with the heavy users at the bottom. Of course, all processes would eventually sink to the bottom with such a system. So the scheduler gradually forgets CPU usage. This means that while a process is sitting in a wait queue, its priority actually rises. This favours interactive processes—even the little CPU time they use is quickly forgotten, so they tend to have highest priorities.

Linux implements this priority adjustment as follows. Each `task_struct` has a `counter` field, which effectively is the quantum for that process. The

counter value of the current process is decremented on each clock tick. When it gets to 0, then the scheduler is called.

Each time it is called, the scheduler examines the run queue of processes in the TASK_RUNNING state, and calculates a factor called the goodness for each one. For a SCHED_RR or SCHED_FIFO process, goodness is always priority + 1000. This will boost it way above any SCHED_OTHER (interactive) process. Otherwise, goodness is just the value of counter. The process with the highest goodness is the next to run. So if there are any SCHED_RR or SCHED_FIFO processes on the run queue, they will get the CPU first, which is what we want. Otherwise the interactive process with the largest remaining quantum will be chosen.

If goodness is 0 for all processes on the run queue, then the scheduler updates the counter field of all processes, including those on wait queues. This is called rescheduling. The formula used is

$$counter = priority + (counter)/2$$

For a process on the run queue, as its counter is already 0, this means that its counter value is set back to its static priority again. For a process on a wait queue, its counter value is actually increased. But to prevent a long-waiting process from acquiring an unreasonably high counter value, half of its previous value is forgotten each time. This means that it continues to increase, but more slowly each time it is rescheduled.

When a process goes back on the run queue after waiting, if its counter value is greater than that of current, then the scheduler is called. Otherwise it just takes its turn with the others, waiting to be selected by the scheduler.

Multiprocessor scheduling

Scheduling for machines with more than one CPU brings in extra difficulties of its own. Two big decisions which have to be made are: should the operating system be given a processor of its own, or should it run on whichever processor is free; and should there be individual queues for each processor, or should there be system-wide queues?

Linux is capable of running on a multiprocessor architecture. Following the Unix philosophy of having very few system processes, most kernel code is executed in the context of the process which calls a system service. So the question of whether or not the kernel should have a processor of its own does not arise. As all processes are equal, and can run on any CPU, there is only one system-wide run queue. This arrangement is known as symmetric multiprocessing.

3.11 Null process

It can happen that at a particular time, the run queue is empty. This may be because there is no work to be done, for example the user is on the phone, or

has taken a coffee break. Or there may be many processes in the system, but all of them are blocked waiting for some resource or other. This would imply that the mix of jobs in the system is not as good as it could be. But there is very little control over such a mix in an interactive system.

What does the operating system do in such a situation? It could execute a do-nothing loop, waiting for one process to become runnable, and then schedule it onto the processor. The problem can be avoided altogether by introducing an extra process, called the null process. This is created when the system is booted. It is guaranteed to be always runnable as it makes no blocking system calls, and does no I/O. It has the lowest possible priority; the lowest user priority is at least one above this. So it can never monopolise the processor; as soon as any other process becomes runnable, the system will preempt the null process, because the new process is guaranteed to have a higher priority.

Such a null process could be just an idle loop. Some operators use it to run system diagnostics or do system accounting. Others use it to calculate prime numbers or expand π.

3.12 Process termination

A Unix process terminates when the program it is running comes to an end. There is a special system service, exit(), by which a child process can let its parent know that it has finished, and also pass back some information about why it finished—whether this was normal or abnormal. The compiler includes a call to exit(), if the programmer does not.

Because of the use of a system call, a process always terminates from kernel mode. First of all, it deallocates resources, such as memory or open files. It then moves to a new state, TASK_ZOMBIE. At this stage it has no memory or program, just its task_struct structure, the exit_code field of which holds the information it wants to pass back to its parent. The scheduler is then called to schedule a new process onto the CPU.

When eventually the parent calls the wait() system service, and picks up this status information, the task_struct is deallocated, and so the last trace of the terminating process is removed from the system.

The programming example from Section 3.6 can be extended, by a call to exit() at the end of the child program. This is one of the few system services which does not return a value. Note that on the manual page it is declared as void. This makes sense. The exit() terminates the process—so there is not going to be any process around to check a return value. A byte of status information can be included as a parameter to exit(), and the system sees to it that that byte is delivered to the parent. It is stored in bits 8-15 of the exit_code field in the task_struct.

Also a call to the wait() system service is included in the parent process. This operates as follows. If the child has already done an exit() before the parent does a wait(), then the parent just picks up the status information, and goes on. On the other hand, if the parent does a wait() before the child

exits, then the parent process is held up until the child does so. This is similar to pthread_join() for a thread.

The wait() returns a value, -1 if it was unable to wait, otherwise a positive integer which is the pid of the child process that exited. If the optional parameter (a pointer to an int) is passed to wait(), then the system puts the value from the exit_code field of the child into this int. The macro WEXITSTATUS(), from <sys/wait.h>, returns bits 8-15 of this integer value.

There are variants of wait(), as well as macros for extracting other information from the status value. See the manual page for wait(2).

Some further ramifications of process termination can be demonstrated by having the parent terminate itself immediately after the fork(), without calling wait(). If the child process works for a few seconds, printing a few thousand numbers, for example, and then calls getppid(), this should now return 1. The parent is dead, so the orphan process has been adopted by the init process, which always has a pid of 1.

If a process dies before its parent, which does not call wait(), then the struct task_struct of the child is not released. The ps command shows it as <zombie>. It cannot be killed, because it is already dead. The init process periodically does a wait() to get rid of such dead orphans.

3.13 Summary

1. A program is a sequence of instructions. A process is a sequence of actions, performed by executing a program.

2. Each user-level activity, and each source of asynchronous events, may be assigned a process of its own. The process manager is itself a process, and the memory manager may consist of several processes collaborating together.

3. As there is normally only one processor, it is shared among all processes.

4. A process consists of a set of system resources, such as a program and memory space, and one or more threads, which are control paths through the program. If a process is blocked in one thread, it can execute another.

5. The system keeps track of each process by means of a data structure called a process descriptor. In practice this can be a fairly complex collection of structures, each representing one aspect of the process. Linux uses dynamically allocated process descriptors, a struct task_struct. These are maintained on a doubly linked list, and also on a hash structure.

6. In Unix, new processes are created as almost exact clones of their parents. The main difference is that they have an identification number of their own. Any process can change the program it is running, by calling exec().

7. Further threads can then be created to run within that process.

8. At any given time, a process will either be runnable, waiting, or stopped. In Unix a process can be running in user mode, or in kernel mode.

9. When a processor is being reallocated from one process to another, it is necessary to save the current state of the machine. This is done in a `struct thread_struct`, which is machine specific.

10. The decision as to which process to run next is known as scheduling. This could be on a first-come first-served, run to completion basis. More commonly, a variation of this called round robin is used, where each process gets a maximum amount of time, the quantum. If it does not finish within the quantum, it is context switched out, and put at the back of the queue.

    Even more typically, priority schemes are used, with a different queue of waiting processes for each priority. Linux has 64 such priorities. The priority of a process is dynamically adjusted to reflect its historical use of the CPU.

11. There may be a null process, which is run when the run queue is empty.

12. When a process terminates, it can send status information back to its parent.

3.14 Discussion questions

1. Unix does not have a system process for the network card. Who then is responsible for handling a network package when it arrives?

2. Figure 3.3 is an oversimplification. Redraw it to include a row representing the operating system itself.

3. When a process moves from running to idle, the state of the machine has to be saved. Obviously this cannot mean the whole state, as there would be no place to save it. Just what information has to be saved?

4. When threads are implemented in the kernel, does the operating system have to transfer control to another thread in the *same* process, or could it transfer control to a thread of another process?

5. One way of implementing a multi-threaded server would be to have a boss thread, which gives out jobs to a number of worker threads. Discuss the tradeoffs involved in having a fixed number of these, as opposed to creating a new one for each job, and terminating it when finished.

6. There are two different implementations of POSIX `pthreads` in Linux. One is at user level, the other is as kernel threads. Which one is installed on the system you are using?

7. Investigate the `clone()` system service. Would the `pthread` interface be preferable?

8. Process descriptors could be kept on hash queues. How would this compare for efficiency with static tables and linked lists?

9. Some operating systems create a new process as a clone of the existing one; others create a new process with a new program. Discuss the advantages and disadvantages of both systems.

10. What would happen if the fork() system call were inside a loop?

11. Why do you think there is no system service which returns the id of a child process?

12. Investigate the different versions of the exec() system service, and distinguish between them.

13. The perror() library function should never be used with thread functions. Why not?

14. What is the difference between a function recursively calling itself, and a function creating a new thread to run another copy of itself?

15. Investigate how to pass parameters to a thread, when creating it.

16. List all the possible combinations of terminating and detaching, which result in the data structures representing a thread being removed from the system.

17. What would happen to a process if all of its threads terminate and are detached?

18. Modern CPUs have special instructions to do all of the copying of registers required at a context switch. Investigate this instruction for a machine of your choice.

19. What happens if a thread uses up its quantum, but is still the highest priority thread in the whole system? How is this situation avoided with multilevel feedback queues?

Concurrency 4

The previous chapter introduced the concept of a process as the unit of work within a computer system. We have seen that it is possible, even likely, that many processes will be in existence at the same time. Each will be somewhere between its initial state and its final state; it is in process. Such processes are said to be concurrent, running at the same time. As there is typically only one processor, we only have apparent concurrency, with the operating system switching between whichever process has control at any one time.

If the processes are unrelated, and never need to interact in any way, then there should be no problem. But frequently they do need to work together to achieve the goal of the concurrent system. For example, many processes may each generate part of a solution; these parts then need to be combined. Another example is a user requesting service from a system process.

So we need to provide for, and control, interaction between concurrent processes.

4.1 Process interaction

Let us begin by looking at why processes may need to interact with each other.

Cooperation

Processes may need to cooperate to carry out some particular job.

1. One process may make a request for service on some other process. It then has to wait for the service to be done. For example, a user process may request an operating system process to read from a disk drive. It has to wait for the data to be available in memory before proceeding.

2. Several processes may be designed to work together. But we cannot predict their relative speeds. There will be points at which one process cannot proceed until another has reached some particular stage. For example, processes may be arranged in a pipeline, with each one doing some processing on a data item, and then passing it on to the next process down

the line. Obviously the second process cannot even begin until the first has finished with at least one data item. Those farther down the line have to wait on the ones up front.

3. In a multimedia system, one process may be reading data from a disk, or from a network connection, and storing it in memory. A second process would be reading the data from memory, and feeding it to the video and audio hardware. Such a temporary storage area in memory is known as a buffer.

There are a number of constraints on the two processes. The first, the producer, must stop work as soon as the buffer is full, and start again as soon as space becomes available in the buffer. It also has to ensure that the buffer is never empty, otherwise there will be gaps in the multimedia output. However, if the buffer ever does become empty, the second process (the consumer) must stop work. It should never attempt to read from an empty buffer, as the results would be totally unpredictable. Finally, the consumer must start again just as soon as some data becomes available in the buffer.

In all of these cases, there is a general requirement for synchronisation. There must be some mechanism by which a process can wait to synchronise with another process, or with the hardware. The other side of this is that one process must be able to signal to another process that some point is reached, or that some task has been carried out.

We have seen an example of such synchronisation already, when a parent waits for a child process to terminate. But that is fairly radical interaction— the child has to die to get the parent's attention. What is envisaged here is a gentler form of synchronisation, which can be repeated over and over again, without any side effects on the process involved.

Competition

Concurrent processes may compete for exclusive use of resources. They may make simultaneous requests for the same resource, or the same service. Several examples will illustrate the basic problem here.

An airline booking system

Two processes, working on behalf of two different clients, can book the same seat at the same time. That is, they can issue instructions to mark that seat booked in the machine's memory.

One process can check that the seat is free, and decide to book it, and be context switched out at that point. The other process can find it free, and book it. When the first process runs again, it will start where it stopped, and the next instruction executed is to book the seat. It will not go back and check again. So the seat will be doubly booked.

Producer and consumer

What is envisaged here is a producer and a consumer process, communicating by means of a shared buffer. A global variable, items, is used by both processes to keep track of how many items are in the buffer.

The producer has a line items++, which compiles to the code shown in Figure 4.1.

```
MOV EAX, items ; load from items into register EAX
INC EAX        ; increment register EAX
MOV items, EAX ; store from register EAX back to items
```

Figure 4.1: Code to increment counter

The consumer has a line items--, which compiles to the code shown in Figure 4.2.

```
MOV EAX, items ; load from items to register EAX
DEC EAX        ; decrement register EAX
MOV items, EAX ; store from register EAX back to items
```

Figure 4.2: Code to decrement counter

Consider the following scenario. There is one item in the buffer, so items has a value of 1. The consumer takes this item. After the DEC instruction, it is context switched out, with a value of 0 in EAX. Meanwhile the producer puts another item in, and increments the old value of items to 2. Then the consumer wakes up and stores its 0 in items. Even though there is one item in the buffer, the global variable says there are none.

The last item is not removed, at least not until the next item is put in. There will always be one item which the consumer does not see. The basic problem is that a single logical operation may not be implemented as a single machine level operation.

Request queue for a system service

One client process is in the middle of putting a new entry on a system queue, and has some pointers updated, and others not. If it is swapped out at that point, and another process comes along and tries to put an item on the same queue, then the pointers will almost certainly be corrupted.

Atomic updates

In these examples, the problem arose because a process could be context-switched out while in the middle of performing a particular operation, and some of the state of the machine (global variables) changed while it is on the wait queue. So when it is context switched back in again, its view of the state

is not consistent with that of other processes. We cannot avoid this possibility if we use global variables.

If we could perform updates in one single instruction, then they would either be done or not done, and there would be no room for confusion. If an update is a single write to main memory, then there is no problem. This is because each such operation is guaranteed to be indivisible and atomic by the hardware. On a uniprocessor, context switches can only occur between instructions. Even with a multiprocessor, the bus controller guarantees that each memory access is atomic.

But an update could involve more than one read or write of memory. Examples would be to write a string, an array, or a struct, book a seat, or write a record to a file. Other processes must be excluded from that specific data structure until the high-level operation is complete. This exclusion may even span across one or several context switches!

Summary of the problem

The foregoing examples show that the operating system must be able to provide for (and control) interaction between concurrent processes, both in the area of mutual exclusion, and of synchronisation.

The system must impose some order on such competing processes. This may involve them taking turns, and waiting when necessary. The system may also have to choose between processes.

Competing processes need to be able to wait to acquire a shared resource, and need to be able to notify the other processes when they have finished with that resource.

Architectures

The implementation of interprocess communication has traditionally been different for machines with and without shared memory. In the former case, processes could share the whole address space, or part of it, and so communicate through that shared memory.

On some machines processes execute in separate address spaces, disjoint from those of all other processes. How can such processes communicate? The operating system has to support the transfer of data, or messages, from one process to another. But this raises some problems of its own. The time required for the operating system to copy data from one address space to another can be significant, compared with the shared memory case.

The problems we have just outlined in this section do not appear to be possible with such a system. But you can never really get away from them. Even if the airline reservation system is working with message passing, it is still possible for two processes to book the last seat.

As shared memory became almost universal on stand-alone machines, so the distinction began to fade. But then distributed systems, with the need for

communication between processes running on different machines, brought it back into focus. Most recent developments in 'distributed shared memory' are blurring it again.

4.2 Software solutions for mutual exclusion

The problem can be summarised as follows. We have a number of concurrent processes. Each has a segment of code, called its *critical section*, containing instructions which may affect other processes, for example updating common variables, etc.

Historically, the problem of mutual exclusion was first tackled in software. Attempts were made to design a protocol, or a set of rules and regulations, that programmers would write into the code being executed by each process, and which would guarantee that only one process was in its critical section at any one time.

In general, a program would have the format shown in Figure 4.3. Of course, this whole structure may be within a loop. But a program will never perform a jump into or out of the critical section. It will always execute the entry protocol beforehand, and the exit protocol afterwards. A successful algorithm must include an entry and exit protocol which each process includes in its code, and which guarantees mutual exclusion on its critical section.

beginning section

Entry protocol for critical section

critical section

Exit protocol for critical section

remainder section

Figure 4.3: General structure of a cooperating program

In order to be considered acceptable, an algorithm must meet the following requirements.

1. The solution must work even if context switches occur while the process is in its critical section.

2. It can make no assumptions about the relative speeds of the processes. It is not enough to arrange that they enter their critical sections in some specific order.

3. A process may terminate outside its critical section. This should not affect other processes. It may not terminate in its critical section, nor in the entry or exit protocols.

4. The solution must be free from deadlock—some process must eventually proceed.

5. It must also be free from starvation—it must not be possible for a process to wait forever.

6. The overhead of executing the entry and exit protocols should be minimal— at least when there is no contention.

Solutions were developed, first for two processes, and then generalised to work with any number of processes. Later work concentrated on making these algorithms more efficient.

These software solutions are rarely if ever used nowadays. But a study of these algorithms is well worth the effort involved, as it leads to a thorough understanding of the pitfalls involved in concurrent programming.

4.3 Software solutions for two processes

We will begin with software solutions for two processes. The approach taken here works through a series of algorithms, showing what is wrong with each one, and attempting to solve that problem in the next one, so as to arrive at a solution which meets all of the requirements.

Algorithm 1—using a guard variable

Let two processes share a common integer variable guard, initialised to 0. Before a process enters its critical section, it checks this variable; if it is still 0, it sets it to 1, and goes on. On the other hand, if it finds that guard has a value of 1, that means that the other process has set it on its way into its own critical section, so the current process waits, doing nothing. Each process executes the algorithm shown in Figure 4.4.

```
              beginning section

          WHILE (guard == 1)
              DO nothing
          ENDWHILE
          guard = 1

              critical section

          guard = 0

              remainder section
```

Figure 4.4: First attempt at solution for two processes

This seems to solve the problem, not only for two processes, but for any number of processes. However, things are not so simple. When compiled, the entry protocol translates to the assembler code shown in Figure 4.5.

```
test: MOV EAX, guard
      CMP EAX, #1
      JE  test:
      MOV guard, #1
```

Figure 4.5: Compiled version of entry protocol

The first line loads a value from guard into EAX. The second line compares the value in register EAX with 1. If the value is 1, rather than 0, then it branches back to test. The fourth line stores the value 1 into guard.

On a timeshared uniprocessor, a process can be context switched out between any two instructions. It is possible that a second process may get control of the CPU at this stage, and execute all of the instructions, setting guard to 1. If such a context switch occurred between the first and second instruction, then after being context switched back, the first process is operating on a stale value for guard, and will also go into its critical section. So the idea of using a guard does not work, due to the nature of machine level instructions.

Algorithm 2—using a turn variable

This next attempt gives a different meaning to the shared variable. Instead of indicating 'any process may enter', here the shared variable will indicate *which* process may enter. Let two processes, 0 and 1, share a common integer variable *turn*, initialised to 0. The versions of the algorithm used by both processes are shown in Figure 4.6.

```
         Process 0                          Process 1

      beginning section                  beginning section

  WHILE (turn != 0)                  WHILE (turn != 1)
      DO nothing                         DO nothing
  ENDWHILE                           ENDWHILE

      critical section                   critical section

  turn = 1                           turn = 0

      remainder section                  remainder section
```

Figure 4.6: Algorithms using turn

This solution actually works, and guarantees that only one process at a time will be in its critical section. But it requires strict turn taking on the part of both processes. They have to enter their critical sections in the order 0, 1, 0, 1, . . . While it might be useful for some very specific application, it does not meet the second requirement for a good solution, and is not of general use.

Algorithm 3—using two guards

Let us revisit algorithm 1. The only problem with it was that the two processes could interfere with one another when attempting to write the shared variable. If each had a variable of its own, such interference should not occur. This can be implemented with an array of two flags, such that if flag[0] is set to 1, then process 0 is in its critical section, and likewise for process 1. The algorithm is given in Figure 4.7 for process 0; process 1 would use a similar algorithm.

```
                      beginning section

          WHILE (flag[1] == 1)
               DO nothing
          ENDWHILE
          flag[0] = 1

                       critical section

          flag[0] = 0

                      remainder section
```

Figure 4.7: Algorithm using two flags

Both elements of the array are initialised to 0. In the entry protocol, a process continually checks the flag of the other process in a WHILE loop, and only when it is 0 does it proceed. It sets its own flag to 1 before entering its critical section, to keep the other out.

Unfortunately, this algorithm does not ensure that only one process at a time will be in its critical section. A process could check the state of the other's flag, find it at 0, and then be swapped out between the ENDWHILE and setting its own flag to 1. If the second process then runs, it will go into its critical section quite legally. When the first process runs again, it will set its flag to 1, without any further checking. So this algorithm allows two process to be in their critical sections at the same time.

Algorithm 4—using two indicator flags

But there is some merit in the idea of using a flag for each process. The previous algorithm did not work because it tested before setting. Another possibility is to let the setting of a flag to 1 only indicate that the process wants to enter its critical section. The revised algorithm for process 0 is given in Figure 4.8.

The problem with this is that it can lock. One process can set its flag to 1, and be swapped out. The second process could then set its flag to 1, and be swapped out. This is extremely unlikely to happen, but it could; and if it did, both would loop forever.

beginning section

```
flag[0] = 1
WHILE (flag[1] == 1)
        DO nothing
ENDWHILE
```

critical section

```
flag[0] = 0
```

remainder section

Figure 4.8: Setting the flag before testing

Algorithm 5—flags with turns

The previous algorithm could potentially deadlock. So we need some way of breaking such a deadlock, if it occurs. Let us re-introduce the idea of a turn. We now have a combination of algorithms 2 and 4. Figure 4.9 shows the algorithm for process 0; as usual, process 1 would use a symmetrical version.

beginning section

```
flag[0] = 1
turn = 1
WHILE ((flag[1] == 1) AND (turn == 1))
        DO nothing
ENDWHILE
```

critical section

```
flag[0] = 0
```

remainder section

Figure 4.9: Algorithm for mutual exclusion

Now let us assure ourselves that this algorithm is free of the problems we encountered with the others.

1. It is not possible for two processes to be in their critical sections at the same time. Process 0 will be blocked from entering as long as

$$(flag[1] == 1) \text{ AND } (turn == 1).$$

Process 1 will be blocked from entering as long as

$$(flag[0] == 1) \text{ AND } (turn == 0).$$

If both processes want to enter, both flags will be set to 1, the first half of both conditions will be true. The variable turn will have a value of 0 or 1. It cannot have both. Hence only one of the conditions will be true, the other will be false. Only one process will enter, the other will be blocked.

2. For the same reason, the algorithm cannot deadlock. The conditions tested in both processes cannot be true at the same time. So one will always get in.

3. This algorithm does not impose strict turn taking, as did algorithm 1. If only one process wants to enter its critical section, it cannot be held up on the WHILE. The first part of the condition will be false, hence the whole condition will be false, no matter what value turn has.

4. Now we come to the most difficult problem. Is it possible for the two processes to interleave at the machine code level, so that one or other of them reads stale data, and both go into their critical sections at the same time?

The entry protocols for both processes will compile to the code shown in Figure 4.10.

```
          Process 0                        Process 1

        MOV flag[0], #1                   MOV flag[1], #1
        MOV turn, #1                      MOV turn, #0
test:   CMP flag[1], #1          test:    CMP flag[0], #1
        JNE enter:                        JNE enter:
        CMP turn, #1                      CMP turn, #0
        JE test:                          JE test:
enter:                           enter:
```

Figure 4.10: Entry protocols for both processes

If process 0 is swapped out after its first line, and process 1 runs, it will execute its first four instructions. But it will not branch to enter, as flag[0] has already been set to 1. It will go on to test turn, and there are only two possibilities.

- If turn is 0, then process 1 will loop back to test, and continue doing so. It will eventually be context switched out somewhere in this loop, and when process 0 wakes up it will resume at the second line, and set turn to 1. This will cause process 0 to loop. When process 1 gets to use the CPU again, it will break out of its loop, and branch to enter.

- If turn is 1, then it will go into its critical section. When process 0 wakes up, it will loop.

If process 0 is swapped out anywhere after its second line, and process 1 executes, it will give process 0 the turn. Process 0 will go in, and process 1 will loop until it comes out.

4.4 Software solutions for many processes

Now that we have a watertight solution for two processes, we will attempt to extend this to develop an algorithm which will work for any number of processes.

Algorithm 6—the Eisenberg and McGuire algorithm

This is an attempt to extend the approach of algorithm 5. For the purposes of the explanation here, we assume 8 processes. Once this is understood, it is a simple matter to generalise it to any number of processes. All of the processes competing in this system can be visualised as arranged in a circular array, see Figure 4.11.

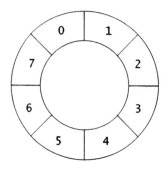

Figure 4.11: Eight contending processes

As before, there is an array flag, with one entry for each of the 8 processes. The element of this array corresponding to each process can be in one of three states. It can be idle, signifying that the process has no interest in entering its critical section. This is the state during the beginning section, and the remainder section. The flag can also have a value of want-in, thus letting all other processes know of its wish to enter its critical section.

Once changed from idle to want-in, the flag is only changed back to idle after the process has been in its critical section, just before it goes into its remainder section. Finally, it can have a value of in-cs, letting all other processes know that it has completed the entry protocol, and is either in, or about to enter, its critical section. Initially, all entries in the array flag are set to idle.

There is also a variable turn, which is initialised to some arbitrary value, typically 0. The turn is always incremented, so it moves clockwise around the circle in Figure 4.11.

The algorithm as given in Figure 4.12 looks at everything from the point of view of process number 4 (of 8). Once the algorithm is understood for 8 processes, it is a simple matter to rewrite it for a generic process i (of N).

beginning section

```
REPEAT
        flag[4] = want-in
        p = turn
        WHILE (p ≠ 4)
                IF (flag[p] == idle) THEN
                        p++ MOD 8
                ELSE
                        p = turn
                ENDIF
        ENDWHILE
        flag[4] = in-cs

        j = 0
        WHILE ((j < 8) AND ((j == 4) OR (flag[j] ≠ in-cs)))
                j ++
        ENDWHILE
UNTIL ((j == 8) AND ((turn == 4) OR (flag[turn] == idle)))
turn = 4

        critical section

flag[4] = idle

        remainder section
```

Figure 4.12: Eisenberg and McGuire algorithm

Entry protocol

Let us assume that process 4 wants to enter its critical section. It expresses this intention by setting its flag to want-in, and taking a local copy of the global variable turn. At this stage turn is pointing to some arbitrary process, which may or may not be interested in entering.

First While Loop The algorithm then checks if any process between turn and itself has expressed a similar intention of entering its critical section. If the process p is currently pointing to has its flag at idle, then it increments p (MOD 8, in order to wrap around), and checks the next one. Otherwise, it takes a fresh copy of turn, and continues checking. Thus it effectively delays by busy waiting until any such processes have been into their critical sections, and come out again, setting their flags to idle.

If turn happened to be 4, then it would not go into this loop at all, as the condition (p ≠ 4) would be false. If turn happened to be 5, then it would have to check all of the other processes.

Once process 4 has started into the first WHILE loop, if another process starts the entry protocol, then one of three scenarios is possible.

1. This process is between process 4 and turn, going clockwise. It will be held up in its first WHILE loop, until process 4 has been in and out. If turn is 0, then processes 5, 6, and 7 would be examples of this.

2. This process is between turn and process 4, but process 4 has not checked it yet. When it does check, the fact that it has set its flag will cause process 4 to idle in the first WHILE loop. If turn is 0, then processes 1, 2, 3 would be examples of this.

3. This process is between turn and process 4, but process 4 has already checked it. This process could get through its first WHILE loop before process 4, depending on processor share, and both processes could set their flags to in-cs. This is the case that has to be checked for later.

Process 4 never lowers its flag to idle anywhere in the entry protocol; hence no process ahead of it in the clockwise order can jump over it. They will always be held up by the first WHILE. Eventually process 4 finds that there are no processes between turn and itself wanting in, so it announces its right to enter its critical section by setting its flag to in-cs. Once process 4 has set its flag to in_cs, no other process can enter its critical section, even if process 4 itself cannot (until process 4 lowers its flag).

Second While Loop But of course between completing its check, and setting its flag to in_cs, some other process may have decided to enter, as in scenario 3 above. So process 4 goes on to check if it is the only process in the system to have asserted its right. It does this in the second WHILE loop.

The condition here is rather complicated. Let us examine what makes a condition of the form A AND (B OR C) false. If A is false, then the whole condition is false, and the loop terminates. If A is true, then it is sufficient for B or C to be true for the whole condition to be true. But if both B and C are false, then the whole condition is false, irrespective of the value of A, and the loop terminates.

Remember process 4 wants to check every other process, so it increments a counter j each time around. The first condition, (j < 8), will be false when all processes have been checked, and will then terminate the loop. This first condition is only concerned with counting its way around the loop.

The second condition is more important. At this point the algorithm is checking that it is the only process with its flag set to in-cs. If it finds any other process with its flag set to in-cs, it wants to terminate this loop immediately.

What about the first half of the OR? This loop is checking all processes, and one of them certainly has its flag set to in_cs, process 4 itself. The algorithm skips over this case, by effectively saying, if process 4 is the one that has its flag at in_cs, ignore that, and keep on looping.

The Repeat Loop Eventually the algorithm comes out of this second WHILE, and we are into the equally complicated UNTIL. If the algorithm comes out of the second WHILE loop with j still less than 8, that means it has found some other process with its flag at in-cs, and so the current process should not enter

its critical section. It fails the first part of the condition, and goes around the REPEAT loop again, lowering its flag to want-in. (The second part is irrelevant in this case, because of the AND.)

If it comes out of the second WHILE loop with j set to 8, that means no other process had its flag set to in-cs when it checked. It is still possible for another process to have set its flag to in-cs *after* this one had checked. But such a late-comer will, in its second WHILE, detect that flag[4] is at in-cs, and will be sent around its REPEAT again.

There is only one hurdle left for process 4. If turn has a value of 4, then process 4 goes ahead. But it is just possible that the process whose turn it is has, at this late stage, decided to set its flag to want-in. In such an exceptional case, process 4 will back off, go around the REPEAT again, and allow this late-comer to enter. This final twist is in the interest of fairness. After all it is the turn of that process. (Note that a process enters its critical section only if no other process has its flag set to in-cs.)

Exit protocol

The essence of the exit protocol is to set its flag to idle. In order to speed up any waiting processes, the one coming out of its critical section could search for some process wanting in, and give it turn. If there is no such process, then its search will end when it gets back to itself, and it will give the turn to itself. For simplicity, this extra complication is not shown in Figure 4.12.

Algorithm 7—Lamport's algorithm

This is an entirely different approach from the previous algorithm, and is much easier to understand. It is based on the practice in some shops and service counters of issuing a number on entry, and serving customers in order. So processes are given a unique number when they declare their intention of entering their critical section, and enter in that order.

The logic of the solution is easy to understand, but implementing it as an algorithm, as shown in Figure 4.13, is quite complicated. It uses two global arrays, number[n] to hold the chosen number for each process, and choosing[n] to flag that a process is actually choosing a number, and thus is manipulating shared variables. This second array is of type boolean. There is also a global variable counter, initialised to 0.

In the first four lines, a process takes a number, and saves it in its own element of the number array. Then in the FOR loop it checks each of the other processes, busy waiting while any of them has a positive number less than its own.

There are two potential problems with the algorithm, both in the part where it chooses a number. The complexity of the implementation arises from the need to prevent these problems from arising.

To understand the first problem, suppose that counter has a value of 3 and process 2 gets as far as incrementing counter to 4, and is then swapped

beginning section

```
choosing[i] = TRUE
counter++
number[i] = counter
choosing[i] = FALSE

FOR j = 0 TO n - 1 DO
        WHILE (choosing[j] == TRUE)
            DO nothing
        ENDWHILE
        WHILE ((number[j] ≠ 0) AND (number[j] < number[i]))
            DO nothing
        ENDWHILE
ENDFOR
```

critical section

```
number[i] = 0
```

remainder section

Figure 4.13: Lamport's algorithm

out. If at that stage process 4 begins the entry protocol, it will increment counter again, to 5, and take that number. Finding no process holding a smaller number, it will go into the critical section. Then when process 2 restarts, it sets number[2] to 4. No process has a smaller number than 4, so it also goes into the critical section.

To remedy this weakness, we introduce the choosing array, and the first WHILE loop. In the previous example, process 4 will be held up in the first WHILE, because choosing[2] is TRUE. Now when process 2 restarts, it will set number[2] to 5, and will be held up in its second WHILE.

While the algorithm can thus prevent one process jumping over another, it cannot prevent two processes getting the same number. As we have seen before, the line counter++ will compile to three machine instructions. It is possible for two processes so to interleave their instructions, that both increment counter in parallel, and end up with the same result. The second WHILE has to be strengthened to recognise this. This can be done by arbitrating between processes by means of their pid numbers.

As another example, suppose process 3 is swapped out in its critical section, and process 5 then begins the entry protocol. It will take a number, and begin checking. When it gets to number[3], it will idle in the loop, because the number process 3 is holding is smaller than its own. Eventually process 3 will execute the exit protocol, and reset its number to 0. Process 5 will then be able to complete the entry protocol, and go into its critical section.

4.5 Summary

1. Processes may need to cooperate to carry out some particular job. But they may also compete for exclusive use of resources. Both situations require a mechanism for processes to communicate between themselves.

   Such a mechanism will be fundamentally different on machines which have shared memory, and on those which do not.

2. Competition between processes can be summarised as the critical section problem. Each process has a section of code, its critical section, and a solution must guarantee that only one process can be executing code from its critical section at any given time.

   Historically, solutions to the critical section problem were first implemented in software.

3. Software solutions for even two processes have to avoid problems which result from context switches occurring at unfortunate places. This can lead to processes using stale values of shared data. Decisions based on such stale data can result in both processes entering their critical sections at the same time, or neither of them ever entering their critical section (deadlock). But there are solutions which meet all of the requirements.

4. The Eisenberg and McGuire algorithm generalises this to any number of processes. Essentially it arranges the processes in a logical ring, and ensures that processes enter their critical sections in order. It uses busy waiting to delay processes until it is their turn.

   Lamport's algorithm is based on the practice in some shops of giving customers a number when they enter, and serving them in order. While easy to understand, implementing it as an algorithm can be quite complicated.

4.6 Discussion questions

1. To insert an item into a singly linked list requires two pointers to be changed. Suppose a process is context switched out after changing the first, but not the second. Draw a diagram of this situation. If the next process to run now tries to traverse this same list, what will happen?

2. The C instruction items-- compiles to the following code

```
MOV EAX, items
DEC EAX
MOV items, EAX
```

   The second instruction decrements the EAX register. What happens if a process is context switched out after the first instruction, and another process executes items-- on the same variable? What happens if the context switch takes place after the second instruction?

3. Sometimes processes cannot share variables, and have to ask the operating system to transfer data to another process. Assume the operating system cannot be interrupted while doing this. Outline a scenario in which it is possible for two clients to book the same seat with such an architecture.

4. If it were possible to guarantee that a process could not lose control of the CPU while in its critical section, then the critical section problem would disappear. How might you go about guaranteeing this?

5. Assume that a particular architecture has a 'memory compare and branch' instruction, which compares a location in memory with zero, and branches accordingly, in one un-interruptible instruction. Would Algorithm 1 work on such an architecture?

6. Show that with Algorithm 2 it is not possible for both processes to be in their critical sections at the same time.

7. Is there any way that Algorithm 3 can deadlock, i.e. keep *both* processes out of their critical sections at the same time?

8. Is there any way that Algorithm 4 can allow both processes into their critical sections at the same time?

9. Consider the code shown in Figure 4.10. If process 0 is swapped out after the CMP flag[1], #1 instruction, and process 1 runs, what will happen?

10. Write out versions of Algorithm 6 for process 0, 1, and 2. Simulate the running of these, using a dice to decide how many instructions each process executes before it is context switched out.

11. Code the Eisenberg and Maguire algorithm in C, and compile it using the -S switch, which produces assembler output. Repeat Question 10 on this assembler version.

12. The implementation of Lamport's algorithm given in Figure 4.13 seems cumbersome. Could you improve on it, using a linked list instead of an array?

Low level IPC mechanisms 5

We have seen in the previous chapter that software algorithms have been developed for the exclusion of processes from critical sections. But there are significant difficulties with all of them.

- They all rely on continuous testing of variables, or busy waiting, which is very wasteful of CPU cycles.

- All of the details have to be implemented by each individual programmer, and the possibility of programmer error is always there.

- More seriously, there is no way to enforce the protocol. It depends on cooperation. A programmer may omit part of it, or leave it out altogether, and just go directly to the critical section.

- Apart from all of that, these protocols are just too complicated.

So programmers began to demand that the operating system help with the interprocess communication problem. One of the reasons why operating systems exist at all is to provide a more user friendly environment for a programmer. And our investigations in the previous chapter have shown that interprocess communication is certainly one area that could be made more user friendly.

In this chapter we will examine the range of low level mechanisms which operating system designers have provided to help with these problems. Then in the following chapter we will look at some high level language constructs that achieve similar effects, but which are easier for the programmer to use.

5.1 The Unix signal mechanism

The first mechanism for interprocess communication which we will examine is the Unix signal. This allows one process to notify another that a particular event has occurred. Signals evolved from a mechanism for terminating misbehaving processes into a primitive IPC system.

Signals became one of the most incompatible areas of Unix system programming. POSIX has now defined a standard interface, which we will follow.

Linux implements the POSIX compliant set of system calls. Most versions of Unix also provide other interfaces for compatibility reasons, but we will ignore them.

The signal mechanism arranges for a user defined function to be called, when some particular event occurs. There is a system defined set of signals, typically 31, each corresponding to a different event. These are identified by integers, defined as symbolic constants, beginning with SIG, and some mnemonic hint of the particular event, e.g. SIGCHLD is the signal sent to a parent when a child process dies. Figure 5.1 gives a selection of signal values, from <asm/signal.h>. Most are reserved for specific purposes, two are available for users.

```
#define SIGINT   2  /* interrupt, generated from terminal */
#define SIGILL   4  /* illegal instruction                */
#define SIGABRT  6  /* abort process                      */
#define SIGFPE   8  /* floating point exception           */
#define SIGKILL  9  /* kill a process                     */
#define SIGUSR1 10  /* user defined signal 1              */
#define SIGSEGV 11  /* segmentation violation             */
#define SIGUSR2 12  /* user defined signal 2              */
#define SIGALRM 14  /* alarm clock timeout                */
#define SIGCHLD 17  /* sent to parent on child exit       */
#define SIGXCPU 24  /* cpu time limit exceeded            */
```

Figure 5.1: A selection of signal values

Synchronous signals

Some signals are caused by synchronous events. These will occur at the same place each time a program is run. Examples of such signals would be floating point exception, such as underflow or overflow, SIGFPE; or an illegal instruction, SIGILL; or a memory segment violation, SIGSEGV. When such an event occurs, the hardware causes an interrupt, which transfers control to the operating system, which then sends the appropriate signal to the process concerned. Such synchronous signals are sometimes called exceptions or traps.

Asynchronous signals

Most signals are caused by asynchronous events. There is no way of knowing in advance when they will occur. There are three main sources of such signals.

- Another process. The system call used to send a signal is kill(). This rather startling name is a reminder of the original use of signals, which was indeed to kill the destination process. While signals can still be used to kill processes, this in not their only use. But the name has not been changed.

A process can send any signal to any other process which has the same owner as itself. The `kill()` system call takes two parameters, the pid of the destination process, and the number of the signal. For portability, it is better to use the symbolic constants rather than numbers. There is no further interaction between the processes. The whole effect of a signal is in the destination process.

- A terminal driver sends a signal when some special key is pressed.

    - The INTR key, frequently mapped to CTRL C, sends SIGINT.
    - The QUIT key, frequently mapped to CTRL \, sends SIGQUIT.
    - The SUSP key, frequently mapped to CTRL Z, sends SIGSTOP.
    - The DSUSP key, frequently mapped to CTRL Y, sends SIGCONT.

    Key mappings can be checked with the `stty -a` command.

- The `alarm()` library function sets a timer. The call resets any previous setting of the timer, and returns the number of seconds remaining on the last setting, if any. The kernel sends SIGALRM to the calling process when the time expires. The default action for this signal is to terminate the process.

Such asynchronous signals are sometimes called software interrupts, as they are as unpredictable as hardware interrupts, and have a similar effect on a process. But they are generated by software, not hardware.

5.2 Implementation of signals

There are a number of phases in the implementation of the signal mechanism. A signal is generated when the event occurs. It is delivered, or handled, when the destination process takes the appropriate action. The response is not instantaneous. In between the signal is pending.

Signal generation

Each process has a number of data structures for implementing the signal mechanism. The first of these we will consider is `task_struct.signal`. This is a 32 bit bitmap, which records pending signals. Normally all the bits in this are cleared to 0. When a signal is sent to a particular process, the corresponding bit in its `signal` field is set to 1. This means that it is only possible to record one outstanding instance of each signal. If two instances of the same signal arrive in rapid succession, only one will be recorded. This may be acceptable for two instances of SIGINT, but not for two of SIGCHLD.

As each Linux thread has a `task_struct` of its own, each has its own set of pending signals. A signal can be generated for a process which is not running, which is currently on the ready queue or a wait queue. Here we have to distinguish different kinds of waiting. If a process is waiting for an event

which may take a long time, such as a keystroke, then it can be woken up to handle a signal (interruptible wait). On the other hand, if it is waiting for an event that is sure to happen, such as disk I/O, it is not disturbed, as it will be notified of the signal very shortly (un-interruptible wait). In either case, it will see the signal when it returns to user mode after being context switched in.

Blocking signals

Individual signals can be masked, or blocked. Such a signal is not lost, it will be delivered when it is unblocked. Blocked signals are recorded in a bit-mask `blocked`, in the `task_struct` of each process. Users cannot access this directly; instead the `sigprocmask()` system call is used to bring a copy of the mask into user space, where it can be examined or changed. Then `sigprocmask()` is called again to copy the new mask back into kernel space.

How does one system call do two different things? In fact what it does is to swap the system value with the user's value. It expects the user to supply pointers to two bitmaps. The first is the new bitmap, which it will read from; the second is where it will write a copy of the old bitmap. If the first pointer is NULL, then it will just copy from kernel space to the bitmap identified by the second pointer; if the second pointer is NULL, then it just copies from the bitmap identified by the first pointer, to kernel space. See Figure 5.2.

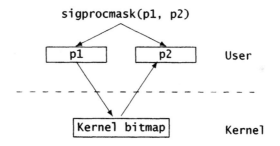

Figure 5.2: Changing the signal mask

There is another parameter to `sigprocmask()` which specifies what is to be done with the other two. This can have three possible values. SIG_BLOCK means that the values in p1 are added to the kernel map; SIG_UNBLOCK means that the values in p1 are removed from the kernel map; and SIG_SETMASK means that the kernel map is replaced by the values in p1.

There are a number of library functions which help in creating the bitmap to pass to `sigprocmask()`. To clear all signals in a bitmap, use `sigemptyset()`, and to set all of them use `sigfillset()`. To add one specific signal to a set, use `sigaddset()`; `sigdelset()` removes one. Finally, `sigismember()` checks if a particular signal is set in a bitmap, or not. It is possible to find out if any blocked signals are pending, using `sigpending()`.

As each Linux thread has a `task_struct` of its own, each has its own set of blocked signals.

Signal delivery and handling

The target process does not explicitly check for signals. Instead, the kernel checks the `signal` bitmap, to see if any action needs to be taken, each time it returns to user mode from kernel mode. If any bits are set in `signal`, it checks if there is a handler. If a handler is registered, it returns the process to user mode, transfers control to the handler, and sets up the stack so that when the handler finishes, control returns to where the program was before the handler ran. If several signals are pending, they will be processed one at a time.

Signal handling

What happens when a signal is delivered to a process depends on the particular signal, and what arrangements the process has made to handle it. Each process has a pointer `task_struct.sig` to a `struct signal_struct`, as shown in Figure 5.3, from `<sched.h>`.

```
struct signal_struct{
        atomic_t            count;
        struct k_sigaction  action[32];
        spinlock_t          siglock;
};
```

Figure 5.3: Data structure tracking signal handlers

- The `count` field tracks the number of processes pointing to or sharing this structure. Such sharing results from a process being cloned with `CLONE_SIGHAND`, which would correspond to the creation of a thread in the process.

- The array `action[]` has an entry for each of the signals supported by the system. Each entry specifies what action is to be taken when the process receives that particular signal.

    If the corresponding entry is set to `SIG_DFL`, then the kernel takes the default action for that particular signal. Each has its own predefined default, from a set of five possible default responses:

    - terminate the process
    - terminate, but save a copy of memory on disk
    - suspend the process
    - continue [if already suspended; else ignore]
    - ignore the signal.

    If the entry in `sigaction[]` is `SIG_IGN` then the kernel just ignores the signal, and does not notify the process.

    Any other value here is interpreted as a pointer to a function which is to be executed to handle that particular signal. In this case, when the

signal arrives, the process stops what it is doing, and executes the handler function. This is similar to what happens when a hardware interrupt occurs, hence the term software interrupt.

- The `siglock` field is used to guarantee mutual exclusion of this data structure. Spinlocks will be discussed in the next section.

Signal handlers

Handlers are ordinary user functions, and are installed using `sigaction()`. This takes three parameters. The first is the signal number. The second points to a `struct sigaction` which specifies the new handler, and a set of signals to be blocked while the handler is running. The third points to another `struct sigaction`, into which information about the old handler will be placed.

A signal handler always returns void, and has one parameter, an `int` specifying the number of the signal. During execution of a handler, the signal which caused the handler to execute is blocked by default.

When the handler function finishes, the relevant bit in the signal mask `signal` is cleared to 0, and control returns to the program at whatever point it was at when the signal arrived.

Handlers are inherited by a child process, after a `fork()`. However, installed handlers cannot be inherited across an `exec()` —old pointers have no meaning in the new program. So `exec()` sets all signals to their default values.

As each Linux thread has a `task_struct` of its own, it can have its own handlers, or can share them with other threads. Note that the field `sig` in `task_struct` is a pointer. How a particular thread behaves is decided by the CLONE_SIGHAND flag passed to `clone()`.

Use of signals

Signals are typically used to avoid busy waiting.

The `pause()` library function suspends a process until it receives a signal, at least one that is not being ignored. If there is a handler registered for that signal, it runs first, then `pause()` returns, always with −1, and EINTR in `errno`.

The combination of unblocking a signal, followed by `pause()`, is a common one. But a signal arriving between these two instructions can have unexpected results, not least deadlock. So in order to provide an atomic implementation of both of these, POSIX introduced `sigsuspend()`. This clears the appropriate bit in the `blocked` signal mask (so unblocking a signal) and suspends the process. When it returns (always with −1), the mask of blocked signals is reset as it was before. So `sigsuspend()` allows a process to wait for a specific signal.

Another POSIX function `sigwait()` suspends a calling process until one of a specified set of signals is delivered—these can be any of the asynchronous signals. It returns with the number of the signal which woke it. It does not run a handler. Note the difference from `sigsuspend()`, which only returns after the handler has run. A process should never wait for a synchronous signal, as it must be running for such a synchronous event to happen.

5.3 Hardware mechanisms

Back in Section 4.3, we looked at the possibility of using a guard variable to guarantee mutual exclusion on a critical section. We came to the conclusion that this simple mechanism would not work, even for two processes. The root of the problem was the fact that the testing of this variable, and its subsequent setting, were two separate instructions at the machine level. And a process could be context switched out between these two instructions. Because of this, it is impossible to guarantee mutual exclusion in this way.

Just as previously the applications programmers threw the problem back at the operating system designers, so now these latter throw the problem back at the hardware designers. We ask them to include some mechanism in the hardware, specifically for this purpose.

Different hardware designers have come up with different solutions.

Interrupt inhibition

On a uniprocessor, mutual exclusion could be guaranteed by disabling interrupts, and enabling them again when finished. In this way a process cannot lose control of the CPU. On the Intel architecture, the CLI instruction causes the CPU to ignore interrupts. The STI instruction causes the CPU to respond to interrupts again. Both of these are privileged instructions.

But such a crude mechanism is not really acceptable. The code for a critical section could consist of hundreds or thousands of machine instructions. If interrupts were disabled for such a significant period of time, many important events, particularly network interrupts, would be lost.

Even if it were acceptable, it would not work on a multiprocessor. So some other solution has to be found.

Test and set

Another possibility is a machine level instruction which tests and sets a variable in one operation. This has to be a special instruction. If conventional machine instructions are used, they could be interrupted between the testing and the setting. Test_and_set always sets the value to 1, irrespective of what was there before.

With such an instruction, one particular location in memory (Key) is used as a flag to denote whether or not you can enter a critical section of code. The entry protocol would be implemented as shown in Figure 5.4.

```
WHILE (Test_and_set (Key))
        DO nothing
ENDWHILE
```

Figure 5.4: Entry protocol using test and set

Test_and_set always returns the previous value, and that is the value used to test the WHILE condition. If the value in Key is 1, this means that another process is in the critical section, and the current one cannot enter, so it loops in the WHILE. If the value of Key is 0, then the critical section is free, so the current process can enter. The program loops, busy waiting, until the value of Key becomes 0.

The exit protocol is a simple assignment, Key = 0. Any compiler will produce one un-interruptible machine level instruction for this.

Both the IBM 360/370 and the Motorola 68000 architectures have such machine level instructions.

Exchange

Yet another possibility is a machine level instruction which, in one operation, exchanges the contents of two locations in memory. If such an instruction is available, then one particular location in memory (Key) is used as a flag to denote whether or not you can enter a critical section of code.

With this, the entry routine is implemented as shown in Figure 5.5.

```
REPEAT
      Local = 1
      Exchange(Local, Key)
UNTIL Local == 0
```

Figure 5.5: Entry protocol using exchange

Key is a global variable visible to all processes. Each process has its own copy of Local. If the value in Key is 1, this means that another process is in the critical section, and the current one cannot proceed. If the value of Key is 0, then the critical section is free, and the current process can proceed. If there is a value of 1 in Local after the exchange, this means that Key was 1 beforehand. Only when there is a value of 0 in Local after the exchange can you be sure that Key was 0 beforehand.

As before, the exit routine is a simple assignment, Key = 0.

Intel microprocessors have an XCHG instruction, which exchanges the contents of a register with a memory location. So Key would be a memory location, while Local would be held in a register.

Problems

Modern CPUs keep private copies of recently read data in a part of the CPU known as a cache. Both of the foregoing mechanisms have a particular problem on multiprocessor machines, as two or more CPUs may have cached copies of Key. Normally, the hardware guarantees that all copies will be consistent. This is typically done by invalidating cached values. When one process writes

to a cached variable, all the other processor caches are informed, and they mark their values as invalid. So writes to shared variables (such as `test_and_set` or XCHG) should be kept to a minimum, otherwise they will be continually invalidating each other's caches, introducing extra overhead, and getting nothing done.

Spinlocks

The two previous mechanisms are known as spinlocks. The CPU spins in a tight loop, waiting to enter the critical section. On a uniprocessor, a process could spend most of its quantum in such a loop. In fact many processes may do this, until the one holding the lock is scheduled to run again, and so releases the lock.

Spinlocks are most useful in situations where it can be guaranteed that a critical section will be at most 20 to 30 machine instructions. This means there is a very high probability that a process will release the lock before its quantum expires, and so there is no contention. They are particularly effective on a multiprocessor machine.

5.4 Semaphores

In the previous sections, we have seen how the signal mechanism can be used to inform a process of an event, and allow it to take some particular action when that event occurs. One process can even wait for an event to occur in another process, and this second process can send a signal when it does occur. We have also seen how spinlocks can be used to control access to a critical section.

While there is the beginning of a synchronisation and mutual exclusion mechanism here, it is not at all adequate to meet the requirements which we discussed in Chapter 4. A far more general system is needed. A process should be able to announce that an event has occurred on which several other processes may be waiting, even ones that are not known to it. If the event happens before any process waits for it, then it should be recorded in some way. If many events happen before the wait, each one should be recorded.

The first general solution for these requirements was by Dijkstra, which he called a semaphore. This can be described as:

> *A non-negative integer, which apart from initialisation, can be acted on only by two standard, atomic, un-interruptible operations, WAIT (which decrements the value of the semaphore) and SIGNAL (which increments the value).*

Instead of users attempting to devise their own synchronisation protocols, which as we have seen is both difficult and treacherous, semaphores are provided as a tool by the system implementor.

Using semaphores, competing or collaborating processes do not have to know even the number of contenders, much less their identities or internal implementation details. All they have to know is the *name* of the semaphore.

However, the two operations defined on semaphores are somewhat more complex than the simple description given above.

WAIT

A WAIT operation is not the same as assignment, s = s - 1. If two processes WAIT on a semaphore with a value of 3, it is guaranteed that the value afterwards will be 1. If two processes use assignment statements to decrement a semaphore with a value of 3, the final result may be 2 or 1.

This is because the assignment statement will typically compile to three machine instructions: a copy to a register, decrement the register, and a copy back to memory. One process could be swapped out after the first instruction, or the second, and another process could complete an assignment, setting the value of the semaphore to 2. When the first process runs again, and completes the assignment, it too will set the semaphore to 2. This is referred to as the 'lost wait' problem.

However, a WAIT does not always decrement the semaphore. It can only do this if the result would be non-negative. If the value of the semaphore before the WAIT is 0, then the WAIT cannot complete, and the process must be context switched out, and moved to a wait queue.

Note that the definition of a semaphore does not allow for its value to be read (although some implementations have provided for this).

SIGNAL

A SIGNAL operation increases the value of the semaphore by 1, again in an indivisible operation.

However, if there is even one process waiting on the semaphore, SIGNAL has a different effect. It wakes up that process, marks it runnable, and moves it to the run queue.

If several processes are waiting, which one proceeds? This is implementation specific—the definition of a semaphore does not decide.

5.5   Applications of semaphores

Having introduced the idea of a semaphore, we now go on to see how they can be used to solve problems introduced in Chapter 4. We will then look at how they are implemented.

Semaphores for mutual exclusion

To arrange for mutual exclusion, a single semaphore, initialised to 1, is used. In the examples here the semaphore is called *Guard*. A commonly used name for a mutual exclusion semaphore is *Mutex*.

Each process uses it as shown in Figure 5.6. Note the similarity with the solutions in Chapter 4. But here the entry protocol is simply a WAIT, while the exit protocol is a SIGNAL.

```
                    beginning section

                    WAIT(Guard)
                    critical section
                    SIGNAL(Guard)

                    remainder section
```

Figure 5.6: Semaphore for mutual exclusion

The state of the semaphore immediately after initialisation is shown in Figure 5.7(a). The value is 1, and there are no processes on the wait queue. After the first contending process has done a WAIT, the value of the semaphore is 0. The state of the semaphore is now as in Figure 5.7(b).

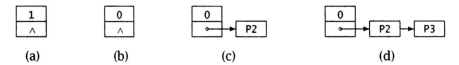

(a)   (b)   (c)   (d)

Figure 5.7: Successive states of a mutual exclusion semaphore

If a second process then does a WAIT, the semaphore is not decremented further, but that process is blocked, and put on the semaphore wait queue, as in Figure 5.7(c). Any subsequent processes that WAIT on that semaphore are added to the tail of that queue, see Figure 5.7(d).

When the first process leaves its critical section, and does a SIGNAL on the semaphore, one of the waiting processes is woken up, and moved from the wait queue to the run queue. The value of the semaphore is unchanged.

When that process does a SIGNAL in turn, another is woken up, and so on. Eventually there will be no processes on the queue, the semaphore will have a value of 0, as in Figure 5.7(b). Then the final process does a SIGNAL, and the value is restored to 1, as in Figure 5.7(a).

Note that the correct working of the mutual exclusion algorithm depends on all of the programmers doing everything correctly. If anyone omits a WAIT or a SIGNAL, or inserts an extra WAIT or SIGNAL, then mutual exclusion will not be guaranteed.

Semaphores for synchronisation

The requirement here is that process A must not pass a point P1 in its code until process B has reached a point P2 in its code. For example, A may require an item at P1 which is only provided by B at P2.

The solution is to use one semaphore, S, initialised to 0.

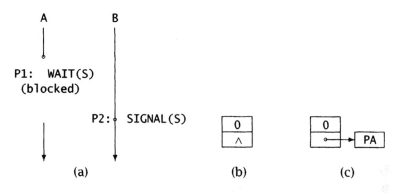

Figure 5.8: Semaphore for synchronisation

There are two possible scenarios. The first is shown in Figure 5.8(a). Process A may get to P1 before B gets to P2. In that case, when A executes a WAIT on the semaphore, it is blocked (on a 0 valued semaphore), and put on a wait queue. The semaphore changes from the state shown in Figure 5.8(b) to 5.8(c). When B eventually gets to P2, and does a SIGNAL on the semaphore, A will be woken up, and continue execution. The semaphore returns to the state in Figure 5.8(b). Note that the value of the semaphore is always 0 in this case.

The other possibility is that B can get to P2 before A gets to P1. This is shown in Figure 5.9(a). In this case, the value of the semaphore is incremented to 1. It changes from the state shown in Figure 5.9(b) to 5.9(c). Then when A does a WAIT, it is not held up, but the semaphore is decremented to 0, and returns to the state shown in Figure 5.9(b).

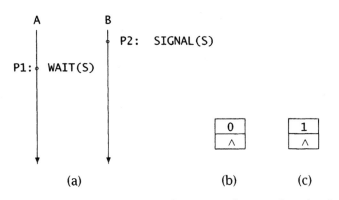

Figure 5.9: An alternative for synchronisation

If the two processes were running on a multiprocessor, then they could attempt to WAIT and SIGNAL at exactly the same time. It is left to the implementation to decide which goes first. Remember that the definition of a semaphore requires that WAIT and SIGNAL be indivisible. So there is no possibility of their being interleaved.

Semaphores for resource management

Semaphores can be used to control the allocation and deallocation of resources. These can be physical resources, such as printers, but they can also be virtual resources such as slots in a buffer.

The semaphore is initialised to the number of instances available. A process requests resources by a WAIT on the semaphore. As long as there is a resource available, it will not be held up. Eventually, when all resources have been allocated, the value of the semaphore will be 0. Any further processes doing a WAIT on that semaphore will be blocked, and put on a wait queue.

A process returns a resource by a SIGNAL on the semaphore. If no process is waiting, then the value of the semaphore (number of instances available) will be incremented. If there are processes waiting, then one will be woken up and given the newly returned resource.

For example, suppose there are two printers available. A semaphore P, to control printer allocation, is initialised to 2. See Figure 5.10(a).

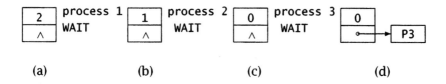

| (a) | (b) | (c) | (d) |

Figure 5.10: Semaphore for resource allocation

As each process requests a printer, it does a WAIT on the semaphore P. The first process changes the state of the semaphore to Figure 5.10(b), and is granted the first printer. The second process changes the state of the semaphore to Figure 5.10(c), and is granted the second printer.

When the third process requests a printer, and does a WAIT on the (zero valued) semaphore, it is not allowed to continue, as there is no printer available. It is put to sleep (see Figure 5.10(d)).

When one of the processes returns a printer, it does a SIGNAL on the semaphore. This wakes up the waiting process, and moves the state of the semaphore to Figure 5.10(c).

5.6 Producers and consumers

In Section 4.1 we introduced a whole class of problems in which producer
processes place data in a buffer, and consumer processes take it out. This
has both synchronisation and mutual exclusion implications. A process taking
data from an empty buffer must block. A process putting data into a full buffer
must also block. And always, the buffer must be protected from simultaneous
access by more than one process. We will now look at how semaphores might
be used to control such situations.

In the following examples, we will assume a circular buffer, with N fixed
size slots, numbered 0 to N − 1. After slot N − 1 has been filled (or emptied),
the next slot to be used is slot 0 again.

Figure 5.11 shows an eight slot buffer, on the left as it would actually be
laid out in memory, and on the right as it might be envisaged in the algorithms
which follow.

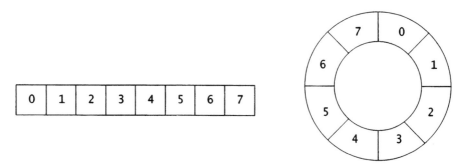

Figure 5.11: Circular buffer with eight slots

One producer, one consumer

We will begin with a situation in which there is only one producer process, and
likewise one consumer process.

This needs two semaphores: SlotFree, which is initialised to the maximum number of slots in the buffer, and ItemAvailable, which is initialised
to 0, as there are 0 items available at initialisation time. These values reflect
the initial state of the system. At any given time, the value of ItemAvailable
is the number of un-consumed items in the buffer, and the value of SlotFree
is the number of free slots available for use.

There are also two pointers. NextIn points to the next slot in the buffer to
be used by the producer. NextOut points to the slot from which the consumer
is to take the next item. Both are initialised to point to slot 0. When each of
these gets to the end of the buffer, it wraps around to point to slot 0 again.
This complication is omitted from the algorithms, which stress rather the use
of semaphores.

Producer

The algorithm for the producer is given in Figure 5.12.

```
Produce an item
WAIT(SlotFree)
Put item in buffer at NextIn
NextIn++
SIGNAL(ItemAvailable)
```

Figure 5.12: Algorithm for producer

Consumer

The corresponding algorithm for the consumer is given in Figure 5.13.

```
WAIT(ItemAvailable)
Get item from buffer at NextOut
NextOut++
SIGNAL(SlotFree)
Consume the item
```

Figure 5.13: Algorithm for consumer

Synchronisation

When the buffer is empty, the consumer will be forced to pause by the WAIT on ItemAvailable, which has a value of 0. It will only get past this point when the producer does a SIGNAL on ItemAvailable, which it only does after depositing an item in the buffer.

When the buffer is full, the producer will be held up by the WAIT on SlotFree, which now has a value of 0. It will only get past this point when the consumer does a SIGNAL on SlotFree, which it will only do after it has removed an item from the buffer, thus making a slot available for reuse.

Mutual exclusion

There is no mutual exclusion semaphore in the implementation given here. This may seem to contradict previous statements that to avoid interference, processes should only access shared resources under mutual exclusion. But in this case, the structure of the code, and the fact that there are only two processes, guarantees that they cannot be accessing the same slot at the same time. It is worthwhile considering this in some detail, as it helps to understand some of the implications of using a shared buffer.

The only way both processes can be accessing the same slot in the buffer at the same time is when NextIn and NextOut have the same value, and are pointing to the same slot.

There are only two possible occasions when this can happen. One is when the buffer is empty, and NextIn and NextOut are both pointing at the next empty slot: the producer to put in there as soon as something is produced, and the consumer to take from there as soon as something is put in. In this case the consumer is held up by the semaphore ItemAvailable, and so cannot get on to the line where it takes from the buffer. Before the producer does a SIGNAL on this semaphore, it will already have incremented NextIn to point to the next slot.

The other possibility is when the buffer is full, and both are pointing at the next full slot: the producer to put in there as soon as it becomes free, the consumer to take from there as soon as it is ready for another item. In this case the producer is held up on the semaphore SlotFree, and cannot get on to the line where it actually uses the buffer. Before the consumer does a SIGNAL on this semaphore, it will already have incremented NextOut to point to the following slot.

While a mutual exclusion semaphore is not strictly required in this example, it is probably good practice to always include one when there is a shared resource involved. Understanding why it is not strictly required in this example helps to understand what semaphores are all about.

Multiple producers, multiple consumers

We use the same two semaphores, and pointers, as in the previous example. But in this case we must introduce a mutual exclusion semaphore, Guard, initialised to 1. This is because two or more producers could try to put an item into the same slot at the same time, or two consumers could try to take from the same slot at the same time.

The algorithm for a producer is given in Figure 5.14; that for a consumer in Figure 5.15.

```
Produce an item
WAIT(SlotFree)
WAIT(Guard)
Put item in buffer at NextIn
NextIn++
SIGNAL(Guard)
SIGNAL(ItemAvailable)
```

Figure 5.14: Algorithm for one of many producers

With only one Guard, only one process, producer or consumer, can be active in the buffer at any time. It would be possible to have two mutual exclusion semaphores. One would be for producers, to guarantee that only one

```
WAIT(ItemAvailable)
WAIT(Guard)
Get item from buffer at NextOut
NextOut++
SIGNAL (Guard)
SIGNAL(SlotFree)
Consume the item
```

Figure 5.15: Algorithm for one of many consumers

producer could be putting an item into the buffer at any one time. The second semaphore would be for consumers, and would guarantee that only one consumer could be getting an item from the buffer at any one time. In this case, one producer and one consumer could be active in the buffer at the same time. They would be prevented from operating on the same slot, by the reasoning of the previous subsection.

Note that the order in which a WAIT is done on the semaphores in both algorithms is critical. If a producer did the WAIT on Guard before the WAIT on SlotFree, and if the buffer were full, then no consumer could get past the WAIT on Guard, and the system would deadlock. Likewise if a consumer were to do a WAIT on Guard before the WAIT on ItemAvailable, and the buffer were empty, no producer could get past the WAIT on Guard, and the system would deadlock.

5.7 Readers and writers

Here we are dealing with one resource, such as a file. For example, it could be a price list file, containing item numbers and prices. In this situation, it is normally acceptable to have multiple readers. It is also commonly accepted that there should be only one writer at any time. Solutions can be implemented at various levels, increasing in severity.

Solution 1

At most one writer, with any number of readers, at the same time. The readers are never held up, but only one writer at a time is allowed. All this requires is a semaphore, Writing, initialised to 1. Each writer does a WAIT on this before writing, and a SIGNAL afterwards. Readers need no controls.

Solution 2

We can tighten the requirements so that the writer must have exclusive use. For this it must wait until the number of readers falls to 0. But new readers are still allowed access, and if this happens continually, then the writer could wait forever.

To implement this we need a global variable, readers, initialised to 0, to keep track of the number of readers. As this variable is incremented and decremented by the various reading processes, any checking or manipulation of it needs to be done under mutual exclusion. So we introduce a mutual exclusion semaphore, Guard, initialised to 1. We also need to guarantee that only one writer process is writing at a time, and any other contending writers are held up, so we will use another semaphore, Writing, initialised to 1.

Reader entry

The entry protocol for a reader is given in Figure 5.16.

```
WAIT(Guard)
readers++
IF (readers == 1) THEN
        WAIT(Writing)
ENDIF
SIGNAL(Guard)
```

Figure 5.16: Entry protocol for a reader

The incrementing and testing of readers is done under the protection of Guard. It increments the number of readers, and checks for the only critical condition, if this is the first reader (readers == 1). If not, then it just releases the mutual exclusion, and goes ahead to read. But if it is the first reader, then there are two possibilities.

1. If a writer is currently writing, then we want to hold up this reader. So it does a WAIT(Writing). This looks like bad practice, blocking on Writing while holding Guard. But it works in this case. Any further readers will be held up on Guard. When the writer finishes, it will release this reader, who in turn will release Guard and allow all the other waiting readers in.

2. The other possibility is that there is no currently active writer. In this case it is not held up by the WAIT(Writing). However, it does lock this semaphore against any future writers, which is just what we want.

Reader exit

The exit protocol for a reader is given in Figure 5.17. It decrements the number of readers, and checks for the only critical condition, if this is the last reader (readers == 0). If not, then it just releases the mutual exclusion on Guard. Otherwise it does a SIGNAL(Writing). This wakes up one writer, if there is one waiting. If no writer is waiting, then it returns the semaphore Writing to its initial value of 1.

```
WAIT(Guard)
readers--
IF (readers == 0) THEN
      SIGNAL(Writing)
ENDIF
SIGNAL(Guard)
```

Figure 5.17: Exit protocol for a reader

Writers

The entry protocol for a writer is very simple. It just does WAIT(Writing). If no other process is active, then it will slip through this. Otherwise it is held up until the last reader, or the current writer, does a SIGNAL(Writing).

The exit protocol for a writer is equally simple, just SIGNAL(Writing). This wakes up the next process, either reader or writer, if any one is waiting. If not, it just resets the semaphore Writing to its initial value.

The overall situation envisaged with this solution is illustrated in Figure 5.18.

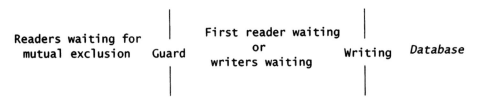

Figure 5.18: Solution 2

Solution 3

We can tighten the requirements even more, so that once a writer makes a request, no new readers are allowed in until that writer has been allowed to write. But when it has finished, then all waiting readers are given access, and any further writers must wait until all of these have finished.

Data structures

The following data items are shared by all readers and writers:

- wr, the number of processes that wish to read.

- ar, the number of processes that are actually reading. This will not always have the same value as wr. For example, while writing is in progress, ar will be 0, but wr may not be. So we need two separate counters.

- ww, the number of writers that wish to write.

- To enforce exclusive access to this shared data, we use a semaphore Guard, initialised to 1.

- Processes wishing to read when a writer is writing must be held up; for this we use a semaphore R, initialised to 0.

- Processes wishing to write when readers are reading must also be held up; for this we use another semaphore W, initialised to 0.

The situation may be visualised as in Figure 5.19.

```
        wr                           ar                      ww

  Readers waiting for                          Writers waiting for
    writer to exit        R    Database    W    last reader to exit
```

Figure 5.19: Solution 3

Reader entry protocol

The protocol that is executed by a process when it wishes to read is given in Figure 5.20.

```
WAIT(Guard)
wr++
IF (ww == 0) THEN
        ar++
        SIGNAL(R)
ENDIF
SIGNAL(Guard)
WAIT (R)
```

Figure 5.20: Reader prologue code

The WAIT and SIGNAL on Guard bracket all manipulations of shared variables. A reader first increments wr, the count of processes that wish to read, so declaring its interest in acquiring the resource for reading. If even one writer has expressed an interest in writing (ww > 0), then the potential reader releases the mutual exclusion on Guard, and waits on the semaphore R. As this was initialised to 0, the reader will be held up here. If no writers have expressed an intention of acquiring the resource for writing (ww == 0), then the reader can proceed. It increments the ar count, and does a SIGNAL on the R semaphore. This latter action is a dummy, to guarantee that the reader will not be blocked on the upcoming WAIT(R). The reader can now release Guard. It will then slip through the WAIT, and go on to read.

This dummy SIGNAL(R) may seem an unnecessary complication. Remember that what we want to do is hold up the reader if any writer has expressed an interest in writing (ww > 0). It would seem more logical to code this as in Figure 5.21.

```
WAIT(Guard)
wr++
IF (ww > 0) THEN
        WAIT(R)
ELSE
        ar++
ENDIF
SIGNAL(Guard)
```

Figure 5.21: Incorrect reader prologue

But such a solution would deadlock. The reader is held up, holding mutual exclusion on the shared variables. An exiting writer would be held up on Guard, and would never get as far as the SIGNAL(R) to release the waiting reader.

Reader exit protocol

The protocol executed by a reader process when it has finished reading is given in Figure 5.22.

```
WAIT (Guard)
ar--
wr--
IF (ar == 0) THEN
    IF (ww > 0) THEN
            SIGNAL(W)
    ENDIF
ENDIF
SIGNAL (Guard)
```

Figure 5.22: Reader epilogue code

The WAIT and SIGNAL on Guard bracket all manipulations of shared variables. It decrements both of the read counts on the way out. If there are no further readers (ar == 0), then if there is a writer waiting, it wakes it up. In this way, the last reader wakes up one waiting writer.

Writer entry protocol

The protocol executed by a writer when it wishes to write is given in Figure 5.23. The WAIT and SIGNAL on Guard bracket all manipulations of shared variables.

```
WAIT(Guard)
ww++
IF (ar == 0) AND (ww == 1) THEN
      SIGNAL(W)
ENDIF
SIGNAL(Guard)
WAIT(W)
```

Figure 5.23: Writer prologue code

First of all it declares its wish to write, by incrementing ww. If there are no actual readers (ar == 0), and it is the first writer (ww == 1), then it can go on to write. The SIGNAL(W) within the IF is so that it will slip through the corresponding WAIT(W). Otherwise, if there are readers, or if it is not the first writer, it is held up on W, until either the last reader or the current writer signals.

Once again we have the unusual construct of the dummy SIGNAL(W). We really want to test for (ar > 0) OR (ww > 1), and if so WAIT(W). But this would lead to deadlock, and the solution presented avoids this, at the cost of added complexity.

Writer exit protocol

The protocol that is executed by a writer when it has finished writing is given in Figure 5.24.

```
WAIT(Guard)
ww--
WHILE (ar < wr)
      ar++
      SIGNAL(R)
ENDWHILE
IF (ar == 0) AND (ww > 0) THEN
      SIGNAL(W)
ENDIF
SIGNAL(Guard)
```

Figure 5.24: Writer epilogue code

Under mutual exclusion, it decrements the count of writers. If there are readers waiting, it increments the count of processes actually reading, and wakes them up by signalling R. Each of the waiting readers will have done a WAIT(R) at the end of its entry protocol. If there are no readers waiting, and there is at least one writer waiting, it wakes up the first writer by signalling W. Finally it releases the mutual exclusion on the shared counts.

Solution 4

This final solution is biased totally in favour of writers. Once a writer is given access, no new readers are allowed in until all those processes which wish to write have written. While this seems severe on readers, it does guarantee that the data they are reading is as up to date as possible.

Data structures

We use the same data structures as in the previous example. We introduce a semaphore Writing, initialised to 1, to enforce mutual exclusion on writers. Also a counter pw, the number of writers that have got permission to write, but are actually waiting their turn.

There is a fine distinction between ww and pw. The first counts the number of writers which are held up on the semaphore W, waiting for the last reader to exit. The second counts writers held up on the semaphore Writing, waiting for the current writer to exit: see Figure 5.25.

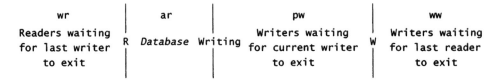

Figure 5.25: Solution 4

Reader entry protocol

The protocol executed by a reader process when it wishes to read is the same as in the previous example, Figure 5.20.

Reader exit protocol

The protocol executed by a reader process when it has finished reading has to be modified slightly, and is given in Figure 5.26.

```
WAIT (Guard)
ar--
wr--
IF (ar == 0) THEN
        WHILE (pw < ww)
                pw++
                SIGNAL(W)
        ENDWHILE
ENDIF
SIGNAL (Guard)
```

Figure 5.26: Reader epilogue code

If there are no further readers (ar == 0), then if there are some writers waiting, it increments the count of writers with permission, pw, and wakes them up one by one. Each waiting writer will have done WAIT(W) at the end of its prologue code. The last reader continues to do this in the WHILE until the number of writers with permission to write (pw) is equal to the number wishing to write. In this way, the last reader wakes up any waiting writers.

Writer entry protocol

The protocol that is executed by a writer when it wishes to write is also slightly modified, and is given in Figure 5.27.

```
WAIT(Guard)
ww++
IF (ar == 0) THEN
      pw++
      SIGNAL(W)
ENDIF
SIGNAL(Guard)
WAIT(W)
WAIT(Writing)
```

Figure 5.27: Writer prologue code

If there are no actual readers (ar == 0), then it can skip over the WAIT(W), by means of the dummy SIGNAL, and go on to compete for the mutual exclusion semaphore to write, when its turn comes. Otherwise it is blocked on the W semaphore, until the last reader wakes it up.

Writer exit protocol

The protocol that is executed by a writer when it has finished writing is given in Figure 5.28.

```
SIGNAL(Writing)
WAIT(Guard)
pw--
ww--
IF (pw == 0) THEN
      WHILE (ar < wr)
            ar++
            SIGNAL(R)
      ENDWHILE
ENDIF
SIGNAL(Guard)
```

Figure 5.28: Writer epilogue code

If it is the last writer (pw == 0), and there are readers waiting, it increments the reader count, and wakes them up, by signalling R. Each reader will have done WAIT(R) at the end of its prologue code. Finally it releases the mutual exclusion on the shared counts. So the last active writer wakes up any waiting readers.

5.8 Implementation of semaphores

Having seen how semaphores can be used to solve interprocess communication problems, we now go on to examine how they are implemented.

The definition of a semaphore, and its associated operations, implies that the implementation is not trivial. Apart from the incrementing or decrementing of the semaphore value, there is the interaction with the scheduler implied by the requirement that a process doing a WAIT on a zero-valued semaphore must not continue processing. A SIGNAL on a semaphore with processes waiting on it also has implications for the scheduler. One and only one of these must be allowed to run.

Semaphore data structure

To keep track of all of the waiting processes, the data structure representing a semaphore must also contain a queue header, as well as an integer. The queue itself is implemented by a link field in each process descriptor. This could be the same field as used for the run queue, as a process can never be waiting on a semaphore and runnable at the same time.

How this queue of waiting processes is organised varies from one system to another. While it can sometimes be organised according to a priority scheme, it is most commonly a FIFO queue. Such an organisation is appropriate where a real-time response is not required, or all processes typically operate at the same priority, or queues can be expected to be very short.

But there can be serious problems with such FIFO organisation. A low priority process may be ahead of higher priority processes in the semaphore queue, and so will get to use the processor before them. This is known as priority inversion.

Different semaphores may require different queue organisations. This could be implemented with an extra field in the data structure representing a semaphore, containing either a coded description of the organisation, or a pointer to the queue code.

Indivisibility

Finally, probably the most significant aspect of the implementation is the requirement that all of this be done as one, single, un-interruptible operation. The implementation must guarantee that no two processes can operate on the same semaphore at the same time. So the code for both WAIT and SIGNAL

must itself constitute a critical section; it must begin with some form of LOCK, and finish with an UNLOCK. For this we can use one of the low level hardware mechanisms which we examined in Section 5.3.

All of these use some form or other of busy waiting for LOCK. So what we have done here is to move the busy waiting from the entry to critical sections of applications programs (as with the software algorithms), to the entry to critical sections of WAIT and SIGNAL.

But, so long as the implementation of WAIT and SIGNAL are simple, the time spent busy waiting should be reasonably short. Any contending processes should execute the code for WAIT and SIGNAL, and release the lock, in a very short space of time. The critical sections of semaphores will almost always be empty, so there should be virtually no busy waiting.

On the other hand, application programs may have very long critical sections, which are almost always occupied. Figure 5.29 tries to illustrate the timing relationship of LOCK and UNLOCK to WAIT and SIGNAL. But it is only an attempt; realistically the representation of the critical section of the application should be tens of thousands of times longer than the implementation of WAIT and SIGNAL.

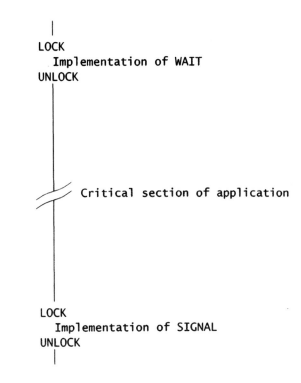

```
|
LOCK
   Implementation of WAIT
UNLOCK



                  Critical section of application




LOCK
   Implementation of SIGNAL
UNLOCK
|
```

Figure 5.29: Timing relationship of locks and semaphores

It is not possible to use LOCK and UNLOCK in place of WAIT and SIGNAL: busy waiting or interrupt disabling is not acceptable over the time-scale involved.

5.9 System V semaphores

Linux provides the System V interface for creating, deleting, and operating on semaphores. This is part of a wider set of facilities known as System V IPC.

The first point to note here is that System V semaphores are system wide resources, managed by the operating system. This has the advantage that any process (with the requisite permissions) can access any semaphore. The downside is that the limit on the total number of semaphores which may exist at one time is system wide, not on a process by process basis. So one group of processes could use them all, while others could not create even one.

System V semaphores are allocated not individually, but in sets; of course it is always possible to request a set containing just one semaphore. All operations are performed on the set. This has the advantage that it permits atomic combinations of operations. The downside is that a simple operation is unduly complicated.

The semaphore table

The next point to consider is how semaphores are identified on a system wide basis. As usual, there is a difference between the way semaphores are identified externally to users, and how the kernel identifies them internally. Users identify semaphores by means of a numeric key. They agree the value of this key among themselves, and use it when creating a new semaphore, or associating with an existing one.

The kernel maintains a table, `semary`, of pointers to semaphores, and identifies them by their position in this table. Each entry in the table is a pointer to a `struct semid_ds`, see Figure 5.30, from `<linux/sem.h>`, and the manual page for `semid_ds`.

```
struct semid_ds{
        struct ipc_perm   sem_perm;
        struct sem        *sem_base;
        struct sem_queue  *sem_pending;
};
```

Figure 5.30: Data structure representing a semaphore set

sem_perm

This is a structure used to define access to the semaphore, see Figure 5.31, from `<linux/ipc.h>`.

- The user supplied key is stored here, in the key field.

- The uid and gid identify the owner of the semaphore, and the group to which the owner belongs.

```
struct ipc_perm{
       kernel_key_t  key;  /* user supplied key */
       kernel_uid_t  uid;  /* owner's user id   */
       kernel_gid_t  gid;  /* owner's group id  */
       kernel_mode_t mode; /* access modes        */
};
```

Figure 5.31: Data structure controlling access to a semaphore

- The mode field specifies which operations the owner, members of the owner's group, or any other users, can perform on this semaphore.

sem_base

This points to the actual data structures representing the semaphores. Sets of semaphores are allocated as an array of struct sem, from <linux/sem.h>, as shown in Figure 5.32.

```
struct sem{
       int semval; /* current value                    */
       int sempid; /* process which last operated on sem */
};
```

Figure 5.32: Data structure representing an individual semaphore

The relationship between the semaphore table semary, the semid_ds representing a particular set, and the actual semaphores in that set, is illustrated in Figure 5.33.

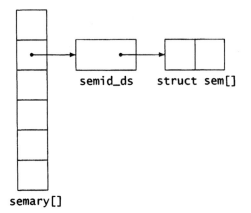

Figure 5.33: System V semaphore layout

sem_pending

The sem_pending field heads a linked list of sem_queue structures, each representing a process which was unable to carry out its operations on the semaphore set, and so has been blocked. See Figure 5.34, from <linux/sem.h>.

```
struct sem_queue{
        struct sem_queue   *next;
        struct wait_queue  *sleeper;
        struct semid_ds    *sma;
        struct sembuf      *sops;
        int                nsops;
};
```

Figure 5.34: Data structure representing a waiting process

- next points to the next entry in this list.

- sleeper points to a corresponding struct wait_queue, and indirectly to the task_struct representing the waiting process.

- sma points back to the relevant semid_ds.

- sops is a pointer to an array of structures representing the operations which this process requested on this set of semaphores. This field is the reason for having a struct sem_queue in the first place. Because of the need to store this information, the standard wait_queue is not enough.

- nsops is the number of operations (the number of elements in the array).

Figure 5.35 illustrates how these data structures fit together.

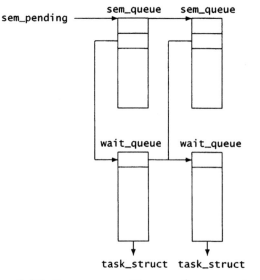

Figure 5.35: Processes waiting on the semaphore set

When the value of the semaphore is increased, all of the processes linked on the `sem_pending` queue for this semaphore set are checked; any which can now go ahead are woken up, and moved to the ready queue.

Indivisibility

The Unix design ensures that when a process is executing in the kernel, it cannot be preempted by any other process. It may be preempted by the kernel itself, or by an interrupt handler; but never by another user process. System V semaphores will only be manipulated by other processes, never by the kernel itself, or by interrupt handlers. So this feature of Unix guarantees indivisibility on System V semaphores.

Operations

The `semget()` system service is used to create a semaphore set, or associate with an existing set. One parameter to this is the user defined key. Others are the number of semaphores in the set, and a flag specifying whether access to the set is exclusive to this process or not. But there is no parameter to set an initial value—this has to be done by a separate system service.

The system does a linear search of its semaphore table. It checks the key field of each `sem_perm` entry, to find if one corresponding to the supplied key already exists. If it finds one, it checks that it matches the other parameters supplied. If there is no such entry, it creates one. In either case, it returns its index in the table. This is known as the id of the semaphore set. It is important to distinguish between the id and the key. The key is used to gain access to the semaphore set. The id is used in all further operations on the set.

There is one generic system service for all operations on a semaphore set, `semop()`. This is passed the id and a pointer to an array of `struct sembuf`. A `struct sembuf` has a field to identify the semaphore in the set, and a field to specify which operation is to be performed on that semaphore. If any one of the operations specified to `semop()` would block, then none of the operations is performed, and the process blocks. This can be a powerful tool, allowing for atomic combinations of operations to be carried out.

It is also possible to examine or change the value of any semaphore in the set, using `semctl()`. This is used for example to initialise the semaphores. Another use of `semctl()` is to remove a semaphore set from the system.

Having only one generic system service means that performing even the simplest operation on a semaphore, such as WAIT or SIGNAL, is unnecessarily complex. Also, the fact that the creation of a System V semaphore is a separate operation from initialising it has always been considered a fatal flaw.

The shell command `ipcs -s` can be used to display information about existing semaphores. The `ipcrm` command removes semaphores from the system.

5.10 POSIX semaphores

POSIX 1003.1b (1993) introduced a new implementation of semaphores. There are two interfaces supplied, known as unnamed and named semaphores. The basic distinction between them is that while unnamed semaphores can only be used within one process, or between related processes, named semaphores can also be used by totally unrelated processes. All they need to know is the name of the semaphore.

Unnamed semaphores

An unnamed semaphore is created by a call to sem_init(). One parameter specifies the initial value. A second parameter is a pointer to a variable of type sem_t, which represents the semaphore to the process from then on. Like all of the POSIX semaphore functions, it returns -1 if it does not work, and puts an error code into errno; otherwise it returns 0.

There are four system services that operate on unnamed semaphores. The standard WAIT and SIGNAL are implemented by sem_wait() and sem_post(), respectively. Then there is a sem_trywait(), which works just like WAIT if the semaphore has a value greater than zero. However, if the semaphore has a value of 0, this call does not block, but returns -1, with errno set to EAGAIN. There is also a function which queries the value of the semaphore, sem_getval().

Finally, when it is no longer required, a semaphore should be deallocated, using sem_destroy().

Currently, Linux implements unnamed semaphores as part of the pthread package. So while such semaphores can be shared between different threads in a process, they cannot be shared between different processes, not even between parent and child.

Named semaphores

A named semaphore is identified system wide by its name. The namespace for semaphores is the same as that used for files, so semaphore names are treated just like file names. The same rules apply. If two different processes, each with a different default directory, use the same name for a semaphore, the system will treat these as two different semaphores, just as it would treat them as two different files. So it is recommended that a full pathname be used for a semaphore name, beginning with /. It is not necessary that there be a file with that name; but the directory specified must exist.

The system call used to create, or associate with, a named semaphore is sem_open(). This returns a pointer to a variable of type sem_t, which represents the semaphore to the process from then on.

All operations are performed using the same system services as those provided for unnamed semaphores. But sem_destroy() cannot be used with a

named semaphore. Instead two other functions are supplied. `sem_close()` deallocates the link between the process and the semaphore. The semaphore itself is not deallocated. It still exists, and retains its value. But it is now inaccessible to the process. A later call to `sem_open()` can connect with it again, with whatever value it had previously (unless changed by some other process).

The `sem_unlink()` system service is used to remove a named semaphore from the system. This always returns immediately.

Named semaphores are not yet implemented in Linux.

5.11   Limitations of semaphores

It may seem that all concurrency problems have been solved with the introduction of semaphores. But they are not perfect. The following are some of the areas in which the semaphore mechanism (at least as described in this chapter) is deficient.

1. Their use is not enforced—it is by convention only. Programmers can accidentally or deliberately not use them, and violate mutual exclusion.

2. Incorrect use can cause deadlock, as noted when dealing with multiple producers and consumers.

3. A low priority process can acquire a mutual exclusion semaphore, and hold it locked against all others, no matter how high their priority. Because it is of low priority, it is also likely to be preempted while holding the semaphore. This phenomenon is known as 'priority inversion', when the lowest priority process is holding up all of the others. One possible, but complicated, solution to this is to give a process a temporary priority boost when it acquires a mutual exclusion semaphore. This is to enable it to reach its SIGNAL as soon as possible, and hold up others as little as possible.

4. A semaphore does not allow a test for busy, without a commitment to blocking. The POSIX `sem_trywait()` addresses this.

5. The semaphore mechanism does not actually pass data to another process. This has to be arranged separately, e.g. using shared memory.

6. Blocking is indefinite; it is not possible to specify a timeout.

So we have to continue our search for other mechanisms.

5.12   Sequencers and eventcounts

Sequencers and eventcounts are another mechanism, proposed as an alternative to semaphores, to overcome some of the problems listed in the previous

section. This mechanism not only keeps track of how many events have oc-curred, but also of which ones. Sometimes it is important to know, for exam-ple, that items 34, 35, 36 are available, and not just that there are three items available.

In effect, this is an attempt to make the operating system responsible for implementing the ticket dispensing mechanism of Section 4.4. It must guar-antee that the dispenser works atomically, and so gives out unique numbers. It also replaces the busy waiting of that section, by putting a process to sleep while it is waiting for its turn to come.

Operations

A *sequencer* is a nondecreasing integer variable, that can be used to totally order events. The value of a sequencer is the value of the next number to be taken. There is only one operation available on a sequencer S, TICKET(S). This returns the current value of S, and increments S.

An *eventcount* always has an integer value E associated with it. The current value corresponds to the event being serviced. There are three operations defined on an eventcount E, AWAIT, ADVANCE, and READ.

AWAIT (E, i) delays the executing process until $E \geq i$. The following code corresponds to a customer entering a shop and waiting for service:

$$i = \text{TICKET(S)}$$
$$\text{AWAIT(E, i)}.$$

This can be written more concisely:

$$\text{AWAIT(E, TICKET(S))}.$$

There must be some way of queueing processes which are waiting. This queue will be ordered according to the value received from TICKET, smallest first.

ADVANCE(E) corresponds to the next offer of service. The eventcount value is incremented; if there are any processes waiting on the eventcount queue, then one is woken and moved to the run queue.

READ(E) is provided for inspecting the current value of the eventcount. A process may find this useful to check whether its turn will come soon. If not, it may do something else before blocking on the AWAIT.

Applications

We will look briefly at how eventcounts and sequencers can be applied to some of the problems seen in previous sections.

Synchronisation

A process specifies which occurrence of an event it is waiting for, rather than just the next event of that type. An eventcount E is initialised to 0. The pro-

ducer advances this each time it reaches a synchronisation point. The consumer keeps a local count i, initialised to 1, and waits for the value of the eventcount to be as least as great as this.

```
    Producer              Consumer

    ADVANCE(E)            AWAIT(E, i)
                          i++
```

Figure 5.36: Eventcount for synchronisation

Figure 5.36 shows the synchronisation code for both. Note that in this case the producer will never be held up, so it presupposes an infinite buffer. The consumer will only be held up when the buffer is empty. For example, if the producer puts in ten items, E will have a value of 10. When the consumer has taken out ten items, i will have a value of 11. So the consumer will be held up on AWAIT(E, 11).

Mutual exclusion

This requires a sequencer S, and an eventcount E, both initialised to 0. Then each process executes the code shown in Figure 5.37.

```
        beginning section

        AWAIT(E, TICKET(S))

        critical section

        ADVANCE(E)

        remainder section
```

Figure 5.37: Eventcount and sequencer for mutual exclusion

The first process will do AWAIT(0, 0), and not be held up. Any other processes coming after it will get values of 1, 2, 3 etc. from TICKET. As E is still 0, they will be held up. When the first process leaves its critical section, it increments E, the process which got 1 from TICKET is woken up, and goes into its critical section.

Producer and consumer

Two eventcounts, IN and OUT, are initialised to 0. These count the items put in by the producer and taken out by the consumer, respectively. The producer has a local counter i, and the consumer has a local counter j, both initialised to 0. Figure 5.38 shows the code used by the producer and the consumer, which assumes an N slot buffer.

Producer	Consumer

```
        Producer                        Consumer

    AWAIT(OUT, i + 1 - N)        AWAIT(IN, j + 1)
    insert at i MOD N            Remove from j MOD N
    i++                         j++
    ADVANCE(IN)                 ADVANCE(OUT)
```

Figure 5.38: Eventcounts with one producer, one consumer

The best way to understand the algorithm is to work through an example with a small buffer, for example with four slots. Have the producer put in a few items, then have the consumer take them out. Let the producer fill the buffer, and see that the algorithm blocks the producer. Check that the consumer is blocked when the buffer is empty.

There is no need for a mutual exclusion mechanism, as the algorithm ensures that the producer and consumer will never be dealing with the same slot in the buffer at the same time.

As with semaphores, the only time i MOD N and j MOD N will be pointing to the same slot in the buffer is when it is empty, or when it is full. When the buffer is empty, the producer will have put in x items, and the consumer will have taken out x items. So IN and j will both have a value of x. The consumer will do AWAIT(IN, j + 1), which is effectively AWAIT(x, x + 1). So it will be held up, and cannot get on to the remove line. It will only proceed when the producer does ADVANCE(IN), by which time the producer has incremented i to point to the next slot.

When the buffer is full, the producer will have put in x items, so i will have a value of x, and the consumer will have taken out x − N items, so OUT will have a value of x − N. The producer will do AWAIT(x − N, x − N + 1), and will be held up until the consumer does ADVANCE(OUT), by which time the consumer has incremented j to point to the next slot.

Evaluation of sequencers and eventcounts

Sequencers and eventcounts have some advantages over semaphores, but they also have their own problems.

1. They allow an operation to wait for a particular event in a sequence, not just for *any* event of that type.

2. The READ operation is an improvement on the standard implementation of semaphores, although POSIX have now catered for this.

3. They still depend on the programmer getting it right. A malicious programmer could jump the queue, by using a lower valued parameter to AWAIT. Even without malice, wrong placing of commands, or incorrect parameters, could render the whole scheme void.

4. If a process acquires a sequencer value, and then dies before using it, the whole scheme could be upset.

5. There is actually very little experience with using sequencers and event-counts, as compared with the vast experience with semaphores.

5.13 Summary

Software algorithms all have the drawback that they rely on cooperation between programmers. There is no way to enforce them. So there is a need for operating system intervention in the area of interprocess communication.

1. The signal mechanism arranges for a user defined function to be called, when some particular event occurs. Such events can be synchronous to the running program, or asynchronous.

2. A signal is generated when the event occurs. It is delivered when the destination process takes the appropriate action. In between, it is pending.

   Each process can register a function to handle any particular signal. Otherwise system default actions are taken.

   Each thread has its own set of pending and blocked signals; they can share handlers.

   Signals are typically used to avoid busy waiting.

3. There are low level hardware mechanisms available for mutual exclusion, such as interrupt inhibition, and spinlocks, which use busy waiting. They are acceptable only over a very short timescale.

4. A semaphore is a non-negative integer, which can only be acted on by two un-interruptible operations. WAIT decrements the value; if it is already 0, the process is blocked. SIGNAL wakes up a process, if there is one waiting; otherwise it increments the value.

5. Semaphores can be used to control mutual exclusion (initialised to 1), synchronisation (initialised to 0), and resource allocation (initialised to the number of instances available).

6. A classic use of semaphores is to control producer and consumer processes, communicating through a shared buffer.

7. The readers and writers problem is another classic situation which can be controlled by semaphores. There are various levels of solution, depending on the severity of the exclusion, and the bias towards readers or writers.

8. The implementation of semaphores involves interacting with the scheduler, for blocking and unblocking processes, and managing the queue of waiting processes.

   Making WAIT and SIGNAL to be un-interruptible requires some sort of locking mechanism in hardware. Spinlocks can be used for this.

9. The user interface to semaphores provided by Linux is the System V set of system services.

10. POSIX has proposed its own interface to semaphores, which can be named or unnamed. This is not yet fully available in Linux.

11. Semaphores are not the ultimate solution to IPC problems. They can be improved on, and there is also room for other mechanisms.

12. A sequencer is equivalent to the ticket dispenser used by Lamport. There is only one operation on it, TICKET, which returns the current value, and increments the sequencer.

    An eventcount is an integer holding the current value, on which three operations are defined. AWAIT delays the executing process until the value of the eventcount is at least as large as the number held by the process. ADVANCE increments the eventcount, and may wake up a waiting process. READ returns the value of the eventcount.

    All of the problems considered in previous sections can be solved using eventcounts and sequencers.

    As with semaphores, they still rely on the programmer getting it right.

5.14 Discussion questions

1. Is it accurate to say that a synchronous event will occur at the same place every time a program is run? Give an example of how a floating point exception (SIGFPE) might occur on some runs of a program, but not on others.

2. On a heavily loaded machine, one or more processes may be swapped out to disk when they are not running. In the light of what you have learned about signal generation, why must the task_struct always be in memory, even when the process is not running?

3. Linux only records one outstanding instance of each signal. Investigate the extensions introduced in POSIX.4 to overcome this deficiency.

4. How does the output from the ps command distinguish between processes in interruptible and un-interruptible wait states?

5. How does Linux remember that a blocked signal is pending?

6. Does the third parameter to sigprocmask() have any effect on the bitmap returned by this function?

7. Describe some situations in which processes would want to share signal handlers with their parent, and some situations in which they definitely would not.

8. What is the difference between ignoring a signal and blocking it?

9. With the Linux signal mechanism as described, is it possible to have process-wide signals—i.e. notified to the process as a whole, and handled by any thread in the process?

10. One thread prints odd numbers, a second prints even numbers. Write an algorithm which synchronises both threads using signals.

11. How does the disabling of interrupts guarantee that a process will not be context switched out in the middle of a critical section?

    Why is it not an acceptable mechanism?

12. Using a semaphore for resource allocation does not in any way control *which* instance of the resource has been allocated, or *which* are free. The semaphore merely guarantees that a requesting process will be blocked if there are no instances of the resource available.

    Write an algorithm which uses a semaphore to allocate printers, and which also maintains information about the status of each printer. Is there need for mutual exclusion?

13. Simulate the use of semaphores for one producer, one consumer, with two people sitting across a table. A card with 0 on one side, 1 on the other, can represent a semaphore. An enlarged copy of Figure 5.11 can represent the buffer. `NextIn` and `NextOut` can be simulated by index fingers.

    You should find that no matter how the two processes interleave their actions, they cannot be putting into and taking out of the same slot in the buffer at the same time.

14. Reverse the order of the WAITs on `SlotAvail` and `Guard` in the algorithm shown in Figure 5.14. Now run the two algorithms and see what happens. Reverse the WAITs in Figure 5.15, and see what happens. What effect does reversing the SIGNALs in either of these have?

15. What are the disadvantages of the first solution to the readers and writers problem given in Section 5.7?

16. Refer to Solution 2 in Section 5.7. When a writer exits, it does a SIGNAL on the semaphore `Writing`. This wakes up the next process, either reader or writer, if any one is waiting. If both a reader and writer are waiting, what decides which will go next?

17. The incorrect algorithm presented in Figure 5.21 is easier to understand than the correct one in Figure 5.20. Is it possible to adapt the incorrect algorithm, so that while retaining its logical structure, it actually works correctly?

18. What precise aspect of Solution 3 in Section 5.7 ensures that waiting readers are given priority over waiting writers?

19. What precise aspect of Solution 4 in Section 5.7 ensures that waiting writers are given priority over waiting readers?

20. The System V interface to semaphores is complicated. Write code to implement a WAIT and a SIGNAL on one semaphore, using `semop()`.

21. How could unnamed POSIX semaphores be used by two different processes?

22. The provision of sem_trywait() in POSIX seems to be a great improvement: a process need never block, if it does not want to. Outline a situation in which a process using sem_trywait() might still find itself blocked unwillingly.

23. Section 5.11 discussed the problem of 'priority inversion', and suggested the solution of temporarily boosting a process's priority when it acquires a mutual exclusion semaphore. How could the operating system recognise such a semaphore?

24. Would there be any advantage in allowing a semaphore WAIT to time out?

25. Suggest a data structure which might be used to represent an eventcount.

26. Run the following sequence of operations through the algorithms given in Figure 5.38, assuming N = 4. P means a producer runs, C means a consumer runs.

    P P P C C C P P C P P C P P P C P P P C

27. Extend the algorithm given in Figure 5.38, to cater for multiple producers and consumers. Be sure to guarantee mutual exclusion.

28. What happens if a process calls TICKET, and then dies?

Higher level mechanisms for IPC 6

The low level primitives discussed in the previous chapter, namely signals, semaphores, eventcounts and sequencers, all offer some assistance in regulating interprocess communication. But there is no guarantee that they will be used correctly. Undisciplined use of any of these mechanisms can lead to errors, as we have seen.

Different processes accessing the same semaphore can get the order wrong, or they may accidentally or maliciously omit a WAIT or insert a SIGNAL. Even when legitimately allowed to access a resource, a process may corrupt it erroneously or maliciously.

Also these mechanisms only deal with the mutual exclusion and synchronisation aspects. Any data transferred between processes has to be catered for apart from this, typically by using buffers in shared memory.

6.1   Data passing mechanisms

One possible development to take from these low level primitives is to make them more powerful, by combining data transfer with mutual exclusion and synchronisation. This can be implemented by some form of structured message passing. The system would arrange both for the transfer of such messages between processes, as well as synchronisation between sender and receiver, and the queueing of messages where required.

Some argue that message passing should always be used, as it is a mechanism which extends neatly to distributed systems.

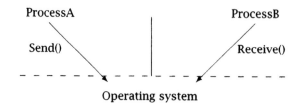

Figure 6.1: Outline of message passing

Figure 6.1 gives the outline of a message passing system. Note that the operating system is involved in all data passing between the two processes. They never communicate directly with each other, only with the operating system. Also the operating system does not force the message on the receiver—it has to ask for it. This is why the arrow on the right-hand side of Figure 6.1 is pointing downwards, to emphasise that ProcessB must actively ask for the message.

There must be some agreement about the size of the message and the structure of the fields in it. Such a structure could consist of a header, which contains for example the id of the source process, the type, which might be request, reply, etc., priority, and then a body containing data. The system must check the source field, so that one process cannot pretend to be another.

Sending a message need not be immediately followed by receiving—the operating system can maintain a queue of waiting messages. This leads to a fundamental distinction in message passing systems.

Asynchronous message passing

With this type of message passing, a sending process is never delayed. So the system must buffer the message, implying the management of buffers. This has implications for space, and for CPU cycles. Messages may need to be copied twice, once from the sender to system space, and then from system space to the address space of the receiver, all of this involving several context switches. So all processes, not just those passing messages, are affected. Facilities provided by the memory manager can be of help in reducing or eliminating this overhead. The ideal is to arrange for buffers to be shared by the two communicating processes. Then all that has to be passed is a pointer to the shared buffer.

It is important that the system distinguish message boundaries. So instead of just buffering a block of data in FIFO order, it buffers a series of distinct messages. The need for the system to buffer messages introduces various possibilities for the designer.

- Should the size of a message be fixed or variable? Should there be a maximum size?

- There could be one buffer in the kernel for the whole system. In this case, access to it by many readers and writers must be synchronised.

  Another possibility is to have one buffer per destination process. There is still a need for synchronisation, as there may be many senders, and a process may have more than one message stream active at a time.

  A third possibility is to have one buffer per message stream. Even here there is need to synchronise access for reading and writing.

- If buffers are implemented as a table, then there is a maximum number of messages that can be outstanding. If they are implemented as a linked list, while there is no fixed limit, messages cannot be added to the list indefinitely.

Synchronous message passing

Message passing can also be implemented in such a way that the sender and receiver must first synchronise, and then the message is copied from one to the other. This avoids the overhead of any buffer management.

However, this type of message passing is not always suitable. Because the receiver must always be ready and waiting, an important server process could be blocked while trying to send a reply, when it could and should be going ahead with work for others.

In a multi-threaded environment, one possible solution would be for the client to create a new thread to handle each request. This sends the request to the server, and then blocks, waiting for the reply. Other client threads can continue execution. The blocked thread is always ready and waiting when the server wants to reply.

6.2   Message queues

A rather down-market implementation of a full-blown message passing system is a message queue. With such a system, a sender cannot specify a destination process for a message. Rather, the system maintains a queue of messages. Processes can add messages to this queue, or take them off. A reader always gets the first message from the queue, or at best the highest priority message on the queue. This situation is illustrated in Figure 6.2.

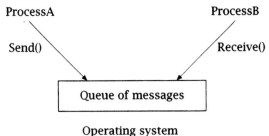

Figure 6.2: A message queue

The following are some desirable features of a message queue system.

- Communicating processes may not know or need to know each other's names. It is sufficient that both know the name of the queue they are using to communicate.

- A process may not want to commit to an indefinite wait if the queue is empty. So it should be possible to specify a timeout period.

- A process should be able to specify which messages in the queue it is willing to receive, and in what order it will receive them. This means being able to specify the priority and type of both outgoing and incoming messages.

It is not really feasible to have duplex communication with a message queue. If one process did a send(), followed immediately by a receive(), then it would get its own message back. Such duplex communication is normally implemented by using two queues, one for each direction.

6.3   System V message queues

Message queues are provided as part of System V IPC. The interface, and indeed the implementation, is very similar to what we have already seen with semaphores. As in the previous chapter, we will first of all examine the implementation, then the interface.

Implementation

Message queues are implemented in a manner similar to System V semaphores. There is a table of pointers to data structures representing queues. Each message queue is identified by a struct msqid_ds, from <linux/msg.h>, see Figure 6.3.

```
msqid_ds{
    struct ipc_perm     msg_perm;   /* access permissions          */
    struct msg          *msg_first; /* first message on queue       */
    struct msg          *msg_last;  /* last message on queue        */
    struct wait_queue   *wwait;     /* blocked writing threads      */
    struct wait_queue   *rwait;     /* blocked reading threads      */
    unsigned short      msg_qnum;   /* number of messages on queue */
};
```

Figure 6.3: Data structure representing a message queue

- The permissions for the message queue are implemented in an ipc_perm structure, as with System V semaphores. The key is also kept here (see Figure 5.31).

- The message queue itself is implemented as a linked list of struct msg, see Figure 6.4, from <linux/msg.h>, with msg_first and msg_last pointing to the first and last messages on the queue.

  - The queue is linked through msg_next.
  - Each message is tagged with a number, known as its type, maintained in the msg_type field. The meaning of this is user defined.
  - The message itself is not contained in the struct msg, which is really only a header. The msg_spot points to the actual data.
  - Each message is time-stamped when it is sent, in the msg_stime field.
  - The length of the message is in msg_ts.

```
struct msg{
        struct msg *msg_next;  /* next message on queue   */
        long        msg_type;  /* as specified by sender */
        char       *msg_spot;  /* message text address    */
        time_t      msg_stime; /* msgsnd time             */
        short       msg_ts;    /* message text size       */
};
```

Figure 6.4: Structure of an actual message

- There are two wait queues associated with each message queue. One, wwait, is for processes blocked waiting to write to a full queue; the other, rwait, is for processes blocked waiting to read from an empty queue.

- msg_qnum is the number of individual messages on the queue.

The system maintains a table of pointers to such structures. The message queue ids serve as an index into this table.

How these data structures fit together is illustrated in Figure 6.5.

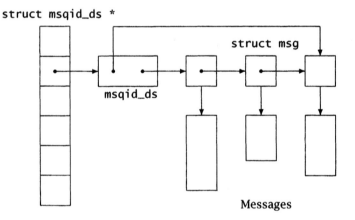

Figure 6.5: System V message queue layout

Interface

A message queue is created using the msgget() system call. This is supplied with a key parameter, just like a System V semaphore. If msgget() is called with a key that is not already in use, then the kernel allocates a new message queue, initialises it, and returns the id that is to be associated with that queue. Otherwise, if it already exists, the function returns the id associated with the existing queue. In either case this id is an index into the system wide array of message queues.

Sending messages

The function msgsnd() is used to put a message on a queue. It is passed the
id of the queue, a pointer to the message itself, the size of the message in
bytes, and a flag parameter. The message must be encapsulated in a msgbuf
structure, from <linux/msg.h>, see Figure 6.6.

```
struct msgbuf{
        long mtype;   /* message type     */
        char mtext[]; /* message contents */
};
```

Figure 6.6: Data structure representing a message

The mtype field can be used to specify the user defined type of the message. This can be used, for example, to implement a priority system.

The flag parameter to msgsnd() determines whether or not the sender
blocks on a full queue.

Receiving messages

The function msgrcv() is used to take a message from a queue. It is passed
the id of the queue, a pointer to a msgbuf structure in user space into which
the message will be placed, the size of this buffer, a type parameter, and a flag
parameter.

The type parameter specifies the type of message the caller wishes to receive. A value of 0 will take the first message on the queue. A value greater
than 0 will return the first message on the queue which has a type field of that
value. A negative value will return the first message of the smallest type less
than or equal to the absolute value of the parameter. The mtype field in the
receiving msgbuf will be set to the type specified by the sender.

The flag parameter specifies whether or not the receiver blocks on an
empty queue, and whether or not over-long messages are to be truncated.

Control functions

There is also a msgctl() function, which performs control operations on a
message queue. This is passed the id of the queue to operate on, and a command parameter. It can be used to query or set values relevant to the whole
queue, such as the maximum size of the queue, or access permissions. It can
also be used to remove the queue from the system.

The shell command ipcs -q displays information about existing message
queues. The ipcrm command removes queues from the system.

Evaluation

With System V queues, message boundaries are preserved, messages can be given a type (priority) and read out of sequence, and the sender and receiver do not have to share a common ancestor.

But there are still some features which could be added. It is not possible to specify a receiver when sending a message. Any process with access to the message queue can read any message. Nor is there any broadcast mechanism. The first process to read a message removes it from the queue, and it is no longer available to any others. The message passing mechanism cannot detect invalid or illegal messages.

6.4 POSIX message queues

There are problems associated with the orderly close-down and removal of a System V queue, so POSIX decided to implement a totally new mechanism, which is not yet available in Linux. A POSIX message queue is identified by name, using the same namespace as POSIX semaphores. These message queues have their own set of system services, different from the System V ones.

A process creates a message queue, or connects to an existing one, with mq_open(). It must supply a unique name, which may be a pathname. Processes specifying the same name will be connected to the same message queue, and so are able to communicate.

The mq_send() system service is used to send a message. Messages are maintained on the queue in order of arrival. It is possible to specify a priority for the message being sent. A process attempting to send a message to a full queue will block.

The mq_receive() system service returns the oldest, highest priority message, and its priority. A process trying to read from an empty queue will block.

After a call to mq_close(), the calling process can no longer access that queue. But it still exists. To remove it, call mq_unlink(). After this, the queue and its contents remain until all processes which are attached to that queue have called mq_close().

6.5 Conditional critical regions

A different approach to the IPC problems we have been investigating would be a programming language construct which forces a programmer to declare explicitly what data is shared, and where the critical sections are in a program. With this information, a compiler could check and enforce that shared data is only accessed from within a critical section, and that critical sections are mutually exclusive.

A first attempt at this is a construct known as a critical region. This involves extensions to the syntax of a programming language, and also to the compiler, so that it can recognise these extensions.

Outline

First of all it should be possible to declare shared as an attribute of any data type. Then it should be possible to declare some scope in the program as critical region <shared data>, using the usual syntax of the language to delimit the beginning and end of such a region, e.g. { . . }, as in C. The compiler would then automatically create a semaphore, and initialise it appropriately. It would also insert WAIT and SIGNAL operations on this semaphore corresponding to the beginning and end of the region.

For synchronisation, what is required is a language construct something like await(condition). The condition would be expressed in the normal syntax of the language. If the condition is true, then the process proceeds. If the condition is false, then the process is blocked until the condition becomes true. The compiler must also see to it that any mutual exclusion locks the process is holding are released while it is waiting.

There is a problem with how the process is woken up. Somehow, the condition on which it is waiting must be re-evaluated every time any process takes any action which might alter the variables being evaluated. This is easier said than done. Also, it must wake up holding the locks it had before it was blocked. In general, the overhead involved in this is considered to be unacceptable. But such an await() would certainly be a useful construct.

Example

For example, if such a construct were available, a solution to the readers and writers problem discussed in the chapter on semaphores would be as simple as shown in Figure 6.7.

Declarations

The shared struct shared_counts contains a count of readers and writers. The shared char writelock is a dummy variable, effectively used as a mutual exclusion semaphore. By declaring a critical region for the use of this variable writelock, only one process can write at a time. Note that writelock itself is never written or read by the program.

Reader code

When a process executes reader code, under mutual exclusion it checks the number of writers; if there are no writers, then it is not blocked on the await, it increments the count of readers, and goes on to read. When finished, it decrements the count of readers, under mutual exclusion.

If there is a process writing, or waiting to write, then the reader is blocked on the await, but its lock on the region is released. Any subsequent readers are also blocked on the await, until the last writer has finished. Note that there is no explicit code for waking up readers; that is all implied in the await().

```
shared struct{
    int writers;
    int readers;
}shared_counts;

shared char writelock;

/* reader code */

critical region shared_counts{
    await (writers == 0);
    readers++;
}

        /* READ */

critical region shared_counts{
    readers--;
}

/* writer code */

critical region shared_counts{
    writers++;
    await (readers == 0);
}

critical region writelock{

    /* WRITE */

}

critical region shared_counts{
    writers--;
}
```

Figure 6.7: Readers/writers using conditional critical regions

Writer code

When a process executes writer code, if there are no current readers, it is not blocked on the `await`, it goes on and tries to get exclusive access to the `shared char writelock`. If there are several competing writers, they will only be allowed access to this region one by one. Note that a process holds its exclusive access to this region all during its writing phase, only releasing it when finished.

If there are any current readers when a writer begins its prologue, it is held up on the `await`. But it has already declared its interest by incrementing `writers`. This will prevent any further readers being allowed in.

When finished writing, it decrements the number of writers, under mutual exclusion. When the last writer has finished, `writers` will have a value of 0. This will cause any waiting readers to be woken up. Again, there is no explicit code for this.

Other solutions

As the code stands, as long as any process is writing, new writers have precedence over readers. This is because readers are waiting for `writers` to drop to 0. So it is implementing solution 4 of Section 5.7.

Now consider the effect of changing the order of the `await` and the increment, in the reader prologue. It would be possible for the system to deadlock, with a reader waiting for `writers` to drop to 0, and a writer waiting for `readers` also to become 0.

But if the order of the increment and the `await` is also changed in the writer prologue, we have a different scenario. Now if there is both a reader and a writer waiting when a writer exits, precedence is given to the reader. This would implement solution 2 of Section 5.7.

Evaluation

All of the foregoing discussion still depends on a programmer writing correct code. It is still possible to manipulate a shared variable outside of a region, either accidentally or on purpose. Nor does it enforce any modularity. It would be better to have all manipulations on shared data done in one place.

6.6 Monitors

All of the mechanisms considered so far have one thing in common. While they each try to control access to shared data in their own way, none of them makes any attempt to control what is done with the data after access is allowed. Monitors were developed to close off this loophole.

Outline

A monitor consists of:

1. The shared data.

2. One or more functions, which can be called to operate on the data.

3. A function which initialises the data; this is executed only once.

The basic idea of a monitor is to provide data abstraction or data hiding. It controls the nature of operations performed on global data, to prevent meaningless or potentially harmful updates. The critical data is accessible indirectly and exclusively through a set of publicly available procedures.

User processes usually have no way of knowing the internal organisation of a monitor, such as the identity or structure of variables or functions.

In addition, in order to guarantee that there is mutual exclusion on the data, the implementation of a monitor must ensure that only one process is active in the monitor at any time. This is implemented by a mutual exclusion semaphore. The mutual exclusion would be arranged by the compiler of a suitable high-level language. Because of this, calling a monitor procedure implies an acceptance of a potential delay.

The critical region and data declarations in each process are replaced by a call to a monitor procedure.

Condition variables

Apart from mutual exclusion, synchronisation is also needed inside the monitor. For example, if a monitor controlled a shared buffer, at times this buffer may be full, and a producer should not be allowed to continue. Such synchronisation could be arranged using semaphores, as in Chapter 5. But we have seen problems with this, where a process waiting on a synchronisation semaphore, and holding a mutual exclusion semaphore, could prevent other processes from synchronising with it, and so lead to deadlock.

Because of this, a variant of a semaphore, known as a condition variable, has been developed. It is particularly useful within a monitor. Condition variables are always used with an associated mutual exclusion semaphore. A programmer, under the protection of exclusive access guaranteed by the semaphore, is able to test some condition, and decide whether to block or not. The condition variable is the mechanism used for this blocking.

Condition variables differ from semaphores, in that they wait on an arbitrary, programmer-specified condition, which could be a combination of AND and OR.

Whenever a process changes the state of one of the shared variables, it signals the condition variable. The signal only means that the variable has changed, not that the condition is TRUE. This wakes up a waiting process, which then checks to see if the condition it is waiting on is now TRUE. If not, it waits again on that condition variable.

Unlike a semaphore, a condition variable is implemented as a header to a queue of waiting processes. There is no integer. There are only two operations on such condition variables, CWAIT and CSIGNAL. As with semaphores, these must be atomic, uninterruptible. So they use LOCK and UNLOCK, just as semaphores do.

Figure 6.8 illustrates what happens when a process calls CWAIT—it always blocks itself, and calls the context switcher to give the CPU to some other process. This is different from WAIT on a semaphore, which only blocks when the value is 0. Also, a condition variable automatically gives up the mutual exclusion semaphore it was holding when it blocked. It remains blocked until some other process does a CSIGNAL.

```
CWAIT(conditionvar)
    LOCK
    Mark process unrunnable
    Queue the process on the condition variable
    Release mutual exclusion on the monitor
    UNLOCK
    Call context switcher
```

Figure 6.8: Implementation of CWAIT

Figure 6.9 illustrates what happens when a process calls CSIGNAL. It has an effect only if there is at least one process waiting. Not only does it wake it up, but it also returns to that process the mutual exclusion it was holding when it was put waiting. This is different from a SIGNAL on a semaphore, which always has some effect, either waking a process up, or incrementing the value.

```
CSIGNAL(conditionvar)
    LOCK
    IF there is a process waiting on conditionvar THEN
        Mark one runnable
        Mark current process unrunnable
        Transfer mutual exclusion on the monitor to selected process
        UNLOCK
        Call context switcher
    ELSE
        UNLOCK
        Return
    ENDIF
```

Figure 6.9: Implementation of CSIGNAL

As CSIGNAL causes the process executing it to give up the mutual exclusion on the monitor, normally it is the last instruction executed by a function before leaving the monitor. The compiler enforces this.

CSIGNAL can also be implemented in such a way that the waiting process is not woken up, but is transferred from the condition queue to the head of

the mutual exclusion queue. This guarantees that it is the next to run. In this case the signalling process continues until it exits the monitor.

The programming of monitor procedures still needs great care. But, it is only done once, hopefully by a specialist and competent programmer. Ordinary programmers only have to call procedures and pass parameters. They have no need to worry about mutual exclusion or synchronisation.

Figure 6.10 illustrates the different parts of a monitor.

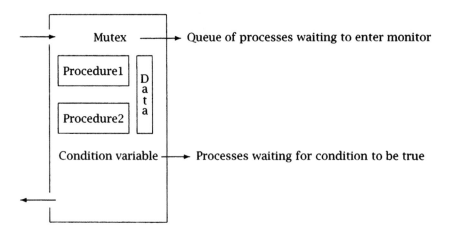

Figure 6.10: An illustration of a monitor

POSIX condition variables

POSIX provides condition variables as part of the `pthread` package. They are always used in conjunction with a POSIX mutex, a specialised mutual exclusion semaphore. These are created using `pthread_mutex_init()`, manipulated by the `pthread_mutex_lock()` and `pthread_mutex_unlock()` functions, and removed by using `pthread_mutex_destroy()`.

Condition variables are created using `pthread_cond_init()`, and are manipulated with `pthread_cond_wait()`, which must also be informed of which mutex to unlock, and `pthread_cond_signal()`. When no longer required, they are removed with `pthread_cond_destroy()`.

6.7 Examples using monitors

Single resource allocator

This simple example could be used to control allocation of a printer, for example. We have already seen this implemented with a semaphore initialised to 1. The monitor implementation would be as in Figure 6.11.

```
MONITOR allocator{

boolean busy = FALSE;
condition free;

reserve(){
    while (busy == TRUE)
        CWAIT(free);
    busy = TRUE;
    }

release(){
    busy = FALSE;
    CSIGNAL(free);
    }
}
```

Figure 6.11: Monitor to allocate a single resource

Note that there is no express mention of mutual exclusion. This is all taken care of by the compiler, once it sees the keyword MONITOR. The use of a while in reserve() means that when the process wakes up after the CWAIT, it will test the condition once more before going on and claiming the resource.

Remember that no part of the implementation shown here would be visible to a user process. All the user would know would be the names of the two functions, reserve() and release(), and the effect of calling them. When control returns from a call to reserve(), the process has exclusive rights to the resource. When control returns from a call to release(), the process no longer has any rights to the resource.

Note that in this implementation the actual resource is not in the monitor; there is nothing here to prevent an unscrupulous programmer from accessing the resource without permission.

Bounded buffer manager

This is a problem seen several times already. The monitor solution is shown in Figure 6.12.

The implementation does not deal with where in the buffer to insert or remove. This is omitted for simplicity. Nor does it deal with mutual exclusion on the buffer. This latter is included in the keyword MONITOR. But synchronisation over the state of the buffer, when it is full or empty, has to be explicitly programmed.

Note that in this version, only one process, of any type, may be active in the monitor, and accessing the buffer, at the same time.

Once again, all a user process has to do is make a call to producer(), or consumer(), as appropriate.

```
MONITOR  buffer{

int count = 0;
condition spaceavail;
condition itemavail;

producer(){
      while (count == MAX)
            CWAIT(spaceavail);
      /* Put item in buffer */
      count++;
      CSIGNAL(itemavail);
      }

consumer(){
      while (count == 0)
            CWAIT(itemavail);
      /* Get item from buffer */
      count--;
      CSIGNAL(spaceavail);
      }
   }
```

Figure 6.12: Monitor to manage a bounded buffer

Readers and writers

We have seen various solutions to this problem in Section 5.7. In the monitor implementation given in Figure 6.13, the resource to be read or written is not part of the monitor. This is because a monitor by definition always enforces mutual exclusion, and including the resource in the monitor would mean that only one process at a time could access the resource—which is not what we want. Of course the downside of this implementation is that an undisciplined process can access the resource at any time.

The logic is reasonably straightforward. A reader is only held up if there are writers active or waiting to write. The CSIGNAL at the end of StartRead(), while it is executed each time, only has an effect if there is another reader waiting on the condition variable. This only happens when a number of readers have been held up, waiting for a writer or series of writers to finish. The last writer wakes up the first reader, which then wakes up the next, and so on.

Similarly the last reader to finish wakes up a writer, if there is one.

A writer is held up if there is an active writer, or active readers.

An exiting writer wakes up the next waiting writer, if there is one, or else the first waiting reader. If there is no reader waiting, then that CSIGNAL has no effect.

Note that this implements the semantics of solution 4 of Section 5.7.

```
MONITOR  readers-writers{

int       readers = 0, writers = 0;
boolean   busy-writing = FALSE;
condition readers-waiting, writers-waiting;

StartRead(){
      while (writers > 0)
            CWAIT(readers-waiting);
      readers++;
      CSIGNAL(readers-waiting)
      }

EndRead(){
      readers--;
      if (readers == 0)
            CSIGNAL(writers-waiting)
      }

StartWrite(){
      writers++;
      while ((busy-writing == TRUE) || (readers > 0))
            CWAIT(writers-waiting);
      busy-writing = TRUE
      }

EndWrite(){
      busy-writing = FALSE;
      writers--;
      if (writers > 0)
            CSIGNAL(writers-waiting);
      else
            CSIGNAL(readers-waiting);
      }
}
```

Figure 6.13: Monitor to implement reader/writer interlock

Evaluation of monitors

The advantages of monitors have been outlined already, but there is also a
downside.

1. The fact that only one process can be active in the monitor at any one
   time can be restrictive. For example, it may be perfectly legitimate for a
   consumer and producer to be accessing a shared buffer at the same time,
   but the simple implementation of a monitor, as used in Figure 6.12, will
   not allow this.

One solution is for the shared resources to be outside the monitor, which only controls the granting and taking back of permissions to access the resource, as in Figure 6.13. But this does not *enforce* mutual exclusion.

2. As with semaphores, a process calling a monitor is committed to wait if the monitor is in use, and again if the resource is not available.

One possible solution to this is to create a child thread which calls the monitor, while the parent thread proceeds in parallel. Of course at some stage the parent has to be assured that the work has been done, so it needs to resynchronise using the `pthread_join()` function.

3. In the examples given here, we have assumed a single shared data structure associated with each monitor. For example, a monitor for managing a file system might have procedures to open, read, write, close a file. As well as that, each file might be subject to readers/writers exclusion.

Now if only one process can be active within the monitor at any one time, then only one operation on one file can be in progress at any time. This is ridiculously exclusive.

One possible solution would be to associate a monitor with each file. But there would be considerable overhead with this, probably unacceptable.

It might be possible to parameterise the monitor, so that the specific file, or other data object, would be identified to the monitor. The monitor would then wait on a specific semaphore, not just on a monitor-wide semaphore.

6.8 Active objects

Monitors, as so far outlined, are passive structures. They consist of code and data. There is no process associated with a monitor. The code is executed in the context of the process calling the monitor.

A monitor could also be implemented as a process in its own right, and could execute code that is independent of any caller. Thus background housekeeping could be done by the monitor in its own time, not at the expense of the caller. It could also decide which operations are possible at any given time (due to the state of the resource).

So far in our work, we have a potential delay on entry to a monitor, and a potential delay inside, if the data is not in an appropriate state, for example if the buffer is either full or empty. It would be an improvement if an operation on an object were allowed to begin only if the object is in such a state that the operation can complete, and if it is not going to block somewhere later on.

Such a monitor process would be sent a message asking it to perform some operation, and it would reply with a message indicating success, or refusal.

This idea of an active object has developed into the remote procedure call. As RPC is more usually found in distributed systems, it will be considered at a later stage, in Chapter 14.

6.9   Path expressions

While monitors provide both mutual exclusion, and data hiding, they still have to be programmed in detail, even if this is done by expert programmers. Ideally, we would like an even higher level mechanism, whereby the order of operations, and their dependencies, can be specified to a compiler, which then produces suitable code. Such a language structure is called a *path expression*.

We will look at some examples of such path expressions, to see the extent to which they simplify programming. All such expressions begin with the keyword path, and finish with the keyword end.

Independent operations

The expression

path first, second, third end

means that procedures first, second and third may be executed in any order, and any number of them may be executing at the same time. Basically it means that they are totally independent.

Pipelines

path first; second; third end

The number of instances of second that are allowed to have begun at any one time cannot be greater than the number of instances of first that have finished at that time. More formally, the number of initiations of what appears to the right of the ';' may not exceed the number of completions of what appears to the left. Concurrent executions of first, second, and third are allowed, provided this restriction is observed. So the expression

path insert; remove end

implies that two different processes can be inserting and removing at the same time, but that you cannot remove from an empty buffer. It places no limit on the number of insertions.

Concurrency restrictions

The expression

path N: (operation) end

restricts the number of concurrent executions of operation to N. If we combine this with the first expression, then

path 1: (first, second, third) end

means that only one of the three can be active at any one time. Taking this a step further, the path expression

path 1: (insert); 1: (remove) end

states that only one process can be inserting at a time, and only one can be removing at a time. But it is possible for one to be inserting at the same time as another is removing, which is allowable. However, the ';' implies it is still not permissible to remove more items than have been put in. But there is no restriction on how far insert can get ahead of remove. If the buffer is bounded, this is not acceptable.

The final example

path N: (1: (insert); 1: (remove)) end

specifies that only N operations can be active at any one time, where an operation is an insert/remove pair. This means that only N inserts can begin before at least one remove begins, and inserts can at most be N ahead of removes.

Path expressions certainly make the specification of concurrency restrictions very concise. The main drawback with them is that very little work has been done on implementing them.

6.10 Summary

1. The next step up from the low level primitives considered so far is to add data passing capabilities to them. Such mechanisms implement interprocess communication, and add features such as distinguishing between message boundaries, and priority among messages. Message passing can be synchronous or asynchronous.

2. A message queue is a simpler mechanism, which does not allow a sender to specify a receiver.

3. System V IPC provides a set of system calls for passing messages between processes.

4. POSIX provides a different interface for message queues.

5. Conditional critical regions allow a programmer to explicitly declare which data is shared, and where the critical sections are in a program. A compiler could then enforce mutual exclusion.

6. A monitor consists of the data corresponding to a shared object, which is accessible indirectly and exclusively via a set of publicly available procedures. The implementation ensures that only one process is active in the monitor at any one time.

   For synchronisation, a mechanism known as a condition variable is provided. This allows a process, under the protection of guaranteed exclusive access, to test some condition, and to decide whether to block itself or not.

7. Monitors can be used to solve all of the classic problems examined in previous chapters, such as resource allocators, bounded buffer management, and the readers/writers problem.

8. Monitors are passive, consisting of code and data, executing in the context of the calling process. A monitor could also be implemented as a process in its own right. Such a mechanism is known as an active object.

9. A language construct called path expressions allows the order of operations, and their dependencies, to be specified to a compiler, which will then produce appropriate code.

6.11   Discussion questions

1. Broadcasting a message can be implemented by sending a copy of the message to each destination. This can be very expensive in use of memory, particularly as the size of messages, and the number of destinations, grow. Suggest an optimisation.

2. Discuss the possibility of developing a messaging system to distinguish between requests and replies, as opposed to just sending and receiving.

3. Discuss the implementation of a function `request_serviced()`, which both sends a request, and blocks waiting for a reply.

4. Discuss the respective advantages of having one system wide buffer for all messages, one buffer per destination process, or one buffer per message stream, when using asynchronous message passing.

5. If a System V message queue is set up to be nonblocking, investigate the return value, and the value in `errno`, when an attempt is made to write to a full queue.

6. With reference to the `struct msqid_ds` for System V message queues, would it be possible to have processes waiting on `wwait` and `rwait` at the same time?

7. Investigate how to set the flags parameter to `msgrcv()`, so that it is nonblocking, and so that it truncates over-long messages. In the latter case, is the receiving thread given any indication that the message has been truncated?

8. Investigate the problems associated with the orderly close-down and removal of System V message queues.

9. POSIX message queues are asynchronous. Propose a set of system calls (including parameters) which would implement synchronous messaging. Add a broadcast facility to this.

10. Discuss the problems involved in implementing the `await()` operation in a conditional critical region, and suggest some approaches to the implementation.

11. What is the essential difference between a monitor and an object?

12. Instead of blocking, a monitor could return a message saying 'busy—try again later'. Discuss the implementation of this.

13. What is the essential difference between doing a CWAIT() on a condition variable, and the await() operation in a conditional critical region?

14. Give an implementation of CSIGNAL, in such a way that any waiting process is not woken up, but is transferred to the head of the mutual exclusion queue, so guaranteeing that it is the next to run.

15. Investigate the pthread_cond_timed_wait() function, as supported in the POSIX pthread library.

16. Investigate the pthread_cond_broadcast() function, as supplied in the POSIX pthread library.

17. Could the CWAIT in the monitor examples of Section 6.7 be put in an IF, instead of a WHILE?

18. Rewrite the example in Figure 6.12 so that one producer, *and* one consumer, can be accessing the buffer at the same time.

19. Is it possible to adapt the program in Figure 6.13 so that *one* writer is allowed in, and then readers again? This would implement the semantics of solution 3 of Section 5.7.

Deadlock 7

What do we mean by deadlock? The simplest possible example would involve two processes and two files. Each process has one of the files open for exclusive writing, and each wants to open the other. They will both wait forever.

A more formal definition would be:

> *A set of processes is in a deadlock state when every process in the set is waiting for a resource which is being held by another process in the set.*

Note first of all that every process is waiting; if even one of them could run, then the set would not be deadlocked. Note also that all of the resources being waited for are being held by a process or processes within the set. If even one of these resources was being held by some process outside the set, then they would not be deadlocked.

7.1 Terminology and tools

Let us develop some terminology, and some tools, for dealing with deadlock between sets of processes.

Resources are divided into different *types*. Each type consists of some number of identical *instances*. If a process requests an instance of a resource type, the allocation of any instance of the type will satisfy the request.

Normally, the following sequence must be followed: request, which may result in a wait; followed eventually by allocation; followed by use; followed by release. It is taken for granted that a process may not use a resource without first requesting and being granted it; and that a process will always return a resource after use.

Resource allocation graphs

The state of a system can be represented by means of a system resource allocation graph. This represents processes and resource types as vertices. The

edges represent requests and allocations. An example of such a graph for a
system with three processes and three resource types, one of which has two
instances, is given in Figure 7.1.

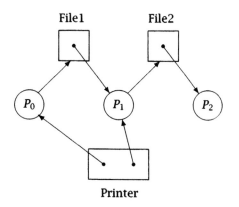

Figure 7.1: A resource allocation graph

In this example, resource types are represented by rectangles, with individual instances shown by dots within the rectangle. Processes are represented
by circles. Arrows from an instance of a resource to a process indicate an allocation to that process, arrows from a process to a resource type represent a
request. When the request is granted, the direction of the arrow is reversed.

If such a resource allocation graph does not have a cycle, then the system
is not deadlocked. If there is a cycle, then it may or may not be deadlocked,
depending on the number of instances of the resources involved in the cycle.

Note the version of the graph shown in Figure 7.2.

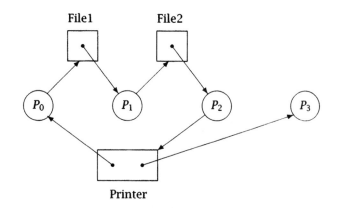

Figure 7.2: A resource allocation graph for four processes

There is certainly a cycle in the graph. But P_3 is not involved in it. P_3 is
not waiting on any resource, so is runnable. It is at least possible that before
requesting any other resources, it will return its printer, which could then

be given to P_2, thus breaking the cycle. So we cannot say that the system is deadlocked. It may be; we just don't know.

Necessary and sufficient conditions

There are four conditions which must be true before a system is deadlocked. These are also sufficient conditions—once all four of them are true, the system is deadlocked, no ifs or buts about it. These conditions are as follows.

1. Mutual Exclusion—the resources involved must be unshareable. Obviously if they are sharable, they cannot cause deadlock, as a process will never have to wait on such a resource.

2. Hold and Wait—the system works in such a way that processes hold the resources they have while waiting for others.

3. No Preemption—resources can only be released voluntarily by a process, they cannot be taken back by the system.

4. Circular Wait—the waiting processes can be arranged in order $P_0, P_1, ... P_n$, such that P_x is waiting for the resource held by P_{x+1}, and P_n is waiting for the resource held by P_0. This is a generalised way of saying that there is a cycle in the resource allocation graph.

There are three possible approaches to the problem:

• Prevent deadlock by arranging that at least one of the conditions given above is not true.

• Avoid deadlock by checking each request for a resource, and only granting it if there is no possibility of it causing deadlock.

• Allow deadlock to occur, but be sure that it is detected as soon as it happens, and then try to recover from it.

Prevention and avoidance go together; both ensure that deadlock does not occur. Detection and subsequent recovery is a suitable strategy when deadlock is very unlikely.

We will consider each of these strategies in the following sections.

7.2 Deadlock prevention

This works by ensuring that at least one of the necessary conditions is false at all times. Let us examine how this might be done for each of them in turn.

Mutual Exclusion To prevent deadlock this way would require all resources to be sharable. But this is not possible for at least some resources, such as a printer. So in general, it is not possible to prevent deadlock this way.

Hold and Wait This condition can be negated by insisting that if a process holding some resources requests another resource that cannot be immediately allocated to it, then all the resources it is holding must be released.

There are many disadvantages to this scheme. Resource utilisation may be very low. Also, starvation is possible, if a process needs several popular resources. It may have to wait forever for all of them to be free at the same time.

But it is relatively easy to implement, and may be most economical in the long run.

No Preemption If a process requests a non available resource, which is allocated to a waiting process, then the system preempts this resource.

This is very useful for resources whose state can easily be saved and restored later, e.g. CPU registers, or a page of physical memory. But it is not applicable to a printer, for example.

If the waiting process is on another machine, then the operating systems on both have to cooperate.

Circular Wait A system wide total order is imposed on all resource types. The order should be defined according to the normal order of use of resources. For example, it could be files, memory, printers. Then insist that a process can only request resources in that order. If several instances of the same type are required, this must be done in a single request.

It is also possible to implement it in such a way that when a process requests a resource, it must release all resources of a higher order.

In either case, a process holding a resource can only be waiting on a higher ordered resource, never on a lower one. So it is not possible for a cycle to exist in a resource allocation graph.

Deadlock prevention is the most restrictive solution from the user's point of view. It leads to low device utilisation and reduced system throughput. But it does guarantee that deadlock cannot occur.

7.3 Deadlock avoidance

Any scheme designed to avoid deadlock completely requires information in advance from each process about the resources it will require.

The simplest possible model would at least require a process to declare the maximum number it would require of each type of resource. A more complex model would require information about the order in which resources will be requested and released.

Then each time a request is made, the system must consider what resources are currently available, the resources allocated to each process, which it may return, as well as possible future requests from each process, and decide whether to grant or refuse the request.

Safe state

Deadlock avoidance is based on the idea that a system always begins in an un-deadlocked, or safe, state, with all resources free, and the algorithm must never allocate a resource which would move it out of a safe state.

This pushes the question back: what is a safe state? A system is in a safe state only if all processes can be organised into a sequence

$$< P_0, P_1, P_2, \ldots, P_n >$$

such that for each P_i, the resources which P_i can still legitimately request can be satisfied by the currently available resources, plus the resources held by all of the previous processes in the sequence.

Another way of putting this is that the system can always see its way out. Even if it has to wait a long time, earlier processes in the sequence will finish eventually, and release resources which will allow later processes to finish, and so on. Such a sequence of processes is known as a safe sequence.

An unsafe state is not necessarily deadlocked; but it may lead to deadlock. So with a deadlock avoidance scheme, if a process requests a resource which is currently available, it may still have to wait. It is not sufficient just to check if granting a resource will immediately cause deadlock; it may not cause deadlock until much later. But if there is even a possibility of deadlock occurring, the resource will not be allocated. Deadlock avoidance is quite conservative.

The simplest example of this is a system with two processes, P_0 and P_1, and two resources, File1 and File2. Suppose both processes have declared that they will need both resources at some stage in their execution, and that File1 has actually been allocated to P_0. This is illustrated on the left in Figure 7.3.

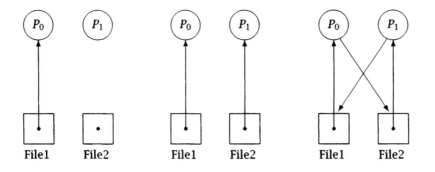

Figure 7.3: Safe, unsafe, and deadlocked system

The system is now in a safe state, $< P_0, P_1 >$. If at this stage P_1 requests File2, it could be allocated, as it is free. The state of the system at that stage would be as shown in the centre of Figure 7.3. It is possible that P_0 might return File1 before P_1 asks for it. But it is also possible that P_0 may request File2 before P_1 returns it, followed by a request from P_1 for File1. The system would then be deadlocked, as illustrated by the cycle in the resource allocation graph on

the right of Figure 7.3. An avoidance algorithm would not grant the request from P_1 for File2, because there is at least a possibility that deadlock might occur later. So P_1 will be held up until P_0 has finished with both resources.

We will now consider actual algorithms for checking and maintaining a safe state in a system. There is a significant difference in the level of difficulty, depending on whether there are several instances, or only one instance, of each resource type. So we will consider the two cases separately.

Single instance of each resource type

A system resource allocation graph is maintained. But as well as current requests and allocations, it also keeps track of requests which processes may legitimately make, at some time in the future. These are also indicated by arrows from the process to the resource. To differentiate them from requests, they could be represented by dashed lines. Figure 7.4 represents the classic situation where two processes, P_0 and P_1, each need the use of File1 and File2 during their processing. The situation after P_0 has been allocated File1 is shown in Figure 7.5.

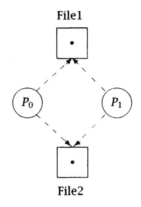

Figure 7.4: A claims graph

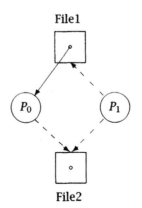

Figure 7.5: One resource allocated

When any further requests are received, the graph is tentatively changed to reflect this, by converting the claim to an assignment. If this new version of the graph has a cycle, then the request would cause deadlock, and should not be granted. Otherwise it is safe to grant this request.

For example, with reference to Figure 7.5, a request from P_0 for File2 would not cause a cycle, and can be granted. A request from P_1 for File2, which is free, would cause a cycle, and so cannot be granted.

Multiple instances of each resource type

The algorithm used in this case is commonly known as the banker's algorithm. It is presumed that a bank never loans its money to such an extent that it would be unable to meet the legitimate demands of its customers, when their deposits become due for repayment. This is what the resource allocation algorithm wants to do—always be able to meet the legitimate requests of processes. It allows for the worst possible case.

The algorithm works on the following data structures, assuming p processes, and r resource types.

Available[r] The number of available instances of each resource type, at a given time.

Max[p,r] The maximum demand of each process for each type. When a new process enters the system, it must declare the maximum number of instances of each resource type that it may need. This is also known as the claim of a process on a resource.

Allocation[p,r] The current allocation of instances of each type to each process.

Need[p,r] The remaining resource needs of each process. Note that Need can be calculated, as Need = Max - Allocation.

Request[r] This array is passed as a parameter by a requesting process. It indicates how many instances of each resource type are being requested at this time.

The algorithm is given in Figure 7.6. It is invoked each time a process requests resources. The algorithm first checks if this request is within the limits agreed with the process when it began; if not, it rejects it. Then it checks if the resources being requested are available; if not, the process must wait.

If the resources are available, the algorithm changes the values in its data structures, so that they now reflect the state the system would be in if the current request was granted. It then checks if this is a safe state.

If it is, then it notifies the process that the requested resources have been allocated. Otherwise it restores the state to what it was before, and puts the process on wait.

When resources are returned, waiting processes are woken up.

```
            IF (Request > Need[i]) THEN
                Error---illegal request
            ENDIF
            IF (Request > Available) THEN
                Wait
            ENDIF

            Available = Available - Request
            Allocation[i] = Allocation[i] + Request
            Need[i] = Need[i] - Request

            Check if this is a safe state
            IF Safe THEN
                Allocate resources
            ELSE
                Restore state
                Wait
            ENDIF
```

Figure 7.6: The banker's algorithm

```
Work[r] = Available[r]
Finish[p] = FALSE (all elements)

REPEAT
    Found = FALSE
    i = 0
    REPEAT
        IF (Finish[i] == FALSE) AND (Need[i] ≤ Work) THEN
            Finish[i] = TRUE
            Work = Work + Allocation[i]
            Found = TRUE
        ENDIF
        i++
    UNTIL (Found == TRUE) OR (i == p)
UNTIL Found == FALSE

Safe = TRUE
FOR i = 0 TO p - 1
    IF (Finish[i] == FALSE) THEN
        Safe = FALSE
    ENDIF
ENDFOR
```

Figure 7.7: Safety algorithm

Safety algorithm

The algorithm to check for safety is shown separately in Figure 7.7. It uses two further data structures. Work is a copy of Available, so that the algorithm can do 'what if' calculations without having to undo them again. Finish is a set of flags, one per process, to indicate when each one has been slotted into the sequence it is building up.

Consider the function of the inner REPEAT loop. Each time it is entered, it attempts to find one more process which can be added to the safe sequence, a process which could be run to completion with the resources currently available in Work. It assumes that such a process will finish eventually, and return all of its resources. So the algorithm sets the Finish flag for that process, recalculates Work, and also sets its Found flag to TRUE. The algorithm loops in the inner REPEAT until it has either found a suitable process (Found == TRUE), or it has checked all processes, and none of them is suitable (i == p).

The outer REPEAT loop always begins with P_0, and works up towards P_{p-1}. Each time around the outer loop it looks for another process which could be run to completion with the new values in Work. It loops in the outer REPEAT until one full cycle through all processes in the inner REPEAT has not found any one meeting the conditions. This is indicated by Found still being FALSE.

There are two possible reasons for this. Either all elements of Finish will be set to TRUE, and it will have found a safe sequence. Or one or more elements of Finish will still be set to FALSE, and there is no safe sequence. The final FOR loop checks this. If all elements of Finish are TRUE, then the algorithm ends with Safe set to TRUE. If even one element of Finish is still FALSE, then the algorithm ends with Safe set to FALSE.

The main drawbacks of the banker's algorithm are a tendency towards over cautiousness, as well as the overhead of applying it.

Example of the banker's algorithm in practice

Take an example with four processes, P_0 . . P_3, and two resource types, A and B. There are in total 10 instances of type A, and 7 of type B, as shown in Figure 7.8.

Available

A	B
3	5

	Max		Allocation		Need	
	A	B	A	B	A	B
P_0	7	5	0	1	7	4
P_1	3	2	2	0	1	2
P_2	9	0	3	0	6	0
P_3	2	2	2	1	0	1

Figure 7.8: State of the system before request

The various steps involved in applying the safety algorithm to this data are illustrated in Figure 7.9.

```
OUTER LOOP              INNER LOOP

1    Work = 3,5    i = 0  Need[0] > Work
                   i = 1  Need[1] < Work      Finish[1] = TRUE

2    Work = 5,5    i = 0  Need[0] > Work
                   i = 1  Finish[1] = TRUE
                   i = 2  Need[2] > Work
                   i = 3  Need[3] < Work      Finish[3] = TRUE

3    Work = 7,6    i = 0  Need[0] < Work      Finish[0] = TRUE

4    Work = 7,7    i = 0  Finish[0] = TRUE
                   i = 1  Finish[1] = TRUE
                   i = 2  Need[2] < Work      Finish[2] = TRUE

5    Work = 10,7   i = 0  Finish[0] = TRUE
                   i = 1  Finish[1] = TRUE
                   i = 2  Finish[2] = TRUE
                   i = 3  Finish[3] = TRUE
```

Figure 7.9: Application of the safety algorithm

The system is currently in a safe state, the processes could complete in the sequence $< P_1, P_3, P_0, P_2 >$. Now suppose a request comes from P_1 for (1,0). The banker's algorithm first checks if this request is greater than Need[1]. (1,0) is not greater than (1,2) so we can proceed.

It then checks if the request is greater than Available. (1,0) is not greater than (3,5). So the requested resources are available. Next it pretends that the request has been fulfilled, and arrives at the state in Figure 7.10, where changes are <u>underlined</u>.

Available

A	B
<u>2</u>	5

	Max		Allocation		Need	
	A	B	A	B	A	B
P_0	7	5	0	1	7	4
P_1	3	2	<u>3</u>	0	<u>0</u>	2
P_2	9	0	3	0	6	0
P_3	2	2	2	1	0	1

Figure 7.10: State of the system reflecting the request

When the safety algorithm is applied, it determines that $< P_1, P_3, P_0, P_2 >$ is still a safe sequence. So the requested resources can actually be allocated. The reader is recommended to try further requests: for example, one from P_2 for (3,0); and one from P_0 for (0,2).

7.4   Deadlock detection and recovery

We have seen that prevention schemes are restrictive, and avoidance schemes are time consuming. Another possible approach, in a situation where deadlock is likely to occur only very rarely, is just to let it occur. However, it is essential that when it does, it will be detected, and then an attempt will be made to recover from it.

The system maintains information about allocations and requests, and then periodically runs an algorithm which examines this information to detect if deadlock has occurred or not.

Such an algorithm could be invoked every time a request for a resource cannot be granted immediately. There is a considerable overhead in this. It could be run at fixed intervals of time, such as once per minute, or when CPU utilisation drops below a certain threshold, or when the wait queue grows beyond a certain size.

As well as the overhead in just running this algorithm, there are potential losses in recovering from deadlock, which will be considered in Section 7.4. As with avoidance, different approaches are used, depending on whether there are several instances of a resource type, or only one.

Single instance of each resource type

As with avoidance, this relies on detecting cycles in a resource allocation graph. Take for example the system whose state is represented by the graph shown in Figure 7.11.

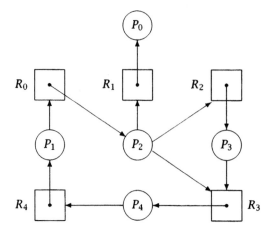

Figure 7.11: Resource allocation graph

For the purposes of deadlock detection, a simplified version of the graph can be used. It is not essential to know *what* resource a process is waiting on—it is enough to know that it is waiting on a resource held by another process. It is possible to remove the nodes representing resources, and collapse the remaining edges, yielding the graph of Figure 7.12: a wait-for graph.

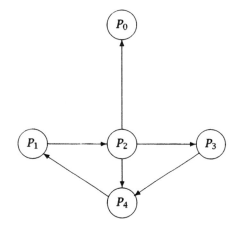

Figure 7.12: Wait-for graph

Deadlock exists if and only if the wait-for graph contains a cycle, as it does in this example. The system must maintain the graph, and periodically invoke the cycle detecting algorithm.

Several instances of each resource type

The algorithm, as shown in Figure 7.13, is very similar to the banker's safety algorithm, and uses similar data structures. There is no question here of processes making claims in advance. So there is no Max or Need. It just tracks the allocation to each process, and if any process is waiting, the Request which caused it to wait. It checks for illegal requests (such as asking for a non-existent resource) each time a request is made, and eliminates them at that stage.

If a process is allocated no resources, it cannot be in deadlock, there is no need to include it in the checks. So the first FOR loop sets the Finish flags of all such processes to TRUE.

Next let us consider the inner REPEAT loop. Processes may be waiting on resources. But this does not mean that the system is deadlocked. So if any process can be found which is waiting on resources which can be satisfied from Work, the algorithm makes the optimistic assumption that if such a process is given these resources, it will return all its resources to the system. So the current allocation of that process is added to Work. The Finish flag for that process is set to TRUE, as we do not want to consider it again. Also the Found flag is set to TRUE, to terminate the inner loop.

```
FOR i = 0 TO MaxProc - 1
    IF (Allocation[i] == 0) THEN
            Finish[i] = TRUE
    ELSE
            Finish[i] = FALSE
    ENDIF
ENDFOR

REPEAT
    Found = FALSE
    i = 0
    REPEAT
        IF (Finish[i] == FALSE) AND (Request[i] ≤ Work) THEN
                Work = Work + Allocation[i]
                Finish[i] = TRUE
                Found = TRUE
        ENDIF
        i++
    UNTIL (Found == TRUE) OR (i == p)
UNTIL (Found == FALSE)

Deadlocked = FALSE
FOR i = 0 TO MaxProc - 1
    IF (Finish[i] == FALSE) THEN
            Deadlocked = TRUE
    ENDIF
ENDFOR
```

Figure 7.13: Algorithm to detect deadlock

Then the algorithm goes around the outer loop again, looking for another such process which can be satisfied from the new, increased, value of Work. If all of the waiting processes can be arranged in this way, then the system is not deadlocked. This is checked in the final FOR loop.

Processes may not meet the optimistic assumptions made here. In such a case, the system may deadlock later. Remember that this is detection, not prevention—it is only determining if the system is deadlocked now.

Example of detection algorithm in practice

Let us follow an example of this algorithm in action. Figure 7.14 shows the initial state of the system, which is not deadlocked at this stage. While two processes are held up waiting on resources, it is possible that the two running processes, P_0 and P_2, could complete and return sufficient resources to satisfy the outstanding requests. One possible sequence in which all processes could run to completion is $< P_0, P_2, P_1, P_3 >$.

Available

A	B
0	0

	Allocation		Request	
	A	B	A	B
P_0	0	1	0	0
P_1	2	0	2	0
P_2	3	0	0	0
P_3·	2	1	1	0

Figure 7.14: A system which is not deadlocked

The calculations performed by the algorithm to arrive at this sequence are shown in Figure 7.15.

```
      OUTER LOOP                  INNER LOOP

1     Work = 0,0    i = 0    Request[0] < Work   Finish[0] = TRUE
                 .
2     Work = 0,1    i = 0    Finish[0] = TRUE
                    i = 1    Request[1] > Work
                    i = 2    Request[2] < Work   Finish[2] = TRUE

3     Work = 3,1    i = 0    Finish[0] = TRUE
                    i = 1    Request[1] < Work   Finish[1] = TRUE

4     Work = 5,1    i = 0    Finish[0] = TRUE
                    i = 1    Finish[1] = TRUE
                    i = 2    Finish[2] = TRUE
                    i = 3    Request[3] < Work   Finish[3] = TRUE

      FINAL LOOP    i = 0    Finish[0] = TRUE
                    i = 1    Finish[1] = TRUE
                    i = 2    Finish[2] = TRUE
                    i = 4    Finish[3] = TRUE    Deadlocked = FALSE
```

Figure 7.15: Application of the deadlock detection algorithm

But if P_2 had also made a request for even one instance of Resource A, then the state of the system would be as shown in Figure 7.16, where the change is underlined. The reader is encouraged to run this new set of data through the algorithm. It should determine that the system is now deadlocked, and that P_1, P_2, P_3 are all involved in the deadlock.

Available

A	B
0	0

	Allocation		Request	
	A	B	A	B
P_0	0	1	0	0
P_1	2	0	2	0
P_2	3	0	1	0
P_3	2	1	1	0

Figure 7.16: A deadlocked system

Recovery from deadlock

When deadlock has been detected, there are two options available to recover from it. Either terminate one or more processes, or preempt some resources from one or more processes.

Process termination

Terminating a process is easy. But it should not be done too lightly, as it may have serious implications for the system. A process may be updating a file, or printing a page, when it is terminated, and it may leave the file or printer in an inconsistent state.

The simplest approach is to terminate all the deadlocked processes. But there is great expense involved in this. It is also possible to terminate one at a time until the deadlock is eliminated. But this involves the overhead of running the detection algorithm after each termination.

The following are some factors which can influence the order in which processes are selected for termination.

- The priority of the process. For example, the lowest priority process could be selected.

- How far advanced it is. If a process is close to completion, it is a poor choice for termination. So it would seem preferable to select a process which had only just begun.

- The number and type of resources released by terminating it. The process holding the largest number of resources, or the most popular ones, would be an obvious victim.

These factors have to be balanced among themselves, and the different weights given to each one will lead to many possible orderings. And all of them have the potential to cause starvation—the same process being chosen over and over again.

Resource preemption

This is not as drastic as terminating a process. Resources are taken from some process, which is put in a wait state. It then has to re-acquire these resources before it can continue. There are several factors to be considered in implementing a preemption scheme.

Selecting a victim The criteria just given for selecting a process to terminate are also relevant here.

Rollback When a resource is preempted, the process must be rolled back to some consistent state, so that it can be restarted from that state later.

The simplest solution is a total rollback to the beginning of the program. But there is a heavy overhead involved in this. It is as if two cars meeting on a narrow road have to reverse all the way to their starting points, instead of the nearest passing out point. In fact such a total rollback is equivalent to terminating a process.

To be able to implement a realistic rollback scheme, it must be possible to identify points within a program to which it can be safely rolled back. These could be points at which it is using no resources, or a minimum number of non-contentious resources. Such points could be identified by the programmer, or by the compiler. This is referred to as dividing the program into jobsteps, and when resources have to be preempted, the process is rolled back to the beginning of the current jobstep. To continue the cars on a narrow road analogy from the previous paragraph, jobsteps are like signposted passing out points on the road.

Of course, rolling back also has implications for the values of variables. The state of a process at the beginning of a jobstep must be saved at least until that jobstep is completed. That way the process can always be restarted exactly as it was at the beginning of the jobstep.

Starvation The same process may always be picked as a victim. One solution to this is to include the number of times a process has already been rolled back as a cost factor in calculating a victim. This is similar to process aging in the scheduler.

7.5 Summary

A set of processes is in a deadlock state when every process in the set is waiting for a resource which is being held by another process in the set.

1. The state of a system can be represented by a resource allocation graph. If there is a cycle in this graph, then the system is deadlocked.

There are four conditions required for deadlock: mutual exclusion, hold and wait, no preemption, circular wait.

There are three possible strategies which can be adopted: prevention, avoidance, detection and recovery.

2. Deadlock prevention works by ensuring that at least one of the necessary conditions cannot hold. But this leads to low utilisation of devices.

3. Avoidance schemes need information in advance about the resource requirements for each process. Where there is only a single instance of each resource type, a resource allocation graph can be used. If there are many instances of each resource type, then the banker's algorithm or equivalent is needed to check each request for a resource, and determine its implications for the future state of the system.

4. Detection schemes need no prior information. They periodically check if the system is deadlocked. A derivation of the resource allocation graph, known as a wait-for graph, is used where there is only a single instance of each resource type. Algorithms similar to the banker's safety algorithm are used for multiple instances of resource types.

   When deadlock is detected, the system can recover either by terminating deadlocked processes, or preempting resources from them.

7.6 Discussion questions

1. A process could be allocated a printer, and hold it unused for long periods of time. Consider ways in which the operating system could preempt the printer.

2. Is it easier to negate the 'hold and wait' condition, or the 'circular wait' condition?

3. Would a programmer have to manually compile the sort of information required by a deadlock avoidance algorithm, or could a compiler be adapted to produce it?

4. The banker's algorithm, as presented, does not deal with the return of resources to the system. Write an algorithm for this, remembering that it has to wake up waiting processes. Should it wake up all the waiting processes, or just those that can now continue? Note that processes can be waiting at two different places in the banker's algorithm, for different reasons.

5. When using the banker's algorithm, if the requested allocation would move the system out of a safe state, the requesting process is put on a wait queue. The algorithm as presented does not deal with what happens next. Extend it.

6. The safety algorithm assumes that processes will return resources in a certain order. What happens if they return resources in a different order?

7. Apply the safety algorithm to the system shown in Figure 7.10, documenting each step as is done in Figure 7.9.

8. With only a single instance of each resource type, is there still a requirement that each process must provide advance information, in order to implement deadlock avoidance?

9. With a deadlock detection system, there is no question of processes having to make claims in advance. How then can a process make an illegal request?

10. Apply the deadlock detection algorithm to the system shown in Figure 7.16, documenting each step as is done in Figure 7.15.

11. Suggest ways of choosing suitable points in a program at which it can be killed off, with the minimum of implications for the rest of the system.

12. If a process is close to completion, it would seem a poor choice for termination. How could you determine how close a process is to completion?

13. How could you avoid terminating the same process over and over again?

14. When a process is rolled back, you want to reset all of its state as it was at the beginning of the jobstep. Suggest ways of implementing this.

15. It may be possible to get the best results by using different strategies to handle deadlocks involving different categories of resource. Discuss this in relation to the different resource types you are aware of.

Memory manager 8

An operating system manages resources. One of these resources is memory. So this is the next part of the system to be studied.

We will first of all look at the objectives of a memory manager—what it is all about, what it should do. At that stage we will conclude that all of these objectives can best be met by providing a virtual memory, so we will look at that concept. Then, in the main body of the chapter, we will look at ways to implement this virtual memory. Finally we will look at how all of this is implemented in Linux.

8.1 Objectives of a memory manager

When a C programmer thinks of a memory manager, the first thing that comes to mind is the malloc() library function. When some bytes of memory are required, it provides them; when no longer required, free() takes them back. We might appreciate that there is some bookkeeping involved in such a service, but not much.

This, however, is only one aspect of what a memory manager does—if the most obvious. There are other areas, of equal if not greater importance. We will now look at all of these in turn.

Memory allocation

The hardware memory in a computer is linear, or one-dimensional. The range of addresses available goes from 0 up to some maximum. See Figure 8.1.

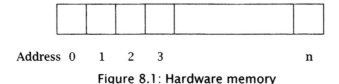

Address   0   1   2   3   n

Figure 8.1: Hardware memory

Programs are not written in this way. They are structured into procedures or functions, and each function is divided into a data area and a code area. Another way of putting this is that the module structure diagram of a program is not linear.

As an example, consider a compiler. First of all, it can be divided into a code section, and a data section. Then the code section might be divided into modules for lexical analysis, syntax analysis, and code generation. The data section in turn might be divided into a read-only area, containing the reserved words in the language, and a read-write area containing the symbol table for the particular program, which it builds as it goes along.

The allocation of memory should reflect this structure. The memory manager should not just give out one large block of memory, big enough to contain all of these segments. If the programmer sees them as separate units, the running system should too. There are all sorts of reasons for this.

- It facilitates top down design and implementation. Different parts of the program can be coded and tested independently of each other.

- It is then possible to give different degrees of protection to different segments of memory, as with the compiler example above.

- Segments can be shared among processes. Otherwise sharing has to be on an all or nothing basis.

- Such segmentation actually facilitates the allocation of memory. It is easier for the manager to find a number of small segments, rather than one very large one.

So the programmer logically divides a program into different segments, and the memory manager must provide separate physical storage for each of these.

Multi-level storage

The situation is further complicated by economic and hardware factors. Memory is expensive. It is not as expensive now as it once was (in real terms), but it is still expensive. Programmers always want more memory, and faster memory, than is available. This has led to four-level systems, as illustrated in Figure 8.2.

We are familiar with the idea of the executable version of a program existing permanently in a directory on a disk. This is normally a somewhat compressed version of the program. When that program is run, it is expanded to its full size, so that space is allocated for empty arrays, and stacks. But it is not expanded into the main memory of the computer—this is done onto a special area of the disk, called the swap area or the swap file, or backing store. So while it is running, all of a program will exist on backing store, or secondary memory. Such backing stores are typically of the order of 1GB, and have an access time around 10ms. They are cheap, but slow.

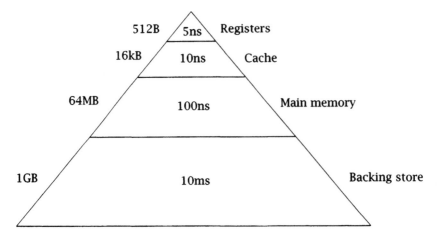

Figure 8.2: The memory pyramid

About 10% of the program will be in main memory. This will consist of the code and data that is currently in use, or has been used very recently. Note that it is not 90% in backing store. It is all in backing store, the 10% is duplicated in main memory. Main memories are typically 64MB in size, with an access time less than 100ns. They are faster than backing store, but more expensive, and hence tend to be smaller.

About 1% of the program, the part currently in use, will also be copied into fast, expensive memory, called cache. So this small piece of the program now exists in three places. Cache memories in modern CPUs tend to be about 16kB in size, but their access times are around 10ns. Again, we have faster, but more expensive and smaller memory.

Finally, there will be one instruction and a few data items in the machine registers, the fastest, smallest, and most expensive part of the pyramid.

Basically, each level is compromising between speed and cost. But note that there will be up to four copies of some parts of a program's code or data. This greatly complicates the task of the memory manager. All of these copies have to be kept consistent. Also, organising the movement of data between the different levels of the pyramid is vital.

Address mapping

Only on the most primitive machines can you be sure that a program will be loaded into memory at exactly the same place each time it runs. In general, programmers cannot know in advance what other programs are in use. For example, there is never the same pattern of usage on a multi-user machine from one moment to the next.

This means that programs as compiled and saved to disk cannot have absolute memory references. For example a program cannot assume that its variable X will be stored at location 1000. It cannot know in advance what

location it will be stored at. It will be different each time it is run. So how can it generate code to reference that variable, if it does not know where it is?

In practice, all memory references, such as JMP or MOV, are relative to the beginning of the program. Another way of putting this is that programs are compiled and linked into executables as if they were going to be loaded into memory at location 0. So the compiler can be quite sure that its variable X is 1000 bytes (for example) from the beginning of the program. And it will always be exactly that far from the beginning.

At run time, a part of the operating system known as a relocating loader could adjust each memory reference to suit the particular location where it is loaded this time.

For example, if variable X is 1000 bytes into the program, then an instruction to read X might be compiled as MOV EAX, 1000. If at load time the memory manager finds a suitable free space at 2500, then the relocating loader will change that instruction to read MOV EAX, 3500. And that is exactly where the variable X now is—1000 bytes on from location 2500.

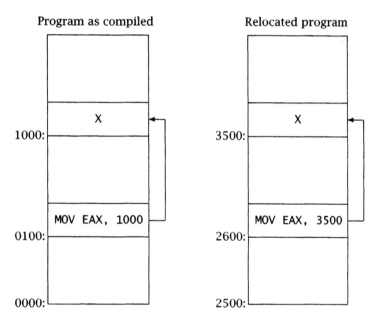

Figure 8.3: Program as loaded by relocating loader

The left-hand side of Figure 8.3 shows the program as compiled and saved to disk. The right-hand side shows it after adjustments have been made by the loader, and it is actually in memory.

This static relocation, which is done once each time a program is loaded, is fine for a single-user machine. But in a multi-user environment, with many programs starting and finishing all the time, it begins to fray at the edges. Programs terminate, returning pieces of memory to the manager, which finds itself owning many small segments, scattered around memory. As time goes on, these tend to become smaller, and there are more of them.

There may be 1MB of memory free, but if it is in 100 blocks of 10kB each, it is not of much use. The solution is to compact memory, gather the small unused bits together. That means moving a program around in memory, after its addresses have been adjusted by the loader. But it will not work in its new location. If the program from the example above is later moved to begin at 1200, the MOV EAX, 3500 instruction will now be pointing into someone else's program. It certainly will not be pointing to the variable X.

Because we have to accept that the region of memory allocated to a process may change during its lifetime, the memory manager must be able to change an address each time it is used, and in a way that is transparent to the process. This is called dynamic relocation, as opposed to static relocation.

Memory protection

At its simplest, this means that one user must not be able to read or write the memory space of another, or of the operating system. This interference can be accidental, or it can be malicious. Protection involves both prevention, and when that fails, at least detection of the intrusion.

It is not sufficient to put the onus for this on the compiler. The compiler can do much of the checking, but there will always be areas it is unable to check. User input supplied at run time is something the compiler cannot reasonably be expected to check. So every memory reference generated by a process must be checked at run time by the memory manager. This is almost impossible without hardware help. But hardware memory protection is a standard on all computers nowadays.

Memory sharing

Despite what was said in the previous subsection, there are times when more than one process *should* be allowed to access the same memory area.

One example is when a number of processes are executing the same application program, such as a compiler. They can at least share the code, even if they have separate data areas, presuming they are compiling different programs. At other times, processes may wish to share a data structure. We have seen that cooperating processes rely heavily on this ability.

So the memory manager has to allow this sharing, without compromising on protection.

Memory extension

The physical address space, or the amount of memory actually installed, is limited by hardware and cost considerations, such as the bus width, the number of expansion slots available, and the power supply.

The logical address space, or the size of a program, is limited by the number of address bits in an instruction.

On simple machines, the logical address space is less than, or in the limit equal to, the physical address space. But most modern memory managers allow the logical address space to be larger than the physical address space. They allow programs to run which are larger than the installed memory. And they allow many of these to run at the same time. How this bit of magic works is something we will have to study in some detail.

8.2 Virtual memory

We have seen that there are six basic functions which a memory manager must support. All of these are highly interdependent. Each solves a problem, but introduces constraints for others.

In order for the memory manager to achieve all of the objectives, it is not sufficient for it to simply allocate memory: it must be involved in every memory access while the program is running. It can then implement protection, and sharing. It can also maintain its multi-level storage system, checking whether the particular part of the program now being accessed is in memory or not.

In particular, it can implement its allocation scheme, dynamic relocation, and memory extension, by using an address translation mechanism, or an address map, to change the addresses used by the programmer into the actual physical memory locations in hardware. This distinction between program addresses, and physical memory locations, is critical. Sometimes the terminology address space and memory space is used to distinguish them. Other times they are referred to as logical addresses and physical addresses. The memory space is linear; the address space need not be. Also, the address space can be less than, equal to, or greater than the memory space.

Such an address mapping allows a programmer to use a range of program addresses quite different from the range of memory locations available. It is designed to produce a virtual memory, which is convenient for the programmer, and also achieves the objectives of the previous section. It transforms the computer into a more convenient virtual machine. Figure 8.4 attempts to illustrate this situation.

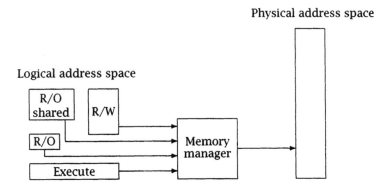

Figure 8.4: Virtual memory

The left-hand side shows memory as it appears to a programmer. A program has a number of components, each of different size, and with differing protection and sharing attributes. The right-hand side shows physical memory, which is just an array of bytes.

The memory manager sits in between, checking each logical address presented to it, and translating it to a corresponding physical address. This address map is maintained by the memory manager. The registers and data structures defining this mapping should not be accessible in user mode.

Various mechanisms have been developed to implement such address mappings. The following sections look at the most common ones.

8.3 Base and length registers

This is the simplest method, but it does not fulfil all of the requirements of a virtual memory. With this scheme, when a program is compiled, it is assumed to begin at location 0. And it is loaded into memory in this format—it is not relocated on the way in. As it is most unlikely that it will be loaded at location 0, this means that program addresses will be incorrect.

Relocation

When it is loaded, the address of where the beginning of the program is in memory is saved in a special CPU register, called the base register. On every memory access, the address provided by the program is modified by the processor. This modification involves adding the logical address to the value in the base register, to produce the correct memory address, which is then put out on the address bus (see Figure 8.5).

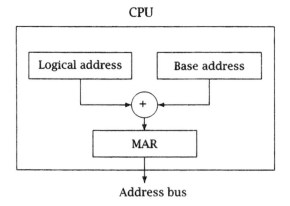

Figure 8.5: Address modification in CPU

So instead of relocating the addresses once and for all at load time, we now relocate each address individually when it is referenced. Address modification is made at run time, instead of at load time.

This has the advantage that during execution, a program can be moved to a new location, if required. For example, this may be needed to compact memory. All that has to be done is to change the value in the base register. This movement is fully transparent to the user, who is totally unaware of it.

The disadvantages are that the adjustment needs to be done over and over again, instead of just once. And the adjustment has to be done at run time, potentially slowing down execution. But specialised fast hardware can overcome this problem almost completely.

It is not economically feasible to have a base register for each process in a multiprocessing system. So in practice the CPU has only one, which is loaded with the information for the current process. When a process is context-switched out, the register value is saved as part of the volatile environment; the value for the incoming process is restored to the hardware base register.

Protection

With the scheme as outlined so far, a programmer could generate an address of any value—a program could access memory outside its own space. In order to protect memory, a second register is needed. This is called a limit register, or more commonly a length register. At load time, the number of bytes of memory allocated to the program is stored here.

When the program generates an address, the hardware not only adds that address to the value in the base register, but also does two tests on the address: see Figure 8.6. Is it positive? Is it less than the value in the length register? Only if both are true will the relocated address be put on the address bus. If either were false, it would imply that the programmer was attempting to access information in memory before or after the block allocated. The memory manager will give a memory violation error message.

CPU

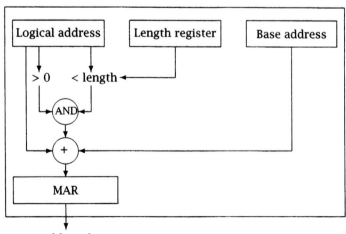

Figure 8.6: Protection and address modification

For example, let the value in the base register be 2000, and the length register contain 1000. This means that the program owns 1000 bytes of memory from 2000 to 2999. Now an instruction such as MOV EAX, -50 would be trying to read from physical location 1950 [2000 + (-50) = 1950] which is illegal. An instruction such as MOV EAX, 1500 would be trying to write to location 3500 [2000 + 1500 = 3500] which is also illegal.

Placement policies

Blocks of memory are allocated when a new program is loaded, and deallocated when a program finishes execution. Because of this, and particularly because of the varying sizes of these blocks, after a while memory becomes a patchwork of allocated and unallocated areas.

The system must keep track of all of this. It links together all of the free areas, into what is commonly called a free list or, as it contains all of the holes in memory, a hole list. Then bringing in a new program involves scanning this list for a hole large enough to hold it. If no hole large enough exists, it may be necessary to compact memory. There are three principal algorithms:

Best fit The hole list is maintained in increasing order of size. The incoming program is placed at one end of the smallest hole in which it will fit. The idea here is that the unused fragment is kept as small as possible, thus reducing waste. But it is unlikely that it will be of use for anything else.

Worst fit The incoming program, irrespective of its size, is placed in the largest available hole. The idea behind this strategy is that the resulting fragment will be as large as possible, and will be useful for something else.

First fit The list is not maintained in order of size. It may be in address order, or creation order, usually as a circular linked list, with a circulating pointer. The first area large enough is allocated. The next search begins where the last one finished. The idea behind this is that when the pointer eventually circulates back to the beginning, so many segments will have been deallocated in the meantime that large regions will have grown up there again.

Fragmentation

This method of allocating memory in blocks means that after a while the memory manager can find itself with a large number of small and useless blocks of memory on its hands. This is known as fragmentation.

The average amount of fragmentation can be reduced by reducing the size of segments. One possibility is to create separate code and data segments. This implies having two pairs of registers, one for code, and one for data.

For example, the Intel 8088 processor had one base register for code, one for data, and one for the stack. But it had no length registers, and hence no protection. This was rectified from the 80286 on.

Systems have been developed which only supply blocks of predefined fixed sizes. These usually differ from each other by a factor of two. Such systems accept a certain amount of internal fragmentation as a tradeoff against simplicity of implementation. Furthermore, a larger block can easily be converted to a smaller one by splitting it in two. Conversely, two smaller adjacent blocks together make up one larger one, exactly. Hence the name, 'buddy system'.

Compaction   The solution to the fragmentation problem is to compact memory. This means to shuffle the memory contents so as to place all free memory together in one large block. Of course, compaction is only possible if programs are relocatable, as they are with a system using a base register. If program addresses had been permanently changed by a relocating loader, then compaction is not possible.

Example   The simplest compaction algorithm is to move everything towards one end of memory, leaving the other end free. Normally the operating system is at one end or the other, so compaction is towards that end. But this can be quite an expensive way of doing things, as the example in Figure 8.7 illustrates.

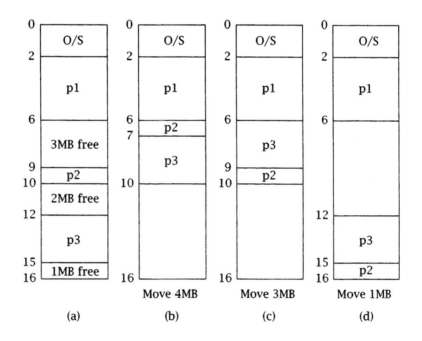

Figure 8.7: Compaction

Figure 8.7(a) shows the original state of memory, before compaction. There are 6MB available, but the largest block is only 3MB. Figure 8.7(b) shows memory after compaction towards the top. Note that 4MB had to be moved. Figure 8.7(c) shows another possibility. This time only p3 had to be moved, a total of 3MB. Figure 8.7(d) shows an even better possibility. We still get 6MB free, but only have to move the 1MB of p2.

However, the amount of checking involved in this begins to outweigh the advantages. The compaction algorithm begins to look like a chess playing program.

Finally, if memory is compacted every time a segment is removed, then there is never any fragmentation, there is no need to maintain or search a hole list. But the other side of that coin is the almost unacceptable overhead of such frequent compaction.

8.4 Segmentation

The base/length mechanism just described had a number of drawbacks. Memory was allocated in one big block (or at best in two or three blocks). Protection was provided, but it was very coarse grained. It covered the whole block of memory, and it either allowed access or not. It did not differentiate between different types of access, whether read, write, or execute. It would be possible to share, but again at a very coarse grained level.

What is needed is a mechanism which would allow a program to be treated by the memory manager as an arbitrarily large number of segments, not just one or two. It should be possible to give each of these different protection, and to share them on a one-by-one basis. And there is still the wish to implement extended memory.

Implementation

The logical way to do this would be by implementing an arbitrarily large number of base/length register pairs in the CPU. But the arbitrary part is technically infeasible, and the large part is economically infeasible. So the solution adopted is to implement these registers in ordinary memory, as a table of base/length pairs. As each entry in such a table is controlling one segment in memory, it is generally known as a segment table. The entries are known as segment descriptors.

Instead of having a base and a length register, the CPU now has a register which points to the beginning of the segment table of the current process. The contents of this register are part of the volatile environment, and are changed at every context switch.

With this scheme, the compiler produces many segments of code and data, of varying size. Each segment corresponds to a function, or a collection of data. Each of these begins its logical addresses at 0. The linker binds them all together into one executable, and gives each segment a unique number. This number is encoded in the high order part of every address. The low order part of an address is the offset within the segment. So a logical address consists of two parts: a segment number, and an offset into the segment, as illustrated in Figure 8.8.

| Segment (s) | Offset (o) |

Figure 8.8: A logical address

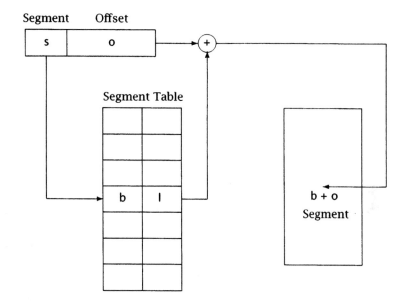

Figure 8.9: Address translation with segment table

The mapping then consists of the followings steps, which should be read with reference to Figure 8.9.

- Break the memory reference into a segment number (s) and an offset within the segment (o).

- Use s to index into the segment table, find b (the base of this segment in physical memory) and l (the length of this segment).

- If o < 0 OR o > l then Error.

- b + o is the required physical address.

For example, a logical address of 4321 might break down to segment number 4, and offset 321. So we go to the 4th entry in the segment table. There we find the base address of the segment (say 12500) and its length (say 400). The offset (321) is not negative, nor is it greater than the length (400). So it passes both of the tests. It is then added to the base, to give 12821. In this way, logical address 4321 is translated to physical address 12821.

Protection and sharing

Different types of access protection can be added to this scheme very easily. Three extra bits can be added to each segment descriptor in the table, signifying read, write, and execute access, respectively. Each descriptor in the table now has the format shown in Figure 8.10.

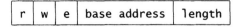

Figure 8.10: A segment table entry

The mapping hardware can be extended to check these bits in parallel with the other operations. So there is no extra time involved. For example, a MOV to memory operation would check if the write bit was set. If not, it would cause an exception.

The use of a segment table also facilitates sharing. First of all, because segments can be of any size, the programmer can indicate just which bytes of data or code are to be shared, and make these a segment on their own. Then each of the two (or more) sharing processes can have entries in their segment tables, pointing to the same physical location in memory.

While the base and length part of the descriptors would be identical, it is not necessary for the protection bits to be the same for the two processes. If one process only ever writes to the shared segment, and the other only ever reads from it, then the protection in the segment descriptor of the first process would be set to write only, while only the read bit would be set in the descriptor of the second process.

Extending memory

Segmentation allows us to achieve another of the objectives of good memory management—it allows us to extend memory. That is, the logical address space can be greater than the physical memory. We can write programs larger then the installed physical memory on the machine.

The essential point is that no matter how many segments there are in a program, at any given time it can be executing an instruction, or using data, from only one of them. So while in theory it may be sufficient to have only one segment in memory at a time, in practice it is certainly sufficient to have only a small number of segments in memory at any given time.

Most commercial programs have large amounts of error-handling code, which may seldom or never be used. There is no point having this taking up valuable space in memory. Because only a fraction of the segments need be in memory at any time, the total size of the program can be much larger than installed physical memory, and still it can run perfectly well.

To handle the mechanics of this, we need to add yet another bit to the segment descriptor, known as the presence (or valid) bit. This is set to 1 when the segment is in memory, and the data in the base and limit fields is valid. When the corresponding segment is not in memory, this bit is cleared to 0. The hardware recognises this bit, and understands whether a segment is currently in memory or not.

Segment fault

When a program address refers to a segment not currently in main memory, the memory management hardware still indexes into the segment table. But now it finds the presence bit cleared to 0. So it generates a segment fault interrupt. The current process cannot continue, so it is marked blocked, and put on a wait queue. The missing segment is loaded into memory, and the corresponding segment descriptor is updated.

How does the operating system know where to find the missing segment? Remember that all the segments of the program are on backing store, on a part of the disk reserved for this, called swap space. When the segment table is first set up, at run time, it contains descriptors for all of these segments, even if none of them is in memory. The presence bits are cleared to 0. The fields for base addresses and lengths are unused.

So the operating system can reuse them to contain the disk addresses of the respective segments. Then when a segment fault occurs, it knows where to find the appropriate segment on disk. It can load it in, and then use the base and length fields for their proper purpose.

The memory manager uses one of the schemes described in Section 8.3 to allocate a free segment in memory.

Segment removal

When a system has been running for a while, it will eventually reach a stage where the amount of free memory becomes so small that it is unable to find a block for the next segment fault. Even compaction is of no use if there are no free blocks to compact. The memory manager has to select some segment in memory, and move it out to disk. Its presence bit is cleared to 0, and its location on disk is recorded in the fields for base and length.

How does it decide which segment to select for removal? Obviously it would like to select a segment which is not currently in active use. This selection is complicated by the fact that the segments will be of different sizes. So the size of the incoming segment will have some influence on which segment to move out.

The simplest rule of thumb would be to find a segment which, together with any holes on either side of it, would free enough space for the incoming segment, and remove it. If there is no single segment large enough, then choose the smallest set of contiguous segments and holes which will provide enough free space.

The problem with this solution is that segments are chosen for replacement on the criterion of size alone. They may be the most active, and may segment fault almost immediately.

In general, there are three factors to be taken into account: the size of a segment, whether it is in active use or not, and the amount of compaction required. The relative emphasis given to each of these produces a variety of algorithms.

8.5 Cache memory

The foregoing description of segmentation will work, and will achieve the objectives set out for memory managers. But it will be unacceptably slow. The time required for each memory reference is effectively doubled. The CPU has to read the segment descriptor, then calculate the real address, then read from that address. Even worse than that, segment faults slow the machine down by a factor of hundreds. If they are frequent, even the fastest CPU will be dragged to a crawl.

We saw in the previous section that it is not economically feasible to hold the whole of a segment table in fast CPU registers. But it is possible to hold some descriptors in the CPU at any time. So the hardware designers generally provide a special, small, hardware memory, called by various names. It is most commonly called cache memory, but it is also known as associative memory or associative registers, content addressable memory, or a translation look-aside buffer. The basic idea is that the descriptors of the most recently accessed segments are saved, or cached, in the CPU, where they can be accessed almost instantaneously—certainly in less than 10ns.

Addressing in a cache

There is one fundamental problem with finding items in a cache. Because they are a random selection, they cannot be in sequential order. When looking for the descriptor for segment 4, for example, the CPU knows that it will always be at position 4 in the segment table. It is sufficient to use a construct such as `segment_table[4]` to refer to it.

Now the CPU cannot be sure that descriptor 1 will be at position 1 in the cache. And it certainly cannot presume that when it has found descriptor 1 in the cache, descriptor 2 will be immediately after it. Descriptor 2 may be anywhere else in the cache. Or it may not be there at all.

So addressing, or finding items in, a cache has to be done on a different basis from main memory. We have to store the number of each descriptor, as well as its contents. This is not necessary for a table in main memory, as it is implied by its position in the table.

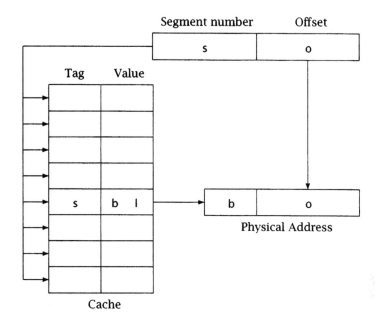

Figure 8.11: Searching a segmentation cache

Each cache register consists of two parts, a tag and a value, as shown in Figure 8.11. The tag is the number of the descriptor, e.g. 1, 4, 7. The value part is the actual contents of the segment descriptor.

When associative registers are presented with an item, it is compared with all tags simultaneously. So if a reference is made to segment 4, all of the cache registers are checked in parallel to see if any of them has the tag 4. If one has, then the CPU has access to the descriptor for segment 4. If none of them has a tag of 4, this implies that segment 4 was not referenced recently. The CPU must then go to the segment table in main memory for the required information.

When it is bringing it from memory, it also puts a copy in the cache, on the assumption that the program will probably reference segment 4 again soon. This adding an entry to the cache implies that some other entry must be discarded. For the sake of simplicity and speed, this is normally done FIFO.

It must be stressed that this is a very fast search, done in parallel on all cache registers at the same time. This makes for expensive hardware, and keeps cache size small.

The cache is normally cleared on each context switch. The new process will have segment numbers similar to the old process, so it is necessary to clear the old entries to avoid confusion.

Segmentation with caching

The whole procedure can be put in the form of an algorithm, as in Figure 8.12.

```
      Present segment number to associative store
      IF no match, THEN
           Use segment number as index into segment table
           IF not present, THEN
                Segment fault---fetch from secondary memory
                Update segment table
           ENDIF
           Update associative store
      ENDIF
      Add offset to base address
```

Figure 8.12: Segmentation algorithm

Timing

Let us look a little more closely at the timing implications of all of this. First of all, let us define *hit-ratio* to mean the percentage of times that the segment descriptor is found in the cache. This will be proportional to the size of the cache. The more associative registers, the more likely there is to be a hit. For the sake of the example, assume that it takes 10ns to search the cache, and 100ns to access main memory.

This means that if the descriptor is in the cache, it takes 110ns to actually access the required data in main memory (10ns + 100ns). If the descriptor is not in the cache, then it takes the 10ns to unsuccessfully search the cache, 100ns to read the segment table in memory, and another 100ns to access the required data in main memory, or a total of 210ns.

Now for an 80% hit ratio, with a sample of 1000 transactions, 800 will be found in the cache, and 200 will be misses. So the average access time is

$$\frac{(110 \times 800) + (210 \times 200)}{1000}$$

or 130ns. This is 30% slower than direct memory access, without any mapping (100ns). So the memory manager is slowing the machine down by 30%. This would normally be unacceptable.

For an 90% hit ratio, the average access time is

$$\frac{(110 \times 900) + (210 \times 100)}{1000}$$

or 120ns. This is 20% slower than direct memory access, which is still significant. It is interesting to note that even for a 100% hit ratio, the effective access time is 110ns—10% slower than direct memory access. This is the price that has to be paid for virtual memory.

Instruction and data caches

There is a further complication, introduced to speed things up even more. Most modern machines have three different caches. One is the translation buffer we have just examined in some detail. Another one caches recent instructions that have been read in and executed. The third caches recent data items that have been accessed.

So the figures in our previous example might be further improved. After finding a translation cached in the translation buffer, the CPU does not always go immediately to main memory for the instruction or data. It first of all looks in the instruction or data cache. If it finds the item it is looking for, then it does not have to go to main memory at all.

For example, assuming a hit in both the translation and instruction cache, the effective time to read an instruction can be as low as 20ns—much faster than direct memory access. But note that this speedup is due to caching—not to segmentation.

8.6   Paging

Now that we have developed such an efficient segmentation system, why is there need to look further? There is still a problem with segmentation, namely the variable size of segments. This has its advantages, in that what the programmer defines as logical parts of the program are kept together by the memory manager. Protection can also be applied on a segment by segment basis. But there is the difficulty involved in finding space for a large incoming segment. Particularly when memory is almost full, it may have to be compacted fairly frequently. And this has a considerable overhead.

A mechanism called paging was introduced to overcome this difficulty. It was first developed on the Atlas computer in Manchester in 1960, and was a significant milestone in the history of operating systems.

The fundamental concept involved in paging is that the virtual address space is divided into fixed size pages, not into variable sized segments. Physical memory is divided into page frames, of the same fixed size. So any page will fit—exactly—into any page frame. The problem of finding a place for an incoming page disappears.

The segment table of the previous sections is replaced by a page table. This has a page descriptor for each page of the virtual address space. Page descriptors are simpler than segment descriptors; they don't need a length field, as all pages are of the same size. But they do have a base field, pointing to the appropriate page frame, as well as protection bits, and a valid bit.

The size of a page is a tradeoff between the following factors.

- Size of the page table. The smaller the page size, the more entries required in the page table.

- Internal fragmentation. The larger the page size, the more will be wasted

on the last page. On average, half of the last page will be unused. This suggests smaller pages.

- Input/Output time. Given that it takes the same time (say 8ms) to locate a small page or a large page on disk, and that it takes 1ms to transfer 1kB; then with 1kB pages, it will take 9ms per kB, while with 8kB pages, it will take 16ms (8ms to find + 8ms to transfer) to load a page, or 2ms per kB. This suggests larger pages.

On the original Atlas, pages were 512 bytes. The Pentium uses a 4kB page, as does Linux. The size is not really important for an understanding of the mechanism. What matters is that on a particular system, all pages and all page frames are of the same size.

As with segmentation, at any given time a process will have all of its pages in secondary memory, and a few of its pages in main memory.

Linux uses paging to implement its virtual memory model, so we will examine it in some detail. First we will look at how the kernel creates and keeps track of page frames. Then we will go on to consider how the actual paging mechanism creates a virtual address space for a process.

Configuring the kernel

When a Linux machine is booted, after memory has been allocated for the use of the kernel, the remainder of the physical memory is assigned to the memory manager, which divides it into page frames. To keep track of these page frames, it creates an array mem_map[]. Each entry in this array is a `struct page`, and represents one page frame. See Figure 8.13, from <linux/mm.h>. The position of the structure within the array indicates which page frame it represents; for example entry 3 represents page frame 3.

```
struct page{
        struct page    *next;
        struct inode   *inode;
        unsigned long offset;
        struct page    *next_hash;
        atomic_t       count;
};
```

Figure 8.13: Data structure representing a physical page

- All page frames which contain pages of the same program or file are kept on a linked list using the `next` field. This keeps track of all the logical pages of that file actually in memory.

- The `inode` field is a pointer to a data structure representing the object backing this page, typically a file on disk. This will be examined in detail

in the next chapter. Here it is sufficient to know that the header for the list of pages actually in memory is in this data structure.

- The offset field indicates the particular part of the file which is backing this page.

- All valid pages are also maintained on hash lists, hashed on *inode and offset. These lists are headed from page_hash_table, and linked through next_hash. This structure is known as the page cache.

- The count field is a reference count of processes using this page. As pages can be shared, this can be greater than 1. A value of 0 here means that this page frame is free. In that case, it is linked on a free list using next.

The kernel allocates a struct page for each logical page when it brings it into memory, and stores it in the corresponding page frame. It uses these page structures to manage the logical pages from then on.

Free page frames are tracked using an array free_area[6]. They are not tracked individually, rather each of the six entries in the array is a header of a linked list of contiguous blocks of 1, 2, 4, 8, 16 or 32 free page frames, maintained on the buddy system. Each entry in free_area[] points to the first struct page representing the block (see Figure 8.14).

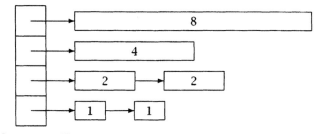

free_area[]

Figure 8.14: Tracking free physical memory

Paging mechanism

Memory management in Linux is clearly distinguished into an architecture dependent part, and an architecture independent part. The former, which we examine in this section, is concerned with

- Maintaining the page tables, which have to be in the format determined by the CPU designer.

- Performing the address mapping: calculating the required page, and finding the corresponding page frame. This is a hardware function.

- Transferring pages from secondary memory as required. This is a software function.

The architecture independent part allows the operating system to maintain much more information about the virtual address space. This will be examined in the following section.

Page table structures

The Linux memory management system on the PC maintains the page table for each process as a tree structure, with two levels. The root of the tree is known as the page directory. With the Intel architecture, the CR3 register in the CPU points to the page directory for the current process. The contents of this register are saved and restored on a context switch. Linux uses 4K pages, and each page table entry is 4 bytes. So as the page directory is always one page in length, there is room for 1024 entries in it.

An entry in the page directory points to a page table, which is similar in size and structure to the page directory. Each entry in a page table points to a 4K page frame. As there are 1K page tables, each pointing to 1K page frames, the tree structure allows for a maximum of 1M page frames. As each page frame is 4K, this allows a maximum virtual address space of 4Mb.

The whole structure can be visualised as in Figure 8.15.

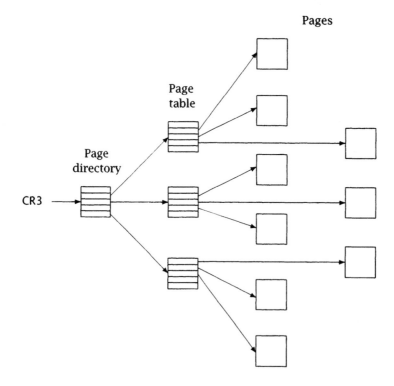

Figure 8.15: Linux page table structure

Such a tree structure allows for a very compact representation of the memory management information.

high order 20 bits of page frame address	page table bits

Figure 8.16: Format of page table entry

The format of a page table (or page directory) entry is given in Figure 8.16. As each page frame is aligned on a 4K boundary in memory, the least significant 12 bits of its address are always 0, and so only the most significant 20 bits need to be recorded.

The 12 bits that are thus freed up in the page table entry are used to record further information about the page of code or data stored in that page frame. The most important of these bits are the following:

- bit 0: the present bit. If set, then the corresponding page is in memory, and the remainder of the entry is valid.

- bit 1: the read/write bit. When set, the page can be written to; when cleared, the corresponding page can only be read.

- bit 2: the privilege bit. When set, the corresponding page is accessible in user mode; otherwise it is only accessible in kernel mode.

- bit 5: the accessed bit. The CPU sets this bit whenever the corresponding page is read or written.

- bit 6: the dirty bit. The CPU sets this bit whenever the corresponding page is written to.

Address mapping

Let us now look at the address mapping function. The CPU calculates the virtual address it wishes to access. It presents this address to the memory management unit, which breaks it into three parts. The high order 10 bits are interpreted as an index into the page directory. The pointer it finds there leads to the appropriate page table. The next 10 bits of the virtual address are used to index into this page table, where the address of the appropriate page frame is found. The least significant 12 bits of the virtual address identify a particular byte within this page.

But as with segmentation, a translation cache is used as well. The algorithm is the same one as used for segmentation. In Figure 8.17, the solid path shows what happens when there is a hit in the cache, and the address of the page frame (f) is found immediately. The dashed lines show what happens when there is a miss in the cache. The page directory is indexed, to find the address of the appropriate page table (t). This page table is then indexed, to find the address of the page frame (f). In either case the offset (o) is added to this, to arrive at the required byte in memory.

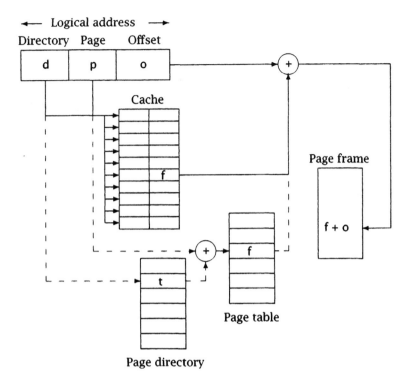

Figure 8.17: Address translation with cache and page table

Page fault

When a program address refers to a page not currently in main memory, as indicated by the present bit in the page table entry being cleared to 0, a page fault interrupt is generated. The current process cannot continue, so it is put on a wait queue, and the page fault handler is called. How this finds the missing page on backing store is architecture independent, and will be described in Section 8.7. A free page frame is found, using the `free_area[]` array. The missing page is loaded into it, and the `struct page` representing this page frame is updated. The corresponding page descriptor is also updated, and a copy of this descriptor is put in the cache. Then the current process is moved back to the run queue.

Evaluation of paging

Page tables take up a large amount of main memory. Because a linear page table has to map the whole of the virtual address space, there could be very many empty entries. But they have to be there, as place-holders in the array of page descriptors. Techniques have been developed for handling such sparse arrays. We have seen that Linux maintains them as a tree structure. Another method is to access them by a hash function.

There is a tradeoff here between the size of the table, and the time taken to access it. If indexed, the time taken to access any entry is fixed. If hashed, larger tables take longer. Yet another possibility is to page the page tables themselves.

Paging should be transparent to a programmer. But there are times when it can influence program performance. Consider the program shown in Figure 8.18.

```
int   array[128][128];

for (i = 0; i < 128; i++)
        for (j = 0; j < 128; j++)
                array[i][j] = 0;
```

Figure 8.18: Program to initialise an array

The array is stored in order `array[0][0]`, `array[0][1]`, etc. Assume an `int` is 4 bytes, and pages are 512 bytes. The program will fill the first page, then the second page, and so on, for a total of 128 page faults. But if the last line is written `array[j][i] = 0`, then the program will skip from page to page each time around the loop, constantly page faulting. It could fault on every assignment, for a maximum of 128×128 or 16,384 page faults.

Paging fulfils the objectives set out for memory management, except that it does not allocate memory as the programmer sees it. Rather it allocates it in fixed size units.

8.7 Architecture independent memory model

As well as the architecture dependent page tables we have seen in the previous section, Linux also maintains much more information about the organisation of memory, which makes the virtual memory look the same on machines of different architectures, even though the underlying models are different.

Within the user segment, blocks of addresses are allocated, known as regions. A Unix process has three regions in its address space by default.

- Text (code) and initialised data, from the executable. In Linux, this is mapped in at 0x 0804 0000.

- Uninitialised data, and the heap (for runtime allocation). This is mapped in above the text region.

- The stack. In Linux, the stack grows down from 0x C000 0000. The kernel segment is mapped in above this.

As well as this, other arbitrary objects such as files or databases can be mapped into the address space. For example, Linux maps shared libraries into a region at 0x 4000 0000 by default.

Linux uses a network of data structures to keep track of the different regions, where they are mapped into the address space, their protection, and where they are on backing store.

Process wide data structures

The root of the whole memory management system for each process is in the struct task_struct. This contains a field mm, a pointer to a struct mm_struct, declared in <sched.h> (see Figure 8.19).

```
struct mm_struct{
        struct vm_area_struct  *mmap;
        pgd_t                  *pgd;
        int                    count;
        unsigned long          start_code, end_code;
        unsigned long          start_data, end_data;
        unsigned long          start_stack;
};
```

Figure 8.19: The root of the memory management data structures

- The mmap field heads a linked list of struct vm_area_struct, each of which represents a region.

- The pgd field points to a hardware-specific page directory for this process.

- The count field keeps track of the number of task_struct pointers referencing this structure, or—equally—the number of threads sharing this address space.

- Other fields identify the beginning and end of code, data, and stack.

Regions

One vm_area_struct, from <linux/mm.h> defines each region (see Figure 8.20).

- The vm_mm field points back to the mm_struct for the process.

- The beginning and end of the address range being mapped by this region are in vm_start and vm_end.

- These structures are maintained as a linked list, headed from mmap in the mm_struct. The link field is vm_next. This makes it possible to map extra regions into the address space at run time, and also to remove them as well. A static table would make this difficult if not impossible to implement. Unallocated regions of virtual memory do not have address map entries.

```
struct vm_area_struct{
        struct mm_struct                 *vm_mm;
        unsigned long                    vm_start;
        unsigned long                    vm_end;
        struct vm_area_struct            *vm_next;
        unsigned short                   vm_flags;
        struct vm_operations_struct *vm_ops;
        unsigned long                    vm_offset;
        struct file                      *vm_file;
};
```

Figure 8.20: Data structure controlling a region

So we have a compact representation of a sparse address space. Such large, sparsely filled address spaces are useful in implementing multi-threaded processes, which need many stacks, and also in implementing shared libraries. Figure 8.21 shows how all of these data structures fit together.

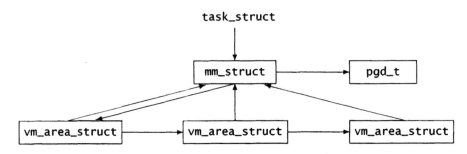

Figure 8.21: Memory management data structures for a process

- Each vm_area_struct describes a region of virtual memory which has the same protection properties. Note that protection is not on a page basis. The vm_flags field determines access to this region. Possible values are given in Figure 8.22, from <linux/mm.h>.

```
#define VM_READ      0x0001
#define VM_WRITE     0x0002
#define VM_EXEC      0x0004
#define VM_SHARED    0x0008
#define VM_LOCKED    0x2000
```

Figure 8.22: Possible values for the flags field

It is possible to change the protection of a subset of a region, but this is done by splitting it into two or three regions, depending where the subset falls, and protecting each individually. Other times adjacent regions with the same protection could be merged.

- Each `vm_area_struct` has a pointer `vm_ops` to an array of function pointers, `vm_operations_struct`, see Figure 8.23, from `<linux/mm.h>`.

```
struct vm_operations_struct{
        void            (*open)();
        void            (*close)();
        void            (*unmap)();
        int             (*swapout)();
        pte_t           (*swapin)();
};
```

Figure 8.23: Operations on a region

- open() is called to create a new region.
- close() is called to delete a region.
- unmap() is used to delete part of a region.
- swapout() and swapin() swap a page to and from disk.

- The `vm_file` field points to a data structure representing the object backing this region, typically a file on disk. But a region does not necessarily map exactly onto an external object. So the `vm_offset` field identifies the point in the object at which the region begins. The file system data structure contains a field `i_pages`, which heads a linked list of `struct page`, representing all of the pages of this region which are actually in memory. This will be seen again in Section 9.4.

Figure 8.24 shows how this set of data structures fit together.

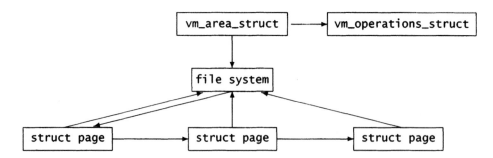

Figure 8.24: Pages actually in memory

Example

For example, suppose a system had three regions mapped, one from 0 to 2FFF, another from 3000 to 4FFF, and a third from 8000 to 9FFF. Note that the range of virtual addresses from 5000 to 7FFF is unallocated. Figure 8.25 illustrates how the memory manager would keep track of such allocations.

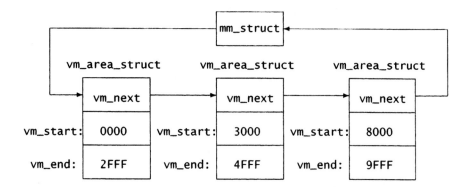

Figure 8.25: Example mapping of three regions

Page faults

When a page fault occurs, the page fault handler checks if the faulting address is valid, by locating the appropriate vm_area_struct. If the address is within some mapped region, it goes on to check the legality of the read/write access, by examining the vm_flags field. Then it locates the object, by following the vm_file pointer. It can calculate the offset into the region, and use that to identify the virtual page in which the faulting address occurs. It can then identify the appropriate part of the object on backing store. It allocates a free page frame, and updates the corresponding struct page. Finally it calls swapin() to copy the page in from disk.

For example, with reference to Figure 8.25, if the faulting virtual address is between 9000 and 9FFF, then the offset into the region is between 1000 and 1FFF (as the region begins at 8000). So it must page in that portion of the backing store.

8.8   System services for memory management

There are a number of POSIX system services which allow the user to interact with the memory manager. One thing they all have in common is that their requests must be aligned on a page boundary.

Memory mapping

The mmap() system service creates a new region in the virtual memory map, and associates this area with a file on disk. It returns a pointer to the beginning of the memory region. So the file appears to be in memory, and is accessed using pointers. But in fact it is paged in and out by the memory manager, as required.

This has the advantage that it reduces the number of system calls which have to be made. With traditional file I/O, the operating system has to be called

for every read or write to a file; this way there is only one system call, to set up the new region; after that all other accesses to the file use pointers.

It also has the advantage that it unifies the data space of a program. Traditionally, a programmer has some data in variables in memory, and some in files, with two totally different ways of accessing them. Mapping a file into virtual memory means that all the data is now accessed in the same way by a program.

The mapping can be performed either MAP_PRIVATE or MAP_SHARED. Normally you would prefer a private mapping, but mmap() allows memory to be shared, if required.

It is possible to instruct mmap() where to map the file within the virtual address space, although it is advisable to allow mmap() select its own range of virtual addresses.

It is also possible to specify the protection to be set on the region of shared memory: PROT_READ, PROT_WRITE, or PROT_EXEC. The protection specified in mmap() must be consistent with the flags used when opening the file. Protection on a mapped region can be changed after mapping, using mprotect(). There are also mlock() and munlock() functions.

The msync() function can be used to force the system to write changes in a mapped region back to disk. With the MS_SYNC flag, when this call returns the memory and disk are consistent. With the MS_ASYNC flag, when the call returns the write has begun, but is not necessarily completed. If more than one process has the same file mapped, then using the MS_INVALIDATE flag causes the other processes to update their mapping, so that they see the new data just updated on disk.

The munmap() function is used to undo a mapping. This can be applied to a subset of the mapped memory, or it can cover many maps, including holes.

Memory mappings are inherited across a fork(), but not an exec().

System V shared memory

Traditionally, shared memory is implemented in Unix using the System V IPC mechanism. The physical shared memory area must first be created, using shmget(), which is similar to the semget() and msgget() functions we have already seen. The particular area of shared memory is identified system wide by a key, a non-zero number.

Then shmat() connects this area of shared memory to the virtual address space of a process. This is passed the identifier returned by shmget(), and it returns a pointer. While it is possible to instruct this function on where to map the shared memory into the address space, it is best to let the system decide where it will put it.

The shmdt() function detaches the segment of shared memory from the virtual address space.

Finally, the shmctl() function, with the IPX_RMID flag, deallocates the area of physical memory.

POSIX shared memory

POSIX introduced shared memory objects, although these are not yet available in Linux. A shared memory object is created or accessed using shm_open(). The object is then mapped into virtual memory using mmap(). shm_open() uses the same naming convention as sem_open() and mq_open(). That is, the name must be a valid file name, but it does not necessarily have to be in the directory structure.

Shared memory is created with a size of 0. It will then be sized using truncate() or ftruncate(), before being mapped. Shared memory is persistent, even after unmapping it. The memory is still available until the last sharer unmaps it. It is finally removed using shm_unlink(). This works on the name, not the descriptor. No new process can open the shared memory after a call to shm_unlink().

8.9 Page replacement

A system which has been running for some time will eventually arrive at a stage when there are no further free page frames available. So it will have to run a page replacement routine, which will eject some pages from memory, and invalidate them. In fact, a system would not wait until it had no page frames available—it would always keep a minimum number of free frames. Otherwise it might have no space in which to run the replacement algorithm, leading to deadlock. When the replacement algorithm is called to make space, it would normally replace a number of pages, not one at a time.

The basic question here is: *which* page to remove? The ideal is to keep the page fault rate as low as possible, so the page should be chosen with this in mind.

Factors affecting page replacement

There are a number of factors which influence page replacement algorithms.

The first is that when replacing a page, there is a big difference between replacing one that has been written to since it was brought in, and one that has not. The former has to be copied out to disk, a time-consuming operation. The latter can just be discarded, written over, as the copy on disk is exactly the same as the copy in memory.

The modified bit, or the dirty bit, in the page table entry allows an algorithm to tell these apart. All other things being equal, it is preferable to remove a clean page rather than a dirty one. It is possible to lock pages into memory, so that they are passed over by the page replacement algorithm. This involves a lock bit in the page table entry associated with each page frame.

Page replacement can be on a local or a global basis. If one process causes a page fault, the replacement algorithm can look only at the pages of the process that caused the page fault, or it can look at all pages of all processes.

Another factor to be considered is how many page frames should a user be allocated. Should allocation be equal for all users, or should it be proportional to the size of the program? Obviously, in whichever scheme is used, allocation will vary according to the number of users.

We will look at several algorithms in this section, and the question of comparing and evaluating them comes up. The method that has been developed is to run the algorithm on a particular string of memory references, and compute the number of page faults. Obviously the algorithm with the lower number of page faults is better.

Such reference strings can be computed artificially, for example using a random number generator. A more difficult method of creating them is to trace a given program. But this will result in a more realistic string. When creating such reference strings, it is only necessary to record the page number—the offset within the page is irrelevant. Also, immediately successive references to the same page need not be recorded, as they cannot cause a page fault.

Apart from the particular algorithm used, the page fault rate will always depend on the number of page frames available, as illustrated in Figure 8.26.

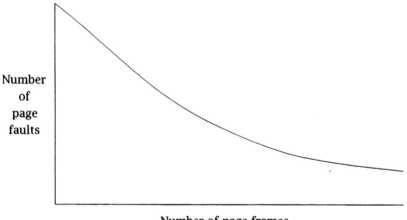

Figure 8.26: Relationship between page frames and page faults

OPTimal

This algorithm can be stated very simply—replace the page which will not be used for the longest period of time. The problem with it is that it is impossible to implement, as it requires knowledge of the future.

But it is the best algorithm, hence the name optimal. It can be used as a standard against which to compare all others. We can rank an algorithm in terms of how close it comes to the optimal.

FIFO

This is the simplest page replacement algorithm. It can be implemented by allocating page frames sequentially, and replacing pages in the same order. One problem with this algorithm is that it ignores the possibility that the oldest page may be the one most heavily referenced, and be needed immediately.

A modified form of the FIFO algorithm is not to write the removed page out immediately, but to add it to the tail of either a list of dirty pages, or a list of free pages. When a page fault occurs, the system searches these before going to disk. The whole dirty page list is written out to backing store at intervals. This method provides protection against the relatively poor, but simple, FIFO algorithm. It gives a second chance.

Least recently used (LRU)

This algorithm uses the recent past as an approximation of the near future. As an algorithm it is quite good. The major problem is how to implement it. One approach is to use counters.

Each page table entry has a time-of-use field, and the CPU has a counter register, which is incremented at every memory reference. When a page is referenced, the value in this CPU register is copied to the appropriate field in the page table entry. The algorithm replaces the page with the smallest time-of-use value. The drawbacks with this are that it requires a search of the page table, which is time consuming; and also the counter register will eventually overflow, and this must be catered for.

There are particular situations in which the LRU algorithm can be counter productive. For example, take a program executing in a loop that extends over 9 virtual pages, on a machine with only 8 page frames. With LRU, it will page fault on every new page.

Not recently used (NRU)

Few machines provide the hardware necessary to implement LRU efficiently. Many provide some help, in the form of a reference bit. When a page is referenced, the hardware sets this bit in the page descriptor. At any time, the system can determine which pages have been used recently, and which have not. We cannot know the order of use. So a reference bit really partitions the pages into used and unused. Still, this hardware mechanism allows the use of an algorithm which tries to approximate LRU, known as Not Recently Used (NRU), as given in Figure 8.27.

The search is circular, and wraps around at the end of the page table. If a page has been referenced since the last time around, then it is not removed immediately. Instead, its reference bit is cleared, and it is given another chance. Only if its reference bit is still clear when the algorithm has circled all the way around the page table, will it be removed. Because of the way it works, this algorithm is sometimes called 'second chance replacement'.

```
REPEAT
  Examine the reference bit in the page table entry for pagenumber
  IF (reference bit == 1) THEN
      reference bit = 0
  ELSE
      remove page
  ENDIF
  pagenumber = (pagenumber + 1) MOD size of page table
UNTIL (required number of pages removed)
```

Figure 8.27: Algorithm for NRU replacement

Linux uses a version of this NRU algorithm. As we have seen in Section 8.6, there is a hardware reference bit (the 'accessed' bit) in each page table entry. The swap daemon (kswapd) is called once per second by the timer interrupt. If sufficient page frames are still free, it goes back to sleep again. If the number of free page frames is below the critical level, then it tries to provide more, by swapping out or discarding the contents of some page frames. The `struct page` representing the physical page frame is then linked into the `free_area[]` structures at the appropriate point for its size. In Linux this algorithm is not implemented globally, but on a process by process basis.

Working set model of program behaviour

As the number of processes running on a system grows, they all compete for a fixed number of page frames. They take these from the free list, causing the page replacement algorithm to remove other pages, which are probably needed by their owners, and so they page fault again very soon, taking frames from yet other processes. As they all queue up for the paging device, the ready queue empties, and CPU utilisation decreases. No work is being done. This situation is described as thrashing, and is illustrated graphically in Figure 8.28.

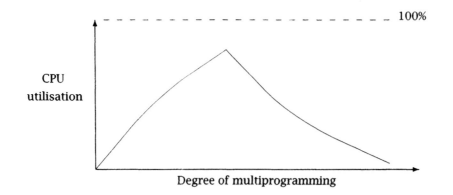

Figure 8.28: Effect of thrashing on CPU utilisation

To prevent thrashing, the memory manager must provide a process with as many page frames as it needs. But how do we decide how many frames it needs?

Working set

There certainly is a minimum number of pages that must be in physical memory before a process can effectively use the CPU. This is called the working set of the process. So we can rephrase the question, how do we determine the working set of a process?

First, we define a parameter Δ, the working set window. Then we examine the most recent Δ memory references. The set of pages in this most recent Δ references is the working set. If a page is in active use, it will be in the working set. If it is no longer being used, it will drop out of the working set Δ references after it is last used.

Accuracy in determining the working set depends on the value chosen for Δ. If this is too large, then many pages will be included in the working set, which are not really part of it. This will waste system resources. If it is too small, then pages which are really part of the working set will be swapped out, leading to thrashing. A typical value for Δ is around 10,000.

How the working set varies with the size of the working set window is illustrated in Figure 8.29.

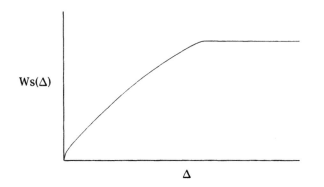

Figure 8.29: Effect of window size on working set

Note that when the window is large enough to include the whole program, the graph levels off.

Demand for frames

If we compute the working set size (W_i) for every process i, then

$$\text{Total demand for frames (D)} = \Sigma W_i.$$

If D is greater than the total of available frames, thrashing will occur.

So, the operating system monitors the working set of each process, and allocates sufficient frames for the working set. If there are enough extra frames available, then another process can begin. If D is greater than the total of the available frames, then some process is chosen, and all of its pages are swapped out. This prevents thrashing, and still keeps the degree of multiprogramming as high as possible.

Any replacement algorithm should never remove a page which is part of the working set of a process.

Implementation

To implement the working set model requires a fixed interval timer interrupt, and reference bits in the page table entries.

For example, assume Δ is 10,000, that the timer interrupts every 2,000 memory references, and that the five leftmost bits in the page table entry are reference bits. The leftmost bit is the hardware reference bit. On each timer interrupt, the bits are shifted right, and the leftmost bit is cleared.

If the page is not referenced between one interrupt and another, then the leftmost bit will remain clear. Any page whose five reference bits are all clear is no longer in the working set, and can be removed.

8.10 Paged segmentation

Now that we have seen both segmentation and paging, a comparison of the two mechanisms should help in understanding both of them.

- Pages are of fixed size, segments vary.

- A programmer is aware of segmentation, not of paging.

- There is one linear address space with paging, whereas with segmentation there are many address spaces.

- Procedures and data can be distinguished and separately protected with segmentation, but not with paging.

- Sharing of procedures is facilitated with segmentation, but not with paging.

- There is automatic overflow from the end of one page to the next; there is no overflow from the end of a segment.

- When segments become very large, it can be quite difficult to find a block of memory for them to fit in. A page will fit in any page frame.

- Segmentation was invented to allow programs to be broken up into logically independent address spaces, to aid sharing and protection, and to run larger programs without having to buy more physical memory. Paging delivers most of these advantages, but with a smaller overhead.

From the foregoing discussion it is obvious that both segmentation and paging have their advantages, as well as their disadvantages. When segments become very large, it can be quite difficult to find a block of memory big enough for them to fit in. So some designers have implemented a paging scheme on top of a segmentation system. This is known as paged segmentation.

Each segment now consists of one or more pages. Each has its own page table. A segment descriptor now points to a page table. The hardware interprets an address as a triple (segment, page, offset), as illustrated in Figure 8.30.

Logical address

Segment (s)	Page (p)	Offset (o)

Figure 8.30: An address interpreted as segment, page, offset

The address mapping algorithm for paged segmentation is shown in Figure 8.31. Note that the first three steps in this algorithm deal with segmentation. The remainder deals with paging.

```
Split the program address into s, p, o
Use s to index into the segment table
IF the presence bit in the segment descriptor is cleared
        (This means there are no pages for this segment in memory,
        nor is there a page table for this segment)
THEN create a new (empty) page table for this segment,
        enter its address in the segment table,
        and set the corresponding presence bit
ENDIF
Extract the address of the page table
Use p to index the page table
IF the presence bit in the corresponding entry
        in the page table is cleared (This means that
        the page is not in memory)
THEN fetch the page from backing store,
        enter its address in the pagetable,
        and set the corresponding presence bit
ENDIF
Extract the page frame address f
Add f to o to give the required location
```

Figure 8.31: Algorithm for paged segmentation

Figure 8.32 attempts to illustrate this in the form of a diagram.

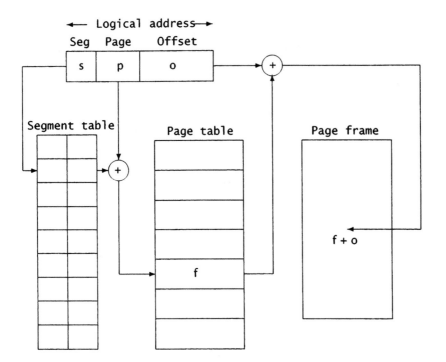

Figure 8.32: Address translation with paged segmentation

There is a considerable overhead in accessing the segment table, then the page table. The use of a cache is essential. The first time a page is accessed, a long and time-consuming address conversion is necessary, but subsequent accesses to the same page can be very rapid. The conversion of virtual to physical address is almost instantaneous if the page has been recently accessed.

Paged segmentation fulfils all the requirements of memory management. The only drawback might be the complexity of the address map, and the space overhead of the tables. But dedicated hardware, especially associative memory, can greatly reduce this.

Strictly speaking, Linux is a paged segmentation system, even if it only has two segments, one for the user (3GB), and the other for the kernel (1GB). Within the user segment memory is accessed using paging. So for practical purposes it has been treated as a pure paging system.

8.11   Fetch policies

A question common to all virtual memory systems is *when* to move data from secondary to main storage. Should it be done all at once, or should it be done when needed? Two different approaches are possible: demand policies, which delay movement until absolutely required; and anticipatory policies, which try to anticipate demands.

Fetch on demand

This is the easiest to implement. A missing page or segment creates a fault. The placement algorithm allocates memory. But fetch on demand can have a significant effect on performance, as illustrated by the following example. Suppose that a page fault occurs on average once every p references. Then

time for p references   =   ((p − 1) × access time) + page fault time

For the purposes of the example, let us take the average page fault service time as 10ms, and memory access time as 100ns. Using these values,

$$\text{time for p references} = (p − 1)100 \text{ ns} + 10 \text{ ms}$$
$$= 100p − 100 + 10,000,000 \text{ ns}$$
$$= 100p + 9,999,900 \text{ ns}$$

$$\text{Average access time} = 100 + 9,999,900/p \text{ ns}$$

Now let us try to put a numeric value on p. Suppose that one access in every thousand causes a page fault. Putting this into the equation gives an effective access time of 10,100ns instead of 100ns. The computer is going 101 times slower! Obviously this is not acceptable. If we want to have less than 10% degradation, then the effective access time must be less than 110ns. Putting this value into the equation,

$$100 + 9,999,900/p \quad < \quad 110$$
$$9,999,900/p \quad < \quad 10$$
$$9,999,900 \quad < \quad 10p$$
$$999,990 \quad < \quad p$$

So, the probability of a page fault occurring must be less than 1 in every 1,000,000 memory accesses.

Anticipatory fetch policies

These rely on predictions of how the program will behave in the future. This can be inferred both from how it has behaved in the past, and also from the nature of computer programs in general.

In any small time interval, a program operates within a particular context— executing instructions from a single function, and using data from a single data area. And almost all programs use loops, some of which may be executed thousands of times. Of course, some programs will operate in context more tightly than others.

Any fetch algorithm should ensure that the whole working set is in memory. When a program is restarted after being swapped out, or when it starts initially, there are a large number of consecutive page faults. In the swapping

case, the swapper can save a list of the working set when swapping out, and can then bring in all of the working set when swapping in. With initial startup, the common practice is to fault in each page as it is referenced. But the compiler could compute the initial working set, and this could be pre-paged in.

8.12 Summary

1. A memory manager has to do more than just keep track of which bytes are in use, and which are free. It must be able to divide up and manage memory in sections that correspond exactly to the divisions and sizes of any particular program. And it must be able to handle a three or four level hardware memory, maintain consistency, and organise the movement of data between different levels.

   It is most unlikely that a program will be in the same physical location in memory each time it runs. Yet the memory manager must ensure that no matter where it is, all loads or stores in the program refer to the correct items of data. It must protect one user from another, and yet at the same time allow them to share data and procedures when required. Most modern managers cater for programs which are larger than the installed physical memory.

2. All of these objectives can be met by making a sharp distinction between addresses as used by the program, and the actual hardware memory locations in which the program is loaded. The memory manager uses a translation mechanism, a mapping, to convert from one to the other, and so is said to implement a virtual memory system.

3. The simplest way to implement a virtual memory is to use base and length registers. The base register allows the program addresses to be adjusted on each memory reference, and the length register implements protection.

   Placement algorithms decide which free space to pick for an incoming program. Common policies are best fit, worst fit, or first fit. But fragmentation is always a problem, requiring compaction.

4. Segmentation provides an arbitrarily large number of base/limit pairs, but in tables in main memory rather than in dedicated registers. Different types of protection (e.g. read, write, execute) can be provided. Sharing is possible by having a single segment referred to in the tables of two different processes.

   Not all segments of a program need be in memory at a given time. So the total of the program can be much larger than installed physical memory. The memory manager needs to be able to recognise when a segment is not in memory, and bring it in from backing store if required.

5. Segmentation as described doubles the time required for each memory reference. It is made practicable by holding the most recently looked up descriptors in the CPU itself—in what is called a cache.

6. The variable size of segments causes difficulties, which can be solved by paging. Programs are divided into fixed size pages, not into variable sized segments. Physical memory is divided into page frames, of the same size. So any page will fit—exactly—into any page frame. Linux uses paging, with a two level tree structured page table.

7. In Linux, the user address space is divided into regions. The data structures representing each region are maintained on a linked list. This provides for a large sparse linear address space.

8. There are system services provided for mapping files into regions of virtual memory, and for sharing regions of memory between processes.

9. Page replacement algorithms decide which page to remove in order to make room in main memory. Common policies are FIFO, least recently used, and not recently used, which is implemented in Linux. There is a certain minimum number of pages, known as the working set, which each process must have in memory before it can effectively use the CPU. With fewer pages than this, it is said to be thrashing.

10. Both segmentation and paging have their advantages and disadvantages. The best aspects of both systems can be combined by paging each segment.

11. Data may be moved up the memory pyramid on demand. This can have a significant effect on performance. It is also possible to anticipate requirements.

8.13 Discussion questions

1. Could the code section of an executable file be used as backing store for a program's code, without the need to copy it into the swap area?

2. If a program used only relative addressing, it would seem that it could be relocated without any difficulty. Why is this not a general solution to the address mapping problem?

3. Every memory access has to be checked for access permission. At first sight this would seem to be prohibitively expensive. How is it implemented in an acceptable time frame?

4. On a particular architecture, the logical address is limited to 16 bits. This would seem to limit programs to 64K. Could you devise some way of writing larger programs, still with 16 bit addresses?

5. Do 'virtual memory' and 'extended memory' mean the same thing?

6. Without progressing to a full-blown segmentation system, could you suggest ways in which the base/limit mechanism could be improved? Consider areas such as more than one linear address space, fine grained protection, and sharing. How about extending memory?

7. The standard implementation of segmentation uses a fixed size segment table, so it is not possible to map extra segments in at run time. Could it be adapted for this?

8. A program generates an address 0xFDE9. The high order 5 bits represent the segment number. Convert the address to binary, and find the segment number. The segment table entry for that segment says that the high order bits of the base address for that segment are 0x213. Perform the address mapping, and find the physical address.

9. When a process terminates, both its segment table, and all of its segments actually in memory, are released. Discuss the implications of this for a shared segment.

10. With memory extension schemes, we can run programs larger than the installed physical memory. Is there any limit to this?

11. The memory manager can use a segment table entry for two purposes— sometimes it contains a segment descriptor, other times a disk address. When it contains a segment descriptor, the disk address is overwritten. How does it know where to write the contents of the segment, when it has to swap it out? Suggest an extension to the mechanism to cater for this.

12. As caches becomes larger, invalidating the cache on each context switch becomes more and more wasteful. Suggest an extension to the mechanism which would enable entries to be kept in the cache across context switches.

13. With a virtual memory system, two programs can have the same virtual address. Could they have the same physical address?

14. If a page table is implemented as an array, it takes exactly one memory reference to access any element in it. If it is implemented as a hash table, what is the minimum number of memory references required to access an element? How large could this grow?

15. Discuss the implications of implementing a page table as a tree structure.

16. If a program is reading sequentially through data stored in a paged system, when it reaches the end of one page, it automatically goes to the start of the next page. What happens when it reaches the end of the last page? If the data actually finishes half-way through the last page, what will happen if the program tries to read beyond the end of the data?

17. Distinguish clearly between the picture of a process address space, as given in Figure 8.15, and that given in Figure 8.21. How can both be describing the same reality?

18. Linux really implements page tables as a three level tree. Investigate how this is collapsed into two levels, to suit the PC architecture.

19. With Linux, when a page is swapped out, the corresponding entry in the page table is used to contain its address in backing store. Investigate the declaration of a page table entry which facilitates this.

20. Why do you think the mmap() function returns a pointer of type void?

21. Regions of the virtual address space mapped by mmap() are inherited across a fork(), but not an exec(). Why?

22. If the OPT algorithm cannot be implemented, how then can it be used as a standard of comparison?

23. A FIFO page replacement algorithm can keep a temporary list of pages which are about to be swapped out, just in case one of them may be needed again almost immediately. Should a page on such a list have its presence bit set or not?

24. Investigate ways of implementing the LRU page removal algorithm, and comment on their efficiency.

25. What is the essential difference between the second chance FIFO, and the NRU page replacement algorithms? Both give a second chance.

26. Calculate successive working sets for the following reference string, with a working set window (Δ) of 5.

    2 6 1 5 7 5 1 6 2 3 4 1 2 3 4 3 4 3 4 1 3 2 3 4 3 4

27. When the total demand for frames is greater than the available physical memory, all the pages of some process are swapped out to backing store. Suggest a mechanism to make this as fair as possible.

28. It is far quicker to remove a clean page, as opposed to a dirty one. Evaluate a strategy which attempts to keep the maximum number of pages clean, by writing back dirty pages when there is no other traffic on the disk channel.

29. A crude algorithm which never removed a dirty page would soon end up thrashing clean pages. Suggest a modification by which it would only remove dirty old pages.

30. Discuss how a compiler might calculate the initial working set of a program, and pass this information on through the executable, so that the full working set is loaded when the program is run, rather than being demand paged in.

Input and output 9

The management of input and output is part of the operating system, for very obvious reasons.

- The hardware interface to most devices is relatively crude. It requires complex setting and clearing of bits. The operating system hides these details. The user program sends a request to the operating system, which then does the required work.

- The operating system provides a simple, consistent, and uniform interface to all devices. The user does not have to know the make of the printer or of the disk drive.

- Devices are shared resources. The operating system allocates and protects them fairly.

This has always been one of the more difficult and unsatisfactory areas of operating systems programming, because I/O brings systems designers up against the real world. It is not possible to define interfaces to suit particular requirements—the designer has no choice but to use the interface provided by the hardware. It is very difficult to design nice, neat, structured programs in this area.

9.1 Design objectives

Before getting into the fine details, it is a good idea to take a broad look at the area, and lay out some of the objectives which should underlie the design of an input/output system.

Efficiency

Input/output is the classic bottleneck in computing, due to the enormous difference in speed between the CPU and memory on the one hand, and the devices attached to the computer, such as a keyboard or printer. So there is great scope here for improving efficiency.

As each piece of hardware is unique, there will be large variations in speed, from disks with transfer speeds of over 1MB per second, to keyboards with a maximum of 3 or 4 bytes per second. Also the unit of transfer may vary from many kilobytes at a time for disks or network devices, to one byte at a time from a keyboard.

The twin aims are to have the CPU idling, waiting for a device, as little as possible; and to a lesser extent to have all devices working as close to their maximum capacity as possible. Mechanisms, such as buffers and direct memory access, have been developed to help achieve these aims.

Device independence

Programs should be independent of particular devices. It should be possible to request a printer, or save a file, without knowing the make of the printer or disk drive. If a system upgrades to a new model of printer, or to a higher resolution monitor, programs should run as before.

A further aim is that the treatment of all devices, though they perform different functions, and have different physical interfaces, should be as uniform as possible. So sending output to a screen, a printer, or a disk drive should appear to a programmer as almost similar operations.

All of this is achieved by presenting the user with an interface which is as independent as possible of particular devices. As with memory management, we envisage a virtual device. The operating system then maps from this virtual device, onto the real one.

Character code independence

Devices may code characters in various ways, for example in EBCDIC, ASCII, Kanji, etc. A programmer should not have to worry about this. The operating system designer hides these differences, by deciding upon one particular code for all internal character representation. This is the 'internal character code'.

If a particular peripheral device does not use this code, the operating system performs translation to and from the internal character code. This is usually done by means of a lookup table, though sometimes it could be a translation algorithm.

Sharing and protection

Many devices are shared resources. The operating system must be involved, to allocate them fairly. All devices, whether shared or not, need to be protected against misuse.

Error handling

While errors can occur in all parts of a computer system, they are particularly common in the area of input and output. There are two aspects to handling errors: detection and correction (or recovery).

Detection

This is achieved by the use of redundant information, such as parity bits or checksums. Some devices are typed by their nature as either input or output devices, and attempts to read from an output device or write to an input device will be illegal. If an error can be detected as soon as possible, before it spreads and causes other errors, then there is a better chance of identifying the fault that caused it. The whole topic of faults and errors will be dealt with in greater detail in Chapter 17.

Correction

Sometimes an operating system is able to correct the error. For example, just retrying an operation may be sufficient to recover from some transient errors. Other times there may be sufficient redundant information available that the system can determine the correct value. Only when it cannot recover from an error does it report it to the process which requested the operation.

9.2   Uniform treatment of devices and files

As far as a user is concerned, all sources of input and output in a Unix system are represented as files. Terminals, disk drives, the more conventional data files, directories, and communications mechanisms such as pipes or sockets, all look alike to the system programmer, and are all treated in the same way. Each of these is accessed through the same set of system calls. Applications can be written without worrying about whether I/O is to a device or to a regular file. This fulfils the requirement set out in Section 9.1.

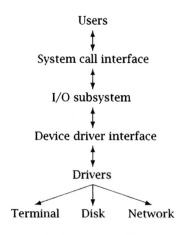

Figure 9.1: Overview of I/O processing

Figure 9.1 gives an overview of how I/O is dealt with in a computer system. User applications communicate with the outside world through the kernel I/O

subsystem, using the system call interface. They need not know whether they are communicating with a device or with a regular file. A program that writes data to a file should be able to write the same data to a terminal or network, without modification. The operating system provides a consistent high level view to user processes.

In the kernel, the I/O subsystem is responsible for all device-independent processing. This subsystem does not know about the characteristics of individual devices. It views devices as high-level abstractions, as virtual devices. It takes care of device naming and access control.

The I/O subsystem interacts with the device specific layer, the drivers, through a standard interface. A device appears as a black box, that supports a standard set of operations. Each device may implement these differently, but this is no concern of the I/O subsystem.

Device drivers are responsible for all direct interaction with devices. A driver consists of data structures and procedures, and it alone knows about the hardware characteristics of a device, such as the number of heads on a disk drive.

In the remainder of this chapter, we will look at generic I/O processing, down to the device driver interface. It must be stressed that throughout this chapter 'file' is used in the generic Unix sense of a source of input or destination of output. Three subsequent chapters will look at device specific processing in the lower layers.

9.3   Directory name space

The unification of devices and files begins at the level of names. In many systems, a filename and a device name are very different things. Filenames are kept in file directories; device names are maintained in separate listings. Unix makes no distinction between the names of devices and the names of files. Both are kept in the directory structure.

Unifying the file and device namespaces has many advantages. Users are presented with a consistent view of the system. They can use their own descriptive names to refer to devices. The access control and protection mechanisms developed for the file system extend seamlessly to cover devices as well.

To enable users to organise and keep track of all files, a logical directory structure is imposed on the file name space. A directory entry contains the properties of each file, such as name, type, owner, access control information, length, date and time of last change, and information about the physical location of the file or device. It must be stressed that directories only contain information about files, particularly their names—directories do not contain the files themselves.

Such directories can be organised in various ways. The functionality provided by different directory systems is proportional to their complexity.

Single level directory

This is the simplest possible organisation. All of the filenames are contained in the one directory. It would generally be implemented as a table, so there is a limit to the number of entries it can contain.

Two level directory

With such a system, each user has a private directory, which contains only files. There is also a master directory, which points to these. When users refer to a particular filename, only their own directory is searched. This effectively isolates one user from another. Such an arrangement has good and bad effects. It helps protection, but it does not allow sharing.

One user can be allowed to reference a file in another directory by using a pathname, which is made up of the user name and the filename. For example, [usera]test or usera/test.

Many systems allow a user to declare a search path. This specifies which directories will be searched for a file, and in what order. Unix has such a feature, the path command.

Tree-structured directory

This is a natural generalisation of the two level directory, and is illustrated in Figure 9.2.

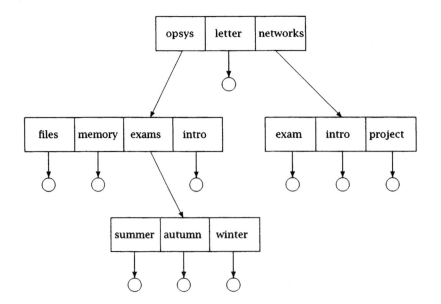

Figure 9.2: A tree-structured directory

The rigid distinction between master directories and user directories is broken down. In this system, a directory (or subdirectory) contains filenames and/or subdirectories.

There is also a notion of a current or default directory. Users think of themselves as being 'in' a particular directory. It is better to think of it as shorthand—the system puts the default directory name before all filenames passed to it. The library function getcwd() returns the current working directory; while the chdir() or fchdir() system services change it. The fs field in the task_struct of a process points to this information.

The introduction of a default directory leads to a distinction between absolute and relative pathnames. An absolute pathname always begins at the root of the directory tree, and names all of the directories in turn, down to the file being specified. With reference to Figure 9.2, an example would be /opsys/exams/autumn. It is quite unambiguous.

A relative pathname always begins implicitly from the current working directory. For example, again with reference to Figure 9.2, if the current working directory is /opsys, then a reference to the file intro refers to a file in that directory. On the other hand, if the current working directory is /networks, then the same reference to intro refers to a different file. Relative pathnames save on typing, but they can lead to confusion.

Most systems treat directories as variable length files, each record being a directory entry. All directories have the same internal format. In Unix, little information about a file is kept in the directory itself, only the name and a pointer to a data structure called an index node, or inode, where the permanent information about the file is stored. One field in this inode defines the entry as either a subdirectory, a regular file, or a device name.

In Linux, directory entry structures are of variable length, to allow for the efficient storage of long filenames. Each contains the number of its inode, the length of the name contained in the entry, and the total length of the entry. These are followed by the name padded to a 4 byte boundary with null bytes.

```
struct dirent{
      long int              d_ino;    /* file number of this entry */
      unsigned short int d_namlen; /* length of string in d_name */
      unsigned short int d_reclen; /* length of this record      */
      char                  d_name[]; /* actual filename            */
};
```

Figure 9.3: Structure of a directory entry

Figure 9.3 shows the structure of a file system independent directory entry, taken from <direntry.h>. Of course, while Linux can handle long filenames internally, the maximum length of a name is limited by the capabilities of the underlying file system on the disk.

The mkdir() function creates a new, empty directory; rmdir() removes a directory, but only if it is empty.

A user with the requisite permissions can read a directory file. POSIX provides file system independent routines, opendir(), readdir(), and closedir(). There is no function to write to a directory file; only the kernel can do this.

All devices are listed in the /dev directory, and have corresponding inodes of their own in the system. Directory entries for devices are created by the mknod() function, which sets a flag in the inode to indicate that this is a device file.

Acyclic graph directory

A tree structure implies that any node has only one parent. We can relax that to an acyclic graph structure, where a node may have more than one parent; the acyclic restriction means that backward pointing links are not allowed.

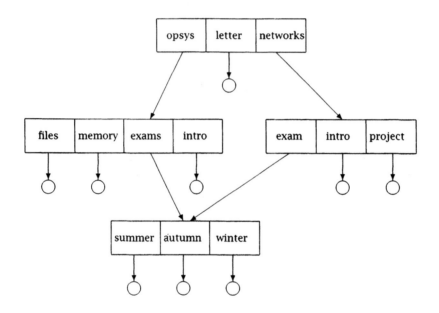

Figure 9.4: A directory with links

Such a directory structure, as shown in Figure 9.4, allows directories or files to be shared. We are not talking here about two copies of a single file. Rather we have separate entries in two different directories, each pointing to the same file. This can be useful, for example, to two programmers working on the same project. All of the project work can be in one directory, which is a subdirectory of both of their home directories.

Such sharing can be implemented in two ways.

Hard links

All of the necessary information can be duplicated in both of the directories. But this introduces a major problem in maintaining consistency. In Unix, this

problem is overcome by having two (or more) directory entries pointing to the same inode. Figure 9.5 illustrates this.

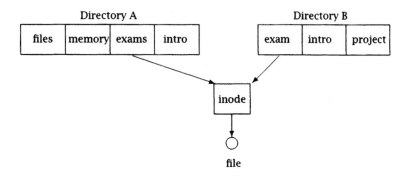

Figure 9.5: How a hard link is implemented

The link() system call creates an additional directory entry for an existing file, and increments the link count in the inode, atomically. There is no way to tell which is the original link. Note that its name is not an attribute of a file, it can have a different name in each of the directories.

Symbolic links

Alternatively, one directory (the owner) may have all of the information, while the other has a special entry called a symbolic link, which is just an ordinary file containing a complete pathname to the entry in the owner directory. See Figure 9.6.

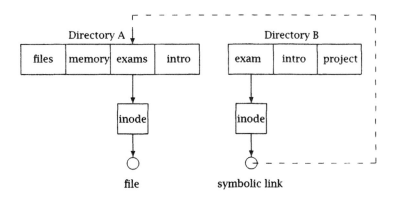

Figure 9.6: How a symbolic link is implemented

If this pathname is short enough, it may fit entirely in the inode. The system call symlink() is used to create such a symbolic link.

When traversing the entire file structure, e.g. when backing up, you do not want to traverse shared structures more than once. Symbolic links solve this problem, as only the owner entry is followed, links are ignored.

Normally, all reads and writes are redirected through the symbolic link to the target file. To open the link file itself, readlink() combines an open, read, and close.

One problem with symbolic links is that there is no way of knowing whether a file has a symbolic link pointing to it or not. So the original file could be deleted, leaving a dangling pointer to it in a symbolic link. Next time the file is referenced through the symbolic link, the file system will return a file not found error.

General graph directory

If backward pointing links are allowed in an existing tree structured directory, then it is possible to get cycles in the structure, as illustrated in Figure 9.7.

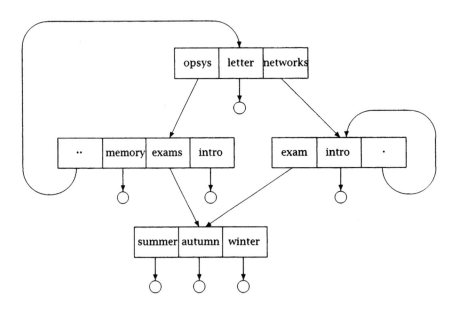

Figure 9.7: A directory structure with cycles

It is a common practice to include two default entries in each directory, one pointing to itself, '.' (dot), and the other pointing to its parent '..' (dot dot). It is best to avoid any other backward pointing links, if possible. Searching software can recognise the dot and dot dot links, but any other backward pointing links could result in infinite searching loops. Also, deletion becomes a nightmare. So only the superuser is allowed to create such links.

Removing entries from a directory

Unix has an unlink() function. This always removes a directory entry, but when can the inode and the space allocated to a shared file be deallocated? They certainly cannot be deallocated whenever anyone unlinks the file. Other users would be left with 'dangling' pointers to a non-existent file.

One possibility is to keep a reference count of the number of users in the inode. When an individual user unlinks the file, this link count is decremented. When the reference count goes to 0, then the inode and the data are actually deallocated.

If the pathname passed to unlink() is a symbolic link, then the link is removed, not the file it points to.

9.4 Inodes

Now that we have looked at how sources of input and output are identified and recorded, we can go on to consider the processing involved in using them.

Once a file has been opened, it can remain open indefinitely. The operating system must remind itself that this file is open, and store some information about it. So it needs to allocate a data structure to hold this information.

In practice this becomes a network of several data structures, as we shall see. In Unix the basic structure representing an open file is the struct inode. One of these is associated with each active executable file, each current directory, each open data file, each device, each network connection.

In the previous section we used the word inode to refer to a permanent data structure on disk; here we are using it to refer to a data structure in memory, which only exists as long as the file is opened. While there is room for confusion here, the context usually makes it clear which one is in question. Also the disk version is typically referred to as the 'disk inode'.

The most relevant fields of struct inode, declared in <linux/fs.h>, are given in Figure 9.8. As this is the most important data structure in the whole I/O subsystem, we will discuss it in some detail. We can break it down into five main areas:

- First there is information about this inode, the links which maintain it on structures of similar inodes, and enable it to be found quickly.

- Next there is information about the file, copied in from the inode which the file system maintains on disk.

- Then there are pointers to operations specific to this particular file system type, for example to maintain the entries in the directory structure.

- There is further information about the open stream, which is not duplicated from the on disk inode. This information is generic to streams of all types.

- Finally there is a section for extra information which is specific to one type of stream or another.

```
struct inode{
      struct list_head        i_hash;    /* link on hash list      */
      struct list_head        i_list;    /* link on inode list     */
      unsigned long           i_ino;     /* inode number           */
      unsigned short          i_count;   /* count of users         */
      kdev_t                  i_dev;     /* device number          */
      umode_t                 i_mode;    /* type and permissions   */
      nlink_t                 i_nlink;   /* hard links             */
      uid_t                   i_uid;     /* owner                  */
      gid_t                   i_gid;     /* owner's group          */
      kdev_t                  i_rdev;    /* if a device file       */
      off_t                   i_size;    /* in bytes               */
      time_t                  i_atime;   /* access                 */
      time_t                  i_mtime;   /* change of contents     */
      time_t                  i_ctime;   /* inode modified         */
      unsigned long           i_blksize; /* size of block          */
      unsigned long           i_blocks;  /* number of blocks       */
      struct semaphore        i_sem;     /* mutex on inode         */
      struct inode_operations *i_op;     /* operations vector      */
      struct super_block      *i_sb;     /* if a mount point       */
      struct wait_queue       *i_wait;   /* wait queue             */
      struct file_lock        *i_flock;  /* locks on this file     */
      struct vm_area_struct   *i_mmap;   /* memory region          */
      struct page             *i_pages;  /* pages in memory        */
      union{
            struct pipe_inode_info   pipe_i;
            struct ext2_inode_info   ext2_i;
            struct msdos_inode_info  msdos_i;
            struct nfs_inode_info    nfs_i;
            struct socket            socket_i;
      }u;
};
```

Figure 9.8: Inode for an open file

Inode identifiers

The first part of the inode contains housekeeping information about the inode itself, irrespective of which file it represents.

- The system frequently has to search its list of inodes, to find a particular one. To facilitate this, inodes are maintained on a hash structure, hashed on the combination of device and inode number. Each element in the hash

table heads a list of inodes, linked through the i_hash field. In Figure 9.9, this is denoted by the dashed line.

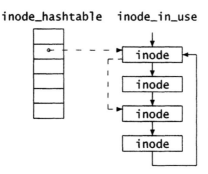

Figure 9.9: Inodes on LRU and hash lists

The struct list_head is a generalised mechanism for linking together lists of any sort of data structures, and we will meet it in other places in the kernel.

It is defined in <linux/list.h> as struct list_head *next, *prev. There are also macros defined in that file for inserting and removing items from lists.

So when searching for an inode by number, that number is hashed into this inode_hashtable, and the corresponding chain of inodes is searched linearly. If there is no inode with that number on the list already, then if appropriate a new one is allocated, and linked in. If there is one there already, the existing structures can be accessed.

- As can be seen in Figure 9.9, active inodes are also maintained on a (circular) linked list, headed from inode_in_use. The link field for this is i_list.

  When an inode is no longer referenced, i.e. when the file it represents is closed, it is moved to another list, headed by inode_unused, but still linked through i_list.

- The i_ino field uniquely identifies this inode within the file system to which it belongs. It is known as the file serial number, or inode number.

- i_count is a reference count of the number of processes holding this file open. It is incremented each time the file is opened, and decremented by close(). When zero, the inode can be released, and moved to the inode_unused list.

Information about the file

The next part of the inode contains information which is copied in from the on disk inode representing this file.

- The `i_dev` field holds the number of the device on which this inode is permanently stored, i.e. the disk which contains a directory entry for this file. This, along with the inode number in the `i_ino` field, uniquely identify the file within the whole system.

- `i_mode` is a very overloaded field. The meaning of each bit in the mode field is given in Figure 9.10, from `<linux/stat.h>`.

```
#define S_IFSOCK 0140000 /* socket                               */
#define S_IFLNK  0120000 /* symbolic link                        */
#define S_IFREG  0100000 /* regular                              */
#define S_IFBLK  0060000 /* block special                        */
#define S_IFDIR  0040000 /* directory                            */
#define S_IFCHR  0020000 /* character special                    */
#define S_IFIFO  0010000 /* fifo                                 */
#define S_ISUID  0004000 /* set user id on execution             */
#define S_ISGID  0002000 /* set group id on execution            */
#define S_IRUSR  0000400 /* read permission: owner               */
#define S_IWUSR  0000200 /* write permission: owner              */
#define S_IXUSR  0000100 /* execute/search permission: owner     */
#define S_IRGRP  0000040 /* read permission: group               */
#define S_IWGRP  0000020 /* write permission: group              */
#define S_IXGRP  0000010 /* execute/search permission: group     */
#define S_IROTH  0000004 /* read permission: other               */
#define S_IWOTH  0000002 /* write permission: other              */
#define S_IXOTH  0000001 /* execute/search permission: other     */
```

Figure 9.10: Mode bit values

The high order six bits identify the type of the file. This can be a regular file, a directory, a block device, a character device, a symbolic link, a socket, or a named pipe. There are seven macros S_ISREG(), S_ISDIR(), S_ISBLK(), S_ISCHR(), S_ISLNK(), S_ISSOCK(), and S_ISFIFO() for testing these bits, defined in `<linux/stat.h>`.

The `setuid` and `setgid` bits are also in `i_mode`; in the case of an executable file these allow the program contained in the file to run with access rights and privileges different from those of the process running it. These bits can be tested against the masks S_ISUID and S_ISGID. Note that these are not macros.

Access permissions are encoded in the low order nine bits of `i_mode`. The `chmod()` system service changes file access permissions for an existing file. To use it, the id of the calling process must be either that of the owner, or the superuser.

Each process has a file mode creation mask. Any bits that are set in this mask are turned off in the `i_mode` field of a newly created file. The `umask()` function is used to set this mask, and returns the previous value.

- `i_nlink` is the number of hard links pointing to this file on disk.

- i_uid and i_gid contain the id number of the owner of the file, and the group the owner is associated with. The access() system service tests these using the id of the current process. It can test for read, write, execute permissions, or just for the existence of the file.

  chown() and lchown() change the owner or group ids of files. Only the superuser can change the owner; the owner can change the group.

- i_rdev is only meaningful for device files; it contains the id number of the device.

- i_size is only meaningful for regular files, directories, and symbolic links; it gives the size of the file in bytes.

- i_atime is the time of the last access to the file; ls -lu returns this time.

- i_mtime is the time the data in the file was last modified; ls -l defaults to this time.

- i_ctime is the time the information in the inode was last changed; ls -lc gives this time.

  The system services utime() and utimes() change atime and mtime; ctime is changed automatically.

  In all cases, time is of type time_t, which is a count of seconds since 1/1/1970.

- i_blksize gives the block size used when storing the file on disk. This is really a property of the file system, rather than the file.

- i_blocks is the number of disk blocks allocated to this file; it is not necessarily the same as the size of the file, as the last block is rarely full.

- i_sem is a kernel semaphore which provides for mutual exclusion on the inode. This is necessary as more than one process may have the same file open at the same time.

There are three system services which can be used to read information from this part of an inode. The first is stat(), which works on a filename. If the filename is a symbolic link, then stat() returns information about the file. If information about the link itself is required, there is an lstat() function, which also uses a filename. The fstat() function is similar to stat(), but it requires the file to be open. All three are passed a pointer to a struct stat, from <asm/stat.h>, which is equivalent to the first 13 fields of inode. They copy the information into the struct stat from the inode.

Inode operations

Even regular files are not all the same. Over the years, different ways have been developed of organising information on disk drives, each suited to a particular purpose. One of the objectives of the I/O manager is to present a consistent interface to all of these file systems. Linux has a virtual file system interface for system programmers, which the kernel then maps on to the relevant file

system on disk. So there may be a number of different physical file systems in use at any time; the programmer does not see any of these directly, but only the virtual file system.

The i_op field in the inode points to an array of pointers to functions, which are specific to the particular file system to which this file belongs. The interface defines a set of abstract operations on each inode, and each file system type supplies an instance of the struct inode_operations. Each element in this points to its own specific implementation of that function.

Most of these extra operations are specific to file systems, and have to do with maintaining the entries in the directory structure. Because of the Unix design feature that all I/O streams, whether regular files, devices, or communication channels, have entries in the directory structure, this extra level of functionality is relevant to all of them, and not just to regular files.

Some elements of the inode_operations structure, from <linux/fs.h>, are given in Figure 9.11.

```
struct inode_operations{
        struct file_operations *default_file_ops;
        int                     (*create) ();
        struct dentry           (*lookup) ();
        int                     (*link) ();
        int                     (*unlink) ();
        int                     (*symlink) ();
        int                     (*mkdir) ();
        int                     (*rmdir) ();
        int                     (*mknod) ();
        int                     (*rename) ();
        int                     (*readlink) ();
        struct dentry           (*followlink) ();
        int                     (*readpage) ();
        int                     (*writepage) ();
        int                     (*bmap) ();
};
```

Figure 9.11: Some functions of the inode interface

- default_file_ops contains a pointer to the default file_operations structure for a file of this type. This will be taken up again in Section 9.5.

- create() is called by the open() system service, when the file does not already exist. It creates a new entry in a directory.

- lookup() translates a name to an inode.

- link() sets up a hard link in the directory structure.

- unlink() decrements the link count in the inode, and if it is zero, also deletes the directory entry.

- symlink() creates a symbolic link file.

- mkdir() creates a new directory file.

- rmdir() removes a directory file.

- mknod() creates a directory entry for a special file, either a device file, or a named pipe.

- rename() changes the name part of a directory entry.

- readlink() reads a symbolic link file, and returns a pathname.

- followlink() translates a symbolic link name to the inode of the target file.

- readpage() copies data from the disk to a specific page in memory.

- writepage() copies data from a page in memory to the appropriate location on disk.

- bmap() is a function which translates a logical block number in a file into a physical block number on a disk.

We will look at implementations of these functions, for the Ext2 file system, in Chapter 10.

Information about the open stream

The next group of fields are not part of the information maintained in the on disk inode. They are only relevant while the file is actually open.

- i_sb is normally NULL. The only time it is used is when a directory file has another file system mounted on top of it (see Section 10.5). In that case i_sb points to a data structure representing the new file system.

- Processes waiting for this particular stream to become ready for I/O sleep on i_wait.

- i_flock heads a linked list of data structures representing locks actually held, or requested, on this file (see Section 9.9).

- We have seen that a program's code and data are paged in and out from the executable on disk. A file mapped into the user's address space by mmap() is also paged in and out to the disk. In Linux, standard file system access to disk files is also implemented internally by mmap(). In all cases the i_mmap field points to the appropriate place in the memory management data structures, namely the vm_area_struct representing the region into which this file is mapped.

- i_pages heads a linked list of struct page. Each entry in this list represents a page of this file which is actually in memory.

Special streams

The union u contains a further data structure, for different kinds of I/O streams. Some possible examples have been included here.

- `pipe_inode_info`, if the stream is used for interprocess communication. This will be examined in Chapter 12.

- `ext2_inode_info`, if the stream represents a file in the second extended file system. This will be examined in Chapter 10.

- `msdos_inode_info`, if the stream represents a file in the MSDOS file system. This will not be considered further.

- `nfs_inode_info`, if the stream represents a file in the network file system. This will be examined in more detail in Chapter 16.

- `socket`, if the stream is used for interprocess communication. This will be examined in more detail in Chapter 12, for processes on the same machine; and in Chapter 14, for network communication.

9.5 Opening files

Before any source of I/O can be accessed, it must be opened. This operation need not necessarily be part of a source language. But it must be part of an operating system, which provides a system call such as `open(pathname, flags)`. The flags field would specify the type of access, e.g. read or write. Unix has a third parameter, which is only used for a new file. This specifies the permissions to be associated with the file. Unix also has a `creat()` function. This creates a new file, and opens it for writing only.

The essence of `open()` is to connect a user's program with its data. An overview of the operations required is as follows.

1. Lookup the directory entry for the file.

2. If the file does not exist, create it (if the correct flags are specified).

3. Check the privileges of the user against the protection on the file.

4. Check if the file is already open. If it is, then depending on the system it may just refuse access, or may refuse access if it is already open for writing, or may only refuse write access if it is open for reading.

5. Create the appropriate data structures to represent this open file, and link them into existing structures representing the process. The sort of information which the system maintains about an open file would include:

   - access mode, is it open for reading and/or writing;
   - reference count, how many processes have it open;
   - location of the file on disk;

- offset into the file, if a sequential file.

6. Provide the caller with some sort of handle to use for further operations on the file.

We will now look at how all of this is done in Linux.

Name translation

The name translation mechanism takes a pathname as input, and indicates whether it is valid or not. This is a recursive process, working through each component of the pathname in turn. At any stage, it can return with a 'no such file or directory' error.

As it is heavily dependent on a knowledge of the internal structure of directories on disk, each different type of file system must provide a function, called lookup(), to do this. We will see this function when we consider the Linux file system in the next chapter.

Because name translation involves searching each directory in the pathname, it is time consuming. So the system maintains a cache of recent lookups of directory entries. This is consulted when resolving a filename.

Each entry in this cache is a struct dentry, as shown in Figure 9.12, from <linux/dcache.h>.

```
struct dentry{
        struct inode    *d_inode;
        struct list_head d_hash;
        struct list_head d_lru;
        unsigned char    d_iname[];
};
```

Figure 9.12: An element in the cache of recent lookups

- d_inode points to the inode corresponding to this entry.

- The cache is maintained as a hash table, dentry_hashtable, declared in fs/dcache.c. The name is hashed to find an entry in this table. The corresponding list of struct dentry, linked through the d_hash field, is then searched linearly, to check if any of the entries corresponds to the name being searched for.

- As well as this, all entries in the cache are on a linked list, threaded through the d_lru field in each entry. This list is maintained in LRU order, so the oldest entry is always the first to be replaced. Each time there is a hit in the cache, that entry is moved to the end of the list. When there is a miss, the first entry in the list is re-used, and moved to the end.

- The name of the file this entry represents is in the d_iname[] field.

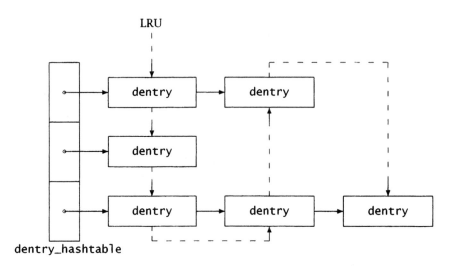

Figure 9.13: Directory name lookup cache

An overview of the name cache system is shown in Figure 9.13.

If the name being sought is not found in the name cache, then the search has to go to disk. Assuming that the file does exist, then eventually the search will encounter the directory entry corresponding to this file. This will contain the inode number of the file, and that inode is read from disk into memory. The name cache is also updated at this point.

In either case, the result of the name translation phase is a pointer to an entry in the name cache, a struct dentry.

Access and security

The question of security only arises when sharing is allowed. The owner of a file must specify which users have access to it, and what kind of access they have.

There is a whole range of possible accesses which a user may have to a file: no access, execute, read, append, update, change protection, delete. These could be arranged in a hierarchy, so that higher permissions imply all lower ones. If this were felt to be too loose, each possible access permission would have to be acquired individually.

To overcome the complexity inherent in controlling access for many different users, it is common practice to group users into classes, such as owner, group, others. Different protection can then be given for the different classes. But it may be difficult to decide who are in group, and who are others. Also there is a problem with overlapping groups.

Typically protection information is recorded as a bitmap. For example, three classes of user, each with three possible types of access, can be coded in 9 bits, as in Figure 9.14.

Protection can be associated with the directory entry, or with the file itself.

Owner   Group   Other

r	w	e	r	w	e	r	w	e

Figure 9.14: A protection bitmap

In the former case, different sharers of a file can have different access. In the latter case, all sharers will have the same access. This is the situation in Unix, where protection information is maintained in the inode on disk.

The rights of a process have to be compared with the protection attributes of the file. In Linux, user credentials, such as the user-id or group-id, are stored in the uid and gid fields of the struct task_struct. Information about the user id and group id of the owner of the file comes from the i_uid and i_gid fields of the file's inode.

If the uid of the current process is the same as that of the file, then the open() system service checks the access requested against the permissions for the owner. All of this information is in the i_mode field of the inode.

If the uid fields do not match, then it can check if the gid field of the current process is the same as that of the file. If it is, it checks the access requested against the permissions for the group in the i_mode field of the inode.

If the process opening the file is neither the owner, nor in the owner's group, then it checks the requested access against the 'other' permissions in the i_mode field.

File descriptors

The connection between the logical stream being opened in a program, and the physical device, is recorded in a stream descriptor list, or a file descriptor table as it is known in Unix. Each process has one of these. One entry in this table is allocated each time a file is opened. The entry is removed from the list when that stream is closed. The descriptor is identified to the calling process by an integer, which is actually an index into the descriptor table. As each process has its own table of file descriptors, the same numbers are reused in different processes. For future operations on the file, the kernel uses the number of the descriptor to index into the descriptor table, and hence locate the data structures associated with the open file.

Such a descriptor might represent a regular file, a device, or a network connection. But the file descriptor mechanism, and a common set of I/O procedures which operate on such descriptors, hide the distinctions between files and devices.

When a new process is created in Linux, it is given a static, fixed size file descriptor table. This can be extended later, if required. The files field in the task_struct points to this table. See Figure 9.15, taken from <sched.h>.

- The count field contains the number of streams open at any given time.

```
struct files_struct{
        atomic_t        count;
        fd_set          close_on_exec;
        fd_set          open_fds;
        struct file *fd_array[];
};
```

Figure 9.15: Definition of file descriptor table

- The fd_set type is a bitmap, with one bit for each possible open file: the close_on_exec field determines whether descriptors remain open after a call to exec().

  - The default is open; that is, the new program gets a copy of the table.
  - If this is not desired, then the close_on_exec field can be set for that file. The fcntl() system service is used for this; with F_GETFD it will get the value of the close_on_exec flag; with F_SETFD it will set or clear it.

- The open_fds field keeps track of which entries in the fd[] table are valid. If a bit is set in this field, then the corresponding entry in fd[] represents an open file; otherwise it is an unused entry.

- The descriptor table itself is essentially an array of pointers to struct file, see the following section.

Two system services which work on file descriptors are dup() and dup2(). These duplicate existing file descriptors, with the difference that dup2() allows the number of the new descriptor to be specified. It will first of all close that new descriptor, if it is currently open. This system service is of use in situations where a program expects a particular file to be associated with some specific file descriptor.

Three default streams are usually opened for each process: standard input (0), standard output (1), and standard error (2). Descriptor 0 is connected to the keyboard; descriptors 1 and 2 are connected to the screen. In POSIX these are defined as STDIN_FILENO, STDOUT_FILENO, and STDERR_FILENO.

All system error messages, such as those output by perror(), are sent to standard error, stream 2. While this is connected to the screen by default, it can be changed (using dup2()), so that error messages go to a printer, or to a log file on disk.

After a fork(), the child gets a copy of this file descriptor table, which it can then manipulate independently of the parent's copy. But if required a process can share this file descriptor table with its parent, by using the parameter CLONE_FILES with the clone() system service.

System open file list

As seen in the previous section, a file descriptor is essentially a pointer to a `struct file`. The actual information about the open stream, such as open mode flags and current position, is contained there. The system maintains a linked list of these structures, known as the system open file list.

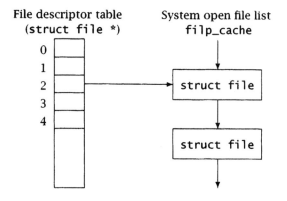

Figure 9.16: Descriptor and open file data structure

Figure 9.16 illustrates the connection between the descriptor table and the open file list. The `file` data structure is declared in `<linux/fs.h>`. A cut down version is shown in Figure 9.17.

```
struct file{
    struct file             *f_next;   /* next struct file           */
    struct dentry           *f_dentry; /* representing this stream   */
    struct file_operations  *f_op;     /* operations on this stream  */
    mode_t                  f_mode;    /* open mode (read/write)     */
    loff_t                  f_pos;     /* current position in file   */
    unsigned short          f_count;   /* number of threads sharing  */
    int                     f_owner;   /* where SIGIO should be sent */
};
```

Figure 9.17: Structure representing an open stream

- All of the `file` structures in a system are kept on a linked list, headed from `filp_cache`, declared in `fs/file_table.c`, and linked through `f_next`.

- The `f_dentry` field points to the entry corresponding to this file in the name cache, and so to the `inode`, which we have already seen in the previous section.

The `struct file` contains a certain minimum of information about an open stream. This is specific to the particular process which has opened that stream. But there is much information about an open stream which is process independent. Hence the need for the `inode`.

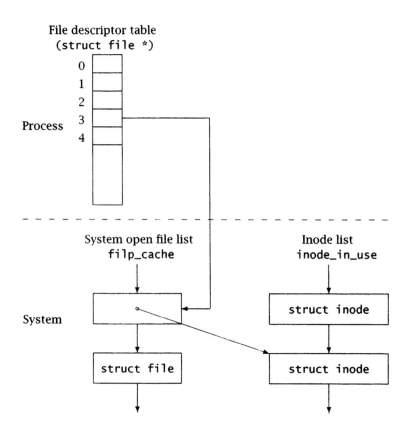

Figure 9.18: File opened by one user

Figure 9.18 shows the relationship between the file descriptor table, the `struct file`, and the `inode`.

- The `f_op` field points to an array of pointers to functions which implement operations on this particular stream, for example for reading and writing. This field is analogous to the `i_op` field in the `inode`. But these functions are relevant not only for regular files, but also for devices and for network communication. See Figure 9.19, from `<linux/fs.h>`.

  When a stream is opened, the kernel arranges that these point to functions specific to this particular stream. For example, if the stream is a device, then the entries will point to functions within the driver for this device. If the stream is a regular file, then the entries will point to functions in the file system code.

```
struct file_operations{
        loff_t          (*llseek) ();
        ssize_t         (*read) ();
        ssize_t         (*write) ();
        int             (*readdir) ();
        unsigned int    (*poll) ();
        int             (*ioctl) ();
        int             (*mmap) ();
        int             (*open) ();
        void            (*release)();
};
```

Figure 9.19: Operations on open files

- llseek() updates the value of f_pos (to be seen shortly).

- read() copies the specified number of bytes from the file into user space.

- write() copies the specified number of bytes from user space to the file.

- readdir() is only defined for directory files. It returns the next entry in the directory.

- poll() is really only relevant to physical devices and network connections. It checks whether an I/O operation would block. See Section 9.8.

- ioctl() is a general purpose function, to deal with operations not handled by any of the others.

- mmap() maps a file, or part of it, into the address space of the caller. We have seen the corresponding system service in Section 8.8.

- open() is called by the open() I/O procedure, to carry out processing specific to this particular stream.

- release() implements the close() system service.

- The f_mode field indicates whether the stream is open for reading, or writing, or both. This is determined by the second parameter to the open() system service.

- The f_pos field is an offset into the file, and indicates where the next read or write will take place.

  The lseek() system service adjusts this current file offset. It is implemented internally by the llseek() function. As it always returns the current offset, it is possible to seek 0 bytes, to get the current offset, or to check if it is possible to seek on a particular stream. No I/O takes place—it only reads or writes the struct file in memory. By seeking beyond the

end of a file, it is possible to create a hole in a file. Such bytes are not written to disk, and are read back as 0.

- As we shall see, a `struct file` can be pointed to from more than one file descriptor. So the reference count, `f_count`, is used to prevent the structure from being deallocated by one routine in the kernel, while another is still using it.

- In some circumstances (see Section 9.8) it is necessary to send a signal to a process waiting on a stream. The id number of the process to which the signal is to be sent is kept in `f_owner`.

Summary

The whole procedure of opening a file is summarised in the algorithm given in Figure 9.20.

```
Set up file descriptor, link to struct file
Search the directory name cache
IF not found THEN
      lookup() (from directory i_op)
      IF not found THEN
            errno = EFAULT
            Return (-1)
      ENDIF
      Create appropriate entry in name cache
      Create inode in memory
      Link dentry to inode
ENDIF
Set up f_op field in struct file
open() (from f_op)
IF no permission THEN
      errno = EACCES
      Return (-1)
ENDIF
Link struct file to dentry
Increment i_count
Return (file descriptor)
```

Figure 9.20: Algorithm for open

Detailed descriptions of all of the steps in this algorithm have been given throughout this section.

9.6   File sharing

File sharing is possible on two levels. Entries in the file descriptor tables of two processes may point to the same `struct file`. This situation is the result of a `fork()`. They share the same value for the current offset.

Another possibility is that two file descriptors, in the same or different processes, each points to its own `struct file`. This is a result of two independent processes performing an `open()` on the same file. Because each process has its own `struct file`, each can have its own different offset within the file. Figure 9.21 illustrates this situation.

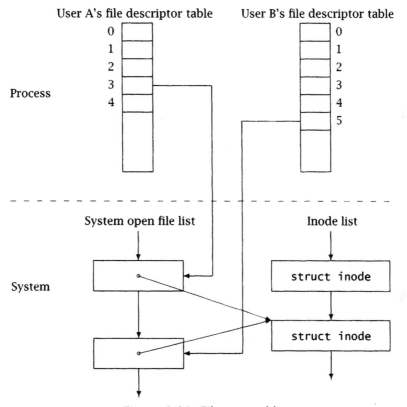

Figure 9.21: File opened by two users

All of the process specific information about an open file is maintained in the `struct file`. Inconsistencies that could result from having the one file represented by two or more data structures are avoided by maintaining generic information about the file in a separate structure, the `inode`.

In Unix, system calls refer to files by giving a position in the file descriptor table. When two users share a file, they both have their own file descriptor table. So one may refer to it as user fileid 3, while another refers to it as user fileid 5. They both have separate entries in the open file list, in which process specific information is held. But there is only one entry in the inode list, and only one file.

Unix guarantees that any individual read() or write() on a shared file will be atomic. It does this by locking the inode for the duration of the read or write, using the i_sem semaphore in the inode. So a reader of a shared file will always see the result of the most recent write().

9.7 File input and output

Opening a file is not an end in itself. It is done so that the file may then be used for input or for output. The I/O procedures are the facilities provided by the operating system to application programs, a subset of the system calls. They are the externally visible interface to the input/output manager, called by the user process. They sit between the user and the kernel, checking and translating.

I/O procedures

The following is an overview of what an I/O procedure has to do:

1. Map the stream or file descriptor number supplied to it onto a file, or physical device. It does this by checking the file descriptor table of the calling process. If this file descriptor number has not been assigned, it returns an error.

2. Compare the parameters supplied by the user with those required or permissible for the stream. Is this operation legitimate for this stream? For example, a read operation on a printer is normally considered illegal. If the operation is not legal, return an error.

3. Identify the appropriate function for that stream, and pass the request on to it.

4. When the data transfer has completed, notify the user process. In addition, for a read, pass the requested data back to the user process.

Different operating system designers have taken different approaches at this point. At one end of the scale, it is possible to have a generalised I/O procedure of the form: QIO(fileid, mode, address, length, errno). The meaning of the parameters is as follows.

- fileid: the number of the stream or channel.
- mode: which operation to perform, e.g. open, read, write, close.
- address: the address of the buffer to be used for the transfer.
- length: the number of bytes to be transferred, if any.
- errno: the address of the location where the number identifying the error is to be written. This location is in the address space of the calling process, and is tested after the return.

```
Map fileid onto stream
IF not open, THEN
        errno = errornumber
        Return (-1)
ENDIF
Check mode and length against stream characteristics
IF not compatible THEN
        errno = errornumber
        Return (-1)
ENDIF
Call stream specific function with appropriate parameters
IF not successful THEN
        errno = errornumber
        Return (-1)
ENDIF
Return (0)
```

Figure 9.22: Generic I/O algorithm

An algorithm for such a generic procedure is given in Figure 9.22.

Some operating systems, such as OpenVMS, do things this way. It has a system service called sys$qio(), which has 12 parameters. But it can do anything in the Input/Output area. Other systems, such as OS/2, have different procedures for each class of device, and for every operation on each class. These have names beginning with Vio, Mou, Kbd, Dos, for example VioWrtCharStr(), to put a character string on the screen.

Input and output in Unix

Unix takes a middle of the road approach, with four main system services for I/O, open(), read(), write(), and close(), each with two or three parameters. Their functions are self evident. There are two other system services for what is sometimes called 'scatter/gather' I/O. The first, writev(), takes data from a number of different places in memory, and writes it to one place in a file; conversely readv() takes contiguous data from a file and reads it into a number of different places in memory.

high-level processing

I/O procedures are supplied with a file descriptor, which was returned by open(). They use this to index into the file descriptor table of the process. If the descriptor is valid, the corresponding entry will contain a pointer to a struct file; otherwise it contains a NULL pointer, and the request is invalid.

The I/O procedure then examines the struct file. The f_mode field specifies whether the stream is open for reading and/or for writing. The specific I/O procedure can determine whether its particular operation is valid on this stream, or not.

The most common I/O procedures, such as read() or write(), just have to call the appropriate function in the f_op field of the struct file. This has been set up when the file was opened. Whether a read, for example, is from a device, a regular file, or an interprocess communication pipe, is transparent to the I/O procedure.

Some I/O procedures, specifically those dealing with file names, and the directory structure, cannot be serviced by the simple functions in the f_op field. In this case, the procedure follows the f_dentry pointer to the struct inode, and on to the struct inode_operations.

All of these routines are invoked in response to specific user requests, and run in the context of the calling process. When any of these routines calls the driver for a physical device, data may not be available. This is most common with reads—a key may not have been pressed, or a message may not have arrived over a network. But it can also happen that a write cannot proceed— a printer may be out of paper, or there may be no disk in the drive. In all of these cases the calling process is put to sleep, inside the driver code. When the device is finally ready, the process is woken up, and the procedure completes.

The actual implementation of these functions, both in file_operations and in inode_operations, will be dealt with in subsequent chapters:

- Regular file systems will be the subject of Chapter 10.

- Physical devices will be dealt with in Chapter 11.

- Chapter 12 will deal with the use of the I/O subsystem for interprocess communication.

- Network communication is the subject of Chapter 14.

Summary

Figure 9.23 summarises the foregoing discussion in the form of an algorithm.

9.8 Synchronous and asynchronous I/O

There is always a delay with input or output. This can range from milliseconds for a disk drive, to seconds or even hours for a keyboard.

In theory, the calling process could continue with some other work during this time. But that would not be practicable, in most cases. With input, the data would not be valid. With output, the buffer could not be reused. So the process must wait for confirmation that the operation has completed successfully. This waiting can be done in different places in the code.

Blocking

One possibility, the one most commonly implemented, is for this to be within the operating system code, either in the I/O procedure, or in the driver itself.

```
Use stream number to index into the file descriptor table
IF not assigned, THEN
        errno = EBADF
        Return (-1)
ENDIF
Follow the pointer from descriptor to struct file
Examine f_mode
IF request not compatible with open mode THEN
        errno = EBADF
        Return (-1)
ENDIF
IF request is for simple I/O THEN
        Call appropriate function in f_op
ELSE
        Follow f_dentry pointer to struct inode
        Call appropriate function in i_op
ENDIF
IF not successful THEN
        errno = EIO
        Return (-1)
ELSE
Return (0)
ENDIF
```

Figure 9.23: Generic algorithm for Unix I/O procedure

The user process is put to sleep, but the user does not see this. It appears
as though I/O is as atomic an operation as an assignment statement. Such an
arrangement is known as synchronous or wait I/O.

This is the situation in a high-level language such as C. When a programmer writes a `printf()` or a `scanf()` statement, it is expected that when the
program goes on to execute the next instruction, the I/O will have completed. It
is also the default situation with system services such as `read()` and `write()`.

Non blocking

This default can be changed to non-blocking I/O, for example by calling open ()
with O_NONBLOCK. In this case, all I/O requests will return immediately, whether
they have actually been carried out or not. If a write is not able to proceed
immediately, or there is nothing to be read, the system call returns -1, with
errno set to EAGAIN. Such a situation is known as asynchronous or nowait I/O.

Signals

When a non-blocking stream returns -1, the programmer can try again later. This is effectively polling. But another option is to set a stream up in such a way that it will post a signal to the process when I/O is possible. Then a signal handler is registered, to read or write the data. This has the advantage that the process can be doing some other work while it is waiting; at the same time the data is processed just as soon as it is available.

Linux, following BSD, uses fcntl() with F_SETOWN to specify which process is to get the signal. The pid of the process to which the signal is to be sent is recorded in the f_owner field of the struct file. Then fcntl() with the F_SETFL command on a specific descriptor sets the O_ASYNC flag in the struct file. The stream then sends the SIGIO signal when I/O is possible. This only works with terminals and networks.

One major problem with this is, how do we tell which stream the signal is coming from? The same signal is sent by each stream. So effectively a programmer can enable only one file descriptor at a time for asynchronous I/O. An alternative solution is discussed in Section 9.8.

POSIX has a simpler interface to asynchronous I/O. It has two new system services, aio_read() and aio_write(). Both can specify which signal is to be sent when the I/O completes. Because the signal is specified on each call, it is possible to use a different signal for each stream. POSIX asynchronous I/O is not yet available in Linux.

Synchronisation

Non-blocking I/O has the advantage that it leads to better utilisation—the program can be doing something else while it is waiting. But the responsibility for synchronisation rests completely with the user. The user must be aware that I/O is not instantaneous, and must not attempt to use data which has not yet been provided. For example, the process could WAIT on a semaphore which the signal handler will SIGNAL.

Where the user process does the synchronisation is important. It can come immediately after the call to read() or write(). This means that the user process is suspended until the I/O completes. The effect is exactly the same as with blocking I/O.

It is also possible for the programmer to put the synchronisation farther on in the code. In this case the program can perform other computations, even make other I/O requests, while the original request is being serviced. This method has the advantage that it leads to better overall utilisation of the computer system.

Multiplexing I/O

A situation can arise in which a process wishes to wait for one of several sources of input. For example, it may have requested input from a keyboard, but also

be willing to accept input from a network, or from a disk drive, if any of these is ready before a key is pressed. With the standard arrangements we have considered so far, if it does a read() from the keyboard, it will be blocked until a key is pressed; it will not be able to read or write any other channel.

Two special system services have been developed for multiplexing I/O. Essentially we build a list of file descriptors we are interested in, and then call a function which does not return until at least one of them is ready. The process blocks; but it will wake up as soon as *any* one of the streams of interest has data available.

Select

The first system service is select(). It is passed a bitmap, with one bit per open descriptor, as well as a timeout value. Bits set to 1 indicate descriptors on which the process is willing to do I/O. If any of these are ready, it returns immediately. Otherwise it sleeps until one of them becomes ready. When it returns, only the bits corresponding to those descriptors which are ready are still set. The return value is -1 on error, 0 if it times out and none are ready, otherwise the number of descriptors which are ready.

There are four POSIX macros for setting, clearing, and checking these bitmaps, defined in <sys/select.h>. The first is FD_ZERO(), which zeroes all bits; then FD_SET() and FD_CLR(), which set or clear one bit. Finally there is FD_ISSET(), which checks whether a particular bit is set or not.

The timeout is specified in a struct timeval, which allows the time to be specified to the microsecond. If the other parameters are NULL, then it is possible to use select() as a very high precision sleeper. Remember that the standard sleep() function is only accurate to the second. Setting a file descriptor to be blocking or unblocking has no effect on select().

Poll

Another system service, originally developed in SVR4, is poll(). It is passed an array of struct pollfd, one for each descriptor on which the process is willing to do I/O. See Figure 9.24, from <sys/poll.h>.

```
struct pollfd{
    int fd;             /* the descriptor we are interested in      */
    short int events;   /* flag specifying events of interest       */
    short int revents;  /* flag specifying events which have occured */
};
```

Figure 9.24: Data structure for polling a descriptor

Each element specifies an open file descriptor, and flags describing the conditions or events we are interested in. For example, POLLIN means wait until data can be read; POLLOUT means wait until data can be written. The available flags are specified on the manual page.

The poll() system service blocks if none of the descriptors are ready. It also has a timeout parameter. The return value is 0 for a timeout, and -1 for failure, with the reason for failure in errno. On success, it returns the number of events which have occurred; the appropriate flags are set in revents to indicate which events occurred. It does not change the events field, like select() does; it still contains the conditions as specified.

Implementation

Both select() and poll() are implemented in the same way. They loop through all the specified descriptors, and check to see if I/O is possible on any of them, by calling the poll() function in file_operations corresponding to each one.

If I/O is possible, they return this information, each in its own way. If no I/O is possible, then the calling process must be put to sleep, but in such a way that it will be woken up when any relevant event occurs. As more than one process could be waiting on a particular event, it must be possible to queue waiting processes. The head of such a queue is always the i_wait field of the inode specific to the device. This heads a linked list of struct wait_queue, each of which points to the task_struct of the waiting process (see Figure 9.25).

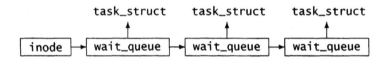

Figure 9.25: Several processes waiting on a device

When the state of a particular stream or channel changes, the driver can find and wake up all the processes linked on its associated queue. Remember that the process was sleeping inside the system service code. When it is woken up, the process loops through all the descriptors again, finds the one that is now ready, and returns.

But there is one further complication. A process may be waiting on more than one device. When the first one becomes ready, the process would proceed, leaving its entries on the other queues. Such an entry could cause spurious processing at a later stage. So when a process is woken up, it must find, and remove, all of its entries on other queues, as specified by the parameter passed to select(), or poll().

9.9 Locks

When many processes wish to open a file at the same time, some for reading, others for writing, there is the possibility of their interfering with each other. This is known as the readers/writers problem. We have examined various levels of solution in earlier chapters.

Internally, Linux provides a lock on the inode (note the field i_sem) so that only one process at a time can be reading or writing any particular file. But this only guarantees atomicity of one read or one write at a time.

POSIX provides locks over specified ranges of bytes in a file. So a process need only lock those bytes of a file it is actually using, and other processes can still access other parts of the same file. Of course a process can always lock the whole range of bytes in the file, from beginning to end, if it wishes.

These locks can be advisory or mandatory.

Advisory locking

Advisory locks do not enforce their use by other processes. One process can find out whether others have a file locked or not, but it can ignore this information. Such an advisory lock can be a read lock, a write lock, or read/write. Read locks can be shared, but write locks are exclusive.

Locking is done using fcntl(), which is passed a pointer to a struct flock, and a request parameter, specifying what it is to do with the information in flock. There are three possibilities.

F_GETLK checks if the specified range of bytes is already locked. If so, the values in flock are overwritten with the existing data.

F_SETLK attempts to set a lock on a range of bytes; if this is incompatible with existing locks, it returns -1 and errno is set to EAGAIN. It is also used to unlock.

F_SETLKW implements a blocking or waiting version of the previous option. If the lock cannot be granted, then the requesting process is put to sleep. So it could lead to deadlock.

Implementation

Internally the system records each lock by means of a struct file_lock, see Figure 9.26, from <linux/fs.h>.

```
struct file_lock{
        struct file_lock    *fl_next;
        struct task_struct  *fl_owner;
        struct wait_queue   *fl_wait;
        struct file         *fl_file;
        unsigned char       fl_type;
        off_t               fl_start;
        off_t               fl_end;
};
```

Figure 9.26: Structure representing a lock on a file

- There is a linked list of such structures, headed from the i_flock field in the inode, linked through fl_next.

- The `fl_owner` field points to the `task_struct` of the process holding the lock.

- But sometimes a lock cannot be granted immediately, and in such a case the process must block. A `struct file_lock` is still inserted in the linked list, but a `struct wait_queue` is also linked in, through `fl_wait` (see Figure 9.27).

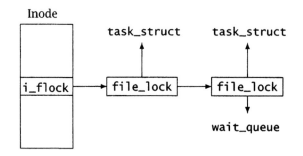

Figure 9.27: A lock request which blocks

- The `fl_file` field points to the `struct file` representing the stream which requested this lock (see Figure 9.28).

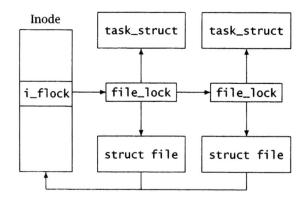

Figure 9.28: How locks are recorded

- `fl_type` is the type of lock, e.g. F_RDLCK or F_WRLCK.

- `fl_start` specifies where the lock begins.

- `fl_end` specifies where the lock ends.

Whenever a lock is released on a file, the linked list of `struct file_lock` is checked for any entries which have a `wait_queue` linked in. This indicates

a waiting process. If the range of bytes it is waiting on is now free, it is woken up, and given the lock.

Locks are not inherited across a fork(). A new task_struct is created by fork(), and the file_lock only points to one such structure, the original. So only the original process holds the lock after a fork(). But they can be inherited across an exec(), if the close_on_exec flag is not set in the file descriptor. The same task_struct exists after the exec(), and the file_lock is still pointing to this. So if the file is still open in the new program, it is still locked.

Mandatory locking

The chmod() system service is used to set the 'set group on execute' S_ISGID bit, and clear the execute permission bit for the group, S_IXGRP, in the i_mode field of a particular file's inode. Clearing the execute bit means that the group cannot execute this file; setting the gid bit means that when the file executes, it runs with the privileges associated with the group, not those of the process which runs it. This is a meaningless combination, and could never arise in normal usage. So it was chosen to indicate mandatory locking.

The implementation of mandatory locks is exactly as described for advisory locks in the previous subsection. But if mandatory locking is in force, the file system then enforces locks, and will not allow a process to proceed if a conflicting lock is held by another process.

9.10 Buffering

The foregoing discussion of I/O procedures assumed that each I/O request from a process caused a physical transfer to or from a peripheral. A process which does a series of I/O operations on the same file, such as sequential writes, or cat to a terminal, will be blocked each time it calls the I/O procedure. This means a context switch each time, which is a very heavy overhead.

One solution is to perform input ahead of requests, and to batch several output requests together into one physical transfer. This technique is known as buffering.

Data for output are accepted into a buffer at the request of a user program, e.g. a write(). The operating system then releases the data from the buffer to the device, when the buffer is full or the device is able to accept it. The user has to wait only if the buffer is full. For example, data is provided by a program in bursts, and accepted by a printer at its own rate.

Input data is accepted from the device as rapidly as it can supply it. It is then provided to the user program on request. The user has to wait only if the buffer is empty.

Space for the buffers is allocated by the operating system. Typically the open() command would fill all buffers. The close() command would flush all buffers, if necessary, and return the space.

Motivation

There is only one real advantage, and that is improved performance. It reduces the elapsed time for a user's program, by reducing the number of waits. This frees resources faster, so speeding up the whole system.

For example, if it takes 10ms to find a block on a disk, and 3ms to transfer it, that is an average transfer time of 13ms per block. With buffering, two blocks can be transferred in 16ms, or 8ms per block.

But buffering can have its disadvantages. If the user's program supplies or needs more data than a device can handle over an extended period, then buffers are of no use. For example, if a data processing program is producing on average more than 100 characters per second, and the printer is rated at 100 characters per second, then the only solution is to buy a faster printer.

When reading or writing random records, buffering can actually be detrimental to performance. Buffering would read in several consecutive records. It is most unlikely that any of these, other than the first, will be used. For example, if it takes 10ms to find a block, and 3ms to transfer it, unbuffered this is 13ms per block. If buffering reads two blocks at a time, but only uses the first one, then the average is 16ms per block.

Buffering algorithm

Buffering requires a variation in the I/O procedure. For example, an input stream handles requests from the user process by reading data from the buffer. Only when the buffer is empty does it call the device handler. Figure 9.29 shows the latter part of an I/O procedure for buffered input.

```
Check parameters against device characteristics
Return if error
IF buffer_empty THEN
        Call device driver (for bufferfull)
        Process any errors
ENDIF
Transfer data from buffer
Return
```

Figure 9.29: A buffered input procedure

Most of the time the IF condition would be false, and the whole algorithm would be executed at memory speeds. It is only on the relatively rare occasions when the buffer is empty that the physical (slow) hardware is involved.

It is a useful exercise to rewrite this algorithm for output.

Unix buffer cache

Unix buffers input and output on a system-wide basis, not on a stream by
stream basis. A fixed number of buffers, about 10% of physical memory, are
allocated when the system is booted. This is known as the buffer cache.

Each buffer has room for one disk block, with a separate header to hold
management information, a `struct buffer_head`. See Figure 9.30, which is
from `<linux/fs.h>`.

- The combination of `b_blocknr`, the physical block number on a particular
  device, and `b_dev`, the device id, uniquely identifies the data in a particular
  buffer. A value of B_FREE in the `b_dev` field identifies a free buffer.

- Like many other data structures in the kernel, buffers are maintained on
  hash lists, based on the combination of block number and device id. The
  `b_next` field is used for linking the hash lists together.

```
struct buffer_head{
        unsigned long       b_blocknr;      /* block number         */
        kdev_t              b_dev;          /* device               */
        struct buffer_head *b_next;         /* hash list            */
        unsigned long       b_state;        /* state bitmap         */
        struct buffer_head *b_next_free;    /* free list            */
        char               *b_data;         /* pointer to data block */
        struct wait_queue  *b_wait;         /* processes waiting    */
};
```

Figure 9.30: A buffer head

- The `b_state` field is a bitmap, with individual bits set to represent the
  state of the buffer. Figure 9.31 from `<linux/fs.h>`, shows the meaning
  of some of these bits.

```
#define BH_Uptodate   0 /* contains valid data  */
#define BH_Dirty      1 /* is dirty             */
#define BH_Lock       2 /* is locked            */
#define BH_Req        3 /* has been invalidated */
```

Figure 9.31: Bits representing the state of a buffer

- When unused, buffers are maintained on a free list, chained through the
  `b_next_free` field. When released, a buffer is placed at the end of this free
  list. But even when free, it still contains data, and is kept on its old hash
  list, so it can be found quickly, if needed again. The example in Figure 9.32,
  with three free buffers, shows how all of this fits together.

- The `b_data` field points to the actual buffer area corresponding to this
  buffer head.

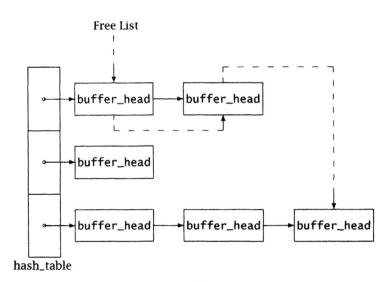

Figure 9.32: Buffer cache

- If processes are waiting to access this buffer, they insert themselves on the wait queue headed from b_wait. When the data becomes available in the buffer, all waiting processes can be found here.

As well as data blocks from files, the buffer cache is also used to hold blocks of system data, such as directory blocks, inode blocks, and indirect blocks. These will be described in the following chapter. The sync() system service writes all system data back to disk; while fsync() writes the data and control information for one specified file back to disk. The contents of the buffer cache is written back to the disk at intervals by the update process.

9.11 Close

This function has to clean up after I/O operations. It calls a file system or device specific release() function, which does the appropriate cleanup operation. For example, if opened for writing, filled or partially filled buffers must be written out to the disk. If opened for read only, data buffers can be discarded.

It updates the directory or inode entry on the disk, e.g. the date field, and possibly the size field. It then zeroes the entry in the file descriptor table, and decrements the f_count field in the struct file. If this is zero, the struct file can be deallocated. It also decrements the reference count in the inode. If this is zero, then it can be released as well at this stage. The kernel automatically closes all files when a process terminates.

9.12 Summary

1. Input/Output is the classic bottleneck in computing, so an operating system tries to be as efficient as possible in this area. Because each piece of hardware is unique, the operating system presents the user with a consistent virtual device interface. Within this it hides any differences in character encoding. It should provide a comprehensive set of error routines.

2. The set of system services that handle I/O make up the I/O subsystem, which takes care of device naming, access control, data transfer, locking, and buffering. It passes the request on to a specific device driver, which knows about the hardware characteristics of a device.

3. Filenames are stored in some form of directory structure. This may be as simple as one single table, but typically it has some form of tree structure, and may allow sharing, even under different names.

    Unix unifies the names of all sources of input and output into one name space, the directory tree. Device names are kept in the /dev directory. Only a file's name is kept in the directory itself. All other information about a file is kept in an index node, or inode. The unlink() system service removes a particular name from the name space.

4. The system represents each file it is dealing with by means of a data structure known as an inode. There is a system-wide inode list, which has one entry (inode) per open file, no matter how many processes have it open.

    There are three system services which can be used to read information from the data structures representing a file: stat(), lstat(), and fstat().

5. The open() system call first checks if the file is already open; if not, it searches the directory structure. If the file does not exist, it may create it. It then checks the privileges of the user against the protection on the file. When a file is opened, the system sets up a network of data structures in memory, which are used for all further accesses to the file.

    Each process has a file descriptor table, which keeps track of all its open streams. There is a system-wide open file list, which has one entry (struct file) per open file per process. This points to the inode representing the file.

6. Unix allows different processes to open the same file at the same time.

7. Input/output procedures sit between the user and the device drivers. In general, they check that the particular stream is open, and that the requested operation is legitimate for that steam. Then the request is passed on to a driver program for a specific device.

    All I/O in Unix begins with a file descriptor, struct file, and an inode, and then differentiates into three main types: regular files, devices, and streams used for interprocess communication. Unix has two main system services for I/O, read() and write(). Each determines, from the

data structures corresponding to the stream, the specific functions which should be called to process that request.

8. There is always some delay with I/O, and there are two possible ways of dealing with this. The calling process can be blocked. This is the simplest approach, known as synchronous or wait I/O. Another possibility is that the calling process can continue with other work, but it has to detect when the I/O completes. This is known as asynchronous or nowait I/O.

   A process may wish to wait for one of several sources of input to be ready. It can do this using non-blocking I/O, signals, or special system services, either select() or poll().

9. POSIX provides locks over specified ranges of bytes in a file. These can be advisory or mandatory.

10. Buffering is a technique which attempts to batch together many small reads (or writes) into one larger physical transfer of data. It adds complexity, but is acceptable because of improved efficiency. Unix uses a system-wide buffer cache.

11. When a stream is closed, the file descriptor entry is invalidated, and the entry in the system file table released. If not shared, the inode can also be freed.

9.13 Discussion questions

1. It is important to distinguish between information *about* a file (metadata), and the information *in* the file. One possibility is to keep the metadata in the directory entry. What other possibilities are there?

2. When is the search path, established by the **path** command, followed? Does an editor use this information when searching for a file?

3. Could each thread in a process have a different default directory, or do they all have to share the same one?

4. Write an algorithm to search through a Linux style directory, looking for a specific name.

5. Discuss the advantages and disadvantages of a general graph directory.

6. How can the unlink() function discover whether there is more than one link pointing to a file?

7. What is the effect of renaming a file to which a symbolic link is pointing?

8. It would be possible to implement file access so that there would be no concept of opening a file. Each read or write would be passed the name of the file as a parameter. Discuss the advantages and disadvantages of this.

9. readdir() (in file_operations) searches a directory for a given file name and, if found, creates a struct file to represent that file. This structure contains a pointer to readdir(). Do we have a chicken and egg

situation here? How did the system know how to call `readdir()`, before `readdir()` created the entry with its own address in it?

10. Could each thread in a process have a different set of open files? What changes would be required in the `task_struct`? What would be the advantages and disadvantages of this?

11. Instead of putting a pointer to the `struct file` in the file descriptor table, and passing back an index into this table, it would be possible to pass back the pointer directly to the calling process. Why do you think it is not done this way?

12. Suppose that a program opens a file for writing, and it returns file descriptor 5. Investigate how you would use the `dup2()` system call to arrange that all output from the program now goes to the file, and not to the screen.

13. With the mechanisms as described, could two threads in the same process open the same file twice? Would there be one or two file descriptors? Would there be one or two instances of the `struct file`? Would there be one or two instances of `inode`?

14. Read the manual page for `stat()`, and outline how you would use it to build a directory listing program. There is one vital piece of information not given by `stat()`. What is it? Where would you get this?

15. The `struct file` contains a set of functions that operate on open streams, and so does the `struct inode`. Is this unnecessary duplication? What is the difference between them?

16. Distinguish between the POSIX `open()` system service, and the internal `open()` function in the `struct file`.

17. What is the meaning of the value returned by the POSIX `write()` function?

18. Can you think of a situation where the `writev()` system service would be useful?

19. Asynchronous or non-blocking I/O sounds complicated. Can you think of any real-life example where it would be worthwhile using it?

20. Setting a file descriptor to be blocking or unblocking has no effect on `select()`. Why is it implemented this way?

21. The `select()` and `poll()` interfaces are just two independently developed ways of doing the same thing. Examine the two interfaces, and argue for which one is most programmer friendly.

22. Why is information about locks maintained in the `inode` (the `i_flock` field) and not in the `struct file`?

23. Some systems implement buffering, not on a system-wide basis, but on a per stream basis. Outline some of the implications of this.

24. If buffering is implemented on a per stream basis, should the information about buffers be kept in the `struct file`, or in the `struct inode`?

25. Rewrite the algorithm in Figure 9.29, for output.

26. How does the kernel know which files to close when a process terminates?

Regular file systems 10

In the previous chapter, we followed the generic processing of I/O down as far as the inode. We saw that from there on the processing becomes more specific. In particular, if the value in the i_mode field is S_IFREG, S_IFDIR, or S_IFLNK, then we are dealing with regular files, directory files, or symbolic links, in effect the standard file systems we are familiar with. This chapter will consider how such disk file systems are implemented.

10.1 The file manager

The memory manager deals with storage, but only for the duration of a running process. At most it maintains information for as long as the machine is powered up. The file system provides a facility for long-term storage.

A variety of demands are placed on file systems. In commercial data processing environments, the emphasis is upon large volumes of data, typically thousands of Gigabytes. University and development environments expect a file system to store many different programs, and many different versions of the same program. These will be source programs, compiled object modules, libraries both of source and object, and linked executables.

The implementation technology has changed. Originally, it was based upon drums, which are now obsolete. Magnetic tapes came later, and are still in use today for long-term storage, though rarely for active systems. Random access disk drives, in their fixed and removable formats are the mainstay of storage today. A newer technology is optical disks: read-only (CD ROM) or writable. The ideal for the future is some sort of storage with no moving parts.

Overview

Getting away from the hardware, the filing system is responsible for organising this data in such a way that the user can access it quickly and easily. This chapter will look at general purpose filing systems, as provided by general purpose operating systems. Specifically, this will not cover database management systems.

A file system is concerned with the physical properties of each file, such as where it is, and how long it is. Such file systems work on a pseudo device, or a logical unit, called a file, which can be of arbitrary size. These files are stored on a block structured medium, with fixed size blocks, typically from 512 to 8k bytes.

Rarely does a file exist in its entirety in one place on the disk. Typically it is scattered more or less at random among the blocks which make up the disk space. There is a parallel with the way pages are allocated at random to page frames. The allocation of files to blocks is a major function of the filing system.

In the context of what has been seen in the previous chapter, the file manager sits between the I/O procedure and the device driver. The I/O procedure sends the filing system a command such as 'read x bytes, beginning at offset y'. The file manager converts this to a command of the form 'read block z'. The device driver reads block z, and makes it available to the file manager. The file manager extracts just the required sequence of bytes from the block, and sends them back to the I/O procedure, for eventual transmission to the user.

Objectives

A good file manager should achieve as many as possible of the following:

- Creation and deletion of files. Even though we have become used to read-only file systems on CD ROM, the ability to create and delete files and directories is still a fundamental ability of general purpose file systems.

- It should be possible to refer to a file by a user-defined name, rather than by machine address. This means that the management of space on the device is the responsibility of the file system, and where a file is on disk should be completely transparent to the user.

- Read and write access to files. This should be generally available, even if write access may be restricted.

- Users may wish to share data and/or programs, and the file system is responsible for this. On the other hand the system should also protect files, when this is required.

- The file system should give a user some insurance against system failure, by providing facilities for backing up files, and restoring them when necessary.

10.2   File system types

Over the years, different ways have been developed for organising information on disk drives, each suited to a particular purpose. These are known as file system types. The system manager makes a decision about which of these will

be needed, and supported, on a particular machine. At boot time, the kernel is told about each of the possible types of file system it may have to deal with; the code to handle each of these systems is loaded into the kernel at this stage. Sometimes it is also possible to load it dynamically into a running system, without rebooting.

In Linux, information about the currently loaded systems is kept in a linked list of struct file_system_type, see Figure 10.1, from<linux/fs.h>.

```
struct file_system_type{
      const char                *name;
      struct super_block        *(*read_super)();
      struct file_system_type *next;
};
```

Figure 10.1: An entry in the linked list of file systems

This list is headed from the global variable file_systems.

- Each file_system_type has a pointer to the ASCII name of the file system it represents, in the name field.

- It has a pointer read_super to a function which is called each time an instance of this type of file system is to be installed. It creates a struct super_block to represent the instance, and returns a pointer to it. The implementation of this function will be considered in Section 10.5.

- The linked list is maintained through the next field.

Each different type of file system which is to be used must have an entry in this list. At present the most common Linux file system is the second extended file system (Ext2). But Linux also supports the Unix file system (UFS), the network file system (NFS), and the CD ROM file system (CDFS), among others.

The sysfs() system service returns information about the different file system types which are currently configured into this list.

10.3 Disk organisation

A disk is a collection of fixed size blocks. There is no structure on a raw disk— it can be used with any operating system on any machine. An operating system imposes a structure on the disk when it formats it. We will look at how disks are formatted, and how information is laid out in the blocks making up a disk.

Block size

The size of a physical block on the disk is decided by the hardware designer. More than one physical block may be transferred to or from the disk at a time. This logical block size is decided by the operating system designer, or by the system manager. Current sizes are 2kB to 8kB.

The choice of block size is a tradeoff between saving on I/O, by having fewer disk accesses, and on the other hand saving memory and disk space by not wasting space inside large blocks. Some of the factors involved are:

- The logical block should be a multiple of the physical block size.

- Internal fragmentation tends to keep block size down.

- The overhead of keeping track of a block forces block size up.

Physical blocks are numbered sequentially from 0 upwards, and are always referenced by the driver in terms of this physical block number. Most of these blocks are used to hold directories and files. But there are also blocks used by the file manager itself.

Boot block

The first block on a disk, block 0, is very special. It is known as the boot block. This contains the bootstrap program, which is run automatically when the machine is powered up, and which loads and runs the operating system.

A disk can be formatted into a number of different partitions, each containing a different file system (see Figure 10.2).

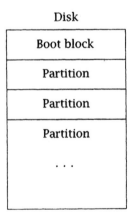

Figure 10.2: Layout of a disk

The file system is the basic unit of data organisation on a Unix disk. This must be distinguished from a file system type, which refers to the way in which data is organised within a file system. There can be many file systems of each particular type.

So there is a standard disk label, also in the boot block. This label includes information about the hardware properties of the disk, and about how the disk is divided up into file system partitions. The disk label is normally specific to the underlying hardware, and not to whatever file system may exist in one or other of the partitions. For example, when Linux is installed on a PC, the boot block contains a standard PC disk label.

Block allocation methods

Now that we have looked at the top level structure of a disk, we go on to consider the internal structure of a partition. While we will examine various ways of structuring a file system on a disk, we will concentrate on the implementation of the default Linux file system type, the second extended file system, or Ext2 (see Section 10.4).

The root directory is usually at some fixed position in the partition. This contains information about the locations of its subdirectories and files. Subdirectories contain information about sub-subdirectories, and so on. A number of different ways have been developed for allocating blocks to files so that disk space is used effectively, and files can be accessed quickly.

Contiguous allocation

This requires each file to occupy a set of blocks that come one after the other on the disk. The directory holds the start address, and the number of blocks. This method supports both sequential and direct access. See Figure 10.3.

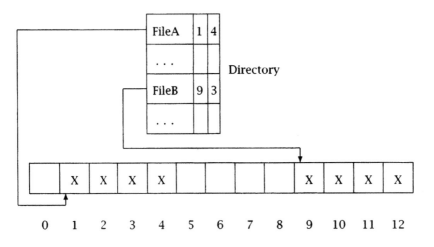

Figure 10.3: Contiguous allocation

For example, with contiguous allocation you know that block 7 will always be immediately after block 6 on the disk. Also, you can always calculate where block 7 is—it is always 7 blocks from the beginning of the file on the disk.

The difficulties are with finding space for a new file, and with extending a file, as well as the need to compact the disk. Similar problems, and suggested solutions, have been seen when dealing with memory management.

A variation on this used by most systems nowadays, is to allocate disk space not in individual blocks, but as a number of contiguous blocks at a time, known as extents or clusters.

This allocation method keeps track of free space by means of a directory of free blocks. Generally, several contiguous blocks are allocated or freed at

the same time. So free blocks are not tracked individually, but as clusters of free blocks. This directory would be maintained in size order. When allocating, policies such as best fit, worst fit, etc., are relevant. If a sufficiently large contiguous area of disk is not available, compaction is necessary.

Block linkage

With this method, the file is kept as a linked list. The directory entry points to the first block. Each block has a pointer to the next block. The last block allocated has a NULL pointer. Figure 10.4 illustrates this.

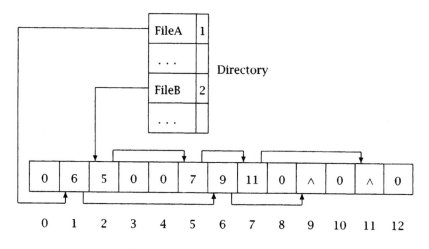

Figure 10.4: Linked allocation

The only information about FileA in the directory is the filename, and the fact that it begins at block 1. This block has a pointer to block 6, which points to block 9, which has a NULL pointer, signifying that it is the last block in the file. Similarly it can be seen that FileB consists of blocks 2, 5, 7, and 11. The directory could also contain a pointer to the last block, which would facilitate appending to the file, and also relinking blocks on to the free list.

This form of organisation may be suitable for small files, or for sequential files which are always read from beginning to end. But for relative files, to read block n, it would also be necessary to read the n − 1 blocks before it. Even more seriously, if a block, or even a pointer, is lost or damaged, then the remainder of the list is lost. Not only that, but it may be linked into another file, or even into the free list.

Some solutions have been suggested to these problems. A doubly linked list would allow some damaged pointers to be restored. A more robust improvement would be to store the file-id and relative block number in each block. Thus even if links to a block are lost, the file it belongs to can still be identified, as well as its position within that file.

With linked allocation, all of the free blocks on a disk are maintained as one linked list. Blocks can be added to or taken from either end of the chain.

File map

This is an attempt to improve on the foregoing, by bringing all the pointers for the whole disk together in one place. A map of the whole disk is maintained, with one entry for each block on the disk. So the nth entry represents block n. If the block is free, then this entry contains 0. Initially, on a blank device, all entries are 0. This map, or at least some portion of it, could be copied into main memory when the file system is mounted.

The directory points to the location in the file map representing the first block in the file. That entry contains either a pointer to the file map entry for the next block, or an NULL marker. Figure 10.5 illustrates this.

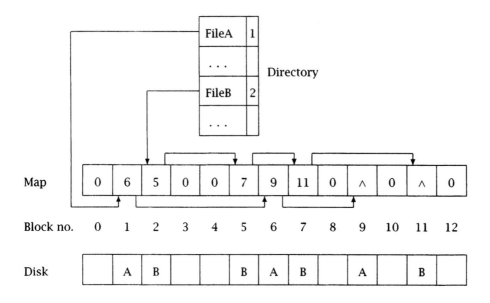

Figure 10.5: Example of a file map

The only information about FileA in the directory is the filename, and the fact that it begins at block 1. This entry in the file map points to block 6, which points to block 9, which has a NULL pointer, signifying that it is the last block in the file. Similarly it can be seen that FileB consists of blocks 2, 5, 7, and 11.

A file map has the same problems as the previous method, in that it is essentially sequential. But at least the sequential search is done in memory, and does not require many disk accesses.

Indexed allocation

This improves on linked allocation, by bringing all of the pointers for a particular file together into one location on the disk, the index block. So it makes the pointers contiguous. The directory points to the first index block. This points to the next, if required. Each index block points to n data blocks.

This method supports direct access. It allows holes in files, without waste of space. A disadvantage is the small time overhead in reading the index block. There is also a small space overhead, internal fragmentation in the index block.

Of course, this puts all of the eggs in the one basket. If the index block is damaged, the whole file may become unreadable. A variation of this method is used in Unix, so it will be discussed in greater detail in Section 10.4.

With indexed allocation, all of the free blocks are linked from one or more index blocks. The overhead is proportional to the number of blocks affected. But the addresses of a large number of free blocks can be found quickly.

Security

It is possible to use more than one form of allocation. For security, both index blocks and links could be used. As the directory is such an important feature in the whole structure, this could be duplicated.

Allocation strategies

The simplest approach to this is to use the first block on the free chain, or in the bitmap. But a somewhat more sophisticated approach would be to use the block which will minimise the amount of disk head movement. In general, disk allocation policies tend to depend on the way in which free space is maintained.

There is some advantage in keeping all the blocks of a file on the same part of a disk. When allocating on a new disk, each file could be given a track of its own.

Blocks scattered all over the disk can greatly decrease performance. The solution is a periodic rebuild of the disk. This involves copying all of the data to another disk, or to tape, and reformatting the original disk. The data is then copied back in such a way that each file is contiguous on disk.

10.4   An Ext2 partition

With the Ext2 file system, a disk partition is divided into a number of block groups, each consisting of one or more cylinders. Each block group contains administrative information, a table of inodes, and data blocks.

The different data structures which go to make up a block group are shown in Figure 10.6, and will be discussed in the remainder of this section.

Figure 10.7 shows how a block group (containing 4 cylinders) would be laid out on disk. In this example there are two blocks of inodes. All of the remainder are data blocks.

Super block

Each block group begins with a super block, which contains information about the whole file system. This is information which does not change, such as the

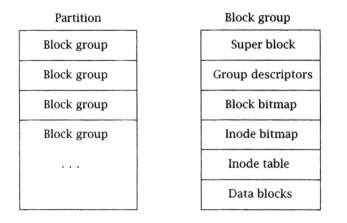

Figure 10.6: Layout of a partition with Ext2

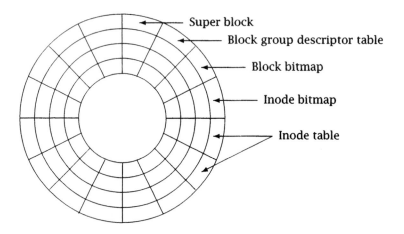

Figure 10.7: A block group on disk

total number of blocks allocated to this file system, or how many of these are data blocks. The super block is duplicated in each block group, so it cannot be lost as a result of any one disk sector becoming unreadable.

The super block is formatted as a `struct ext2_super_block`, see Figure 10.8, from `<linux/ext2_fs.h>`.

- `s_inodes_count` is the total number of inodes in the whole file system.

- `s_blocks_count` is the total number of data blocks in the file system.

- `s_free_blocks_count` is the number of free blocks in the file system.

- `s_free_inodes_count` is the number of free inodes in the file system.

- `s_first_data_block` is the location of the first data block in the file system.

```
struct ext2_super_block{
    u32 s_inodes_count;       /* Inodes count              */
    u32 s_blocks_count;       /* Blocks count              */
    u32 s_free_blocks_count;  /* Free blocks count         */
    u32 s_free_inodes_count;  /* Free inodes count         */
    u32 s_first_data_block;   /* First data block          */
    u32 s_log_block_size;     /* Block size                */
    s32 s_log_frag_size;      /* Fragment size             */
    u32 s_blocks_per_group;   /* # Blocks per group        */
    u32 s_inodes_per_group;   /* # Inodes per group        */
    u16 s_inode_size;         /* size of inode structure   */
    u16 s_block_group_nr;     /* number of this block group */
};
```

Figure 10.8: An Ext2 super block

- s_log_block_size is the size of a disk block in this file system. Such a block size may be a multiple of the physical block size on the disk. Its value is stored in logarithmic form. For example, a 4k block is 2^{12} bytes, so the value in this field would be 12.

- For efficiency reasons, the Ext2 file system allows data blocks to be broken into smaller units. See Section 10.4. The s_log_fragsize field contains the size of such a fragment.

- s_blocks_per_group is the number of blocks in a block group.

- s_inodes_per_group is the number of inodes in a block group.

- s_inode_size is the number of bytes in a disk inode structure.

- The final field s_block_group_nr is the only one which differs in each copy of the super block. It contains the number of this block group, which uniquely identifies it within the whole file system.

The super block is padded out to the size of a full block. It is copied into the buffer cache in memory when the file system is mounted, and remains there until it is unmounted. Mounting a file system will be discussed in Section 10.5.

Block group descriptors

Next on the disk is a table of block group descriptors. Like the super block, this table is also duplicated in each group, so it can be recovered in case of damage. Each entry in this table is a struct ext2_group_desc, as shown in Figure 10.9, from <linux/ext2_fs.h>, and describes a single block group. The group descriptor does not contain a group number; rather the group is identified by its place in this table.

- bg_block_bitmap points to where the bitmap which tracks the allocation of data blocks in this group begins.

```
struct ext2_group_desc{
        u32 bg_block_bitmap;        /* Blocks bitmap block */
        u32 bg_inode_bitmap;        /* Inodes bitmap block */
        u32 bg_inode_table;         /* Inodes table block  */
        u16 bg_free_blocks_count;   /* Free blocks count   */
        u16 bg_free_inodes_count;   /* Free inodes count   */
        u16 bg_used_dirs_count;     /* Directories count   */
};
```

Figure 10.9: Structure of a block group descriptor

- bg_inode_bitmap points to a similar bitmap for inodes in this group.

- bg_inode_table points to where the inode table for this group begins.

- A count of free data blocks in the group is maintained in bg_free_blocks_count.

- Likewise, a count of free inodes is maintained in bg_free_inodes_count.

- The number of directories created in this block group is kept in bg_used_dirs_count. This is used to spread directories as evenly as possible over all of the groups.

The whole table is copied into the buffer cache in memory when the file system is mounted, and remains there until it is unmounted.

Block bitmap

This field, to which bg_block_bitmap of the group descriptor points, keeps track of allocated data blocks in the group. One bit represents each data block in the group. This has the advantage that it uses the minimum amount of space, and free blocks can be found quickly.

The bitmap is always one block in size, so determining the maximum size of a block group. The position of the bit within the map corresponds to the position of the block in the group. A value of 0 means it is free, 1 implies it is in use. Consider a group where blocks 2, 3, 4, 9, 12 are free, all of the others being allocated. The block bit map would be:

$$11000111101101111 \ldots$$

This bitmap is loaded into main memory when the file system is mounted.

Inode bitmap

This field, to which bg_inode_bitmap of the group descriptor points, keeps track of which inodes in the group are allocated, and which are free. The bitmap is loaded into the buffer cache in memory when the file system is mounted.

Inode table

Inodes are stored in blocks that come next in each block group. The `bg_inode_table` field in the block group descriptor points to the first inode block. Disk inodes, although similar to the `inode` structure, have an internal organisation specific to the file system type. They contain only a fraction of the information found in a `struct inode`, only that which must be maintained after the file is closed. The format of an Ext2 inode is shown in Figure 10.10, from `<linux/ext2_fs.h>`. Each disk inode is 128 bytes in size.

```
struct ext2_inode{
        u16 i_mode;             /* File mode            */
        u16 i_uid;              /* Owner uid            */
        u32 i_size;             /* Size in bytes        */
        u32 i_atime;            /* Access time          */
        u32 i_ctime;            /* Creation time        */
        u32 i_mtime;            /* Modification time    */
        u16 i_gid;              /* Group id             */
        u16 i_links_count;      /* Links count          */
        u32 i_blocks;           /* Blocks count         */
        u32 i_block[15];        /* Pointers to blocks   */
        u32 i_faddr;            /* Fragment address     */
        u8  l_i_frag;           /* Fragment number      */
        u8  l_i_fsize;          /* Fragment size        */
};
```

Figure 10.10: Structure of an Ext2 disk inode

Most of the fields in this structure are self explaining. The first nine have already been met with in the previous chapter, when dealing with the `struct inode` in Section 9.4. The disk inode is the permanent home for these items of information. The remaining four fields will now be described.

Pointers to blocks

The field `i_block[]` allows for 15 addresses of 4 bytes each. These 15 addresses are used to track the allocation of the file on disk. This is a standard Unix mechanism, and is not specific to Ext2. Because the vast majority of files in Unix systems are small, the first 12 addresses point directly to data blocks. Once you have accessed the inode, you have all of the pointers. This situation is illustrated in Figure 10.11.

But some files will be larger than this. So the next pointer in the inode, `i_block[12]`, does not point to a data block, but to an index block. This is known as the indirect block. This in turn holds pointers to data blocks, as shown in Figure 10.12. Should the file grow any larger, there is a double indirect block, `i_block[13]`, which points to a block of pointers to blocks of pointers to data blocks, as shown in Figure 10.13.

Finally there is a rarely used triple indirect block, `i_block[14]`, allowing for very large files, but with extra overhead.

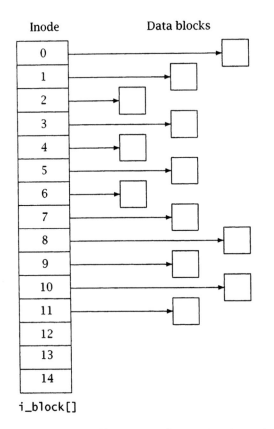

Figure 10.11: Allocation information in an inode

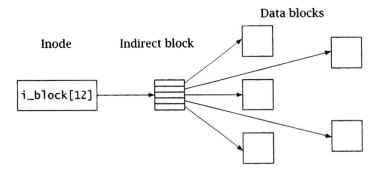

Figure 10.12: Single indirect block

If i_mode is set to S_IFCHR or S_IFBLK, the inode refers to a device, which has no data blocks. In this case i_block[0] contains the device number. If i_mode is set to S_IFLNK, and i_blocks is zero, i_block[] contains the name of the symbolic link. This is used for symbolic pathnames up to 60 bytes in length, saving on the overhead of a complete data block to hold the name.

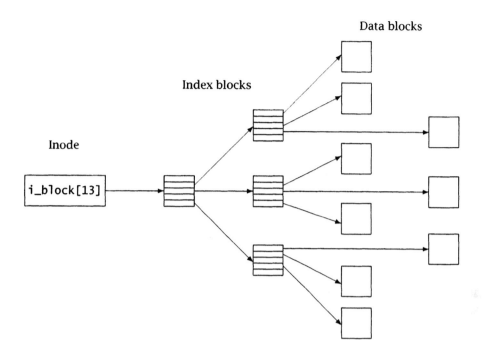

Figure 10.13: Double indirect block

Fragments

A file is composed of complete blocks. But to avoid undue waste of disk space, some data blocks can be divided into fragments, and the end of a file may be allocated only as many fragments as are necessary. These must all, however, be within the same block, and be contiguous. Effectively this means that files may share their last blocks. The final three fields in ext2_inode cater for this.

- The i_faddr field points to the block containing the fragments of this file.

- The l_i_frag identifies the first fragment of this file within the block.

- l_i_fsize contains the number of consecutive fragments to be found at that location.

Figure 10.14 shows a situation where FileA owns the first three fragments of a block, while FileB owns the next four fragments of the same block.

When data is added to the end of a file, the requirement that all of its fragments be contiguous can lead to complications. With the example shown in Figure 10.14, if FileA needs to add a further three fragments at the end, they will not fit in the current block. So a new fragment block, with at least six free fragments, will have to be found. The existing three fragments, and the three new ones, are copied there, and the three fragment fields in the inode are updated.

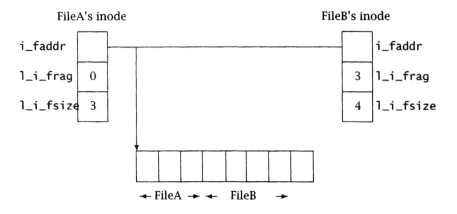

Figure 10.14: Fragments of two files in a block

Data blocks

The remainder of the block group consists of data blocks, which are used both for ordinary data files, and for directory files.

Ext2 directories

Unix treats directories as ordinary files, with a specific internal structure. So space for directories is allocated from the same data blocks as ordinary files. Directory entries in Ext2 are of variable length. This makes it possible to implement file names up to 255 characters without wasting space.

The fixed part of each directory entry consists of a 32 bit inode number, a 16 bit entry length value, and a 16 bit name length value. This is followed by a variable length file name with a maximum of 255 characters. If the filename is less than 255 characters, it is NULL terminated. The structure of an Ext2 directory entry is shown in Figure 10.15, from `<linux/ext2_fs.h>`.

```
struct ext2_dir_entry{
        u32  inode;     /* inode number of the entry */
        u16  rec_len;   /* total length of entry     */
        u16  name_len;  /* length of name            */
        char name[]     /* file name                 */
};
```

Figure 10.15: An Ext2 directory entry

When an entry is deleted, the system merely sets the `inode` and `name_len` fields to zero. If contiguous entries become free, it joins them together, by setting the `rec_len` field in the first one to the total size of the free area.

Block allocation in Ext2

The Ext2 file system tries to keep related information on the same part of the disk. This is the whole reason for dividing the partition into block groups, instead of dealing with it as one large partition, or even one whole disk, in which case blocks of a file could be scattered all over the disk. As far as possible,

- inodes of all files in a directory are allocated in the same block group
- inodes and data blocks are allocated from the same block group
- each new directory is created in the block group with the smallest number of directories.

These policies work well when there is plenty of free space, but deteriorate when the disk is above 90% full.

When a new disk block is needed, the system calculates the ideal one to allocate, according to these criteria. It checks the block bitmap to see if it is available. If it is not available, then it looks for a free block elsewhere in the same block group. After this it searches in other block groups.

When a free block is found, the system tries to preallocate up to 8 consecutive blocks. Then it updates the block bitmap, the block group descriptor, and the super block. If the file does not use all of these preallocated blocks, any still unused are deallocated when the file is closed.

It is important to maintain consistency between the directory, the inode, and the bitmap. When allocating, the bitmap should be updated first, then the inode, and finally the directory. If a crash occurs in between, the block will be marked as in use, but at least the inode and directory will be consistent. Otherwise the inode would show the block as part of a file, but the bitmap would show it as free, and it could be allocated to another file later.

When returning a block, the directory should be updated first, then the inode, and finally the bitmap. The worst that can happen then is that an unallocated block will be marked as in use in the bitmap, and will never be allocated. But the directory and inode will be consistent. Such blocks can be reclaimed by rebuilding the disk: backing up, reformatting, and restoring.

10.5 Mounting a file system

Now that we have examined how data is statically laid out on disk, we go on to consider how this data is made available.

Mounting a file system

The basic unit of data organisation on a Unix disk is known as a file system. Each file system always has a root directory. It usually has a more or less elaborate structure of subdirectories, as well, though this is not necessary. Sometimes a file system takes up a whole disk, although as we have seen, with

larger disks it is common to have several file systems in different partitions on the same physical device. Any medium to large Unix machine will have many such file systems. These may be spread across a number of physical disks, and may even exist on remote machines, in the case of the network file system.

By convention, in Unix these are not visible as distinct systems. They are presented as joined together into one large directory tree, with only one root. Each machine has a root file system; this is the only one whose root directory is visible. It may be the only file system present, though normally there are a number of different file systems joined together, which may even be of different file system types. It is possible to attach them together in any order.

Connecting a file system into some point in the directory structure is known as mounting it. This is usually done at boot time. A file system is attached to the directory tree at a directory known as the mount point, using the mount() system service. It can also be detached, with umount().

Figure 10.16 shows two file systems, A and B; Figure 10.17 shows the situation after B has been mounted over the 'include' directory of A.

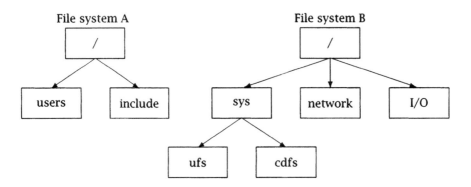

Figure 10.16: File systems as they exist on disk

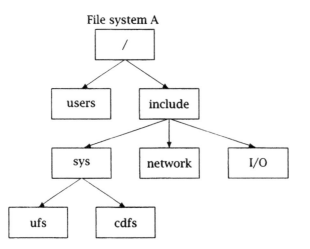

Figure 10.17: Directory structure after attaching file system B

Note that any entries in the 'include' directory are not now visible. They still exist, but cannot be accessed until file system B has been unmounted.

The system services `statfs()` and `fstatfs()` return information about a particular mounted file system.

Mount

The `mount()` system service is used to link a file system into an existing directory tree. Here we will look at how this is implemented in Linux, and specifically mounting an Ext2 file system. The first parameter to `mount()` specifies the file system type. The list of configured types (Section 10.2) is searched, and the corresponding entry found. The `read_super()` function specific to that type is then called, and it carries out the following operations.

1. It finds or allocates an `inode` for the directory onto which the file system will be mounted, as specified by the second parameter to `mount()`. This is done using the standard name translation mechanism, as described in Section 9.5.

2. It checks that this directory is not already in use as a mount point (the field `i_sb` in the `inode` must be NULL).

3. A `struct super_block`, see Figure 10.18 from `<linux/fs.h>`, is allocated and filled in.

```
struct super_block{
        struct list_head         s_list;
        kdev_t                   s_dev;
        struct file_system_type *s_type;
        struct super_operations *s_op;
        struct dentry           *s_root;
        union{
            struct ext2_sb_info  ext2_sb;
            struct msdos_sb_info msdos_sb;
            struct nfs_sb_info   nfs_sb;
        }u;
};
```

Figure 10.18: Data structure representing a mounted file system

The kernel maintains a linked list of these, headed from `super_blocks`, with one entry for each mounted file system. The first entry in this list is always for the root file system.

- The list of `struct super_block` is linked through the `s_list` field.
- The `s_dev` field identifies the physical device on which this file system is stored. This was passed as a parameter to `read_super()`.
- The `s_type` field points to the appropriate `file_system_type` in the linked list of configured file types. See Section 10.2.

- The s_op field points to the appropriate struct super_operations for its file system type. See Figure 10.19, from <linux/fs.h>.

```
struct super_operations{
        void  (*read_inode)();
        void  (*write_inode)();
        void  (*put_inode)();
        void  (*put_super)();
        void  (*write_super)();
        int   (*statfs)();
};
```

Figure 10.19: Operations on a file system

Each file system type will have its own implementation of these functions. They map between file system formats for data structures such as inodes on disk, to the file system independent formats as used in memory. Strictly speaking, the file system does not even have to use inodes (e.g. MSDOS). These functions will map between totally different formats.

- read_inode() is passed a pointer to an inode in memory, and fills it in from the information on disk. Its most important job is to set up the i_op field correctly.

- write_inode() copies the contents of an inode to disk, changing the format on the way.

- put_inode() is called when an inode is no longer required. As well as calling write_inode(), it also has to check i_nlink. A value of 0 in i_nlink means that the file is marked for deletion. So it must deallocate any disk blocks assigned to this file.

- put_super() is called when unmounting a file system. It must mark the struct super_block as free.

- write_super() flushes the contents of the file system super block in the buffer cache (Section 10.4) to disk.

- statfs() returns statistical information about the file system, such as the number of free inodes or data blocks.

- The s_root field points to the name cache entry for the root directory of this new file system. This field will be filled in in step 5.

- The union u in super_block contains file system type specific data. The most important information contained here would involve free space on the disk. There would also be statistical information about the file system.

When an Ext2 file system is mounted, a copy of the super block, of the group descriptor table, the inode bitmap, and the block bitmap, is read into the buffer cache. Then, a struct ext2_sb_info is created in the struct super_block, to reference these. The sort of information

maintained for the Ext2 file system is shown in Figure 10.20, from
`<linux/ext2_fs_sb.h>`.

```
struct ext2_sb_info{
        struct ext2_super_block  *s_es;
        struct buffer_head       **s_group_desc;
        struct buffer_head       *s_inode_bitmap[];
        struct buffer_head       *s_block_bitmap[];
};
```

Figure 10.20: Superblock for an Ext2 file system

- s_es points to the super block in the buffer cache. We have examined an Ext2 super block in Section 10.4.
- s_group_desc points to the buffer head representing the chain of
  buffers containing the table of block group descriptors. All of the
  block group descriptors are read into memory at mount time. We
  have examined these descriptors in Section 10.4.
- s_inode_bitmap[] is an array of pointers to the buffers which contain the inode bitmap.
- s_block_bitmap[] identifies the buffers which contain the data
  block bitmap.

4. The field i_sb in the inode of the mounted over directory is set to point
   to this super_block.

5. It allocates an inode for the root directory of the newly mounted system,
   and calls read_inode() in super_operations to fill it in. It sets up a
   name cache entry for this root directory, and then points the s_root field
   in super_block to this struct dentry, and hence to the inode.

6. As the contents of the directory it is mounted on are no longer visible, it
   purges any entries in the name cache which pertain to this directory.

7. Finally, it passes back a pointer to the super_block for this file system.

Figure 10.21 illustrates the data structures at this stage. It also illustrates
how directory searches cross mount points into other file systems. The inode
for the mounted over directory, which is still in memory, has a pointer i_sb
to the struct super_block of the mounted on file system. This field is NULL
in any other inode. This is how mount points are recognised during directory
searches.

When the search arrives at the inode of the covered directory, it recognises
from the i_sb field that it is a mount point. So it does not search in the contents
of that directory. Instead, it follows the i_sb pointer to the super_block, and
the s_root pointer from there to the root inode of the new file system, from
where the search continues.

The old directory file still exists on disk. An ls of its parent directory now
gives the old name. But an ls of the directory itself goes to the root of the
mounted file system—not to the original.

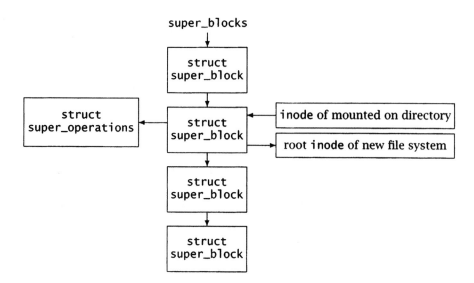

Figure 10.21: Data structures involved in mounting a file system

Umount

The system call to unmount a file system is umount(). This function carries out the following operations.

1. Make sure there are no open files in this file system.

2. Purge any entries in the name cache relating to this file system.

3. Deallocate the root inode for this file system.

4. Write back the super block, and deallocate the copy of the struct super_block in memory, by calling put_super().

5. Set i_sb in the mounted over directory inode to NULL. The original contents of this directory are now visible again.

10.6 Ext2 file operations

The previous section showed how an Ext2 file system is added into the directory structure, and made available to the kernel. We now go on to look at how files in such a system are manipulated. The Ext2 file system provides functions to carry out the file operations discussed in Section 9.5. For many of these the default functions are sufficient. Only those for which Ext2 provides a special implementation will be discussed here.

These functions will be continually referencing the Ext2 specific field in the inode. This is a struct ext2_inode_info, as shown in Figure 10.22, from <linux/ext2_fs_i.h>, which contains data copied from the on disk inode.

```
struct ext2_inode_info{
        u32 i_data[15];
        u32 i_faddr;
        u8  i_frag_no;
        u8  i_frag_size;
        u32 i_file_acl;
        u32 i_dir_acl;
        u32 i_block_group;
};
```

Figure 10.22: Ext2 file system inode data in memory

- The most important field is i_data[], which contains the locations of the file blocks on disk.

- The next three fields identify the block containing any fragments at the end of this file (i_faddr); the first fragment within this block (i_frag_no); and the number of fragments (i_frag_size).

- Note the fields i_file_acl and i_dir_acl, which are currently unused, but are designed for future security enhancements.

- The i_block_group field identifies the block group to which this inode belongs. This allows functions to index into the table of group descriptors, and find the vital information there, such as the data block bitmap for this particular block group.

Read

This function is given the number of bytes to be read, and a location in user space into which they are to be written. It uses the f_pos field to determine the absolute starting byte offset within the file, which corresponds to the data to be read.

We have already seen the memory manager's page cache, which is used for holding pages of program files, in Section 8.10. Linux also uses this page cache for reading from data files on disk. So once it has calculated the offset into the file, it uses this offset, along with the inode pointer, to hash into the page cache. If it finds the page there, then it can transfer the requested range of bytes to the buffer specified by the user.

For example, suppose it is asked to read 100 bytes, and that f_pos is currently 200. So it requires bytes 200-299 of the file. When it finds the struct page corresponding to this offset, it transfers the bytes.

If that particular page is not present, then it sets up a struct page for it, with its associated page frame, and calls the inode function readpage() to read in a whole page from disk.

Write

This function is also given a location in user space from where data is to be written to disk, and the number of bytes to write. It uses the f_pos field to determine the offset within the file, which corresponds to the data to be written.

While Linux uses the page cache for reading from a file, it uses a different mechanism, the buffer cache, for writing to files. So once it has got the offset into the file, it uses it to calculate the corresponding block number in the file, and the offset in that block. The specified range of bytes could actually fall across two or more blocks.

It translates this logical block number to a physical block number on the device, using the i_data[] field in ext2_inode_info, and hashes into the buffer cache. If the required block is in the cache, this returns the buffer head. If the block is not in the cache, then it allocates a cache block, and fills in an appropriate buffer_head. In either case it transfers the data from user space into the appropriate place in the cache.

For example, suppose it is asked to write 100 bytes, and that f_pos is currently 200. So it requires bytes 200—299. With a block size of 4kB, the required range is 100 bytes into block 0. Suppose that logical block 0 translates to physical block number 1234. The buffer cache is then searched for an entry corresponding to this block.

In all cases, it is not concerned with writing to the disk. This will be done at a later stage, by the update process.

As data being read is kept in the page cache, while data being written is kept in the buffer cache, the page cache is going to be inconsistent once a write has been carried out. So this function also checks if there is a copy of this page in the page cache, and if so, it updates it with the changes just made.

Readdir

This function is given a location in user space into which it is to write the next directory entry. The f_pos field tells it where to start reading in the directory file. It translates this byte offset to a logical block number, and then translates the logical block number in the directory, to a physical block number on the device. This, together with the i_dev field, enables it to hash into the buffer cache. If the required block is not in the cache, it allocates a cache block, and calls the disk driver to get the block from disk. In either case it copies the required directory entry to user space.

Mmap

When this function is called, the mmap() system service has already allocated a vm_area_struct for the region. This function merely sets the vm_inode field to point to the inode of the file to be mapped, and sets the vm_ops field to point to the appropriate operations, depending on whether the file is mapped shared or private.

Open

There is no special open() function for Ext2. The generic processing is done by the open() system service call, and the Ext2 specific processing, such as reading disk inodes, and filling in the ext2_inode_info field, is done by the directory inode function lookup(), see Section 10.7.

Release

This function is called by the close() system service, if the i_nlink field in the inode is 0. If the file system has preallocated any disk blocks to this file, but not used them, then it returns them, and marks them free in the block bitmap.

10.7   Ext2 inode operations

We have seen in Section 9.4 that the file system interface defines a set of abstract operations on each inode, and each file system type supplies an instance of the struct inode_operations, which is an array of pointers to these functions. Each element in this array points to its own specific implementation of that function.

We will now look at how the more important of these functions are implemented for the Ext2 file system.

Create

This function creates a new regular file in a directory. First it allocates an inode in memory for the new file. Then it finds a free disk inode, marks it allocated in the inode bitmap, and fills it in. In particular it sets i_mode to S_IFREG.

It uses the inode of the parent directory to hash into the buffer cache, and find the directory block. It searches through this, to find the first free entry, and puts the name in there.

Finally, it sets this directory entry to point to the disk inode.

Lookup

The lookup() function is passed a pointer to an inode representing the current directory, and the next segment in a path name. Its purpose is to find or create an inode representing this segment of the path name, and return a pointer to it.

It searches the directory lookup cache, and if the file has been opened recently and so is present in the cache, it returns a pointer to its inode. If not, it sets up a new inode, copies information into it from the on disk inode, and links it into the inode hash list, as well as the lookup cache, before returning the pointer.

Link

This function is passed pointers to the inode representing the file, and the inode representing the directory in which the hard link is to be created, as well as the name for the link. It creates a new directory entry, as in create(), but sets it to point to the old inode number. It increments the i_nlink field in the file's inode.

Unlink

This function is passed a pointer to a directory inode, and the name of a file in that directory. It finds the directory block in the buffer cache, and searches it to find the entry corresponding to the given name. It sets length and inode in that entry to 0, and if any adjacent entries are also free, it amalgamates them. Then it decrements the i_nlink field in inode. If this is now 0, it calls release(), to return any preallocated disk blocks, and marks the disk inode as free in the inode bitmap.

Symlink

This creates a new disk inode, with an i_mode field of S_IFLNK. If the full symbolic path name is less than 60 bytes, it puts it in the i_block[] field of the disk inode. Otherwise it writes the path name to the new file. This involves setting up a block in the buffer cache, copying the path name to that block, and calling the block write function of the disk drive to copy it to disk. It then adds a directory entry for the new name.

Mkdir

This function is identical to create(), but it first checks that the entry does not already exist, and then sets the i_mode field to S_IFDIR. It also sets up two default entries in the new directory, '.' and '..'.

Rmdir

This function is passed a pointer to the inode representing the parent directory, and the name of the directory entry to be deleted. It finds the inode of that directory, and hashes into the buffer cache to find the directory block. If there are any valid entries in this directory, it returns an error. If the directory is empty, it sets rec_len in the directory entry of the parent to 0. If previous or successive entries are also 0, it amalgamates them. It then releases any buffer blocks and disk blocks, and the disk inode, used by the deleted entry.

Mknod

This function is identical to create(), but it first checks that the entry does not exist. It sets the i_mode field to S_IFBLK or S_IFCHR or S_FIFO, as appropriate.

Rename

This function can rename a file into a different directory. It is passed pointers to two directories (which may be identical). First, it finds the directory block in the buffer cache, and the appropriate entry in the directory, for the old name. If the new name is shorter than the old name, it replaces it, and changes the name_len field. Otherwise, if the immediately following entry is large enough, it expands into that, and changes both name_len and rec_len. If neither of the previous options is feasible, it must find the first location in the directory large enough for the new name, and set up an entry there. In all cases the inode number is unchanged.

Readlink

If the i_mode field of the inode is not I_FLNK, then it returns an error. If the value in i_blocks is zero, then it returns the pathname from the i_data[] field of the struct ext2_inode_info. Otherwise it reads the pathname from the symbolic link file, and returns it.

Followlink

This function gets the pathname, in the same way as readlink(). It then goes ahead and opens the target file. It returns the inode corresponding to this file.

Readpage

This function is called when a read on a file cannot find the appropriate page in the page cache. It is passed a pointer to the struct page representing the page it is to read in, including the page frame into which it is to be placed, and a pointer to the inode representing the file it is to read from.

It maps from the offset field in the struct page, which specifies the logical page in the file, to a physical block number on disk, using bmap(). The actual transfer of data from the disk is file system independent, and is carried out by the disk driver, not the file manager.

Writepage

As Linux uses the buffer cache for writing, this function maps directly onto the block write function of the underlying disk drive.

Bmap

This function translates a logical block number in a file to a physical block number on disk. It is passed a pointer to an inode, and it uses the i_data[] field in the struct ext2_inode_info to determine where that logical block is actually stored on disk.

10.8 Summary

1. The file manager provides a facility for long-term storage. It allows files to be created and deleted, read from and written to, and also caters for protection and sharing.

2. Many different ways have been developed for organising information on disk drives—these are known as file system types. The code to implement these is loaded into the kernel at boot time.

3. Some of the space on each disk is used for administrative purposes. This includes the disk label and the boot block.

   Various schemes are used for allocating blocks to files. One possibility is that a file is kept in contiguous blocks. Another possibility is that the blocks of a given file are linked together by pointers, much like a linked list. Two improvements on that are to bring all the pointers to the whole disk together in a file map, or to bring all the pointers for a particular file together in an index block.

4. The Ext2 file system divides a partition into a number of block groups, each consisting of one or more cylinders. Each contains a copy of the super block, and of all the block group descriptors, also bitmaps, as well as inodes and data blocks.

   An inode contains all of the permanent information about a file, in particular where it is on the disk. Unix provides room for pointers to 12 blocks in the inode. If the file grows any larger, then indirect blocks are used.

   The system tries to allocate inodes for all the files in any directory from the same block group, and also allocates all blocks in a file from the block group in which the file's inode exists.

5. The basic unit of data organisation on a Unix disk is known as a file system. The user sees a seamless combination of several such file systems, into one directory tree.

   Inserting and removing file systems from the directory tree is known as mounting and unmounting. When an Ext2 file system is mounted, a copy of the super block, the group descriptor table, and the bitmaps, is read into the buffer cache.

6. The high-level interface examined in the previous chapter specified a standard set of operations on files or I/O streams, and each file system type is expected to provide its own implementation of these. Ext2 does not provide specific functions for a number of these, but uses default functions.

7. Likewise, there are a standard set of inode operations, and Ext2 provides its own implementation of each of these. They are mostly concerned with maintenance of the directory structure, and information about I/O streams. There are also functions to read or write a whole page of a file.

10.9   Discussion questions

1. Sometimes, the range of bytes requested by a read() may be stored in two (or more) different blocks on a disk. Outline the steps taken by the file manager in this case.

2. There are parallels between the memory manager and the file manager. Could one 'storage manager' be provided, to replace the two?

3. Use the sysfs() system service to determine which file system types are installed on the machine you are using.

4. Investigate how Linux allows a new file system type to be loaded dynamically, while a system is running ('loadable modules').

5. Why is the function read_inode() part of super_operations, and not part of inode_operations, which would seem the proper place for it?

6. It is a common problem that disks formatted by one operating system cannot be read by any other. Would a common disk label (across all operating systems) help?

7. Investigate the whole procedure of bootstrapping an operating system.

8. In a system using contiguous allocation, a file contains 10 blocks. Explain what is involved in adding a block (a) at the beginning (b) in the middle (c) at the end.

9. Repeat Q.8 for block linkage, file map, and indexed allocation.

10. Block linkage is very susceptible to damaged pointers. Could you suggest any extensions which would make it possible to reconstruct files, even if one or more pointers were lost?

11. Explain how indexed allocation allows for holes in files, e.g. it is possible to have record 1, and record 10000, without allocating space for the intervening records.

12. When compaction is required in a contiguous allocation scheme, is it necessary to compact the whole disk, or would it be sufficient to compact each track? Is there any time difference?

13. There is no field in the struct ext2_inode for the inode number. How then is each individual inode identified?

14. What is the advantage in allocating the inodes for all files in the same directory from the same block group?

15. What is the advantage in allocating data blocks for a file from the same block group as its inode?

16. Do you think the space saved by fragmenting the last block of a file is worth the time overhead of keeping track of fragments?

17. Use the statfs() system service to get information about a particular mounted file system.

18. How can the umount() system service know that there are no files open in the file system it is un-mounting?

19. When the file manager has calculated a physical block number it requires, how does it ask the disk driver to read that block? Refer to the following chapter.

20. Develop an algorithm to manage the deletion of a directory record in the Ext2 file system. Your algorithm should cater for coalescing free space before and/or after the record being deleted.

Special files 11

In Unix terminology, a special file is a directory entry which represents a physical device. The processing of such sources of input or output will be different from regular files in a file system, and that is the subject matter of this chapter.

We will begin by considering the permanent data structures and programs that are configured into the kernel to deal with such devices. There are no extra data structures set up in Linux when such special files are opened. We will then look at how input and output is performed.

11.1 Device drivers

Each physical device attached to a computer needs a program specially adapted to suit it, known as a device driver. This driver must be available to the kernel, and there must be some standard way of calling it. It runs as part of the kernel software, and carries out requests when called by an I/O procedure.

In Chapter 3 we encountered the Unix philosophy of having very few system processes, and so executing most kernel code in the context of the user process. The implications of this are most obvious when dealing with device drivers.

When the currently executing process wishes to do I/O, it executes system service code, then I/O procedure code, then device driver code. It is blocked somewhere in the driver, waiting on the device, and so is context switched out. The processor is given to some other process.

When the device is ready, it interrupts. The interrupt routine, running in interrupt context (stolen from the current process), services the device. This part of a device driver is never called directly by a user, and usually has no relation to the currently running process. It is not possible to predict when it will run; this depends on the device.

The interrupt routine also identifies which process was waiting for this device, and moves it from the wait queue to the run queue. Eventually its turn will come, and it will wake up at exactly the point where it was blocked, in the driver. It will return to the I/O procedure, to the system service, and ultimately to the user. Figure 11.1 illustrates this situation.

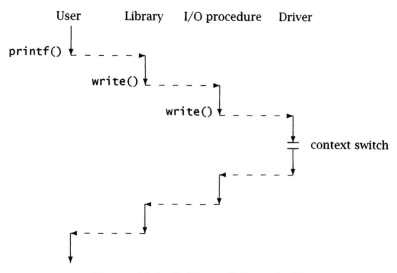

Figure 11.1: Calling a Unix style driver

Other operating systems take a different approach, and assign each device driver a process of its own. Such a driver process spends most of its time asleep. It is woken up when required, by some form of interprocess communication. With this arrangement, some way has to be found to pass data and instructions to the driver process. Typically these are encapsulated in a data structure called an input output request block, or IORB. The simplest IPC arrangement would be a message queue, with the IORB in the message.

The I/O procedure runs in the context of the calling thread. It creates an IORB, and either passes it in a message, or puts it on a queue and does a SIGNAL on a semaphore. In either case, after passing the request on to the driver, the I/O procedure typically blocks itself, until the driver notifies it that the request has been completed.

The driver code is broken into two parts. The first part has already done a WAIT on the semaphore it shares with the I/O procedure, so the SIGNAL on it wakes it up. It removes the IORB from the linked list, carries out the requested function, and puts itself to sleep again. When the device finally interrupts, it is the driver process which is woken up; it now executes the second part of its code. When it has serviced the interrupt, it notifies the I/O procedure that the I/O request has completed, and loops back to read from the message queue, or WAIT on the semaphore again. Figure 11.2 illustrates this situation.

11.2   Configuring the kernel

In many systems, including traditional Unix, driver code is bound into the kernel at compilation time. Changing or adding a driver means recompiling the kernel. Linux allows drivers to be loaded or unloaded dynamically, while the system is running.

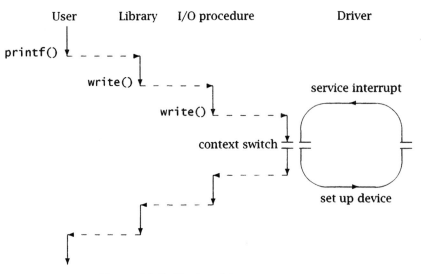

Figure 11.2: Device driver as a process

Devices are divided into two basic types, character and block. Character devices can only be accessed sequentially, for example a keyboard. Block devices can be accessed randomly, and transfer data in fixed size blocks, using the buffer cache. The typical block device is a disk drive. While this traditional distinction is retained in Linux, the interface to both is identical.

The heart of the whole mechanism is a pair of arrays, called the device switch, as shown in Figure 11.3, from `linux/fs/devices.c`.

```
struct device_struct{
        const char              *name;
        struct file_operations *fops;
};

static struct device_struct chrdevs[];
static struct device_struct blkdevs[];
```

Figure 11.3: The character and block device switches

Each driver has an entry in one or other of these arrays. As can be seen, each entry is a `struct device_struct`, which consists of the name of the device, and a pointer to a `struct file_operations`. These are the standard file operations which we saw when considering the `struct file` in Section 9.5. The value from `fops` is copied into the `f_op` field of a stream representing a device, when it is opened.

For supported functions, the driver supplies an implementation specific to its device. If a particular function is not supported by a driver, then there is a NULL pointer in the appropriate position. The entry in these tables is the only link between the driver code and the rest of the kernel.

The system manager assigns each device a unique number in the system, known as its major number. This is one of the parameters to mknod(), which is used to create the special file in the /dev directory which represents this device. The same number is used when the driver is registered with the kernel, which uses it as an index in chrdevs[] or blkdevs[] at which to insert the instance of struct device_struct corresponding to this device. See Figure 11.4.

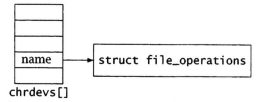

Figure 11.4: An entry in the character device switch

11.3 Operations on devices

In Chapter 9, we traced the implementation of the I/O procedures from the file descriptor, through the struct file, to the inode. In the case of a device file, i_mode will be either S_IFBLK or S_IFCHR. The f_op field in the struct file is used to access the specific driver functions for that device.

These functions are usually written by the hardware engineers, who are familiar with the complex requirements of the hardware. Here we will look at how these functions might be implemented.

The i_op field of the inode for a special file also points to an array of functions. But these are the standard functions of whichever file system type the *name* of the device is stored in; they are not specific to the device.

Lseek

Some devices allow the user to specify a position at which the next input or output will occur. The best example of this would be a tape drive. With such a device, this function adjusts the f_pos field in the struct file. No operation is actually performed on the physical device. If the device is not seekable, then the function merely returns an error.

Read

The read() function is called by the read() I/O procedure. It is implemented differently for character or block devices.

Read for character device

First we will look at the implementation for character devices, or when the i_mode field is S_IFCHR. The device driver is passed pointers to the inode,

struct file, and the memory location to which it is to read the data, as well as a count of the number of bytes to read.

The algorithm for read() is given in Figure 11.5. The following comments refer to this algorithm.

```
IF device busy THEN
        Sleep
ENDIF
Set up the I/O operation
Sleep
IF error THEN
        return value = errornumber
ELSE
        Transfer data to destination
        return value = success
ENDIF
Return (return value)
```

Figure 11.5: Algorithm for reading from a character device

1. Normally a device can perform only one operation at a time. So there must be some way of arranging for mutual exclusion on the device. This could, for example, be a semaphore. Whatever mechanism is used, it must ensure that while a device is working for one process, any other process that calls it will be blocked.

2. Setting up the operation involves writing to the control register of the particular device.

3. The driver then has to wait, even if there are other requests pending, as the device can be doing only one thing at a time. So the calling process is put to sleep. When the device has finished, and generated a hardware interrupt, the interrupt routine will locate the waiting process, and mark it runnable. When it eventually runs, it will take up at the next instruction.

   Another possibility is to have the second part of the driver registered as a handler for the specific interrupt generated by that device.

4. The test for error involves checking the status register of the device. If an error occurred, then the error number relevant to the condition is returned.

5. If there was no error, the data is read from the data register of the device, into the buffer specified by the caller.

Read for block device

The device driver for a block device provides a different implementation of the read() function. It builds the parameters of the request into a struct

request that contains all the information required: see Figure 11.6, from
`<linux/blkdev.h>`.

```
struct request{
        kdev_t         rq_dev;      /* device identifier */
        int            cmd;         /* READ or WRITE     */
        unsigned long  sector;      /* start sector      */
        unsigned long  nr_sectors;  /* number of sectors */
        char           *buffer;     /* buffer address    */
        struct request *next;       /* next IORB         */
};
```

Figure 11.6: Request block for block devices

- The device number is in rq_dev.

- A flag to indicate read or write is set in cmd.

- The starting block number on the device is in sector, and the number of
  blocks to transfer in nr_sectors.

- The location where the data is to be stored in memory is pointed to by
  buffer.

- As block devices tend to be shared, there may be several requests, from
  different processes, pending at any one time. The requests for a particular
  device are kept on a linked list, linked through the next field.

Both reading and writing a block device are carried out by the same routine,
known as the strategy routine. This is asynchronous; it queues the request,
and returns. Typically the I/O procedure puts the calling process to sleep at
this stage; it is woken up by the interrupt handler when the operation has
completed.

The algorithm for the strategy routine is given in Figure 11.7.

```
Put struct request on device queue
IF device idle, THEN
      Select struct request from queue
      IF (cmd == WRITE) THEN
          Transfer data from user space to device memory
      ENDIF
      Set up the device for specified operation
ENDIF
Return to caller.
```

Figure 11.7: Algorithm for strategy routine

1. As more than one process, as well as the interrupt routine, may be manipulating the queue at the same time, they need to synchronise their access. So the queue must be protected by a mutex (not shown here).

2. As there is no device specific process in Unix, the actual handling of the device has to be done in user context, as here, or else in interrupt context later.

3. The device driver normally handles each request as it comes. But, for example, a disk driver may select IORBs from the queue in an order which minimises movements of the head.

4. Setting up the operation involves writing to the control register for the particular device. The request is carried out by the device in its own time.

When the device is finished, it interrupts. The interrupt service routine has to check whether it is cleaning up after a read, or a write, and act accordingly. The algorithm for such a routine is given in Figure 11.8.

```
Check for error
IF (cmd == READ) THEN
        Transfer data from device memory to user space
ENDIF
Move user process from wait queue to run queue
IF request queue not empty THEN
        Select struct request from queue
        IF (cmd == WRITE) THEN
                Transfer data from user space to device memory
        ENDIF
        Set up the device for specified operation
ENDIF
```

Figure 11.8: Algorithm for interrupt service routine

1. The test for error involves checking the status register in the device.

2. If the cmd field in the struct request specified that the operation was a read, then data has to be moved from the device to the user buffer, as specified by the buffer field of struct request.

3. If there are further requests on the queue, the next operation is begun in interrupt context, before the interrupt service routine completes.

Write

As with read(), block devices are dealt with by the strategy routine, which we have already seen. Here we will consider the driver function for writing to a character device.

This function is called by the write() I/O procedure if the i_mode field is S_IFCHR. It is passed the same set of parameters as read(). The algorithm for write() is given in Figure 11.9. It is similar to the character read algorithm, and the comments made in Section 11.3 are also relevant here.

```
IF device busy THEN
        Sleep
ENDIF
Transfer data from user buffer to device memory
Set up the device for writing
Sleep
IF error THEN
        return value = errornumber
ELSE
        return value = success
ENDIF
Return (return value)
```

Figure 11.9: Algorithm for writing to a character device

Readdir

This function is meaningless for devices. So there is a NULL pointer in the corresponding entry in the struct file_operations.

Poll

We have seen the high-level implementation of the poll() system call in Section 9.8. This device-specific function is called to interrogate the device, and check if it is ready to be read from or written to. So it reads only from the status register. If the device is ready, then it returns 1. Otherwise, it returns 0.

Ioctl

Each device has its own characteristics, hence this catch-all function. It is used to execute driver functions which are not catered for in the standard file operations. Examples would be setting baud rates on communications lines, or writing labels to disks or tapes.

Mmap

Some devices have a significant amount of physical memory installed on their interface cards. The mmap() system service can be used to map this device memory into the address space of a process. The drivers for such devices provide this low level function. It sets up the appropriate memory management

structures, such as a vm_area_struct and page table entries. It points them to the physical memory on the device. Presumably a function written specifically for this device will know where the physical memory is. In effect, it gives this physical memory a virtual address, at which the process can read or write it.

Open

When a process calls the open() system service for a device file, it performs most of the operations associated with opening a regular file. It looks up the filename on disk, sets up the inode, struct file, and file descriptor.

It uses the device number, from the i_rdev field in the inode, and the relevant bits from the i_mode field, to index into either chrdevs[] or blkdevs[]. This gives it a pointer to the struct file_operations for this particular device. It puts this pointer into the f_ops field of the struct file, which makes the driver functions accessible for future operations. It then calls the open() function for the device.

While the processing performed by this open() function is obviously very device specific, it always has to check that the device is powered up and on line, i.e. that it is responding to commands. Then it resets the device to a known state. For example, a printer driver might send an eject or page feed command, and move the print head to the extreme left position. This guarantees that printing will begin at the top left-hand corner of a page.

Release

Typically all the release() function does is reset the device, and maybe put it off line. If output were being buffered, then it would flush the buffer. It might also flush any queues of waiting requests.

11.4 STREAMS

The device driver mechanism described above has problems. There is a lot of device-independent processing in each driver. There is little support for sharing code between drivers, and much functionality is duplicated. Particularly with character I/O, there is no recognition of boundaries in the stream of bytes, or of control or priority information. The mechanism was just about adequate for terminals and disk drives, where it was assumed that data passed unchanged between the device and the user. The most that was envisaged was translation from one character code to another.

When network devices were added to computers, shortcomings began to show up. Networking software has developed as a layered structure; some processing is done by each layer. This involves at least reading, interpreting, and stripping off headers and trailers on input, and creating such headers and trailers on output. The traditional mechanism was just not up to this.

Overview

What was required was a more complex driver, one which could in turn be built up of layers of software modules. Each module would take output data from the one above, process it, and pass it on to the one beneath. Each module would also take input data from the one beneath, process it, and pass it on to the one above. The module at the bottom would be a raw driver for the device, and the one at the top would provide the standard file interface.

The STREAMS mechanism was developed as such a generalised architecture, providing a full duplex communications path between a stream head at one end, and a device interface at the other.

The traditional `open()`, `read()`, `write()`, `close()` user interface, and the high-level processing, is maintained—it is the implementation of the driver which has changed. A STREAMS device appears to an application as a character special file. It is identified as `S_IFCHR`—there is no special `IFSTREAM`.

Figure 11.10 gives an overview of a stream.

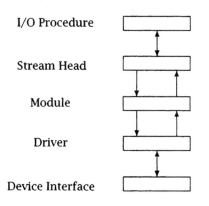

I/O Procedure

Stream Head

Module

Driver

Device Interface

Figure 11.10: A basic view of a stream

A module is the basic component in a STREAMS implementation. Each module provides some specific processing for the data supplied to it. The modules in a stream are not implemented as processes or threads in their own right. The code of a module is executed in the context of the calling process. If any operation cannot be carried out immediately, then the data is put on a queue, and processed at a later stage. So the original system call always returns promptly, and does not block.

STREAMS do not have to be constructed statically, like the rest of the kernel. It is possible to insert extra modules into a stream, and remove modules from a stream, as and when required. This requires standardisation of the interfaces between modules, as you never know in advance just where a module may end up. The STREAMS mechanism has not been implemented in Linux.

Opening a stream

A stream is usually built in two steps. The first step creates just the stream head and the stream end or driver. The second step adds modules to produce an expanded stream. If the driver performs all of the required processing, then no modules are needed.

When a process opens a STREAMS device, the kernel recognises from the directory entry that it is a character special file. An entry is allocated in the user's file descriptor table and a `struct file` is created. An `inode` is allocated and initialised to represent a file of type character special. When the device specific `open()` function is called, a standard stream head structure is allocated.

Then a pair of queues are allocated for the stream head. Each module, head, or driver, is allocated two **queue** structures, to hold messages on their way up or down. A pair of queues is also allocated at this stage for the driver, and linked to the head's queues. Figure 11.11 shows how the structures representing a minimal stream are linked together. It also shows some messages waiting on the stream head write queue.

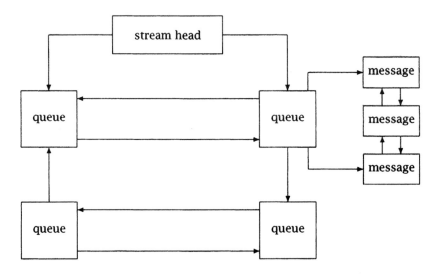

Figure 11.11: Data structures constituting a minimal stream

As with all Unix I/O, processes can share streams. A second process calling `open()` on the same stream will be assigned its own file descriptor, and `struct file`, which will point to the existing `inode`. A process may also inherit an open stream after a `fork()`; in this case it will have its own file descriptor, which will point to the common `struct file`.

The system service `isastream()` can be used to determine if a file descriptor refers to a STREAMS file or not.

Adding and removing modules

Modules can be added to a stream, using the `ioctl()` `I_PUSH` system call;
they are inserted immediately below the stream head. An `ioctl()` `I_POP`
system call removes the module immediately below the stream head: STREAMS
connects the stream head to the module below the popped one. It is also
possible to alter the standard connections between the queues in a stream.
An example is a loop-back pseudo driver whose write queue would connect
directly to its own read queue; such a configuration might be used for test
purposes. (Irregular queue connections of this kind are called welds.)

Multiplexing streams

Streams have been described so far as linear connections of modules, where
each module is connected to one upstream module and one downstream module. While this configuration is suitable for most applications, some require
the ability to multiplex streams, both upwards and downwards. This can be
done using `ioctl()` `I_LINK`. There are three types:

- A many-to-one multiplexor, see Figure 11.12, multiplexes data from several upper streams to a single lower stream. A terminal windowing facility
  might be implemented in this way, where each upper stream is associated
  with a separate window.

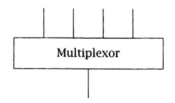

Figure 11.12: A many-to-one multiplexor

- A one-to-many multiplexor routes data from a single upper stream to several lower streams: see Figure 11.13. A networking protocol could be
  implemented like this, where each lower stream links the protocol to a
  different physical network.

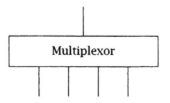

Figure 11.13: A one-to-many multiplexor

- A many-to-many multiplexor routes data from one of many upper streams to one of many lower streams, as shown in Figure 11.14.

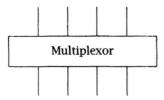

Figure 11.14: A many-to-many multiplexor

Figure 11.15 shows a realistic example. The IP module in the diagram is an example of an upper multiplexor because it has multiple streams above it. It is also a lower multiplexor, as it has multiple drivers below it, and it can send data to either the token ring or ethernet driver.

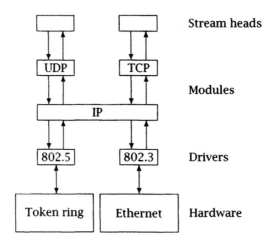

Figure 11.15: Networking multiplexor

Processing messages

With STREAMS, all input and output data is packaged into messages, consisting of one or more message blocks. What are actually passed between modules are pointers to messages. So only the minimum amount of copying has to done as data moves up or down a stream.

Requests from application programs are routed through the current device's struct file_operations to the stream head. This may fulfil the request immediately, e.g. a read request when there is data available at the head. Otherwise it creates a message block, puts it on the queue of the next module

down, and calls its processing routine. This processes the message, and moves it to the next queue. Eventually the driver is called. All of this is done in the context of the calling process. When the driver has sent the request to the device, control returns to the stream head, which may put the calling process to sleep, waiting for a reply.

When a device interrupts, the driver processing routine is called. This passes the message on to the next module up, by linking it on its queue, and passing control to it. Eventually the stream head is called, and may wake up a waiting process, which has previously made a system call for input. All of this is done in interrupt context. The stream head translates incoming messages into a format appropriate to return to a system call.

System services

The `read()` and `write()` system calls just deal with sequences of bytes, there is no concept of messages or boundaries. Because STREAMS can distinguish messages, there is need for special system services if users are to avail of this.

The `putmsg()` system call enables a user to create messages and send them downstream. The user supplies the contents of the control and data parts of the message in two separate buffers. There is a special version, `putpmsg()`, to send priority data down a stream.

The `getmsg()` system call is used to retrieve the contents of a message located at the stream head read queue, and place them into two user specified buffers, one for control information, one for data. There is a corresponding `getpmsg()` to receive priority data from a stream.

The `ioctl()` function is used to perform a variety of control functions on streams. There are in fact 29 different `ioctl()` requests relating to STREAMS, each of which is encapsulated as a message, and sent downstream.

Closing a stream

A stream is closed when the last process associated with it issues a `close()` system call. Dismantling consists of popping any modules on the stream, and closing the driver. Finally the user's file descriptor table entry, the `struct file`, and the `inode` are deallocated.

11.5 Terminal I/O

Terminals are somewhat different from what we have considered so far. For example, requests for output to a screen or printer, or for input from a disk drive, all originate from a running process. But in the case of a terminal, input originates with the device.

A terminal interrupt is not in response to requests from above, it is totally independent of a running process. Such data must be processed and stored by the operating system, until it is requested by a process.

Processing

There are two common levels of processing which the operating system can perform on characters typed at the keyboard. The first is canonical mode, cooked mode, or line-at-a-time mode. Characters are buffered until a full line has been entered, typically denoted by the RETURN or ENTER key. The process is sleeping in the meantime, giving the user the opportunity to edit the line before it is passed to the program. Such canonical processing is done in a 'terminal line discipline' module.

The second level of processing is non-canonical, or raw, or character-at-a-time mode. Each character is passed through to the process when it is typed. The operating system does not attempt to interpret any special characters, such as backspace or arrow key. An editor, for example, would need this.

While these are the two extremes, there are also a large number of combinations in between them. POSIX introduced the `struct termios`, which encapsulates all the characteristics of terminal I/O that can be changed: see Figure 11.16, from `<asm/termbits.h>`. Each field is a bitmap, with each bit controlling one aspect of the terminal line discipline. For example, depending on the setting in `termios`, it will do canonical or non-canonical processing.

```
struct termios{
        tcflag_t c_iflag;
        tcflag_t c_oflag;
        tcflag_t c_cflag;
        tcflag_t c_lflag;
        cc_t     c_cc[];
};
```

Figure 11.16: Data structure controlling terminal characteristics

- `c_iflag` bits define the processing that can be done to a character on its way in from a terminal.

- `c_oflag` bits define the processing that can be done to a character on its way out to a terminal.

- `c_cflag` defines control characteristics as baud rate, stop bits, and parity.

- `c_lflag` specifies how characters are interpreted, for example whether they are to be locally echoed or not.

- `c_cc` allows certain control characters to be redefined.

Along with this, there is the `tc` series of system calls, such as `tcgetattr()`, which reads values from `termios`; and `tcsetattr()`, which sets new values in `termios`, and so ultimately controls the operation of the line discipline. Others include `tcdrain()` and `tcflush()`.

The `isatty()` library function is used to determine if an open file descriptor refers to a terminal device. The `ttyname()` function returns a pointer to the pathname of the file representing the terminal device.

Pseudo terminals

It is common practice today for users to log on over a network, not from a directly connected terminal. Such an arrangement is known as a pseudo terminal. It is built into servers that provide network logins.

A pseudo terminal is divided into two halves, the slave and the master. Each has its own entry in the /dev directory. The master is /dev/ptyp0; the corresponding slave is /dev/ttyp0. But they are built in such a way that anything written to the master is presented as input to the slave; anything written to the slave is passed as input to the master.

The slave presents an interface to a user process which looks just like a standard terminal. But there is no hardware at the other end, rather the master, which emulates the hardware, typically is a network connection.

For example, the telnetd daemon waits for connection requests from a remote machine. When one arrives it forks a new process, and the parent continues to wait for further requests: see Figure 11.17.

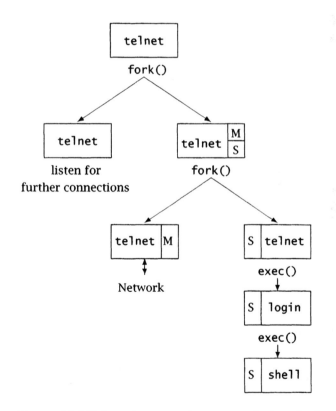

Figure 11.17: Logging on using a pseudo terminal

The child process, which is still running telnet, opens a master-slave pair of pseudo devices. It then forks into two processes. File descriptors 0, 1, and 2 are set to the master pseudo terminal in the parent; they are set to the slave pseudo terminal in the child. The two processes are connected through the

pseudo terminal. The parent process continues to run `telnet`, and handles communication over the network. It writes any data which comes in over the network to the master, which presents it to the slave, in the child process. Any data written to the slave is presented to the master, and is then copied to the network by `telnet`.

The child execs the login program. This asks for a username and password. When these come in over the network, `telnet` writes them to the master, and so they are read by the slave, which verifies them, and then execs a shell program.

11.6 Summary

A special file is a directory entry which represents a physical device.

1. A device driver is the part of the operating system that is specially tailored to each individual piece of hardware.

2. Each configured device has an entry in `chrdevs[]` or `blkdevs[]`, containing pointers to device specific functions.

3. Each device driver implements the standard `file_operations` functions specified in the `struct file`, in so far as these are applicable to the particular device. There is a significant difference in the way the `read()` and `write()` operations are implemented for character devices, and for block devices. The former normally work synchronously; while the latter queue requests asynchronously.

4. The STREAMS mechanism allows drivers to be built from predefined modules. This is particularly useful where some processing has to be done on the data as it passes in or out, e.g. networks or terminals.

   A stream is created by opening the special file associated with the driver. Such a minimal stream consists of just a stream head and the stream end or driver.

   Modules can then be added (or later removed) by using the `ioctl()` system call. Streams can be multiplexed, upwards and/or downwards.

   With STREAMS, all input and output is encapsulated in messages. Each module processes data by putting the message on the queue of the next module (up or down), and calling its processing function.

   As well as `read()` and `write()`, there are extra system services for use with STREAMS. These allow control information, and priority data, to be sent.

5. Terminals are an example of an application where the driver may need to do some processing on the data, e.g. interpret the backspace key.

   A pseudo terminal is used for network logins, where there is no hardware terminal. This consists of two halves, a slave and a master, connected together as a feedback loop. The slave is in the user process; the master is in a process handling communication, such a Telnet or Xwin.

11.7   Discussion questions

1. Discuss the advantages and disadvantages of implementing each device driver as a separate kernel process, as opposed to running the driver in the context of the calling process.

2. What is the advantage of having device drivers implemented as separate modules, as opposed to having them compiled into the kernel?

3. Why are device driver functions implemented as operations on the `struct file`, and not on the `inode`?

4. How does the interrupt routine identify the process waiting for a particular device?

5. Investigate some of the algorithms which have been developed for ordering the request queue for a disk drive.

6. Investigate some of the uses of the `ioctl()` system service.

7. STREAMS introduces simplicity and clarity into the design of an I/O system, but also increases the amount of processing required. Discuss the tradeoffs between these.

8. Modules are always inserted at, and removed from, immediately under the stream head. How would you remove a module nested more deeply down a stream?

9. Investigate how you would use the `tcsetattr()` function to disable the echoing of characters to the screen.

10. By default, CTRL-S allows a user to stop output to the screen, and CTRL-Q restarts the output. Find the appropriate bit in the `termios` structure which controls this. Check if it is set or not. Write a program which turns off this facility.

11. Use `tcsetattr()` to allow any key to restart suspended output, and not just CTRL-Q.

12. Clear the `ICANON` bit in the `termios` structure, to turn off canonical processing. This makes the basic unit of input to be the single character, rather than the logical line.

13. With the `ICANON` bit turned off as in Question 11.12, investigate how to set a value for the minimum number of characters the terminal driver must receive before a call to read from the terminal returns.

14. With the `ICANON` bit turned off as in Question 11.12, investigate how to set a timeout period for a read from the terminal.

15. Use a master/slave pair of pseudo terminals to implement data passing between two processes.

In Unix, some mechanisms for interprocess communication are integrated into the I/O subsystem. These are pipes and sockets. Like the types of I/O we have examined previously, they are assigned a file descriptor, a `struct file`, and in some cases a directory entry and an `inode`, and are accessed using the standard I/O procedures. But they do not use the standard `open()` function; instead they are created by special system services `pipe()` and `socket()`.

12.1 Unix pipes

The pipe was the first interprocess communication mechanism developed in Unix. Essentially it is only a first in first out buffer. It is created by the `pipe()` system call, which returns an array containing two open file descriptors: one for the write end and the other for the read end. The `open()` system service is not used with such pipes. The pipe exists as long as one of these descriptors remains open. Data is put into the pipe using the standard `write()` function, and removed using the standard `read()` function, just as with a regular file. There is no structure on the data in a pipe, it is just a stream of bytes. There is no distinction between where one write ends, and the next begins.

The pipe mechanism does add synchronisation to the data transfer. A process doing a `write()` on a full pipe will be blocked by the system until some other process removes sufficient data. A process doing a `read()` on an empty pipe will be blocked until some other process puts data in. The size of the pipe buffer is system dependent; it is defined as PIPE_BUF. The `pathconf()` system service will return the value of this. The default under Linux is 4kB.

Programming with pipes

When a process creates a pipe, the input and output ends are both in the same process. This situation, which is illustrated on the left of Figure 12.1, is not really very useful. The next step is normally to `fork()` a child process. Pipes are inherited by children, so now we have read and write ends of the pipe in both processes. This situation is illustrated in the centre of Figure 12.1.

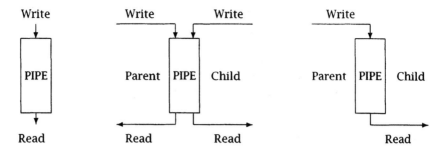

Figure 12.1: Setting up a pipe for interprocess communication

The child can read what the parent writes, and the parent can read what the child writes. But because there is no structure in the pipe, each process could get its own message back. Cooperating processes could invent their own protocols to prevent this—but it has to be done by the programmers, it is not supplied by the pipe mechanism.

A common practice is for the parent to close one end of the pipe after the fork(), and the child to close the other. For example, if the parent closes the read end, and the child closes the write end, then we have a one way pipe from parent to child. This situation is illustrated on the right in Figure 12.1. For two way communication we use a second pipe.

When there are no further file descriptors pointing to the read end of a pipe, it is not possible to write to the other end. But it is possible to read from a pipe with the write end closed, as long as there is data still in the pipe.

Implementation

The pipe() system service sets up two file descriptors, each with its own struct file, one opened for reading, the other for writing. Each points to the same inode. But there is no directory entry, or on-disk inode. The inode contains a struct pipe_inode_info in the u area, as shown in Figure 12.2, from <linux/pipe_fs_i.h>.

```
struct pipe_inode_info{
      struct wait_queue *wait    /* for blocked threads    */
      char              *base  /* buffer                */
      unsigned int      start  /* next byte to read     */
      unsigned int      readers /* number of readers     */
      unsigned int      writers /* number of writers     */
};
```

Figure 12.2: Data structure representing a pipe

- The wait field heads a linked list of struct wait_queue, each representing one sleeping process waiting to access the pipe, whether for reading or writing.

- The data is stored in a page sized buffer. The `base` field points to this.

- `start` is a circulating pointer, which always points to the next byte to be read.

- The `readers` and `writers` fields track the number of processes which have the pipe open for reading or writing, respectively.

The number of bytes in the buffer is contained in the `i_size` field of the inode. The macro `PIPE_LEN()` returns this size. So a new write always begins at `(start + PIPE_LEN(inode)) MOD PIPE_BUF`. See Figure 12.3.

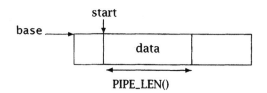

Figure 12.3: Representation of a pipe

Named pipes

Pipes can be inherited by child processes, and by grandchildren. But there is always the limitation that processes wishing to communicate by pipe must have some common ancestor. To overcome this limitation named pipes, or FIFOs, were developed. Such a mechanism is essential for a server process, as it is not possible to establish a common ancestor between a client and a server, and still any client process must be able to communicate with the server.

The basic problem is, how do two totally unrelated processes associate with the same pipe? The solution is to allow pipes to be uniquely named. Then once two programs use the same name for the pipe, they will be communicating with each other through that pipe. As there was already a mechanism in place for storing filenames (the directory structure), it was decided to use that for storing pipe names as well. While their names are part of the file system, the data being passed through such pipes is stored in system memory.

FIFOs look like regular file system entries, with a directory entry and inode in the file system on disk, but there are no associated data blocks on disk. The directory entry representing such a named pipe or FIFO is created by using the `mknod()` system call. These entries are distinguished by the p in the first column of the output from the `ls -l` command. It is important to note that only the *name* of the FIFO is maintained on disk; the data is still buffered in memory, as with unnamed pipes.

FIFOs are opened in the same manner as other I/O channels, with the `open()` system call, not `pipe()`. Any process, with the requisite permissions, can open, read, write the FIFO. And the processes do not even have to be running at the same time. Both ends of the FIFO must be opened separately, one

for reading, the other for writing. Each opening returns a file descriptor, with
its own struct file; but as they are using the same name, there is only one
inode.

Evaluation of pipes

- As the data passing through a pipe is buffered in memory, the maximum
  size of a pipe tends to be kept small. So they are most useful in situations
  where a large backlog of messages is unlikely to build up.

- There is no system support for structure in the data being passed. Any
  boundaries between messages must be implemented by the programmer.

- Traditionally, it was not possible to test if a pipe is empty (or full). So a
  process always risked blocking on a read() or a write(). We have seen
  the select() and poll() system services, which allow a process to test
  the status of a number of I/O streams, including pipes.

- Pipes cannot be used for broadcast communication. The first process
  which reads from a pipe removes the data; it is not available to any other.

12.2 The socket mechanism

The designers of 4.2 BSD set out to provide a standard communication interface between any programs running under Unix, on the same machine, or on
different machines. The abstraction they came up with is known as a *socket*.

Introduction

Sockets are an extension of the Unix file access mechanism. Like pipes, they
are allocated file descriptors, and the traditional read() and write() system
calls can be used with them.

The implementation of the socket mechanism is extremely complex. This
is because it has been designed to communicate between processes on any machine, using any of a wide variety of networking systems. While in this chapter
we are only concerned with socket communication between two processes on
the same Linux machine, we cannot escape the complexity entirely. A later
chapter will look at socket communication between different machines.

It is not surprising that sockets have been implemented as a layered structure, something like the virtual file system we have examined in some detail.
The top layer is generic, and treats a socket as an interprocess communication channel. So it is possible to abstract from whether the communicating
processes are on the same machine, or on different machines.

And if communication is over a network, the socket layer abstracts away
the differences between the possible networking protocols which may be used
in the lower layers.

We have seen that the virtual file system links the device independent upper layer with the device specific drivers, by defining a standard set of functions. Any particular file system, or a driver for a particular device, provides its own implementation of these functions. The socket mechanism involves a similar standard interface between the generic upper layer, and the protocol specific lower layers.

A protocol is a set of rules and data formats that regulate the transfer of information between the two ends of a communication connection. We have already seen POSIX message queues, for example. Many different protocols have been developed for communicating over networks, and the socket mechanism itself must be able to handle any or all of these. For example, the Unix domain protocol, which we examine in this chapter, is a form of interprocess communication, which uses the socket interface. We will examine the Internet domain protocols in a later chapter.

From our point of view here, the most important property of a communication protocol is how it identifies the endpoints of a communication. How is a particular socket, in a particular process, uniquely identified in the whole system? This is the problem of addressing a socket. All sockets which use the same form of addressing are said to belong to a particular address family, or domain.

The many possible address formats are represented by predefined constants in <linux/socket.h> (see Figure 12.4). The only one to concern us in this chapter is AF_UNIX, the Unix domain.

```
#define AF_UNSPEC     0 /* Unspecified           */
#define AF_UNIX       1 /* Unix domain sockets   */
#define AF_INET       2 /* Internet IP Protocol  */
#define AF_IPX        4 /* Novell IPX            */
#define AF_APPLETALK  5 /* Appletalk             */
```

Figure 12.4: Supported address families

Setting up the kernel

At boot time, certain address domains and protocols are configured into the kernel. Each one is described by a net_proto_family structure, as shown in Figure 12.5, from <linux/net.h>.

```
struct net_proto_family{
        int family;
        int (*create)();
};
```

Figure 12.5: Data structure representing a protocol family

- The `family` field identifies the protocol family by its literal constant, such as `AF_UNIX`.

- The `create` field is a pointer to a function which customises a new socket for this particular family.

There is one such structure for each domain. The system maintains an array `net_families[]` (declared in `net/socket.c`) of pointers to these structures, with one entry for each domain. See Figure 12.6.

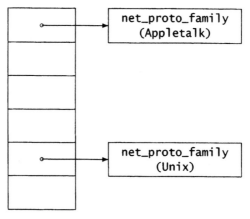

net_families[]

Figure 12.6: Domains registered in the kernel

12.3   Interprocess communication using sockets

We will now go on to look at the interface which the socket mechanism provides to a programmer, and the top level, domain independent processing.

We will break the discussion down into three phases. First, we will consider the processing involved, and the data structures which are set up when a socket is created. Next, we will consider how one socket is connected to another. Finally, we will consider how data is actually passed from one socket to another, in both directions.

Creating a socket

A process creates a socket by means of the `socket()` system call. Just what kind of socket is created is decided by the values passed as arguments.

The first parameter determines the address family to which this particular socket will belong. This will be one of the options from Figure 12.4.

Even within a particular address family, or domain, there are different ways in which the communication can be regulated. This is determined by the

second parameter. Different domains may supply various options, but there are two types supplied by all domains.

SOCK_STREAM This sets up a permanent, two way, connection between two sockets. However, it does not recognise record boundaries, i.e. data is treated as a continuous stream of bytes. This is sometimes likened to setting up a connection between two telephones.

SOCK_DGRAM This provides connectionless communication, or datagrams; the record boundaries are preserved. This is sometimes likened to the postal service.

The third parameter specifies which protocol is to be used with the socket. Currently, there is only one protocol for each type within an address family, or domain. By setting this argument to 0, or PF_UNSPEC, the default protocol is chosen.

When an application calls socket(), the kernel uses the first parameter to index into its net_families[] array of net_proto_family structures, to find the one that corresponds to the parameters specified by the caller. If that domain has not been configured, then it returns an error.

The operating system now allocates new data structures to hold all of the information needed to represent the socket to the kernel. First of all an inode is allocated. The i_mode field is set to S_IFSOCK. This inode contains a struct socket in the u area. Figure 12.7 shows the struct socket, from <linux/net.h>. It either contains or points to all the information associated with the communications link.

```
struct socket{
    socket_state        state;   /* current state of connection */
    struct proto_ops    *ops;    /* domain specific functions   */
    struct sock         *data;   /* domain specific data        */
    struct wait_queue   **wait;  /* waiting processes           */
    short               type;    /* SOCK_STREAM, etc.           */
};
```

Figure 12.7: Data structure representing a socket

- The state field will have one of the values from Figure 12.8, which is also from <linux/net.h>. Initially it will be in the SS_UNCONNECTED state.

- The ops field points to a set of functions which implement operations in the particular domain. See Figure 12.9, again from <linux/net.h>.

  Most of these operations are initiated by system services of the same name. This is the interface between the domain independent socket layer, and the domain specific lower layers. Implementations of these functions for the Unix domain will be considered in Section 12.4, and for the Internet domain in Chapter 14.

```
typedef enum{
      SS_FREE,            /* not allocated               */
      SS_UNCONNECTED,     /* unconnected to any socket   */
      SS_CONNECTING,      /* in process of connecting    */
      SS_CONNECTED,       /* connected to socket          */
      SS_DISCONNECTING    /* in process of disconnecting */
}socket_state;
```

Figure 12.8: State values for a socket

```
struct proto_ops{
      int family;
      int (*bind)();
      int (*connect)();
      int (*socketpair)();
      int (*accept)();
      int (*listen)();
      int (*shutdown)();
      int (*setsockopt)();
      int (*getsockopt)();
      int (*sendmsg)();
      int (*recvmsg)();
};
```

Figure 12.9: Data structure representing a protocol

- The data field points to a domain specific control block, a struct sock, which will contain information about the state of the connection for this particular socket. This structure will be considered in detail when we come to look at the domain specific processing.

- The wait field points to the head of a list of processes sleeping on this socket, waiting for data to become available.

- The type field is filled in from the second parameter of the socket() call.

At this stage, the create() function in the net_proto_family is called. This performs protocol specific processing, such as setting up the struct sock as required by the particular family. It sets the ops field of the socket to point to the appropriate proto_ops structure, which contains an array of functions which are specific to the communication domain to which this socket belongs.

When this create() function returns, the system then sets up a file descriptor, and a struct file. The f_op field in this struct file points to a set of file operations specific to sockets. The data structures allocated at this stage are as shown in Figure 12.10.

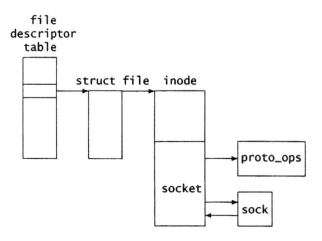

Figure 12.10: Data structures after socket is allocated

Connecting two sockets

Now that we have set up a socket, the next step is to connect it with another socket. This can be done passively, or actively. One process can wait to be contacted by another process, or it can take the initiative.

In this section we will follow the procedure from assigning an address to a socket, then look at how a socket can wait passively to be contacted, how it actively connects to another socket, and finally see how a socket is closed and removed from the system.

Binding

Each socket must be uniquely identified within a particular machine. This unique identifier is known as its address. So a connection between two sockets is fully specified by source and destination addresses.

The system service which connects a particular address with a particular socket is bind(). It is passed a pointer to a struct sockaddr, see Figure 12.11. Each individual domain has its own address format, which maps onto this generic one.

```
struct sockaddr{
        sa_family_t sa_family; /* address family, AF_xxx */
        char        sa_data[]; /* protocol address       */
};
```

Figure 12.11: Generic format of a socket address

The actual system service does little or no work, it just calls the bind() function in the proto_ops of the particular domain. The address bound to a socket can be found using the getsockname() system service.

Accepting connections

Let us first look at the passive situation. This is typical with server processes, where they create a socket, bind an address to it, and wait for clients to contact them. One very important feature of the socket mechanism is that when a request for connection comes in from a client, a new socket is created to handle it; the original one continues to listen at the original address for further requests.

A process can specify that connections are to be accepted on a socket with the listen() call. This only applies to a stream socket, and it must be bound, and in the SS_UNCONNECTED state. When listen() returns successfully, the socket is accepting requests for connection.

The server process then repeatedly calls accept(). If no other process has initiated a connection, then it sleeps until some one does request a connection.

If there is a connection waiting to be accepted, this will be indicated by a message queued on the accepting socket. This message will identify the socket which is requesting the connection. There may be several such messages on the queue; accept() will take the first one each time it is called.

The high-level, generic code creates a new inode, complete with a struct socket, sets its state to SS_CONNECTING, and its type to SOCK_STREAM, then calls domain specific code, the accept() in proto_ops.

When the domain specific accept() returns, the high-level code changes the state field to SS_CONNECTED, and sets up a struct file, and a file descriptor. Finally it returns the file descriptor to the caller, which can now use it to communicate over the connection which has just been set up.

The process which requested the connection has been sleeping in the meantime. It is now woken up, and moved to the run queue.

Requesting a connection

We now look at the process which takes the initiative in establishing a connection, the client. The client uses the connect() system call, passing it the name of the socket listening at the other end, in the server. The high-level code calls the domain specific connect() function in proto_ops. When this returns, the connection has been established. So the high-level code sets the state field to SS_CONNECTED, and returns to the caller.

The remote address to which a socket is connected can be found using the getpeername() system service.

Socket pairs

The socketpair() system service creates two connected sockets, without the user having to specify addresses. Both are by definition in the same process, on the same machine, in the Unix domain. It takes the same parameters as socket(), and returns two file descriptors. It creates two socket structures, with their associated sock structures, and connects them together. The state field in both is set to SS_CONNECTED.

Closing a connection

When the connection is no longer required, the socket can be closed using
shutdown(), which disables receive and send operations, and discards pending data, depending on its parameters. But the socket still exists. This is
finally removed from the system by the close() system service.

Sending and receiving data

Now that we have seen how sockets are created and connected together, it is
time to look at what, after all, is the reason for the whole mechanism—the
actual transmission of data between two processes.

First we will examine how data is sent across a connection established
between two sockets. Then we will consider the system call by which a process
on the other side declares itself ready to accept this data.

Sending data

Let us follow what happens when the standard write() is used with connected
sockets.

Using the first parameter, the system follows the path from the file descriptor table, to the struct file, from where the write() function for a socket
is called. This write() function first builds a msghdr structure, as shown in
Figure 12.12, from <linux/socket.h>.

```
struct msghdr{
        void            *msg_name;     /* name of destination socket */
        int             msg_namelen;  /* length of name              */
        struct iovec    *msg_iov;      /* array of data buffers       */
        int             msg_iovlen;   /* number of buffers           */
};
```

Figure 12.12: Message header

The msg_iov field points to an array of one or more struct iovec, each
of which points to a block of data. This allows a message to be constructed
from a number of non-contiguous areas in memory. But the whole reason for
introducing the struct msghdr is to make the mechanism compatible with
the sendmsg() system service, which will be introduced next.

The write() function then follows the pointer to the inode, where it finds
the struct socket. From the socket, the ops field leads to a list of pointers
to domain specific functions in proto_ops, and the sendmsg() function is
called.

Apart from write(), there are other system services which can be used
to send data between sockets. Each has slightly different functionality. The
send() system service can also be used only with connected sockets, but it
allows priority data to be sent. It has an extra flags parameter.

To send data to a non-connected socket, the sendto() system service is used. It allows the address of the peer socket to be specified.

The sendmsg() system service is the interface with the greatest functionality. It can be used with connected or unconnected sockets. The control information for sendmsg() is specified in a msghdr structure. Because of this there are fewer parameters to the actual system call.

Receiving data

The simplest interface is read(). This can only be used with a connected socket. It follows the chain from the file descriptor table, to the struct file, from where the read() function for a socket is called. This follows the pointer to the inode, where it calls the domain specific recvmsg() function in proto_ops. When it returns, it copies the data to the address specified by the caller.

The recv() system service has an extra flags parameter, which allows data to be read out of sequence, as well as peeking at the data waiting to be read (non-destructive read).

For non-connected sockets, recvfrom() allows the address of the peer socket to be specified, and recorded.

The system service interface with the greatest functionality is recvmsg(). When data becomes available, this copies it to a msghdr structure in user space.

12.4 Unix domain sockets

The software for any particular communication domain provides an implementation of the standard set of functions described in the previous section. These are the create() function from net_proto_family, and the array of functions in struct proto_ops. In this section we examine how these functions are implemented for sockets in the Unix domain.

Create

The main work it does is to set up a domain specific control block, a struct sock, see Figure 12.13, from <net/sock.h>, and link it from the data field of the socket.

- All allocated control blocks for the Unix domain are maintained on hash lists, headed from unix_socket_table[], which is declared in net/unix/af_unix.c. The next field is the link for the hash chains (see Figure 12.14).

- The receive_queue field heads a linked list of incoming data blocks, and rcvbuf contains a count of the number of bytes on this queue.

```
struct sock{
        struct sock             *next;
        int                     rcvbuf;
        struct sk_buff_head     receive_queue;
        int                     sndbuf;
        struct sk_buff_head     write_queue;
        struct proto            *prot;
        struct unix_opt         af_unix;
        struct socket           *socket;
};
```

Figure 12.13: Domain-specific control block

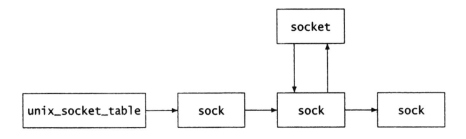

Figure 12.14: Hash chain of Unix domain control blocks

- Likewise the write_queue field heads a linked list of outgoing data blocks, and sndbuf contains a count of the number of bytes on this queue.

- The prot field points to a struct proto, see Figure 12.15.

```
struct proto{
        void            (*close)();
        int             (*connect)();
        struct sock*    (*accept) ();
        int             (*poll)();
        void            (*shutdown)();
        int             (*setsockopt)();
        int             (*getsockopt)();
        int             (*sendmsg)();
        int             (*recvmsg)();
        int             (*bind)();
};
```

Figure 12.15: A protocol specific structure

This contains pointers to functions specific to a particular protocol within the Unix domain, either stream or datagram.

Many of the functions here have the same names as those in proto_ops, and something must be said about this overlap.

The functions in proto_ops are generic ones. They are called for operations on any type of Unix socket. In general they only deal with fields in the struct sock. They call the corresponding functions in proto. The latter handle the lower level specifics of dealing with either stream or datagram communication over a Unix socket connection.

- The af_unix field is a structure containing Unix specific information, see Figure 12.16, from <net/sock.h>.

```
struct unix_opt{
        struct unix_address *addr;
        struct sock          *other;
};
```

Figure 12.16: Links for a Unix specific socket

- The addr field will later be used to point to the unique name given to this socket; see Section 12.4.

- The most important field here is other, which will point to the struct sock at the other end of a connection, when one is eventually set up.

- The socket field points back to the struct socket.

Bind

In the Unix domain, socket addresses are pathnames in the file system. This means that the protection attributes of the file system can be used to limit access to sockets as well. The actual address itself is specified by the user in a struct sockaddr_un, as shown in Figure 12.17, from <linux/un.h>.

```
struct sockaddr_un{
        unsigned short sun_family;    /* address family, AF_UNIX */
        char           sun_path[104]; /* pathname                */
};
```

Figure 12.17: Structure containing address of a Unix domain socket

Because the format of an address depends on the underlying domain, this structure first identifies the address family, then allows for address information. For example, Unix domain addressing allows a pathname of up to 104 bytes. Internally, the sockaddr_un structure is wrapped into a larger data structure, struct unix_address, from <net/af_unix.h>.

The bind() function puts a pointer to this struct unix_address into the af_unix.addr field of the struct sock corresponding to the socket. It also calls mknod() in the i_op field of the inode to create a socket entry of this name in the directory tree. This entry is of type S_IFSOCK. The shell

command ls -l shows an s in the leftmost position. It cannot be opened, nor is it removed when the socket is closed. Such a socket entry must not exist before bind() is called, otherwise it will fail with errno set to EADDRINUSE.

Accept

This function is called after the high-level code has set up a struct socket for a new connection. It creates and fills in a struct sock. This new socket does not have any address bound to it, so the af_unix.addr field is NULL.

It links in the appropriate struct proto for a stream connection, and calls the accept() function in that struct proto to do stream specific processing. The most important part of this processing is to point the other field in the struct unix_opt of the new sock, to the sock of the requesting socket. Control then returns to the high level code.

Connect

This uses the file system name cache to translate the name to the inode of the other socket. This will work only if the server socket file exists, and has the requisite permissions. This in turn presupposes that the server has been properly bound.

If this client socket is of type SOCK_DGRAM, the protocol specific connect() checks that the other socket is also of type SOCK_DGRAM; then it stores a pointer to the peer address in the af_unix.other field of its own struct sock, for use when sending data, so that it does not have to be supplied each time. A datagram socket can be disconnected, and then assigned a different address, by a second call to connect().

If the client socket is of type SOCK_STREAM, the protocol specific connect() checks that the other socket is also of type SOCK_STREAM. If so, it tries to set up a connection with it: it creates a message block, which contains the address of the client sock; it puts this block at the tail of the receive queue of the socket it wants to connect to; the state of the client is set to SS_CONNECTING, and it stores a pointer to the sock structure of the other socket in the af_unix.other field of its own struct sock.

The process then blocks, waiting for an accept() on the other side. When it is woken up, its state is set to SS_CONNECTED, and data can now be passed. The links between two connected sockets are shown in Figure 12.18.

Sendmsg

The sendmsg() function in proto_ops has been written specifically to transfer data between Unix sockets.

First of all, it copies data from user space into an sk_buff structure. This consists of a header, shown in Figure 12.19, from <linux/skbuff.h>, followed by a data area which contains the actual message.

unix_socket_table[]

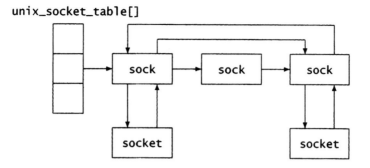

Figure 12.18: A pair of connected sockets

```
struct sk_buff{
        struct sk_buf *next;      /* Next buffer in list    */
        struct   sock  *sk;       /* Socket we are owned by */
        unsigned long len;        /* Length of actual data  */
        unsigned int  truesize;  /* Buffer size            */
        unsigned char *head;      /* Head of buffer         */
        unsigned char *data       /* Data head pointer      */
        unsigned char *tail       /* Tail pointer           */
        unsigned char *end        /* End pointer            */
};
```

Figure 12.19: Buffer used for communication over sockets

- A long message may occupy several buffers, and these are linked together through the next field.

- The sk field points to the sock of the owner; this is the sender while the message is being built up, the receiver after it has been sent.

- truesize is the size of the data buffer part of the sk_buff, which may be greater than len, the number of bytes of actual data in the buffer.

- head and end point to the beginning and end of the data buffer part of the sk_buff.

- data and tail point to the beginning and end of the actual data within the buffer.

Figure 12.20 shows the relationship between these last six fields.

These sk_buff structures are really designed for the situation when sockets are used over networks. For compatibility reasons they are also used in the Unix domain, even if not strictly needed.

At this stage the sendmsg() function in struct proto is called. For a connected socket, it queues the packet from receive_queue in the struct sock of the destination socket, which it identifies by using the af_unix.other field

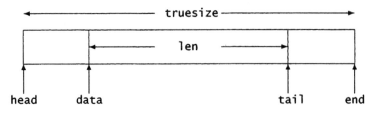

Figure 12.20: Data part of an sk_buff

of the struct sock of the source socket. It wakes up any process blocked wait-ing for input on that socket, and marks it runnable. If the destination stream has been set non-blocking, the destination process is notified by SIGIO.

The sendmsg() for datagram sockets uses the file system name cache to find the inode corresponding to the destination name. When it finds a match, it has identified the destination socket, and can queue the packet from its receive_queue. If no match is found, then the address is invalid—at least it is not currently bound to any socket: a value of ENOENT is returned in errno.

Recvmsg

This follows the pointer to the struct sock, where the protocol-specific func-tion recvmsg() in proto is called. If there is no data on receive_queue, the calling process is blocked. It is woken up when data arrives at the socket.

The requisite number of bytes are then copied from the receive buffer of the socket to a struct msghdr, and passed back to the file read() function. If there are any bytes remaining in the sk_buff, then it remains at the head of the queue.

12.5 Summary

1. A Unix pipe is essentially a FIFO buffer, which is inherited by a child pro-cess after a fork. Synchronisation is also provided for situations when the buffer is full or empty. Named pipes are an extension of this mechanism for unrelated processes.

2. The socket facility is an interprocess communication mechanism, which can be extended to processes on different machines.

   At boot time, the kernel sets up a net_proto_family structure for each address family it is prepared to handle.

3. The socket() system call creates a socket. As with all Unix I/O, it returns a file descriptor pointing to a struct file and an inode, which contains a struct socket. This is a generic data structure, common to all types of socket. But it is linked to the struct proto_ops, an array of functions specific to the appropriate domain. It is also linked to a struct sock, which contains domain specific information for this connection.

A socket can then be assigned an address, which is a file system path-name, using bind(). A user may passively accept connections, by calling listen(), and then repeatedly calling accept(). Or a user may actually take the initiative and use connect() to establish a link with a socket which is listening. The close() system service removes all of these data structures.

The standard read() and write() system services can be used with sockets, but there are also socket specific system services, with enhanced functionality.

4. Unix domain sockets can be used to communicate between two processes on the same machine. The domain specific functions in proto_ops set up and manipulate a struct sock. This contains queues of incoming and outgoing messages, the name bound to the socket, and a pointer to the peer socket it is connected to, if any.

Data is passed between sockets in an sk_buff structure. These are of fixed size, and can be chained together to hold large packets.

On output, the data is copied into an sk_buff, which is first queued from the write_queue of the source sock structure. The destination information is read from the sock associated with the socket, and the appropriate sendmsg() function is called, which then moves the sk_buff to the receive_queue of the destination sock.

When a user requests input, using read(), the data is transferred from the receive_queue to user space. If no data is available, the calling process is blocked.

12.6 Discussion questions

1. Discuss the advantages and disadvantages of integrating interprocess communication with the I/O system.

2. Investigate the size of a pipe buffer on the system you are using.

3. Devise a protocol by which a writer to a pipe could communicate the length of a message to a reader.

4. Suggest a protocol which would prevent a reader blocking on an empty pipe.

5. Do the two file descriptors returned by pipe() have to come one after the other in the file descriptor table of the process?

6. Suggest how you would implement a peek() function for pipes. This looks at the contents of the pipe, but does not remove it.

7. Investigate the address formats used in other domains besides AF_UNIX.

8. Could you see any use for a socket type which is connected, but also preserves record boundaries? Investigate if such a socket type exists.

9. Investigate the options which can be set with setsockopt().

10. If you are only ever going to use a particular socket for output, do you have to bind an address to it?

11. What is the essential difference between calling `connect()` on a socket of type DGRAM, and one of type STREAM?

12. Compare the functionality of `socketpair()` and `pipe()`.

13. Transmission of data from one socket to another uses two formats, `struct msghdr` and `struct sk_buff`. Explain the difference between them, and justify the need for two such structures.

14. Using the `read()` system service with sockets, it is possible to read data from two or more messages, if the `size` parameter is large enough. Is this a feature or a bug?

Distributed systems 13

Computer systems have developed from stand-alone machines, to direct connections between two machines, to networks where one machine can communicate with any other networked machine.

Figure 13.1 illustrates the basic hardware configuration, with some workstations and a server connected together, using a bus network.

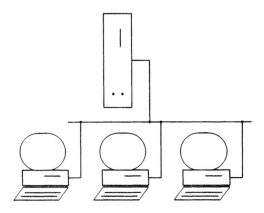

Figure 13.1: Networked computers

But even with this, the user is always aware of the connection, and has to issue explicit commands for the movement of data.

Now we are on the verge of the next development, building on networking. This involves groups of machines acting together as one. A distributed system is a collection of individual computers, which are networked together not just to share data, but to cooperate, to distribute computation among themselves.

The hardware configuration remains as in Figure 13.1. But instead of each system running its own autonomous operating system, there would be a distributed operating system controlling all of the machines.

To the user it appears as one system—the interface remains unchanged. The system software for this is just emerging.

13.1 Features of distributed systems

Distributed systems have some features not found in centralised systems, and these are influencing the pace of development.

Economy

The single most important argument for the move towards distributing computing resources is the economic one. At present the ratio between price and performance is in favour of multiple small machines. A microcomputer can provide only limited performance, but if microcomputers can be added together to provide greater performance, they will do so at a fraction of the cost of a mainframe. The fall in the cost of high speed networks is another factor in the development of distributed systems.

Reliability

While distributed systems are not necessarily any more reliable than stand-alone ones, they can be made to offer the high reliability and fault tolerance needed by critical applications. The secret is to have as few critical components as possible, and as many as possible of the others interchangeable.

This applies to hardware, and also to the redundant storage of data. One copy of a database may be destroyed, but with proper systems in place it can be ensured that other up-to-date copies exist, and are immediately available. The user need not even be aware that there was a problem.

It is possible and desirable to have redundant servers, although this introduces the problem of keeping them consistent with each other. Central control schemes, or centralised servers, put all of the eggs in one basket.

Resource sharing

This is another factor driving the development of distributed systems. Such sharing can be for purely economic reasons, for example an expensive printer, or other specialised hardware. A multi-user licence for one shared copy of a piece of software is much cheaper than buying many single-user licences.

Apart from economic reasons, it can often be very convenient to share resources. The whole area of computer-supported cooperative work depends crucially on distributed systems. The ideal is to have a number of people at different sites all working on the same project, with updates immediately visible to all.

Sharing the workload over idle workstations is one of the long-term goals of distributed systems. The ideal here is that when a personal workstation is idle, it could undertake work for other, busier, machines. But it would always be fully available for its owner, when required.

Performance

Some applications are very suitable to distributed systems, by their very nature. If a job consists of many sub-jobs, each of which is independent of the others (e.g. matrix arithmetic), then all of the parts can be processed at the same time on a distributed system. This is known as partitioning a computation, with the ultimate goal of speeding up the overall computation. It would be difficult for a centralised system, no matter how powerful, to compete with hundreds or thousands of microcomputers in such a case.

While performance can be improved by using more machines, there is a downside. Communication is the great bottleneck here. So processes and the resources they use should still be on the same machine, as much as possible.

Another critical factor is the ability to adapt to increased load. The system should not just collapse when the load on it goes above a certain point. Performance should degrade gracefully. For example, a doubling of the load should mean roughly twice the time—not ten times longer.

Incremental growth

Distributed systems allow for the incremental growth of a computer installation. It is not necessary to buy all the processing power, memory, or disk drives at the one time. It is possible to install just what is necessary to begin with, knowing that the system can expand to keep pace with growing demand, into the foreseeable future. And it is possible to do this without any major disruption.

In order for a system to be able to scale to larger and larger numbers of machines, it is necessary to avoid centralised elements such as tables, schedulers, etc. In general, systems which rely on decentralised algorithms scale better than centralised ones, which tend to develop bottlenecks.

13.2 Transparency

Distribution should be transparent, both to the user, and to programs at the system call interface. Like glass in a window, you should enjoy its effects, but not even notice it is there. The user or programmer must not be able to tell that a remote machine is involved. Ideally, a distributed system should look like a conventional system to users. It should support user mobility—any user should be able to log on anywhere.

An ideal distributed system would be transparent in terms of:

Access Local and remote resources should be accessed in exactly the same way. Users should not even be able to know whether a resource is local or remote. Ideally the network should be fast enough to mask any speed differences.

Location A user cannot tell, nor is there any need to know, where hardware resources, such as a CPU or printer, or software resources such as a file, are. There should be no distinction between remote and local resources.

Migration Resources should be free to move from one location to another without changing name. Programs which use these resources should continue to work, without any changes.

Replication It must be possible to have multiple copies of a resource, such as a file, without any side effects. These copies must remain consistent. A program may use one copy now, and another later, and still work.

Concurrency Concurrent processes should work just as well when distributed; it must be possible to implement read/write locks across the whole distributed system.

Failure A distributed system should continue to function correctly in case of failure of a component in the system. It should be fault tolerant, see Section 17.3.

Performance The system should detect imbalances between the loads on different processors in the system, and automatically move work from a heavily loaded machine to a lightly loaded one. The user should not be involved in, or even aware of, this process migration.

Scaling The system should be able to grow without disrupting work in progress. It should not be necessary to change algorithms, or even to recompile programs.

13.3 System architecture

When we come to discuss just how computing power can be distributed, we find that two very different architectures have developed. These are known as the workstation model and the processor pool model. Some people favour one, some favour the other. Both are based on very different ideas of what a distributed system is all about.

Workstation model

In our historical overview in Chapter 1, we saw that computers developed from single user machines to multi-user machines and back again to single user machines, all under the influence of economic factors. The norm today is single user machines, known as workstations.

Stand-alone workstations

In most cases, these are stand-alone machines. They have sufficient disk capacity to store all of the user's programs and data, and each user has their own copy of all of the application software.

It is becoming more and more common for groups of such machines to be connected together over a LAN. All of a user's personal files, and frequently used programs, are held locally. Shared databases and larger, rarely used programs, are stored on a remote server or servers. Figure 13.2 illustrates this situation.

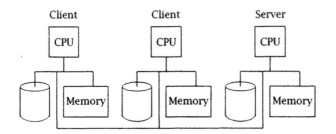

Figure 13.2: Workstations connected on a LAN

Diskless workstations

Another configuration, not so common, is the diskless workstation. As the name implies, this has its own CPU and memory, but no disk drives—typically not even a floppy drive. (Sometimes there may be a small local fixed disk, used for paging, file caching, and temporary files.) It does all its file system access, both for programs and data, over a network. It even boots its own operating system across the network, when it is powered up: see Figure 13.3.

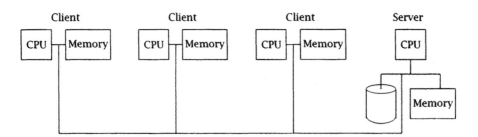

Figure 13.3: Diskless workstations on a LAN

There are a number of reasons for such a configuration. There is the saving on the cost of the disk; then there is the saving on the cost of a multi-user software licence; it is also easier to handle software upgrades—only the one copy needs to be changed. Because all files are centralised, any user can work at any workstation, giving great flexibility.

But perhaps the greatest advantage of this scheme is security. With no local disk access, files can only be put into or taken out of the system at one carefully controlled point. The extra control this gives to a security conscious organisation is of inestimable value.

Process migration between workstations

Either of the two previous arrangements can lead to uneven allocation of processing power. Machines are idle while their users are reading, writing, on the telephone, taking a coffee break—even thinking. Is there some way of using such idle processors? A first possibility might be for another user to log on to an idle machine remotely, for example using `telnet`. But for a true distributed system, we want a solution which is transparent to the user.

With such a system, a process may not be executed at the site at which it is submitted. This process migration, as it is called, may take place for a number of reasons.

- Load balancing. The distributed operating system may decide that the local machine is overloaded, while some remote machine is idle.

- Computation speedup. A large job may be broken into subprocesses, and these distributed.

- Parallelism. In theory the system should detect potential parallelism in a program, split it into a number of subprograms, and distribute these over different machines. This would imply cooperation between the compiler and the operating system. In practice, explicit intervention by the programmer is still required, at least to get the best use of distribution.

- Hardware preference. There may be a machine on the network with specialised hardware more suitable for the particular job.

- Software preference. The required software may only be available at one particular site.

There are a number of aspects to such a distributed solution.

Processor allocation

Which process should be run on which machine? There are many factors involved in such a decision. As we have seen so often before, the relevant importance given to different factors results in many different arrangements.

- First of all, a system may be made up of machines all of the same architecture. Or there may be different architectures involved. This latter situation obviously limits the choices available, as a particular program will only run on the architecture it was compiled for.

- Then a process could be non-migratory, in that it always stays where it starts, until it finishes. In a migratory system, a process moves as the load changes.

- When a new process is created, the machine on which it is to run can be chosen by the user, or by the operating system.

- Finally, there must be some way of assuring that processes which communicate frequently run simultaneously.

System load

How do we measure idleness, or load, anyway? Load may be the average number of processes on the run queue. Or it could be the percentage of time that the CPU is busy. Idle can be taken to mean that there has been no keyboard activity for a certain length of time.

Identifying an idle machine

Next, how is such an idle workstation found? One possibility is that a coordinator maintains a usage table for all machines in the system. Then a user asks the coordinator to allocate a processor for a new process.

Another possibility is that each machine could monitor its own keyboard, and broadcast a message when it detects that it is idle. Or it could leave such a message on a bulletin board which all other machines can read.

Yet another possibility is for a busy machine to broadcast a message asking for an idle machine to identify itself. This message could contain details of the work to be done, such as processor type, memory requirements, etc. This will mean that unsuitable machines will not get involved. Remote machines could delay their response for a time proportional to their current load, so that the lightest loaded machine replies first.

Sender initiated algorithms generate a large number of messages just when the system is heavily loaded. Receiver initiated algorithms are better from this point of view.

Moving a process

When an idle machine is found, how can a remote process be run transparently? Moving code to the idle machine is no great problem. But setting up the correct environment there is a different matter. It must be arranged that all disk accesses will be sent to the home machine, or at least to the correct file system. Obviously all system calls dealing with the keyboard, mouse, or screen must be redirected to the home machine. All of this overhead may offset any advantage to be gained from the move.

Refusing work

What happens when the remote machine is no longer idle, and does not wish to carry the extra load? It must close the foster process down in an orderly fashion, not just stop it.

It might be possible to migrate it back home, or somewhere else, still alive. But gathering all of the relevant operating system data structures, and setting them up again on the new host, is a very difficult if not impossible task.

No matter what, the departing process must leave the host exactly as it was before it came.

Processor pool model

Even with the best possible load balancing, there will still be unused processing power, and unused memory. For much of the time a few machines are busy, even overloaded, but most are idle. So a totally different architecture has been developed, known as the processor pool model. It is based on the idea that if the file system can be centralised on one server, so can the processors. This has not become very common, but it has its advantages.

With this model, each user would only have a terminal, maybe a graphics X terminal. All of the CPUs are installed in one central location, along with all of the memory. This is the pool of processors (see Figure 13.4).

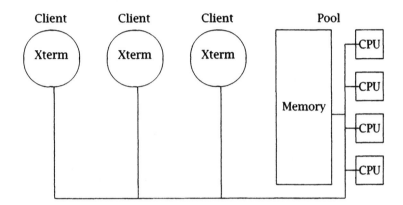

Figure 13.4: Processor pool model

A user is allocated whatever processing power and memory is required to run its current process, from this pool. The single operating system has all of these resources directly under its control, and does not have to be continually checking with other 'owners' about the status of their resources. So CPU and memory allocation can be optimised.

It is a much cleaner way of getting extra computing power than looking around for an idle machine.

Combination

It is possible to combine the two models. Each user would have a workstation, with or without a disk, and the processor pool is there as well (see Figure 13.5).

For general purpose work, the local operating system on the workstation would use its local CPU and memory without bothering the rest of the system. But when a particular user switched to high performance, heavy duty work, then it would request extra CPUs from the pool, and run some processes on them. This is a possible 'best of both worlds' scenario. But only time will tell which of these organisations, if any, will prove to be most suitable for the computing needs of the future.

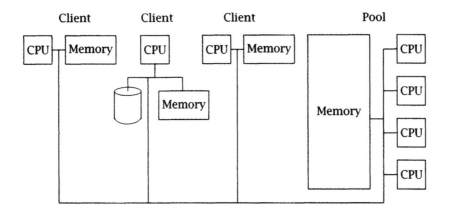

Figure 13.5: Combined model

13.4 Client/server systems

The simplest possible architecture used to structure a distributed system is to arrange for some processes to provide services to others. Those which provide services are known as servers, naturally enough. Those which use these services are known as clients. The whole arrangement is known as a client/server system. What the server does and what it sends back to the client (if anything) can vary enormously. But all of the different models of distributed computing can be reduced to this.

Such a system could be implemented on a single, stand-alone machine. But it is more common to implement it over a network, with the server process or processes on one machine, and the client processes on others. However, it must be stressed that the distinction is between client and server processes—not client and server machines.

The sender can be held up until the reply arrives—synchronous operation. It is also possible for the client to go ahead with some other work, until the reply arrives from the server—asynchronous. The client can be informed of the arrival by means of an interrupt, or it could have to find out for itself, by testing the value of a status variable. In all cases there will have to be some way of giving up on a faulty server, such as a timeout.

The client could create a separate thread to handle each request to the server. This thread would block, but other threads in the same process could continue to run. In any case, it is a common practice to use a multi-threaded server, which creates a new thread to handle each request.

The server can send data—bringing the data to the process. Or a server can process data sent by the client—transferring the computation, which may be more efficient. Typically client/server systems use remote procedure call, which executes a predefined procedure on the remote machine. Another possibility is to send a message to the remote site. The operating system there creates a new process, which processes the data, and sends back a result.

Note that in all of this we have stand-alone operating systems on both machines, even if they are specially adapted. They communicate with each other, but they are fully independent. Also, users are aware of the multiplicity of machines. The level of transparency provided can vary. At the very least, users can log in to a remote machine, and work on it, using for example the `telnet` server. It is also possible to transfer data between a remote machine and their own, using for example the `ftp` server. This is not real file sharing, rather it results in potentially inconsistent copies.

A step up is the ability to mount file systems from a remote server on a local machine, where they appear as part of the local directory structure. The user sees no difference between local and remote files. All of this is run on the server side by a network operating system, which is really just a general purpose operating system with enhancements. It only transfers those portions of a file which are actually necessary for a task. If the file is modified, then it is written back afterwards. There is a similarity between this and paging. Unix provides all of these services, as does NT Server.

13.5 Naming

In a distributed system, it is necessary to be able to identify uniquely all of the resources—individual machines, processes, files, printers. At the system level, these identifiers are binary numbers. There are two problems with such identifiers. One is that humans find such binary numbers, or even their decimal equivalents, difficult to remember and input. We are much more at home with names.

The second problem is more serious. Suppose a process on a remote machine is providing some service. A client needs to know the identifier of the server machine, and also the identifier of the process on that machine which is providing the required service. If this server process crashes, and restarts, it will now have a different process id, and clients will not be able to reach it. Another possibility is that the machine itself may crash, and the system administrator may move the server process to another machine. Clients would continue sending requests to the old server, with no results.

There is one solution to both of these problems, and that is to provide a name server in the system. At the human level, resources are identified by meaningful names, such as 'timeserver' or 'laserprinter'. At the machine level they are still identified by binary number. The link between a name and a number is called a binding. Then we add in a name server process, somewhere in the system. This maintains a database of such bindings, and performs translations on behalf of clients. For example, a process sends the name server the string 'laserprinter', and it sends back the unique id of that printer. If the id changes, it is only necessary to inform the name server. As long as a process can find the name server, it can find any other resources in the system.

There are two different name servers commonly found on networked Linux systems, DNS for the Internet, and NIS for the Network File System.

Internet names and addresses

All of the computers attached to the Internet can be identified by a name, and
also by a number.

Let us look at the numeric identifiers first. Each machine attached to the
Internet is given a unique 32 bit identifier, known as its Internet protocol address, or IP address. How these are actually allocated by administrators need
not concern us. But all communication between machines on the Internet is
carried out using these identifiers.

When humans do get involved with these numbers, they are usually written
in 'dotted decimal' form. Each of the four bytes making up the 32 bits is
separately converted to decimal format, and written down separated by dots.
For example, 136.201.24.2.

Machines also can be given names. All of the names given to computers on
the Internet are arranged in a tree structure, just like the directory structure
of a file system. Each non-leaf node in this tree is known as a domain. Unlike
Unix file names, domain names are built from the bottom up. Domain names
can be relative (to the local domain), or they can be absolute. Absolute domain
names always terminate with '.', just as absolute Unix file names begin with
'/'. There is a root, then first-level directories, or domains, such as com, org,
edu, etc.

There are also first level domains for individual countries, such as us, ie,
etc. Each of these domains is divided into sub-domains, and so on. Figure 13.6
illustrates a part of this tree of names. A typical name for a computer attached
to the Internet would be shannon.cs.ul.ie.

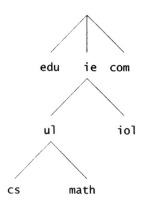

Figure 13.6: Part of the Internet name space

Internet domain name system

The Internet domain name system (DNS) keeps track of all of the computers attached to the Internet. Its role is to translate a name such as shannon.cs.ul.ie
into an IP address, such as 136.201.24.2.

Figure 13.7 illustrates the procedure. A client knows the name of a server. But in order to send a request to that server, it must know its address. So it first sends a request to the name server, asking it to translate the name to an address. The name server looks up the required address in its database, and sends it back to the client. The client is then able to send a request for service.

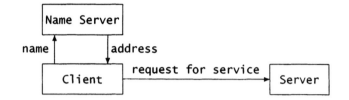

Figure 13.7: Using a name server

These name servers also do reverse translation. Given the IP address of a machine, they will give back its name. A machine may have more than one name; the DNS only keeps track of the address corresponding to the first one.

The DNS also keeps track of domains, and translates domain names into the IP address of mail servers for the particular domain. For example, when an email program is presented with an address such as John.OGorman@ul.ie, it will consult its name server, and be told to send all mail for ul.ie to machine number 136.201.1.23. The DNS is not part of the operating system; it is just a standard process, running in the background, that makes life easier for users.

Distributed database

Having one server to cater for the whole of the Internet just would not work. So the designers came up with the idea of breaking up the overall database of name/number pairs, and keeping parts of it on many different machines around the world. This may seem to make the problem even worse, but in fact it is a very elegant solution, as we shall see.

Each sub-domain, or zone, of the Internet has an administrator, who undertakes to assign names and numbers to machines in that domain. The administrator also undertakes to provide a name translation server for that domain, on at least two different machines. The chances of both being unavailable at the same time are very small.

To avoid inconsistencies growing up between different servers for the same domain, one of them is the primary server; the others are secondary servers. The primary reads its information from a file on disk. Changes are only made at the primary; the secondary servers update themselves from the primary at fixed intervals. There is a short interval after an update of the primary, in which the database is inconsistent.

Some domains are so large that it would be inconvenient to keep all of the information on one server. So these are divided into several sub-domains, each of which has its own server. The domain server need have no information

about machines in a sub-domain, but it must know the address of the server for each of its sub-domains. Like a good librarian, the server may not have some particular information, but it must know where to look for it.

To tie the whole system together, there are a number of root servers in different parts of the world, which know the addresses of the servers for all of the first level domains—org, com, us, ie, etc. All servers the world over have the addresses of these root servers.

The whole system is rather like phone books. We know the name of the person we want to phone, but we need a number. All of the phone numbers in the world are not listed in the one book. Each subscriber has a book of local numbers (the name server for the local domain). If they need a number not in the local book, they can apply to directory enquiries (higher level domain server). If directory enquiries do not have the number, they know where to get it (the root servers).

Resolving a name

If a name server is presented with a name in its own domain, it can give a reply immediately. However, if the name is in some other domain, then there are further steps involved.

For example, a server presented with the name shannon.cs.ul.ie will first of all query a root server for the address of the name server for the ie domain. Then it will query that server for the address of the name server for the ul.ie domain. Then it will query that server for the address of the name server for the cs.ul.ie domain. Finally it will query that server for the address of the machine shannon.

The full procedure is outlined in Figure 13.8.

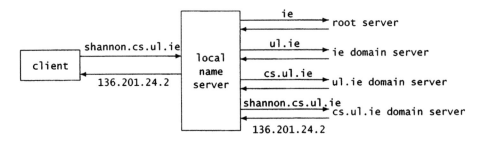

Figure 13.8: Translating an Internet name

Caching

To reduce the overhead of repeatedly looking up frequently accessed names, the DNS relies heavily on caching. Each server stores every translation it looks up. Now if it is asked for the same translation sometime in the future, it already has it, and does not need to send messages around the world to look it up.

Of course this brings up the problem of stale data. So every time a server gives out information, that information is given a time to live. The information may be cached by another server, but once its time to live expires, it will be discarded. This means that data may be temporarily inconsistent between one server and another. But with relatively short lifetimes for data, typically a few days, the inconsistency will soon be corrected.

Implementation

The most widely used implementation of DNS is the Berkeley Internet name domain software, or BIND. The server process, or daemon, is called named. From the shell prompt, nslookup is the user interface to the DNS system. It allows users to query the DNS interactively

For programmers who wish to interface with the DNS directly, there is a set of functions in the standard C library collectively known as the resolver. The two most straightforward functions are gethostbyname(), which translates a name to an address, and gethostbyaddr(), which translates an address to a name.

Sun network information system

The Sun network file system allows shared access to a common set of files. The NIS manages names assigned to various elements in the NFS environment. These can be machines, users, services, directories, or files. It is not worldwide like DNS, rather it is restricted to a local group of machines, known as a domain. Membership of a domain is defined by the set of files a machine shares. All machines which share the same files are in the same domain. The shell command domainname shows the name of the current domain. Normally it is a valid Internet domain name.

Server

Each domain has one master server. As it is essential to have access to NIS at all times, there may be slave servers as well. Changes can only be made at the master, which then pushes them to the slaves. The daemon process which runs on a server is ypserv. The NIS was originally known as the yellow pages; traces of this can be found in the yp part of many of the function and command names.

The following are some of the files which it manages.

- /etc/hosts, which associates machine names with IP addresses. This duplicates some of the functionality of the DNS.

- /etc/passwd is the traditional Unix password file, which maps user names to internal id numbers. But once we move into a distributed environment, there is room for confusion. Two (or more) different user names, on differ-

ent machines, could be mapped to the same id number. This would lead
to chaos, not least to major holes in security.

So the administration of the password files on different machines is
taken over by NIS. This centralisation prevents such duplication.

- /etc/group, which maps group names to id numbers.

- /etc/exports lists the files which a particular server is willing to make
  available to clients.

- /etc/rpc lists remote procedures which are available on a particular host.

- /etc/services contains information about standard Internet services
  provided by that host.

NIS builds databases from these files, for ease of access. The NIS server is then
called to read information from the database.

The shell command ypcat prints all values from an NIS database. The
ypmatch command prints the value of one or more entries from an NIS database,
for example ypmatch username passwd.byname will return the information
about the user in the password database.

Client

Each client machine runs ypbind. This first finds the IP address of an NIS
server, using broadcast, and stores it —this is called a binding. From then
on, all NIS requests from client processes are sent to this server. The shell
command ypwhich identifies the host which is the current NIS server.

13.6 Distributed operating systems

A true distributed operating system must, at the very least, begin to blur the
boundaries between machines.

Obviously it will be responsible for managing all local resources, such as
the CPU, and peripheral devices, including network interfaces. As well as this,
it is responsible for advertising resources which are free and available, as well
as importing and exporting processes from and to other machines. And it
should do all of this transparently.

There are a number of systems which claim, to a greater or lesser degree,
to be distributed operating systems. All of them provide more transparency
than merely connecting machines or sharing files; none of them are yet fully
fledged distributed operating systems.

Mach

Mach is a stand-alone microkernel, which handles processes, memory, I/O,
and communications. It is designed to allow transparent access to network resources, and be portable. A layer which emulates a particular operating system
interface can be built above this.

Mach was designed to be as compatible as possible with Unix, so a Unix application program should run anywhere on a network of different computers running Mach. It was also designed to make efficient use of multiprocessors.

Interprocess communication

In the Mach microkernel, interprocess communication is the most important kernel function. Instead of the operating system supplying such a mechanism to users as a system service, Mach provides an interprocess communication facility which supports most of the operating system.

The Mach interprocess communication subsystem is a message passing facility, used to pass data between separate processes, or between different threads in the same process. But this message passing is regulated by the kernel, which must first give permission.

Two fundamental parts of the system are the message, which is the data transferred, and a port, the mechanism used to transfer the data.

Messages

If a message contains a small amount of data, it is transferred by physically copying the data through a buffer in the kernel. Large amounts of data can easily be passed between processes, because in such a case, Mach does not physically copy the data. Instead it maps the data into the address space of both processes. As long as the data remains unaltered, there is only one physical copy. As soon as one or other process alters a part of the data, a second copy of it is made. This is *lazy evaluation*: delay performing an operation until the last minute, in the hope that it may not need to be performed at all.

Mach ports

A port is essentially a message queue within the address space of the kernel. A process can have send or receive rights to a port. Only one process can receive messages from a particular port, although any number of processes can write to a port. Send or receive rights are known as capabilities.

Ports are used to represent system objects such as processes, threads, or memory. When a process creates one of these objects, the kernel gives the process access to the object by giving it rights to the port representing that object.

Distributed systems

Mach interprocess communication extends very nicely to distributed systems. Instead of messages passing from a process on one machine to another process on the same machine, through the kernel on that machine, now messages pass from a process on one machine to a process on another machine, through the network. From the point of view of a process, work is still done by passing messages.

So users can communicate with processes on remote machines as easily as with local processes, using the same interface and system calls. It is not possible to determine whether a message came from a local or a remote process. A process only knows that it came in on a port it has read rights for. A process sends a message using a local name. All of the complexity of translating this to a remote port is hidden from the user.

Chorus

This is also a stand-alone microkernel, with Unix emulation on top, designed to allow Unix programs to run on a collection of machines on a network. Like Mach, it uses message passing as its IPC mechanism. Threads send messages to ports, so it can be extended to distributed systems. A thread still sends a message to a local port, but now to one which represents a remote object.

In both Chorus and Mach, network communication is handled by a user level process, not by the microkernel itself.

Clouds

This system takes a different approach from the two previous ones. There is no message passing. It is based on objects, which are passive entities, with an address space of their own, containing code and data. Threads are separate entities, which execute within an object. But a thread is not associated with a particular object, it can move from object to object.

The really nice feature of Clouds is that a thread can execute an object which exists on another machine, passing it the appropriate parameters. Such execution is fully transparent. Execution of a local object, or a remote one, look the same to the user.

Amoeba

This is oriented more towards making a collection of distributed machines act like a single computer; so it is a complete distributed system.

It was developed from scratch, so there is no problem with backward compatibility. Later, Unix compatibility was added, so that existing applications could run on it. But this is not essential.

Amoeba is based on the processor pool model, but it can use workstations as well. There is no concept of a 'home' machine. The user deals with the system as a whole. In the course of a logon session, a user's work may run on many machines.

The standard Amoeba microkernel runs on every machine in the distributed system. It provides the minimum management necessary for processes and threads, memory, I/O, and communications.

Then there are specialist user-level servers, which are distributed using RPC. The RPC mechanism makes remote functions look like local functions, thus providing network transparency.

13.7 Environments for distributed computing

At present, the way forward is not clear. Several different alternatives have been proposed as the basis for the distributed systems of the future. We will examine two of these. But only time will tell exactly how the whole area will develop.

CORBA

In a distributed system, a server typically manages resources on behalf of clients. One obvious approach is to encapsulate these resources in modules, and provide distributed access to these modules. In this way the details of their management is hidden from the clients, only the interface is publicly available. This is an extension of objects to distributed systems, known obviously enough as distributed objects.

Overview

An association of computer manufacturers known as the Object Management Group (OMG) drew up a specification for a common object request broker architecture. As its name implies, CORBA provides access to objects distributed across a system. It is envisaged that CORBA would be used both for building distributed systems, and also for integrating existing and new applications.

Like all object oriented systems, CORBA encapsulates resources in modules, and makes them available only through interface procedures. This allows a large application to be broken down into subsystems with clearly defined interfaces. Each of these subsystems can then be implemented on its own, possibly on different machines, with the assurance that they will all work together. The designer decides which objects are to be made available, and defines the interface for them. The interface is object oriented; the implementation need not be.

These interfaces are specified in an interface definition language, or IDL, which is similar to C++. An interface specified in IDL can be translated to any other language, e.g. C, by an IDL compiler.

CORBA has been described as acting like a software bus. Just as hardware components all communicate with each other over the system bus, so software components communicate with each other through CORBA.

Object request broker

At the core of the CORBA specification is the object request broker (ORB). The ORB is responsible for locating the object, passing parameters to it, and returning the reply to the client. It allows a client to make a request across the network, despite differences in operating systems and programming languages (see Figure 13.9).

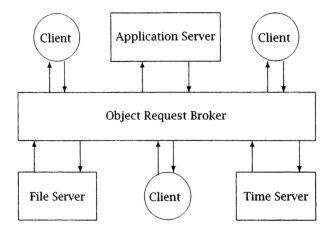

Figure 13.9: Overview of CORBA

The client does not have to know where the object is located, or anything about its implementation—just its interface.

There are many commercially available CORBA implementations. Each vendor's implementation must be able to communicate with all others, so that any client can communicate with any object developed in any CORBA environment.

The OMG have defined a set of 15 services, which support the ORB and cover most of the common functions that are needed when developing distributed systems. These include familiar services such as naming, time, security, transactions, and messaging, as well as distributed concurrency control. Objects are location transparent; all the user needs to know is the interface. To implement location transparency across a distributed system, CORBA supplies its own nameserver.

To facilitate the porting of legacy applications to a distributed environment, the code of such applications can be wrapped with a CORBA style interface. This makes it compatible on the outside with all the other modules supplied by the ORB.

DCOM

Microsoft has its own distributed object architecture, DCOM, which is the distributed version of Microsoft's component object model (COM) technology. COM specifies a binary standard for software objects, or components, which allows them to communicate regardless of the language in which they were programmed. COM objects can transparently request services from COM servers over a network, using DCOM. Objects are location independent.

As with CORBA, DCOM has a number of services to support it in a distributed environment. For example, it uses the Windows NT security service, and the Microsoft Transaction Server.

The most recent version, supported only on Windows 2000, is COM+.

While originally developed for the Windows platform, dedicated bridge software now allows it to interoperate with CORBA, so that CORBA client or server objects can communicate with COM/DCOM server or client objects. This opens up the way to cross platform development.

Distributed computing environment

The Open Software Foundation was set up to develop a new version of Unix, known as OSF/1, which would not be subject to copyright restrictions by previous owners and developers. Then when the need for distributed systems became apparent, OSF developed DCE, which could run on top of OSF/1, but also on other operating systems. It has been ported for example to Tru64 Unix, OpenVMS, MS-Windows, and OS/2.

So in theory you can take a number of existing machines, of different architectures, each running its own operating system, and just by putting the DCE software on top of these, you have an instant distributed system, without disturbing any of the existing applications. In most cases this can be done at user level, without affecting the kernel (see Figure 13.10).

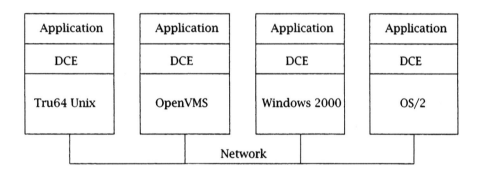

Figure 13.10: The distributed computing environment

DCE is a layer of software sitting between the operating system and the distributed application. It expects a transport layer below it, such as TCP/IP or one of the OSI transport protocols. While it can work with any of these, all of the machines involved must have at least one network protocol in common (or they cannot communicate).

The underlying model is client/server. Clients are ordinary programs, linked with a special library. Servers can be provided by DCE, or by other applications.

DCE provides tools for building distributed applications, such as its own threads facility, and remote procedure call, which is the basis for all communication in DCE. It also provides services for running such distributed systems, including security and protection, directory, and a time server. The advantage is that all of these are integrated, and do as much work as possible for the programmer.

There are seven components in the DCE system.

1. Threads

If the host operating system does not already provide threads, then the DCE threads package can be used. As it sits on top of the operating system, it is obviously a user level implementation. The operating system does not know about these threads. The interface is based on the POSIX `pthread` standard.

2. Remote procedure call

RPC allows a user to access a remote service, by calling a local procedure. The RPC system finds the remote server, and handles message passing, all transparently to the client. DCE RPC provides both a development tool, and a runtime service.

Development tool The interface definition is at the heart of developing an RPC system. It specifies all the functions which a server exports, with the types of the parameters. Typically it also includes comments describing the semantics of the function. It is written in an interface definition language, IDL. The IDL compiler then processes this definition, and produces code segments for both the client and the server, known as stubs, which handle all the distributed aspects. All the user has to write is the actual client and server code.

Run time service When a server boots, it registers itself with the DCE RPC daemon. Each machine keeps a database of available services, managed by this daemon. At run time, the process on the client machine first asks the RPC daemon for information about the server it requires. It can then communicate directly with the server.

3. Directory service

This server maintains information about all of the users, machines, and other resources available to the distributed system, in a hierarchical name space. This is both distributed and replicated. DCE can also use DNS as a directory service, and can integrate it into its own namespace.

4. Distributed time service

This server synchronises time on the different machines in the system, and also maintains a reasonably accurate time of day clock. See also Section 15.1.

5. Security service

This caters for authentication, allowing processes on different machines to be sure of each other's identity. It also handles authorisation, or what privileges should be given to an identified process. It uses access control lists for this. A user's security status is established at login, verified by password.

6. Distributed file system

It provides a single global namespace which covers all files on all participating machines, thus providing full location and migration transparency. It uses replication and caching for high performance. DCE also provides its own physical file system, the Episode file system. See Section 16.4 for more detail.

7. Diskless support

DCE provides support for diskless workstations. This includes providing a copy of the kernel at boot time, along with the appropriate configuration files for the particular machine, providing for remote paging and swapping, as well as a remote file system.

13.8 Summary

1. There are a number of reasons leading to the development of distributed systems. There are economic reasons, as a network of small machines is cheaper than the equivalent large machine. Also, they can offer greater reliability. The ability to share resources is another factor, as well as their ability to grow little by little.

2. Ideally such a distributed system should be totally transparent to a user.

3. On the hardware side, the workstation model is currently the most popular. These can be diskless, or have some local disk capacity. In either case, load balancing can be used to share the power of idle workstations.

   It is also possible to pool processors and memory, and allocate resources to users from this pool.

4. The most common architecture used is client/server. One process (server) provides some service to another (client). Typically these will be on different machines. Both clients and servers can be multi-threaded.

   Network operating systems provide some distributed applications, such as remote login, file transfer, and even remote directory sharing.

5. We prefer to identify machines and resources by human readable names. At the system level, this is more conveniently done by numeric identifiers. A nameserver maps between the two.

   DNS is the nameserver used for the Internet. It maps between names and addresses, and vice versa. It also maps between mail domains, and the appropriate mail servers.

   NIS is the nameserver used for the Network File System.

6. A true distributed operating system must at least begin to blur the boundaries between machines. Mach, Chorus, Clouds, and Amoeba are examples of distributed operating systems.

7. There are a number of competing environments for distributed systems being proposed at present.

   CORBA provides access to distributed objects. It can be used both for building new systems, and for distributing legacy systems. The interface definition is at the heart of the CORBA system. Any particular implementation of the CORBA standard is an ORB. These run on top of existing operating systems.

   OSF DCE is a similar proposal, which also runs on top of existing operating systems. It provides tools for building distributed applications, as well as run time services to support them, such as threads, RPC, directory, time, and security services, a distributed file system, and diskless support.

13.9 Discussion questions

1. Suggest some applications which would be particularly suitable for distribution over a network of microcomputers.

2. A distributed system can be built to be so reliable and fault tolerant that a user need not even be aware that a fault has occurred. Is this a good thing?

3. Assess any distributed system you are familiar with against the criteria in Section 13.2.

4. Investigate how a diskless workstation boots its operating system when it is powered up.

5. With the knowledge you have of I/O in Unix, suggest ways to arrange that all I/O of a process which migrates to another machine is redirected to the correct devices.

6. A computer attached to the Internet may be given more than one name. May it have more than one IP address?

7. When you present a name to your browser or mailer, how does it find the address of the machine it has to communicate with? Work out all of the steps involved.

8. Investigate the nslookup program, and use it to obtain information about different sub-domains of the Internet, and particularly the names of the root servers.

9. Use the nslookup program to find the time to live on information given out by your local DNS server.

10. Use ypmatch to find your own entry in the password file. From this read your user-id and your group-id. You can also read the encrypted form of your password, but it is unlikely to make much sense to you.

11. In what sort of applications would a client send data to a server for processing, and when would a server send data to a client for processing?

12. Mach and Chorus, as presented here, seem to be very similar. Investigate both systems further, and draw up a list of the areas where they differ.

13. For any of the interprocess communication mechanisms we have examined on stand-alone machines, what would be involved in developing a distributed version of it?

14. Is it accurate to describe CORBA as 'distributed monitors'?

15. What is the essential difference between Clouds and CORBA?

16. Does the ORB run on the server or the client machine?

17. Is there any fundamental difference between CORBA and DCE?

Communication 14

Any distributed system relies totally on the ability of different machines to communicate with one another. So we will begin with an examination of how such communication is implemented by the operating system on each machine. Then we will go on to consider how a distributed system could be built on top of the facilities provided by this layer.

The whole area of communication between machines is the province of computer networks. The fundamental design abstraction which has developed there is layered protocols. From our point of view, the important thing is that processes at both ends of the communication must use the same protocol.

14.1 Sockets for networking

We have examined various mechanisms for interprocess communication on stand-alone machines, such as message queues or pipes. In particular, we have examined sockets. Unix domain sockets only allowed communication between processes on the same machine. But the socket mechanism can be extended, so that it allows processes to send and receive data, across a network, without having to worry about any of the underlying protocols. Sockets have become a *de facto* industry standard, and are used in many network applications.

Despite the best efforts of the standards organisations, there are many different protocols or rules in use for communication between computers, and for identifying computers, and processes on them. These are known as domains, or address families, and are represented by predefined constants in <linux/socket.h>. Refer back to Figure 12.4.

When the kernel is configured for any particular machine, the system manager makes a decision about what networking software is to be loaded. This may be just one particular suite of software, if that is all that is required. Or it may be an extensive selection, if it is foreseen that this machine will be communicating with a wide range of other machines, and hence will need software to match all of them. The system keeps track of these networking protocols in the net_families[] array, as discussed in Section 12.2.

Internet domain

In particular, we have examined AF_UNIX, the Unix domain, in Chapter 12. But there are many other possibilities, such as AF_INET, the Internet domain, which we will concentrate on here.

Underlying all communication in the Internet domain is the Internet protocol, IP. This works at the network layer of the OSI model, and is concerned with getting packets to the correct destination machine. The Internet uses a set of transport protocols built on top of this IP networking layer; the principal ones, and the only ones we will consider, are the user datagram protocol (UDP), used for datagram communication; and the transmission control protocol (TCP), used for connection oriented communication.

All of the system services discussed in Section 12.3 are also relevant to Internet domain sockets.

Network interface

Software must also be installed to control the particular network interface card in use on the machine, including an interrupt service routine.

Drivers for network cards are handled differently from the drivers for all other devices. They do not have entries in either chrdevs[] or blkdevs[], nor do they have an entry in the /dev directory.

Information about the hardware interface itself is maintained in a device structure, as shown in Figure 14.1, from <linux/netdevice.h>.

```
struct device{
        char            *name;
        struct device   *next;
        int             (*init)();
        unsigned short  type;
        unsigned char   dev_addr[];
        int             (*hard_start_xmit)();
};
```

Figure 14.1: Data structure describing a network interface

- The name field points to the ASCII string representing the name of the particular device.

- If there is more than one network device installed on the machine, the corresponding structures will be linked through the next field.

- The init field points to a function which is called at boot time. It checks that the hardware actually exists, and initialises the other fields in this device structure.

- The type field identifies the type of card, e.g. ethernet.

- The `dev_addr` field holds the hardware address of the device, for example the 48 bit address of an ethernet card.

- The `hard_start_xmit` field points to a function which actually manipulates the hardware to send a packet.

There is a linked list of such structures, one for each network card installed, headed from `dev_base`. Information about installed network devices is given by the shell command `ifconfig`.

14.2 IP sockets

We have seen in Chapter 12 that the interface between the high-level socket mechanism, and any individual communication protocol, is implemented by means of a set of predefined functions. In Section 12.4 we considered the implementation of these functions for the Unix domain. Here we will look at how these same functions are implemented for the Internet domain.

Create

This customises the socket to be an IP socket. It creates a new `struct sock`, holding all of the relevant information. We have seen this before, in Figure 12.13, but the Internet domain uses fields that the Unix domain does not; we show a fuller version of it in Figure 14.2, from `<net/sock.h>`

```
struct sock{
        struct options      *opt;
        struct sock         *next;
        struct sk_buff      *partial;
        struct sk_buff_head receive_queue, write_queue;
        struct proto        *prot;
        u32                 daddr;
        u32                 rcv_saddr;
        u16                 dport;
        unsigned short      num;
        u32                 saddr;
        struct socket       *socket;
        void                (*data_ready)();
};
```

Figure 14.2: An Internet protocol control block

- The opt field points to a data structure that records options set for this socket. The values in this structure can be queried with `getsockopt()`, and options selected with `setsockopt()`. The various options are specified on the manual page.

- The next field is used to link the struct sock on a list of all allocated Internet control blocks. There are separate lists for UDP and TCP control blocks. These are used to find the struct sock to which an incoming packet is to be sent.

- TCP uses the partial field to queue packets which have arrived out of sequence.

- receive_queue and write_queue are headers for linked lists of packets on their way in or out.

- prot points to a struct proto containing the functions for the specific protocol, within the Internet domain. We have seen the struct proto in Section 12.4. Here the structure is identical; the functions pointed to are of course specific to TCP (for stream sockets) or UDP (for datagram sockets).

- daddr is the destination IP address for an outgoing packet.

- rcv_saddr contains the IP address bound to the socket.

- dport contains the remote port number, to which an outgoing packet is to be sent.

- num contains the port number bound to this socket.

- saddr is the source address, from the incoming packet.

- The socket field is a back pointer to the struct socket.

- The function data_ready() is called whenever incoming data arrives at the socket.

Bind

Each socket must be uniquely identified within a particular machine. Packets are sent on a network to a host, identified by an IP address, which is a unique 32 bit number. But each packet also has an identifier for the protocol which should receive this packet, such as UDP or TCP. Then within the particular Internet protocol, a 16 bit number, called a port number, is used to identify the specific socket. So a connection between two sockets is fully specified by source IP address, source port, protocol number, destination port, and destination IP address.

The port number used by a server is usually well known in network circles, and any requests coming in to that machine for connection to that port will be sent to that particular socket.

An IP address is contained in a struct sockaddr_in, as given in Figure 14.3, from <linux/in.h>. This identifies the address family (AF_INET), the port number on the host machine, and the IP address of that machine.

```
sockaddr_in{
     short int          sin_family; /* Address family, AF_INET */
     unsigned short int sin_port;   /* Port number             */
     struct in_addr     sin_addr;   /* Internet address        */
};
```

Figure 14.3: Internet socket address structure

When the IP specific bind() is called, it copies the IP address into the rcv_saddr field of the sock structure, and copies the port number into the num field.

The shell command netstat displays information about all active (bound) IP sockets in a system.

Accept

By the time the IP specific accept() is called, a new socket has been created to handle the requested connection. This function attaches a struct sock to it, and assigns a new, unused, port number to the num field. It then sends a message back to the remote socket, informing it that it is to use this port number for all future communication. The accepting process then sleeps, waiting for an acknowledgement.

When finally the remote process acknowledges this message, the connection is fully set up, and control returns to the socket level.

Connect

If this client socket is of type DGRAM, then connect() just stores the foreign address in the daddr field of the appropriate struct sock, for use when sending data, so that it does not have to be supplied each time. Such a UDP socket can be assigned a different foreign address, by a second call to connect().

If the client socket is of type STREAM, then connect() tries to set up a connection with the specified remote socket. The TCP specific connect() function, from proto, sends a message to the remote machine. This message contains the IP address and port number of the client. The caller is blocked until a reply arrives.

Because of this, connections appear synchronous to a user. When the server replies, with the port number to be used for all future communication, the client acknowledges this message to the new port number. Then it stores this port number in the dport field of its struct sock. Finally it returns a success value to the connect() system service which called it. Normal communication can now begin.

The three phases of setting up a connection between TCP sockets are outlined in Figure 14.4.

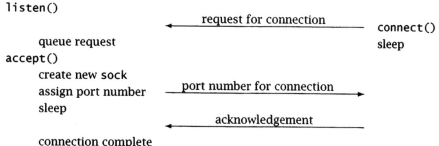

Figure 14.4: Connecting two sockets

Sendmsg

When the sendmsg() function for the INET domain is called, it copies the data from the msghdr structure into an sk_buff. We have already seen the sk_buff data structure when dealing with Unix domain sockets. This is also used for moving all data between the socket layer and the physical interface, and vice versa.

Messages have to be processed by four different layers on their way in or out. These four are the socket layer, the transport layer (UPD or TCP), the IP layer, and the hardware layer. The last three will be adding headers on the way out, and stripping them off on the way in.

For larger messages, more than one sk_buff can be chained together; this facilitates the adding of protocol headers. For example, if there is no room at the front of an sk_buff, IP and TCP/UDP headers are attached by adding an sk_buff at the head of a chain, and copying the packet header to it. The length of the chain is now longer, by the size of the IP or TCP/UDP header. The header is stored at the end of the data area of new sk_buff. This allows a lower level protocol such as ethernet to put its header in before.

The prot field in the struct sock points to a struct proto, which contains a vector of operations for the specific type of INET socket this is, i.e. TCP or UDP. The sendmsg() function in struct proto is called, which carries out protocol specific processing. First of all a TCP or UDP header is prefixed to the data; then an IP header is prefixed to this, and a checksum added. All headers are contiguous.

Finally a physical layer frame, e.g. ethernet, is constructed. The internal structure of the sk_buff at the physical layer is shown in Figure 14.5.

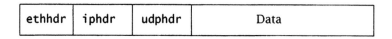

Figure 14.5: A physical frame

The function hard_start_xmit() (see the struct device in Figure 14.1) actually sends frames. If the device is idle, this function is called directly at this stage. If the device is busy, it is called automatically when the device finishes with the current frame.

Recvmsg

The recvmsg() function for the INET domain does very little work itself. If the receive_queue in the struct sock is empty, then the process is put to sleep. Otherwise it just calls the protocol specific recvmsg() in the struct proto.

For a stream socket, the requested number of bytes are transferred from the sk_buff queued there, and transferred to a msghdr structure. In this format it is passed back to the socket specific read() function, which transfers the data to the buffer specified by the user, and returns.

For a datagram socket, the whole message contained in the sk_buff is returned.

14.3 Network interrupt handler

Data arrives over a network asynchronously from any running process, and this data must be handled asynchronously. We will now follow incoming data from the ethernet layer, through the IP layer, then the transport layer (UDP or TCP), up to the socket layer.

Ethernet

When a complete packet has been received from the network, the interface card generates an interrupt. The handler for this interrupt constructs an sk_buff, and moves the packet off the ethernet card into this sk_buff, making the card ready to receive the next packet.

The interrupt handler then examines the ethernet header, see Figure 14.6, from <linux/if_ether.h>. This contains the destination and source ethernet addresses; more importantly, h_proto identifies the protocol stack the packet should be sent to, for example IP, or OSI, or some other protocol.

```
struct ethhdr{
        unsigned char  h_dest[];
        unsigned char  h_source[];
        unsigned short h_proto;
};
```

Figure 14.6: An ethernet header

The ethernet driver maintains a hash structure of struct packet_type, see Figure 14.7, from <linux/netdevice.h>, which identifies all of the possible packet types.

```
struct packet_type{
        unsigned short      type;
        int                 (*func)();
        struct packet_type *next;
};
```

Figure 14.7: Structure identifying a packet type

This hash table is ptype_base[], declared in net/core/dev.c. The interrupt handler hashes the h_proto field in the ethernet header into this list, and checks the type field in each entry. For IP, the type value is 0x8000. When it finds a match, the corresponding func() is called. Packets which do not match any of the known types are discarded.

IP

We are only considering IP packets, so in our case the IP handler will always be called by the ethernet interrupt handler. It examines the IP header, see Figure 14.8, from <linux/ip.h>.

```
struct iphdr{
        u8  protocol;
        u16 check;
        u32 saddr;
        u32 daddr;
};
```

Figure 14.8: An IP header

If the checksum in check is not valid, that means that the packet is damaged or erroneous. If so, it silently discards it. The protocol field then determines whether this packet is for TCP or UDP. The official Internet protocol names and numbers can be found in /etc/protocols. For example, TCP is 6, UDP is 17. It strips off the header. The appropriate protocol receive function is then called, either the UDP rcv(), or the TCP rcv().

UDP

The IP layer calls the UDP rcv() function, passing it a pointer to the sk_buff. This function examines the UDP header, see Figure 14.9, from <linux/udp.h>. If the checksum in check is not valid, it discards the packet.

The hash table of struct sock corresponding to UDP sockets (udp_hash[] from net/ipv4/udp.c) is then searched. If no match is found between the

```
struct udphdr{
        u16 source;
        u16 dest;
        u16 check;
};
```

Figure 14.9: A UDP header

dest field of the incoming header, and the num field of the sock, the packet is discarded. Otherwise, when a match is found, the sk_buff is queued from the receive_queue of the corresponding sock.

The data_ready() function in the struct sock is then called. If any process is waiting on this socket, it wakes it up; or it is notified by SIGIO, if it had been set non-blocking.

TCP

The processing for TCP is very similar to that just described for UDP. When a TCP datagram arrives, the TCP specific rcv() function is called by the IP layer. It examines the TCP header, see Figure 14.10 from <linux/tcp.h>. If the checksum in check is not valid, it discards the packet.

```
struct tcphdr{
        u16 source;
        u16 dest;
        u32 seq;
        u16 check;
};
```

Figure 14.10: A TCP header

It searches its hash table of TCP sock structures (headed by tcp_ehash from net/ipv4/tcp_ipv4.c) to find the appropriate one, corresponding to the dest field in the tcphdr of the incoming message.

But before it queues the data from the receive_queue of this sock, it must examine the seq field, and check that it is in correct sequence. If not, then it is queued from the partial field in sock. On the other hand, the arrival of this packet may complete a sequence, and so several packets may be passed to receive_queue at once.

As with UDP, the data_ready() function in the struct sock is called, which wakes up any process waiting on this socket, or notifies it by SIGIO, if it had been set non-blocking.

14.4 Extended transport interface

SVR3 introduced a transport level interface (TLI), as an alternative to the socket interface. It is based on the OSI standards. X/Open introduced an improved format, the Extended Transport Interface (XTI). It is not yet part of POSIX, nor is it available in Linux.

XTI is designed as a generic interface to any underlying transport protocol, not just TCP or UDP. It can be synchronous or asynchronous.

The system services are similar to those used with sockets. The more important are t_open(), which establishes a transport endpoint, and returns a file descriptor, used in all subsequent calls. Then t_bind() assigns an address to a transport endpoint, t_listen() waits for a connection request, t_accept() accepts a connection, and t_connect() establishes a connection with another transport user.

Both normal or priority data are sent and received over a connection using t_snd() and t_rcv(). A transport endpoint is disabled by t_unbind(), which reverses the t_bind() operation; it is finally torn down by t_close().

14.5 Remote procedure call

The client/server mechanism looks very much like the traditional I/O system to a user. A request is sent, to a local device or to a remote server, and then the requesting process waits until the result arrives. It was one logical way to develop distributed systems, building on what programmers were used to.

But programmers are probably even more familiar with function calls. Such a function call diverts control to an out of line function, possibly passing parameters to it as well. When the function finishes, control returns to the main program, and a result value is also made available in the main program. So another possible way to develop distributed systems is to implement a mechanism which would allow programs to call functions on other machines.

The remote machine has a module with an interface which exports a set of procedures. This gives the mechanism its name—remote procedure call, or RPC. The normal semantics of a function call are maintained as far as possible— input and output parameters, and a return value. In this way all the details of how the network operates (even its existence) can be hidden from the application program.

Overview

With a conventional procedure call, the compiler will generate code to push the parameters onto the stack. If these are passed by value, i.e. literal constants, or the names of variables, then the actual value is put on the stack. For example, if x contains the value 5, and x is passed as a parameter, then 5 is put on the stack. If a parameter is passed by reference, then a pointer to the parameter is put on the stack. With the same example, if &x is the parameter, then the

address of variable x is put on the stack. Finally the compiler will generate an instruction to call the subroutine. The special machine instruction for this on the PC, for example, is CALL.

The called subroutine can then either access these parameters directly on the stack, or it can copy them into its own workspace, with the former being most common. When finished, the called subroutine makes the return value available to the caller, in some architecture specific way.

For example, on the PC it puts the return value into the EAX register, where it is available to the caller. It then returns to the calling program at the next instruction after the CALL. The special instruction for this on the PC is RET. The simple flow of control in either case is illustrated in Figure 14.11.

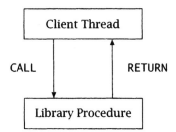

Figure 14.11: Function call/return

One fundamental requirement with RPC is that it should be transparent to the programmer, that is it should look exactly like a local procedure call. This is achieved by the sender having a dummy procedure in a library on its own machine, known as a stub. The sender calls this in the usual way, passing parameters on the stack, as before.

As far as the sender knows, this is the procedure which is doing the work. But it is not. All it does is to format the parameters into a message, add some identification of the procedure it wants executed on the remote machine, and send the message off to that machine, using an interface such as a socket or XTI. The sender stub then blocks, waiting for a reply.

When the message arrives at the remote machine, the RPC server process there unpacks the message, and identifies which procedure is being requested. It then calls that library procedure in the normal way, passing parameters on the stack.

The procedure returns as normal, passing back a return value to the RPC server process. This in turn packages the result as a message, and sends it to the communication layer for transmission to the stub on the requesting machine. This stub unpacks the message, and passes back the result to the client process in the normal way. Figure 14.12 illustrates the flow of control in this case.

The server may have one general purpose module which receives requests, and passes them on to the appropriate local procedure. Or it may have a separate unmarshaller (a stub) for each procedure.

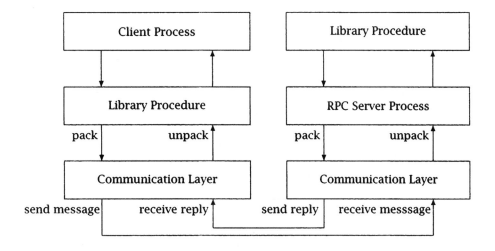

Figure 14.12: Call/return with RPC

Parameters

There are problems with data types in parameters. Different machines can encode characters in EBCDIC or ASCII, and even that in 7 bits or 8 bits. There are also differences in how integers and floating point numbers are represented. There is no agreement about the order in which array elements are stored. Also some machines can be big endian, others little endian. But both the client and the server stubs know the types of the parameters, and their order. So they must agree a standard for representing basic data types.

One possibility would be to devise a standard network format. All parameters would then be translated into this format, before being transmitted. This could be inefficient sometimes, if both the sender and receiver use the same native format, different from the network format. So another possibility is that the sender uses its own native format, but indicates what it is. Then the receiver only translates if necessary. DCE RPC uses this method to avoid the double translation.

Reference parameters cause their own problems. One possibility is to copy the value into the message, even for arrays. This is replacing call by reference with copy/restore. There is a heavy overhead in this. But it can be reduced. An input parameter need not be copied back. Output parameters need not be sent in the first place.

Transport: UDP or TCP

Is the RPC protocol to be connectionless or not? On a LAN it generally is connectionless. But the decision is influenced by the requirements of the particular application.

Some procedures can be repeated over and over again, with no side effects. An example would be reading a block from a file. Such procedures are said to be idempotent. Others have a different effect each time they are executed, for example reading the *next* block from a file, or incrementing a counter. These are said to be non-idempotent.

So if procedures are idempotent, the arguments in both directions less than 8K (the maximum UDP packet size), and there is a high volume of requests, then many systems use UDP over IP.

If procedures are non-idempotent, or the arguments are greater than 8K, or the application needs a reliable transport mechanism, then TCP can be used. But because TCP retains state, it places a greater load on the server.

Binding

The next problem is, how does the client locate the server? Hardwiring the network address of the server into the client stub is not good enough. So some form of dynamic binding is required. We know the name of the remote procedure. This does not change. But it must be translated to a specific id on a remote host, such as a socket at a particular IP address. This needs to be done each time the client runs.

So we need a binder service, or a registration service, a name server which has a table of such mappings. When it starts up, a server program registers its name, and the port at which it is listening, with the binder. It should also be possible to de-register procedures. The registration server can also be responsible for authentication.

When registering, a server program can specify which users, or groups of users, it it willing to serve. The binder will refuse to identify the server to any unauthorised client.

The system should be able to handle multiple servers exporting the same interface. Binders should be fault tolerant, for example they should cache their information in a file. Even better would be a distributed binder service like DNS—and replicated.

A client specifies a name and a version number to the binder, which returns a machine address and a local port number on that machine.

But how does the client find the binder? One possibility is that it has a well-known IP address, hard-coded into all clients. However, this implies the need for re-compilation if the binder is moved to another machine. So a better mechanism is to have the address of the binder in an environment variable; then only this variable needs to be changed.

Another possibility is that when a client wishes to find the binder, it broadcasts a message over the network, effectively saying 'would the binder please identify itself to the machine at such an address'. The binder listens for such messages, and sends its IP address to the requesting machine. The client can then ask the binder to translate procedure names in the usual way.

Failures

Like anything else in a computer system, we have to expect that RPC will fail from time to time. But it rarely fails cleanly. Remember there are three components involved, the client machine, the server machine, and the communications network. Normally one fails, but the other two continue working. So the results can be decidedly odd.

Lost messages

Let us first of all consider the loss of a message. The client can detect this, by using a timeout interval. If no reply arrives in this time, it knows something is wrong. But it cannot know whether it was the request or the reply which was lost. All it can do is send the request again. However, in order to help the server to distinguish between original requests and repeats, it must mark the repeat in some way. This could be a sequence number, or just a repeat bit, in the message header.

To help it handle situations like this, the server maintains a list of recent transactions, both the request and the reply. When a repeat request comes in, the server checks its recent transaction list. If it finds the recent request there, then it knows that the original reply was lost, so it resends a copy of that reply, without carrying out the operation a second time.

On the other hand, if it does not have an original copy of the request in its recent transaction list, it knows that the original request was lost. So it treats the repeat as the original, carries out the operation, and sends back a reply.

This procedure works for both idempotent and non idempotent operations. One possible loophole is that a series of lost messages could mean that a repeat request arrives at the server after it has flushed the information from its recent transaction list. This could result in a non-idempotent operation being carried out more than once.

Server crash

If the server crashes before carrying out the operation, there is no consistency problem. The client knows, from the absence of a reply, that the operation has not been carried out. The client will probably retry a maximum number of times, and then give up. The operation has not been carried out, and the client knows this.

Also, if the server crashes after carrying out an idempotent operation, but before sending the reply, there is no problem. When the server eventually comes back up again, the client will ask it to repeat the operation, and both sides will be consistent.

However, the server could crash between carrying out a non-idempotent operation and sending the reply. When the server comes back up, it may or may not be able to detect that a request is a duplicate. The non-idempotent operation will be carried out twice in that case.

Client crash

If the client crashes after sending a request, the server completes its work, sends back a result, and considers itself finished with that request. When the reply arrives at the communications layer of the client machine, it will find that there is no process there to receive the reply, and most systems will just quietly discard it. Even if it does officiously tell the server that it cannot deliver its message, the server will just ignore this.

14.6 RPC programming

All of the work involved in building RPC programs could be done by hand, in a conventional programming language, but it would be very prone to error. The order, type, and encoding of parameters must be the same in all four modules that deal with them. If all four are coded independently, there is certainly room for inconsistencies to creep in, particularly over time, as changes are made in one place but not in all.

The ideal is to automate as much of this as possible. The programmer only writes the client program and the server procedure. Stubs and socket calls for communication can all be generated automatically, and also any differences in the way data types are represented on the two machines can be masked.

A number of different, incompatible, systems are available, which facilitate the development of RPC programs. The OSF developed a system for their DCE, which we have already mentioned in Section 13.7. This is also used by Microsoft, which is a member of the OSF.

Sun Microsystems developed an RPC system which has become a *de facto* standard. It was originally designed to underpin their network file system, but the specification for it was put in the public domain, and it has been widely used for many other applications. To avoid the proprietary implications of the name 'Sun RPC', it is now distributed under the title 'Open Network Computing', or ONC. As it is the RPC system commonly available on Linux, as well as most Unix systems, we will examine it in some detail.

Identification

Each remote procedure is identified by a <program, version, procedure> triple. This allows one server program to supply a number of different related procedures, and even different versions of them at the same time. The file /etc/rpc contains a list of recognised programs, and the numbers assigned to them.

Program numbers are allocated as follows:

- 0x00000000 - 0x1FFFFFFF are defined and administered by ONC
- 0x20000000 - 0x3FFFFFFF are defined by the user
- 0x40000000 - 0x5FFFFFFF are defined once off by programs
- 0x60000000 - 0xFFFFFFFF are reserved for future use.

The version number allows the client and the server to check that they are using the same version of the software. This is to protect against possible changes in parameters, for example.

To identify which procedure is being requested, both the client and the server agree a unique integer for each procedure; this is included in the request. It is expected that each server program will have a NULL procedure, which is numbered 0 by default. The first real procedure then is numbered 1.

Rpcbind

ONC RPC does not have a network wide binder. Each machine runs a process, known as rpcbind, which keeps track of which RPC programs are using which port numbers on that machine. It itself listens at a well-known port, 111.

A server calls rpcbind to register its program and version number, and the port it is listening at. A client calls rpcbind to find the port at which a specific server is listening.

The client and the server both communicate with rpcbind using RPC, program 100000, version 3. Version 2 of that program refers to an earlier binder known as portmapper.

The shell command rpcinfo lists the programs registered on a particular machine, along with their version numbers, and the transport protocol they are using. Only the superuser can delete registrations, using rpcinfo -d.

Interface specification

As we have outlined above, there are four different procedures involved in RPC. There is the client function, and the client stub, both of which will run on the client machine. Then there is the server stub, and the server function, both of which will run on the server machine.

Neither of these two stubs needs to know anything about what the server function is actually doing. They are only concerned with passing parameters over a network. So they can be written and compiled as long as the parameters of the call are known.

RPC language

The work of building an RPC program begins with a specification of the interface in RPC language, which is similar to C. Figure 14.13 shows how this language is formally specified. The interface specification must include the name of the server program, its unique id number, and the version number. Also, for each function that program supplies, the type of the input parameter and return value must be specified. Note that it is only possible to specify one input parameter. As most practical applications require more than this, both the input parameter and the return value are typically defined as a struct.

```
program-definition:
     "program" program-name "{"
          version-list
     "}" "=" value ";"

version-list:
     version ";"
     | version ";" version list

version:
     "version" version-name "{"
      procedure-list
     "}" "=" value ";"

procedure-list:
     procedure ";"
     | procedure ";" procedure-list

procedure:
     type-ident procedure-name "(" type-ident ")" "=" value ";"
```

Figure 14.13: Format of RPC specification language

Example

The format of such an interface definition can be illustrated by the following example, which we will use as a running example throughout the remainder of this section. Suppose we have a server program called MATH, with an id number of 0x20000001. Let us also assume that this is the first version of that program. It has only one procedure, which takes an int as input, and returns an int. The interface definition for such a program is shown in Figure 14.14.

```
program MATH{
     version MATHVERSION{
          int DOUBLE (int) = 1;
                         } = 1;
          } = 0x20000001;
```

Figure 14.14: Interface definition for MATH program

This will serve as an interface definition for procedure 1 in version 1 of program 0x20000001. Note the use of uppercase for the program name, the version, and the procedure name. This is not obligatory, but is used by convention in the RPC language.

This definition is saved in a file with a .x extension—typically math.x.

Program generator

The tool that generates C code to implement the RPC protocol is the rpcgen program generator. It processes the definition file from the previous example, and produces three further files.

One is a header file, math.h, which will be used to specify the program number and version, and the procedure number, to both the client and server programs.

The second file, math_clnt.c, is a standard C program file, so it is possible to examine it, and see what rpcgen is producing. It contains a function double_1(). This is the client stub, complete and finished. The client stub name is from the interface definition, lowercase underscore version number. But there is no need to examine this function. It is possible to produce a functioning RPC client without knowing anything about the internals of the stub.

The third file, math_svc.c, is the server stub. This contains a main() function, which creates a socket for incoming requests, then informs the local rpcbind of the procedure name, the version number, and the portnumber at which it is listening. It then waits for incoming requests. When such a request arrives, it checks the version and procedure numbers specified, and calls the particular procedure corresponding to that procedure number, e.g. double_1().

By default, rpcgen generates server stub code for both UDP and TCP. The -s switch can be used to specify one or the other.

If the -a switch is used with rpcgen, then it will produce two further files, math_client.c and math_server.c. These are skeleton C programs for the client and server, which can then be filled out with code written by the programmer.

External data representation

ONC RPC translates all data types in parameters into its own network format, known as external data representation, or XDR, which is independent of any machine architecture. Converting from a particular machine format to XDR is called serialising; the opposite is deserialising.

A library of filter routines is supplied, for serialising data items such as integers, floats, enumerations, strings, structures, unions, and arrays. These routines are named xdr_xxx(), where xxx descibes the type, e.g. int. Routines are direction independent—the same routine is used to serialise, and to deserialise.

So for standard data types, such as int, XDR routines already exist. But if the data types are user defined, declared in the RPC specification file, then rpcgen creates a file of XDR routines, in C code. In our example it would be named math_xdr.c. This has to be compiled to object format, ready to be linked with the client and server.

As both of the parameters used in the foregoing example were of the predefined type int, there was no need for rpcgen to produce the file math_xdr.c.

Client program

Now that the stubs are ready, all that remains is to write the client and server programs for the foregoing example. Let us begin with the client. There are some points to note here. The header file <rpc/rpc.h>, as well as the header generated by rpcgen, in our example math.h, must always be included.

Handle

Then the client has to take one extra step, not required when calling a local function. It must call the RPC library function clnt_create(). This call takes four parameters. The first is the network name of the server. This can be passed as a literal string. The second and third are the remote program number, and version. These can be passed as MATH and MATHVERSION; they are meaningful here because they are defined in math.h. The final parameter specifies the transport mechanism to use for the call, or in effect what kind of socket to create; this parameter is usually specified as a literal string, either 'tcp' or 'udp'.

The clnt_create() function calls the portmapper (rpcbind) on the remote machine to find the port number at which the server is listening, and it returns this as a 'handle'. If it returns NULL, then clnt_pcreateerror() will show the reason why. This can be passed a string, just like perror().

It is good programming practice to deallocate the handle, when the client program is about to terminate, by calling clnt_destroy().

Calling the stub

When the client comes to call its stub function, remember that its name is double_1(). It is called with two arguments, the input parameters (if more than one) as one struct, and the handle. Also, the stub expects its arguments to be passed by reference—i.e. pointers to the arguments. Notice that at this stage we have specified all the information needed: server, program number, version number, transport protocol, procedure name.

The stub then sends a datagram to the appropriate port. When a reply datagram arrives, the stub will pass back a pointer to the result. Return values are packed into one struct, if necessary. The client only declares a pointer to this return value.

If the RPC or network fails, the client stub will return NULL. The library function clnt_perror() can be called to print an explanation of the error.

If the transport mechanism carries the message without fault, but there are problems with the remote procedure, then error information can be passed back in the return parameter struct.

Memory leaks

Some of the complex XDR filters used in client stubs generated by rpcgen allocate memory dynamically. They cannot deallocate this memory themselves, as

it is still needed by the client. So the client program must deallocate it, when finished with it. Otherwise repeated calls to the stub could result in serious memory leaks.

There is a generic freeing routine in the XDR library, xdr_free(). This can be called in the client main program. It takes two parameters, the XDR routine for the object being freed, and a pointer to the object itself.

Client authentication

The client stub created by rpcgen does no authentication. Different forms of authentication can be used; the default is none. If the client needs to authenticate itself to the server, then after the call to client_create() returns a handle cl, the following assignment must be made:

$$cl\texttt{->}cl\_auth = authunix\_create\_default();$$

Each RPC call includes a struct authunix_parms, from <rpc/auth_unix.h>, as shown in Figure 14.15.

```
struct authunix_parms{
        u_long aup_time;        /* time credentials were created */
        char   *aup_machname;   /* host name of client's machine */
        int    aup_uid;         /* client's Unix user id         */
        int    aup_gid;         /* client's current group id     */
        int    *aup_gids;       /* array of client's groups      */
};
```

Figure 14.15: Unix style credentials

This includes a timestamp, the name of the local host, the uid of the client, and a list of all groups the client belongs to.

Server program

Finally we come to the server program itself. The header file <rpc/rpc.h>, as well as the header generated by rpcgen, in our example math.h, must always be included. The server program does not have a main() function; remember it is only a function which will be called by main() in the stub.

Its name is double_1(), in lowercase. It expects its argument to be passed by reference, and it will return a pointer to the result. This result will be read by the server stub *after* the server function has finished. So the variable into which the server will place the result cannot be automatic (on the stack). It should be declared as static.

The finished programs

Now that all four C programs are written, they are compiled to produce two executables, as follows.

```
cc client.c math_clnt.c -o client
cc server.c math_svc.c -o server
```

When the server is run, it first of all registers itself with rpcbind; then it arranges to run in the background. The ps command will show this. It should be removed when no longer needed. Note that if a server crashes, as opposed to closing down gracefully, it remains registered with rpcbind.

Figure 14.16 gives an overview of the whole system.

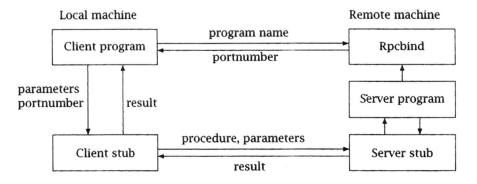

Figure 14.16: Overview of RPC system

It is also possible to link the client main program and the server procedure together, for testing purposes. When everything is working as local procedures, then they can be linked with the stubs, and distributed.

Inetd port monitor

Instead of having the server process waiting for a request, which may come rarely or never, it is possible to ask the port monitor inetd to do the listening. When a request arrives for the specified port, inetd then forks a process to run the server. When finished, the server waits a default 2 minutes, and if there are no further requests, it terminates, leaving inetd to continue listening.

The -I option to rpcgen creates server code to run in this fashion. The -K option changes the waiting time.

At boot time, the inetd daemon reads information from its configuration file, /etc/inetd.conf, about which ports it is to listen for. The manual page for inetd.conf gives more information.

14.7   Low level RPC programming

At a lower level, programmers can do all of their own coding, without using rpcgen.

Library routine

The most useful library function for this is callrpc(). This takes 8 arguments, as follows:

- Name of the remote machine on which the server is running
- Number of the remote program
- Version of the remote program
- Number of the procedure to be called
- XDR procedure to encode the argument
- Address of the parameter to be sent
- XDR procedure to decode the result
- Address of where to put the result.

Note that it always uses UDP. It is not possible to control timeouts when using callrpc(). It tries five times at 5 second intervals. It defaults to using no authentication, and the user has no control over this either. On success, callrpc() returns 0; otherwise it returns an error number, which can be interpreted by clnt_perrno(). Do not confuse this with clnt_perror().

Message structure

The structure of a raw RPC message, from <rpc/rpc_msg.h>, is shown in Figure 14.17.

```
struct rpc_msg{
        u_long                      rm_xid;
        enum msg_type               rm_direction;
        union{
                struct call_body   RM_cmb;
                struct reply_body  RM_rmb;
        }ru;
};
```

Figure 14.17: Structure of an RPC message

- Both the call and reply use the same structure, but different parts of the union ru.

- The field rm_xid contains a unique id number; the reply message contains the id of the call it is replying to.

- The rm_direction field contains 0 for a call, 1 for a reply.

The format of a call message is given in Figure 14.18, from <rpc/rpc_msg.h>.

```
struct call_body {
        u_long                  cb_rpcvers; /* RPC version number */
        u_long                  cb_prog;    /* program number     */
        u_long                  cb_vers;    /* version number     */
        u_long                  cb_proc;    /* procedure number   */
        struct opaque_auth cb_cred;         /* authentication     */
};
```

Figure 14.18: Body of a call message

The rpcvers field identifies the version of the RPC protocol itself which is in use, currently 2. The other fields are self evident. This is followed by the parameters specific to the particular remote procedure being called.

The format of a reply is given in Figure 14.19, from <rpc/rpc_msg.h>.

```
struct reply_body{
        enum reply_stat                 rp_stat;
        union{
                struct accepted_reply RP_ar;
                struct rejected_reply RP_dr;
        }ru;
};
```

Figure 14.19: Body of a reply message

- The field rp_stat is 0 if the message was accepted, 1 if it was refused.

- In the former case RP_ar contains the result; otherwise RP_dr contains the reason for the rejection.

14.8 Summary

Interprocess communication between different machines is an essential prerequisite for any distributed system.

1. The socket facility allows processes to send and receive data across a network without having to worry about any of the underlying mechanisms.

At boot time, the kernel sets up an array `net_families[]`, in which it maintains information about each address family it is prepared to handle, e.g. IP. Information about the hardware interface itself is maintained in a `device` structure, not in the traditional `chrdevs[]` or `blkdevs[]` arrays.

2. There are IP specific functions for IP sockets.

The `create()` function links the `socket` to a `struct sock`, which contains information specific to the IP domain.

A socket can then be assigned an IP address, and port number, using `bind()`.

A user may passively accept connections, by calling `listen()`, and then repeatedly calling `accept()`.

Or a user may actually take the initiative, and use `connect()` to establish a link with a remote socket which is listening.

Data and control information is passed between the socket layer and the hardware in an `sk_buff` structure. These are of fixed size, and can be chained together to hold large packets.

On output, the data is copied into an `sk_buff`. The destination information is read from the `sock` associated with the socket, and the `sendmsg()` function for the required protocol is called.

When a user requests input, using `recvmsg()`, the data is transferred to user space from `receive_queue`. If no data is available, the calling process is blocked.

3. On input, the hardware interrupts when a complete frame has been received. The ethernet driver copies the packet into an `sk_buff`, and passes it on to the IP handler. This function determines which protocol the packet is destined for, either TCP or UDP. It is then queued on the `receive_queue` of the appropriate `struct sock`, where it is available for the user.

4. The extended transport interface (XTI) is another mechanism for interfacing with a range of networking protocols. It is very similar to the socket interface.

5. Remote procedure call is a mechanism which allows programs to call functions on remote machines in a transparent manner. The caller has a stub procedure to marshal the arguments into a message, which it sends to the server. The server has a stub which unmarshalls the arguments, and calls the actual worker procedure.

Any of the three components, client, server, or network, can fail. So arrangements have to be made to handle errors from any of these sources.

6. The *de facto* standard is ONC RPC.

It is useful to have a central registry of what servers are exporting which procedures. ONC RPC does this on a machine-by-machine basis, using `rpcbind`.

Much of the work involved in writing RPC programs can be automated. The programmer specifies the interface, using XDR to describe the parameters. The `rpcgen` compiler uses this specification to generate client and

server stubs. The client program includes a call to its stub. By default there is no authentication of RPC calls, but it is possible to change this.

The inetd port monitor can be used to listen for requests. When a request arrives, it forks a process to run the server.

7. It is of course possible to write RPC programs, without using rpcgen. The callrpc() library function is provided for this.

14.9 Discussion questions

1. Which communication protocol(s) are in use on the machine you use?

2. The socket facility can be built on top of many different communication domains. Why does this not allow a machine using DECNet to communicate with a machine using AppleTalk? What extra arrangements would have to be made to allow this?

3. Consult the manual page for socket(), or a textbook, to find out more about the differences between stream and datagram sockets, as well as any other types which might be available.

4. There are fields in struct sock concerned with sequencing, which is more the concern of networks rather than operating systems. Investigate how TCP uses sequence variables, and also the purpose of keep-alive probes.

5. The same system service, bind(), is used to associate an address with a socket, no matter which address domain is in use. How can one function be so universal?

6. Would it be possible to have a handler configured for incoming ethernet packets which do not belong to any known domain? What sort of processing would such a handler carry out?

7. Only the minimum amount of processing is done on an incoming packet at the hardware interrupt priority level (copy to an sk_buff, and put it on a queue). All further processing is done at a lower priority. Why is this?

8. The checking for erroneous or damaged packets is done at software priority level. Would it not seem more sensible to do this even before queueing the packet?

9. An ethernet card has no way of determining whether an incoming packet is UDP or TCP—nor does it try to differentiate. How then do they arrive at their correct destinations?

10. An RPC server could have one general purpose module which receives all requests, and then passes them on to the appropriate local procedure. Or it may have a separate stub for each procedure. What are the advantages and disadvantages of each method?

11. When calling a subroutine on a local machine, a pointer to a variable can be passed as a parameter. Why is this not possible with RPC?

12. A binder or registration server can also do authentication. Discuss the implications of this.

13. If a client resends a request, the server knows that a message has been lost. How can it tell whether it was the original request, or the reply, which was lost?

14. Why do you think a server program is expected to provide a NULL function?

15. Examine a client stub produced by `rpcgen`, and identify what each line of it is doing.

16. Examine a server stub produced by `rpcgen`, and identify what each line of it is doing.

17. The handle returned by `clnt_create()`, and passed to the client stub, is opaque, i.e. its structure is not available, and is not of interest to the user. What fields do you think are in this handle?

18. With ONC RPC, all parameters are passed to and from stubs by reference, i.e. pointers to the data are passed. Is it possible that the value one of these is pointing to could be overwritten, or the memory space deallocated?

19. If a server process is removed using `kill`, it will still be registered with the binder. How could this inconsistency be avoided?

20. If RPC were implemented asynchronously, suggest some mechanism in the client stub for accepting, identifying, and dealing with asynchronous replies.

Concurrency in distributed systems **15**

We have considered the problems of concurrent systems on a single machine in some detail. Single machine solutions all relied, in one way or another, on shared memory. Now we turn to the extra complications introduced by interactions between concurrent processes running on different machines.

15.1 Event ordering

On a single processor machine, the CPU clock determines all activity. Only one instruction can be executed at a time, by whichever process. There can be no ambiguity about the order in which instructions have been executed. This property was assumed in all of our earlier reasoning about mutual exclusion and synchronisation.

Universal time

In a distributed system, there are many CPU clocks, all in different places. How can we decide whether an instruction has been executed on one machine before or after a particular instruction has been executed on another machine?

This may seem trivial: all we have to do is establish a global or universal time. But this is easier said than done. Even if we could set it up, we could not maintain it, as different clocks will slowly get out of sync. This is known as clock skew, or drift. Some work has been done on synchronising clocks using radio signals, but this is too cumbersome, and anyway is not accurate enough to distinguish between instructions on two machines running at 500MHz.

DCE time service

One service to be provided by a distributed computing environment is a time service. In DCE, one or more machines act as time servers. They maintain consistency by repeatedly exchanging time with each other. They also keep themselves consistent with the time of day. They maintain time internally as a 64 bit integer.

The time clerk is a daemon which runs on local machines, and keeps the local clock synchronised with server clocks. It resynchronises by contacting all the time servers on its own LAN, and averaging out their values. It does not make abrupt changes, but runs its clock slower or faster until it is in sync with the value given by the time server.

Time in Unix

Unix supports a number of time services, which are mainly intended for maintaining time of day clocks.

Internet daytime protocol

The server listens on port 13, either TCP or UDP. When a remote process connects to that port, it sends back an ASCII string containing the date and time. The TCP version then closes the connection.

Internet time protocol

This is similar to the daytime protocol. It uses port 37. It returns a 32 bit value representing the number of seconds elapsed since 1/1/1900.

Network time protocol

Machines running this protocol send each other UDP messages at regular intervals, exchanging their current local time. Allowing for the transmission delay, each can then calculate its clock drift, and compensate accordingly.

It is envisaged that one machine on the network will have access to a very accurate clock, such as broadcast by satellite. This is known as a stratum 1 machine. Those that get their time directly from this are designated stratum 2. Others use a stratum number one larger than the machine they are in direct contact with.

The daemon which runs this service is ntpd; it listens on UDP port 123. While the system guarantees to be accurate to within a few milliseconds, this is not good enough for distinguishing between events in distributed processes.

Time synchronisation protocol

This protocol relies on one master server, which periodically collects times from all of the others. It then works out the average of these times, and adopts that time as its own. Finally it orders all of the others to synchronise with it. Then the whole process is repeated all over again.

Consistency is guaranteed between the different machines. But as there is no external point of reference, accuracy of time of day is not guaranteed. They can all drift off together. This protocol is used by the timed network time daemon, which listens on UDP port 525. As it only provides for compatibility, NTP is preferred.

Happened before relationship

But remember that we are not really interested in time in itself—we are only using it to compare two events, and to decide if one happened before the other. There are other ways of achieving that goal besides the difficult, if rather obvious, one of establishing a universal time on all machines.

If two processes never communicate, there cannot be any question of synchronisation. It is only when they communicate that the question of ordering events in the two of them arises. No matter how they communicate, the message will have to be sent before it can be received, so we can always say that the sending of a message happened before its arrival. For distributed processes, the important events are the arrival and departure of messages.

This leads us to the idea of a 'happened before' relationship, denoted by $\rightarrow$. If two events a and b happen in processes which never communicate, then it is not possible to say $a \rightarrow b$. Nor is it possible to say $b \rightarrow a$. So they are considered to be concurrent. Note that 'happened before' has no implication of one event causing another.

Example

Figure 15.1 shows three events x_1, x_2, and x_3, in a process running on machine X. Event x_1 involves sending a message to a process on machine Y.

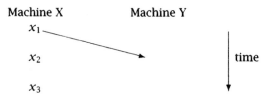

Figure 15.1: Events in process X

Figure 15.2 shows three events y_1, y_2, and y_3 in a process running on machine Y. Event y_2 is the arrival of the message from machine X, and event y_3 is the sending of a message to a process on machine Z.

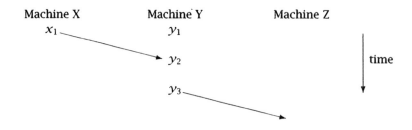

Figure 15.2: Events in process Y

Figure 15.3 shows three events z_1, z_2, and z_3 in a process running on machine Z. Event z_3 is the arrival of a message from machine Y.

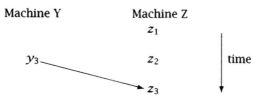

Figure 15.3: Events in process Z

For any individual process, we can determine a total ordering on events:

$$x_1 \rightarrow x_2 \rightarrow x_3$$
$$y_1 \rightarrow y_2 \rightarrow y_3$$
$$z_1 \rightarrow z_2 \rightarrow z_3$$

In the distributed system, we can also say:

$$x_1 \rightarrow y_2$$
$$y_3 \rightarrow z_3$$

Because the 'happened before' relation is transitive, we can say:

$$x_1 \rightarrow y_2 \rightarrow y_3 \rightarrow z_3$$

Unless there were other messages, we cannot know about the relative ordering of any of the other events. For example, we have no way of knowing whether $x_3 \rightarrow y_3$ is true or not. Even less intuitively, it is not possible to say whether $y_1 \rightarrow x_3$ is true or not.

Implementation

Each machine keeps its own time counter. This is not necessarily a time of day clock. Remember that the aim of the protocol is not to maintain physical time, rather to order events. But it must be an integer counter of events. It is incremented whenever an event occurs. Whenever a message is sent, this timestamp is added to it.

When a message arrives, the timestamp on the message is compared with the value of the local counter. If the message timestamp is less than the local counter, then the relative ordering of the two processes is correct. The message was sent before it was received, so the sending timestamp should be less than the receiving timestamp.

The situation can be described as follows:

IF A $\rightarrow$ B, THEN timestamp(A) < timestamp(B).

If, however, the timestamp on an arriving message is equal to, or greater than the local timestamp, this implies that the local counter is falling behind. In order to maintain the 'happened before' relationship, the local counter must be adjusted so that it is greater than the message timestamp. So it is set to be at least one greater than the timestamp of the incoming message. The relative ordering of the two processes is now correct.

For example, suppose a message arrives with timestamp 11. If the counter on the local machine has a value of 12 or greater, then no action needs to be taken. The relative ordering of the two processes is correct. But if the local counter has a value of 11 or less, then it must be incremented to at least 12, so that the relative ordering of the two processes is correct.

15.2 Distributed mutual exclusion

When studying mutual exclusion on stand-alone machines, we based our solutions on the idea of critical sections within programs. Then once we had guaranteed that at most one process could be executing a critical section at any time, we could guarantee mutual exclusion. Mechanisms such as semaphores were introduced to control this.

The concept of critical sections will extend to cover mutual exclusion in distributed systems. But mechanisms such as semaphores are very difficult to distribute. They rely on shared variables, which by definition exist in one place. Guaranteeing indivisible, uninterruptible access to them over a network is difficult, if not impossible.

The algorithms which have been developed to control mutual exclusion in distributed systems fall into two classes. Some are centralised, with one controller which handles all requests. These are simpler to implement, but suffer from the drawback that they have a single point of failure. Fully distributed algorithms, on the other hand, rely on getting agreement among all the distributed processes. This is much more difficult to implement, but has the advantage that it can still work, even if some processes crash.

Centralised algorithm

With this arrangement, there is one dedicated coordinator process, somewhere in the system. Such a process could control one critical section, or many. It listens for requests at a well-known port. A process asks permission, gets it, enters the critical section, and then informs the coordinator when it leaves its critical section.

So there are three different messages used: a request, a reply, and a release message (see Figure 15.4).

When a request comes in, the coordinator checks its own tables, to see if some other process is currently in that critical section. If not, it grants the request. Otherwise the coordinator can refuse permission by simply not replying, or it can actually send a refusal message. Or it could queue the request.

Figure 15.4: Centralised control of mutual exclusion

When the critical section is free, then it gives permission to the process at the head of the queue.

When a process gets a refusal message, how will it know when the critical section becomes available? One possibility would be to time out, and try again. There could be some form of exponential back-off, as used by ethernet to avoid clashes. But it is important to ensure fairness here.

Such a system will work if there are no crashes or lost messages. Of course the whole system will deadlock if a process fails while in its critical section.

Elections

A problem with any centralised algorithm is that the coordinator process may crash. Such systems are usually built so that any process can act as coordinator, but only one does so at a time. So when the current coordinator crashes, it is necessary to ensure that another one takes over—but only one other.

The first assumption is that there is some way of recognising that the coordinator is no longer functioning. This can usually be detected by failure to receive an acknowledgement after a timeout period. Then a successor is identified from among all of the others, based on the combination of process id and IP address, which we assume is globally unique. Generally, the process with the highest combination is selected as coordinator. Two processes can discover a dead coordinator at the same time, but only one will be elected.

The main problem is getting all of the others to agree to accept this new coordinator. We will consider two possible algorithms for this.

Bully

Whenever a process notices that the coordinator has died, for example an over-long delay in a reply arriving, it broadcasts an election message to all processes. Such a message identifies the sending process, and states that it is proposing to take over as coordinator. If even one process with a higher id is alive, it will send back a response, and the current process gives up its claim. If no response comes back, then the process broadcasts an announcement that it is the new coordinator.

When a failed process restarts, it holds an election, and the process with the highest id wins again. As the highest always wins, it is known as the bully algorithm.

Ring

This algorithm assumes that all cooperating processes are arranged in a logical ring, so that each process knows the identity of at least two others. A process calls an election by sending a claim message around this ring, to all the other processes. As each process receives this message in turn, it can either add its own id to it and send it on, or if its id is larger than the incoming id, it can replace it and pass it on. When the message gets back to the original sender, it will either contain the id of the highest process, or it will be obvious which is the highest in the list. An announcement is then sent on the ring declaring that process to be the new coordinator.

If two processes discover simultaneously that the coordinator has died, each will run the algorithm, but it will select the same new coordinator in each case. Two announcements will then be sent out, each identifying the same new coordinator.

Distributed algorithm

Because of the drawbacks associated with centralised algorithms, attempts have been made to develop fully distributed algorithms. With these, each process takes its share of the responsibility for arranging mutual exclusion on a critical section or a resource. Such an algorithm assumes that all processes know the identity of each of the others; and that each process maintains a logical clock, so that it is possible to establish a 'happened before' relationship between events.

The algorithm

When a process wants to enter its critical section, it multicasts a request to all of the others, stamped with its pid and logical timestamp.

When such a request arrives, there are three possible courses of action.

- If the receiving process is not in its critical section, or not wanting to enter, then it sends back permission.

- If a process is in its critical section, then it queues the request, and sends a message saying the request is queued.

- If the process is waiting to get into its critical section, it compares the timestamp on the incoming message with the one it sent in its own request, and the lowest one wins. It either gives permission, or puts the request on a queue.

The requesting process waits until it has got permission from all of the others, then it enters its critical section.

When a process exits its critical section, it gives permission to all processes on its wait queue. This of course does not mean that all can enter. Rather they are building up permissions.

Example

In the example illustrated in Figure 15.5, Process A sends a request to enter its critical section with timestamp 10, and very shortly afterwards Process B sends a similar request with timestamp 11.

Process B gives permission to request 10, which has a timestamp lower than its own request, and continues waiting. Process A queues request 11, as it has a timestamp greater than its own. When all the permissions arrive, it goes into its critical section. When it comes out of its critical section, it then gives permission to request 11.

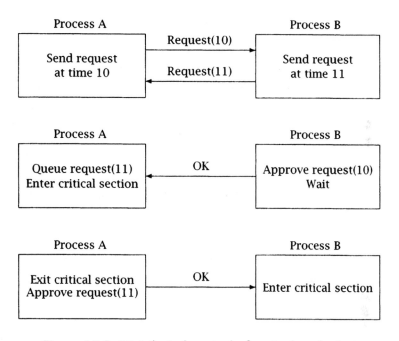

Figure 15.5: Distributed control of mutual exclusion

Evaluation

There is no single point of failure in this algorithm; but any process can fail, so we have n points of failure. If a requesting process were to wait forever for a message from a dead process, the system would quickly deadlock. The requester can use a timeout to recognise failed processes.

A process may need to know if a message has been received and understood. For this purpose, it can include with the message the maximum time it is willing to wait for a reply. But in general it is never possible to be completely sure that a particular message has been received. It might be possible to work on a majority decision, but it is not possible to be absolutely certain the process has failed, and is not just a long time in its critical section.

One of the drawbacks of this algorithm is the large number of messages it requires, $2(n-1)$. Another problem is the need to know all the processes involved. It is suitable for small, stable sets of cooperating processes.

Token ring algorithm

This is another possible distributed algorithm. All processes are configured as a logical ring. This is initialised with one holding a token, which then circulates around the ring. A process can only enter its critical section when it is holding the token.

The algorithm itself is very simple, but of course it has its problems. There must be some protocol to deal with the loss of a token. First of all it must be possible to distinguish between a lost and a delayed token. Timeouts are not acceptable, unless there is a bound on the time a process can be in its critical section. It would be possible for a process to circulate an 'in-cs' message, followed by an 'out-of-cs' message. This way all processes would know if the critical section was occupied or not. Then if no process was in its critical section, and the token does not appear within the maximum circulation time for the ring, it can be assumed that it is lost.

The next question is, who regenerates the token? It is very important that this is only done by one process, as more than one token in circulation would nullify the whole mechanism. It is possible to use the ring election algorithm of Section 15.2.

If a process crashes, the ring must be reconfigured. Failure to acknowledge the token indicates that a process has crashed. The problem then is to discover who is second next on the ring. Multicasting could be used to discover this.

Processes can leave the ring by sending appropriate messages to the ones before and after them. Each process knows the identity of its predecessor and successor, as it has been in constant communication with them.

How do new processes enter the ring? Periodically the token holder broadcasts an invitation to join. Any processes which reply to this invitation are inserted in the ring immediately after the current token holder.

15.3 Atomic transactions

So far, we have been looking at low level mechanisms for distributed concurrency, equivalent to semaphores on stand-alone systems. We now move on to look at the possibility of developing high-level mechanisms, the equivalent of monitors.

Transaction model

The simplest possible form of distributed system is where a server on one machine maintains data on behalf of clients on other machines. It exports procedures, by means of which the clients can perform operations on this

data. It must be possible to guarantee that operations performed by the server are atomic. This must be so, even if the server is multi-threaded, and despite delays and messages lost on the network.

The basic mechanism provided by the system is the transaction. This is a group of instructions with the requirement that either all of them are executed, in which case the transaction is said to commit, or none of them is. If a transaction cannot complete, then it will undo any partial work, and leave the state as it was before the transaction began.

A transaction has four essential properties.

Atomic It is effectively indivisible; it does all or nothing, even when the server fails.

Consistent It always leaves the system in a consistent state.

Isolated Concurrent transactions do not interfere with each other; intermediate effects are not visible.

Durable Once it commits, the effects are permanent.

These are referred to as the ACID properties of a transaction.

When a transaction begins, it is given a private copy of all of the relevant data in its own private workspace. If it aborts, this copy disappears. If it commits, the private copy becomes the public permanent copy.

Distributed transactions

A distributed transaction involves operations on several different servers. For example, a transfer of funds operation on one server may involve a withdrawal on a second server, and a deposit on a third. When there is more than one server involved, directly or indirectly, they have to reach a joint decision on whether to commit or not. Either all commit, or none does.

All of this needs a coordinator, which is normally the first server involved in the transaction. It knows all the other servers involved, and they know it. So it can collect the information required at commit time.

For example, a customer at Bank A wants to move money from an account in Bank B to an account in Bank C. The servers in all three banks must agree before the transaction commits. One of the servers acts as coordinator of the whole transaction. In our example, the server at Bank A would be an obvious candidate for the role of coordinator; but it need not be so.

The coordinator tells all the other servers to do their work. Each server ensures that its local transaction has been properly carried out, and then it commits. The coordinator waits until all have notified it of their commit. They are not free to abort. This way it guarantees that the whole distributed transaction has been carried out. This is known as one phase commit.

Two phase commit

We can extend this to a two phase commit, in which any worker can abort its part of the transaction. Before the coordinator asks all workers if they are prepared to commit, it writes a log entry saying that it is starting to commit. Then it sends each of the others a message saying prepare to commit. The subordinates check that they are ready to commit. When they are, they write to their logs, and send back their decision, yes or no.

The coordinator must ensure that all vote, and it logs the results as they come in. When the coordinator has all the replies, it knows whether it can commit or not.

In order for the whole transaction to commit, all of the workers must agree to commit. The coordinator then authorises all of them to commit. The sequence of operations is illustrated in Figure 15.6.

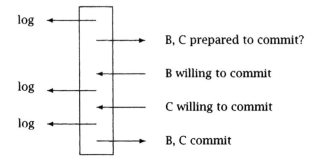

Figure 15.6: Successful two phase commit

If even one of the workers is unwilling to commit, then the whole transaction must be aborted, and the coordinator must tell all of the other workers to abort their part of it. The sequence of operations in this case is illustrated in Figure 15.7.

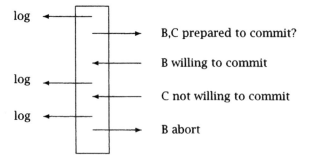

Figure 15.7: Aborted two phase commit

Because of the use of logs, this is very resilient. If any of the workers, or the coordinator, or the network, crashes, it is always possible to recover.

Example

A wedding ceremony is an example of two phase commit. The minister asks
the groom if he is willing to marry the bride. The groom commits. Then he
asks the bride if she is willing to marry the groom. The bride commits. Then
the minister announces that the whole transaction is committed. If either of
them were unwilling to commit, the minister would announce that the whole
event was aborted.

15.4 Concurrency control

The transaction model guarantees that any particular transaction either completes totally, or not at all. But many different transactions can be in progress
at the same time.

We have examined some of the classic problems this can cause on stand-
alone machines. The lost update problem is one of these. If two transactions
on a bank account, for example, happen to run concurrently, then with just the
wrong interleaving it is possible that the effect of one or other of them could
be lost. Another example is the inconsistent retrievals problem. When transferring cash between two bank accounts, if another client reads the balance on
either of them when only half of the transaction has been done, it will get an
incorrect figure.

The aim of any concurrency control protocol is to achieve *serial equivalence* between transactions. This does not necessarily mean that the actions
of one transaction are all carried out before any actions of another transaction
begin; but the effect must be the same as if each transaction finished before the
next began. This prevents lost updates and inconsistent retrievals. There may
be more than one valid serially equivalent interleaving of two transactions.

There are two common concurrency control protocols for achieving serial
equivalence, locking, and optimistic concurrency control. We will now look at
both of these in turn.

Locking

Locking data while it is in use is a simple, easily understood way of guaranteeing mutual exclusion. But undisciplined use of locks can lead to deadlock.
Possibly the best way to avoid deadlock is to take care with the granularity
at which locking is performed. This means taking out more locks on smaller
items of data, rather than locking whole records or even whole files.

A number of different locking protocols have been developed.

Two phase locking

A transaction is divided into two phases, a growing phase and a shrinking
phase. It must acquire all the locks it needs during the growing phase. Then
it releases locks in the shrinking phase.

With such a mechanism, a transaction could lock some item of data (A) in its growing phase, and write to it. Then it could release the lock on A at the beginning of its shrinking phase, while continuing to work on other items of data it holds locks on. Now if the whole transaction aborts for some reason, it has to go back and reset the value of data item A to what it was before the transaction began.

Some other transaction may have taken out a lock on it, after the first released it, and this transaction must now be invalidated, and begin again. See Figure 15.8.

Transaction 1   Transaction 2

Lock A

Lock B

Lock C

Write A

Unlock A
                          Lock A
Unlock B
                          Read A   ◄───────┐
                                                  │
Abort   │
                                                  │
                          Read A again   ────────┘

Figure 15.8: A cascaded abort

The effects may spread even wider, so the phenomenon is known as cascaded aborts, where an abort in one transaction invalidates data another transaction is working on, causing it to abort in turn.

Strict two phase locking

This problem of cascaded aborts has led to the development of a strict two phase locking protocol. With this mechanism, all locks must be held until a transaction either commits or aborts. The shrinking can only begin at that stage. This means that any other transaction only ever gets a lock on, and reads, committed data.

Implementation of locking

There is one lock manager in the distributed system, which maintains a table of locks. Each entry contains an identifier for the item of data being locked, data-id, a condition variable, and a header of a linked list of locks held on that

item of data. Each element in the linked list consists of an identifier for the transaction holding the lock, trans-id, and the type of lock (R or W). Figure 15.9 illustrates how such a lock table might be maintained.

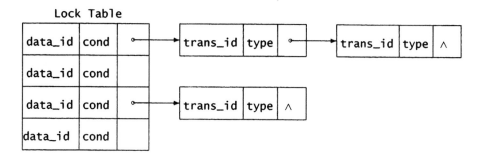

Figure 15.9: A lock table

The algorithm for Lock is given in Figure 15.10.

```
Lock (data-id, trans-id, lock-type)

        MUTEX_LOCK(table)
        IF (data-id already in table) THEN
            WHILE conflicting
                CWAIT(condvar-data-id)
            ENDWHILE
            Add trans-id to existing entry
        ENDIF
        Add new entry to table
        MUTEX_UNLOCK(table)
```

Figure 15.10: Algorithm for lock

If there are no locks currently held on the particular data, then it just adds the entry to the lock table, and grants the lock. However, if there are existing locks on this data item, then it checks if the request conflicts with the existing lock. Really the only two that do not conflict are an existing read lock and a read request. In this implementation, the lock manager queues requests, rather than rejecting them. To facilitate waiting, each request runs in a separate thread, and then does a CWAIT on a condition variable associated with the data it is waiting to get a lock on.

The algorithm for Unlock is given in Figure 15.11. It releases all locks together, so it is implementing strict two phase locking. If this transaction is the only holder, then it was either a writer or the last reader, so it does a CSIGNAL on the condition variable in case any other request is waiting. If there are other holders, then they must be readers. In this case it does not CSIGNAL, as only a writer would be waiting.

```
Unlock(trans-id)

    MUTEX_LOCK(table)
    FOR (each entry in table belonging to trans-id) DO
        Remove the entry
        IF (trans-id was only holder) THEN
            CSIGNAL (condvar-data-id)
        ENDIF
    ENDFOR
    MUTEX_UNLOCK(table)
```

Figure 15.11: Algorithm for unlock

Lock and Unlock must be atomic. For this reason the algorithms just presented are bracketed by LOCK and UNLOCK on a mutex, so that they have mutual exclusion on the table.

Optimistic concurrency control

The use of locks has a number of disadvantages, such as the overhead of a lock manager, the possibility of deadlock, and the fact that (at least with strict two phase locking), locks can only be released on commit, so reducing potential concurrency.

When there is a low probability of transactions clashing, a method known as optimistic concurrency control can be used. This allows transactions to proceed without taking out locks. Each transaction has a tentative version of the data, in its own private workspace. Then at commit time, the validation phase, it checks if any other transaction has written to or read from this data in the meantime. This requires all accesses to the data to be timestamped. If there are no conflicts, it can proceed to write the data, and commit. Otherwise it must go back and begin again. Note that transactions never wait. So the whole procedure is deadlock free.

If clashes occur very infrequently, this can be a quite acceptable method.

15.5 Distributed deadlocks

Deadlock is a problem even in stand-alone systems. When we move to a system of cooperating machines, the situation becomes even more complicated, as do the solutions. There is also the possibility of deadlock in the communications subsystem, but we will leave the analysis and solution of that to the network engineers.

We have seen that deadlock prevention is so restrictive that it is rarely used even in stand-alone systems; we will not consider its use in a distributed environment.

Nor is deadlock avoidance used either in distributed systems. Remember, avoidance algorithms need advance knowledge of all the resources required

by processes. This is difficult if not impossible to know even in a stand-alone system, and is really only relevant to batch systems. Once we move into distributed computing, it is not feasible to talk about advance knowledge of all resource usage.

The only approach to deadlock which is relevant in a distributed system is detection and recovery. The algorithm to implement this can be centralised or distributed.

Centralised algorithm

This requires a coordinator process somewhere in the system, which checks for distributed deadlocks. It could implement the algorithm of Figure 7.13, if there were many instances of each resource type. For simplicity, we will assume one instance of each type. This means that we only need to maintain a wait-for graph, and check it for cycles from time to time. Of course that begs the question of how to maintain and check a wait-for graph for a whole distributed system.

Each individual machine maintains its own local wait-for graph, and could even implement local detection and abortion. The coordinator process maintains the union of these graphs, and checks for cycles in it. There are three possible approaches to maintaining such a global graph.

A process could send a message to the coordinator each time a local graph is changed. Or it could sent messages about the state of the local graph periodically. Or the coordinator could ask for information at fixed intervals.

There could be a cycle in this distributed graph which is not in any local one, so indicating a distributed deadlock. The coordinator examines the distributed graph periodically, and takes appropriate action.

For example, the resource allocator on machine A sees the graph on the left of Figure 15.12.

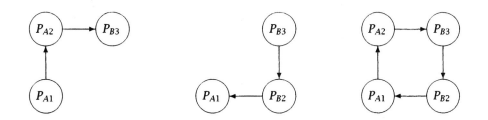

Figure 15.12: Local and global wait-for graphs

The resource allocator on machine B sees the graph in the centre of Figure 15.12. Neither of these has a cycle, so there does not appear to be any deadlock. But the coordinator sees the union of the two graphs, as shown on the right of Figure 15.12. Clearly there is a system-wide cycle, and these four processes are deadlocked.

A centralised algorithm like this can lead to phantom deadlocks, if messages arrive in the wrong order. While building up the graph, some information could be out of date. Such a deadlock tends to repeat itself, as the sequence of actions which caused it are likely to occur again. To avoid this, messages could be timestamped, using the 'happened before' relationship. Another possibility is to wait to see if the deadlock is persistent.

Two drawbacks of a centralised algorithm are the high volume of message traffic involved, and the fact that the coordinator process introduces a single point of failure.

Distributed algorithm

Every time a process has to wait for a resource which is allocated to a remote process, it sends a message, known as a probe, to the process holding it. This probe contains the id of the blocked process. If the recipient is waiting on something, it updates the probe with its own id, and forwards it. If the probe comes back to the original sender, then there is a cycle.

The scheme is attractive, but sending a probe when you are blocked is not exactly trivial. The high volume of message traffic as a result of invoking this algorithm each time a process has to wait is also a drawback.

Recovery in distributed systems

With a centralised algorithm, the coordinator is responsible for breaking the deadlock, by terminating one or more processes.

One possibility when a cycle is discovered by the distributed algorithm is for the process running the algorithm to terminate itself. But this could be overkill if more than one process discovers the cycle. Another possibility would be for each blocked process to add its pid to the probe, instead of replacing it. This way the ids of all processes involved in the cycle would be known. The highest or lowest could then choose itself as victim.

15.6 Distributed shared memory

We have seen how shared memory is implemented for processes running on the same machine. And we have seen how this is the basic mechanism underpinning all interprocess communication on stand-alone machines. Data is passed between cooperating processes through shared buffers. Synchronisation and mutual exclusion are implemented using semaphores, which are basically shared variables.

Effort is now being directed towards allowing memory to be shared by processes on different machines. This would allow a shared memory programming model to be used by cooperating processes in a distributed system. With such a distributed shared memory, an existing system could be distributed

with minimum effort. But note that the runtime support for implementing distributed shared memory is typically based on message passing, using sockets.

Implementation

To a programmer, there should be no difference between distributed shared memory, and shared memory on a stand-alone machine. Each process has its own virtual address space. Some of the physical memory backing this address space is also mapped into the address space of other processes. Whether these are on the same machine, or on remote machines, is not really relevant to a programmer.

On a stand-alone machine, there is no question about where the shared memory will be physically located—it will have to be somewhere in the physical memory of that machine. But with a distributed system, it could physically exist on any of the machines. This could be one fixed machine, chosen when the shared memory is first created. Copies would be sent to sharing machines, and reclaimed after use. It is also possible for different parts of the shared memory to belong on different machines (see Section 15.6).

The simplest way to implement distributed shared memory is to have one server machine, which manages the shared memory on behalf of client processes on remote machines. These communicate with the server by means of RPC.

The initial mapping of a range of such distributed shared memory into the address space of a process can be handled in a manner very similar to POSIX shared memory. An initial RPC identifies the block of shared memory which is being requested. The server checks permissions and access mode, etc., and then returns a handle. This is a unique identifier, generated by the server, which is used to identify and authenticate all further accesses to that block of distributed shared memory.

The server exports three further procedures. One, for reading, is passed the handle, an offset within the shared memory, a byte range, and a location in the local machine into which the bytes are to be stored when the RPC returns. The other procedure, for writing, is passed similar parameters, and changes the value of the appropriate range of bytes in the shared memory. Finally there is a procedure which lets the server know that the client has no further use for this block of shared memory.

Local runtime support

While easy to understand, the foregoing scheme would be very inefficient, and can be improved on in a number of ways. So far, the local memory manager is not involved at all—the client process has to make an RPC for every read and write. Ideally, distributed shared memory should be transparent to a process. Assignment to variables in such shared memory should be identical to assignment to variables in local memory—the memory manager should take care of all of the necessary overhead.

Such a goal could be accomplished by a slight extension to the local memory manager, and to the `mmap()` system service. This would be passed the handle returned by the server, and information about the size and access permissions of the shared memory. It would map this shared memory into the address map of the process, possibly setting it up as a region in its own right. Then it returns a pointer to this region. From here on the process accesses the distributed shared memory using standard local pointers.

The first time a program references an address within this shared region, a remote page fault occurs, and the distributed shared memory runtime fetches the appropriate page. To a user, this looks exactly like the traditional system. It is transparent to the running process; the distributed shared memory runtime system does it all. The main difference from conventional systems is that the backing store interface is to a remote server, not to a local disk. Such a server is known as an external pager. The local kernel handles frame allocation, and replacement. The external pager supplies pages on demand, and guarantees consistency if several kernels are paging the same object.

Local physical memory will eventually fill up, and it will be necessary to replace some pages of shared memory. The choice of which page to replace can be made using the same algorithms as used for stand-alone systems. But the distinction between clean and dirty pages is even more important in this context. A clean page can just be overwritten. A dirty page has to be copied somewhere over a network. This is a significantly greater overhead than copying it to backing store.

Granularity of sharing

For simplicity, a server would share memory in units of pages. So the read and write RPCs would always work on a unit of one page.

Of course, a more structured approach would be to share only those items of data which are required. This could certainly be done, at the cost of increased overhead, both on the server and the client. The server could keep a list of all such shared variables, indexed by name.

Caching

The simplest model would use no caching. When a process acquires a segment of distributed shared memory, it is given exclusive access to it. When finished, it releases this segment, which is then available to be acquired by another process, which can read any changes made by the previous one. Such shared memory would typically be persistent, it would exist on its server even when no processes are attached to it. So communicating processes could have non-overlapping lifetimes, as with POSIX shared memory on stand-alone machines.

Things get more complicated when we consider the possibility of caching copies of the shared memory on more than one machine at the same time. As usual, there is no problem with read-only pages. Caching writable pages is more problematic.

The simplest solution would be a distributed version of the multiple readers/single writer algorithm.

If this is too restrictive, and there is a requirement for concurrent distributed writing, then write-through caching is the next simplest mechanism. This is commonly used with CPU caches on multiprocessors, and its implementation is well understood. Each time a process on a machine with a cached copy of shared memory writes to it, the write is copied back to the home machine. This causes an invalidation message to be multicast to all the other sharers, and it has to be acknowledged by all of them before the write can complete. They must then acquire a clean copy before they can continue. This, however, could lead to a form of distributed thrashing.

Systems can be built in different ways, so that the effect of a write followed by a read may not be the same in each. Because of this, the way a distributed shared memory behaves may be somewhat different from what we have come to expect in a stand-alone machine. Various models are in use, trading ease of implementation against performance.

Ring based implementation

Using a centralised server to implement distributed shared memory is a bottleneck, with the manager being a single point of congestion and failure. It is also possible to share memory using a distributed algorithm. All of the machines are arranged into a logical ring, with a circulating token. Each block of shared memory has a home machine, on which it has a permanent allocation of physical memory. But it may be cached on a machine other than its home machine.

On a read, if the required data is not present on its local machine, a process waits until the token arrives, then it puts its request on the ring. Each machine checks as the token circulates. If it has the requested block, it puts it in the token. Because a block has to be somewhere, this mechanism is guaranteed to pick it up in one circuit.

On a write, if the page is present, it may not be the only copy, so an invalidation message is sent around the ring. The write does not complete until the token returns again. If the page is not present, then a combined read/invalidate packet is sent out in the token.

15.7 Summary

1. Distributed concurrency needs some way of ordering events on different machines. DCE attempts to provide a global time on all machines. Unix provides a number of services for time of day.

    It is only when processes communicate that the question of ordering events arises at all. The 'happened before' relationship, →, is implemented by each process keeping a counter of local events, and timestamping each

message sent. A receiving process advances its counter, if necessary, so that it is at least one greater than the sender.

2. The algorithms which have been developed to control mutual exclusion in distributed systems fall into two classes. Some are centralised, with one controller which handles all requests. If this controller crashes, a new one can be elected using the bully algorithm, or the ring algorithm.

   Another possibility is to control mutual exclusion using a fully distributed algorithm. For example, a process could request permission from all of the others, before entering its critical section.

   It is also possible to arrange processes in a logical ring, and circulate a token between them. A process may enter its critical section only when it has the token.

3. A transaction is a group of instructions, with the ACID properties: atomic, consistent, isolated, durable.

   With a distributed transaction, involving more than one server, one acts as coordinator. With one phase commit, the coordinator just waits for all of the others to notify it that they have committed. With two phase commit, they first tell the coordinator that they are prepared to commit. When it has got such notification from all, it sends a commit message. Only then do they commit. Otherwise it sends an abort message.

4. Serial equivalence requires that the effects of multiple transactions must be the same as if each transaction finished before the next began.

   Locking data while in use is a simple way of achieving serial equivalence. With two phase locking, a transaction must acquire locks in the growing phase, and releases them in the shrinking phase. It is possible to distinguish read locks from write locks, for greater granularity. This requires a lock manager.

   Optimistic concurrency control allows transactions to proceed without locks, when there is a low probability of their clashing. But a transaction must check for conflicts at commit time.

5. Deadlock is a problem even on stand-alone systems; it is even more so in a distributed system.

   Deadlock detection and recovery is the mechanism used in distributed systems. Algorithms can be centralised, using a global wait-for graph; or they can be distributed, using probes.

6. A server manages distributed shared memory for a group of clients. These send requests to the server using RPC. On a local machine, the onus could be put on the memory manager, to mask any difference between local and remote memory.

   Sharing could be at the level of a page, or individual variables could be shared.

   For efficiency, clients cache copies of the distributed shard memory. A distributed version of the multiple readers/single writer algorithm could be used to maintain consistency; or write-through caching could be used.

The effect of a write followed by a read may be different from the strict consistency we find on stand-alone machines, where all writes are instantaneously visible to all processes.

It is also possible to implement distributed shared memory without a central server, using a token passing algorithm.

15.8 Discussion questions

1. Suppose the timestamp used to implement the 'happened before' relationship is declared as type int. If a sufficiently large number of events occur, this will eventually overflow. What effect will this have? How can a system be adapted to cater for this eventuality?

2. Find a machine in your local domain which provides a time service, and write a program to query it.

3. A centralised coordinator can take three courses of action when unable to grant a request. It can ignore it, queue it, or send a refusal message. Discuss the advantages and disadvantages of the three approaches.

4. A coordinator could send a message granting a request, but that message might be lost in transit. The client interprets the failure to receive a reply as a refusal. The server and client now have different views of the state of the system. How can they get back in sync again?

5. Investigate some algorithms for electing a new coordinator, when a centralised algorithm is used for mutual exclusion.

6. What happens if a centralised coordinator crashes, is replaced, and then starts up again, acting as if it were still the coordinator?

7. Is the distributed algorithm for mutual exclusion (Section 15.2) fair?

8. Develop a version of the distributed algorithm for mutual exclusion, which works on a majority decision.

9. Develop a distributed algorithm for mutual exclusion, based on token passing.

10. Suggest some way in which a process crashing in its critical section does not deadlock the whole distributed system.

11. Why is it never possible to be completely sure that a particular message has been received, and acknowledged?

12. With reference to the two phase commit protocol illustrated in Figure 15.6, if the server crashes after a message arrives from C saying it is willing to commit, but before this is logged, show how the server can complete the transaction after it recovers.

13. Develop an example of a cascading abort, i.e. where an abort in one transaction invalidates data another transaction is working on, causing it to

abort in turn. Show how two phase locking, when applied to the same example, prevents this.

14. Draw up a reasonably realistic example of what a lock manager's table might look like (i.e. at least six locks).

15. What extra information would a system have to maintain, to implement optimistic concurrency control?

16. Discuss how each of the four necessary conditions for deadlock might be negated in a distributed system.

17. Develop a situation in which a phantom deadlock occurs in a distributed wait-for graph (i.e. a process sends a coordinator a message giving its state, and immediately afterwards releases some resource).

18. What happens if a probe arrives at a process, which is waiting on *two* resources, each on a different machine?

19. Sending a probe when you are blocked is not exactly trivial. So how can it be done?

20. It seems simpler to manage all of the distributed shared memory from one machine. Is there any advantage in having different parts of it physically based on, and managed by, different machines?

21. Outline the requirements of such a distributed shared memory system, in which different parts of the memory are owned by different machines.

22. Outline how the local runtime support for distributed shared memory could be extended so that a program could actually declare a distributed shared variable, and refer to it by name.

23. To implement a distributed version of the multiple readers/single writer algorithm would need some distributed shared variables, which presumably would exist in distributed shared memory. Is this a chicken and egg problem?

24. Develop an algorithm for write-through caching of distributed memory.

25. With the token ring based version of distributed memory, how could a process determine that its copy is not the only one?

Distributed file systems 16

We have already studied file systems in a previous chapter. A first step up from such a stand-alone system is the ability to copy files between different machines, such as provided by the file transfer protocol, ftp. This makes a second copy of the file, on the local machine. A distributed file system is much more than that. There is only one copy of the file. But it appears as if it exists on all of the machines in the system. Such a file system can be part of a distributed operating system, but this is not necessary.

16.1 Introduction

Different parts of the system exist on different machines. The simplest way to implement a distributed file system is to have the files on one machine, managed by a server process, and the user or client processes running on other machines. In a realistic system, there will be many clients, and possibly more than one server. Servers can run on dedicated machines, or a machine can have both server and client processes running on it.

Typically, a user would make normal system calls, which the system software on the local machine translates to RPC calls to the server.

Stateful or stateless service

A server can track each file being accessed by each client. It can implement locks, and perform readahead for sequential reads, just like a stand-alone file system. All of this implies that it must maintain information about every file each client has opened. And this information must be maintained until the file is closed. Because of this, it is known as a stateful server. If such a server were to crash, it would be in difficulties afterwards, when all of this information is lost. It would not know about which files any particular client has open.

Another possibility is that it can simply provide blocks as requested. In this case the server does not keep track of which clients are accessing which files. Such a stateless server is slower. But it is more robust, in that it simplifies the recovery procedures after a server crashes and reboots. A client must

provide a stateless server with the name of the file, and a current offset, at each request. Open or close requests are not sent to the server.

Transparency

A distributed file system should look like a conventional file system, including its performance. Ideally, it should be able to operate across different hardware platforms. So a true distributed file system must show transparency, at the following levels.

Access Files on local or remote machines must appear identical to a client.

Location The client need not know where any particular file is located. The pathname should have nothing to do with the physical location, nor give any indication of where the file is.

Migration A file may move from one machine to another during its lifetime, without the user having to know anything about it. If the location changes, there should be no need to change the name of the file. This is not easy, but it is desirable.

Replication The system may wish to maintain more than one copy of a file, but the user should have no idea of this.

Concurrency The sort of read/write interlock implemented on stand-alone machines should also be applicable on a distributed system.

Failure One or more servers may fail, but the system should continue to function.

Performance A distributed system should not be noticeably slower than a local one. But of course it can never be as fast.

Scaling As the distributed file system grows in size, with more users, more files, and more servers, it should continue to provide the same level of service to its clients.

Naming schemes

One basic problem for any distributed file system is to provide a namespace that uniquely identifies each file in the system. File systems have traditionally used directories for this, organised in some form of tree or graph structure.

At one end of the scale, such a distributed system could be implemented by integrating all files and directories into a single global namespace spanning all machines in the system. This means that there is only one directory tree, shared by all machines, and each file has its own unique place in this. The complexity of administering such a namespace, particularly if the file system is distributed over a large number of machines, outweighs any benefits it may bring.

At the other end of the scale, a two part scheme, such as host:localname, would be relatively easy to implement, but would not meet the requirements for location transparency. In order to access any file in the system, a user would have to know the name and location of the machine on which it was stored. Such a scheme would also make migration transparency impossible, as a file's identifier would change when its location changed.

A middle of the road approach is normally acceptable. We have seen how different local file systems can be attached together, to form one coherent directory tree. This idea can be extended to distributed systems. Remote directories could be attached to local directories, and appear seamlessly as subdirectories. A user should not be able to tell the difference between a local directory, and a remote one. Obviously both the exporting and the importing machine would need extra software.

Figure 16.1 shows two simple file systems, one on a local machine, and the other on a remote machine.

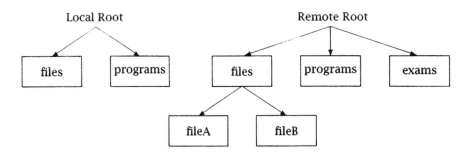

Figure 16.1: Situation before attaching remote files

Figure 16.2 shows the situation after the local machine has attached the contents of the remote directory 'files' to its directory 'programs'.

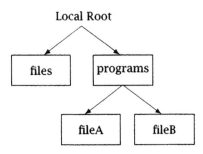

Figure 16.2: Local file system after attaching remote files

Note that both fileA and fileB still exist on the remote machine; they only appear as if they were attached to the local 'programs' directory. Note also that the local machine must know where they are in order to attach them; but after that all references to these files are transparent.

As more than one machine could attach different parts of the remote directory tree to their own directory tree, different clients can have different views of the file system. The same file can have different pathnames on different machines.

16.2   Caching

A server will normally cache blocks of files, or directories, to save on disk accesses. This is just normal file system caching, to reduce disk I/O, and presents no extra problems.

A client will also cache file blocks, to avoid the delays associated with using a network, and to reduce the volume of traffic on the network. The value of caching depends on CPU speed, and the network speed. If the CPU is slow relative to the network, then it becomes more likely that the network will be able to provide file I/O before the CPU is ready for it. In this case there is little advantage in caching on the client. On the other hand, if the network is a speed bottleneck, then client caching is a very useful technique for improving overall efficiency.

A local cache could be implemented at two levels, with some of a file in main memory, and more or all of it on a local disk. Diskless workstations of course have to have all of their cache in main memory. Even when there is a local disk, the downward trend in the cost of memory means that memory caches will become larger.

A client cache can be maintained on a process by process basis. This is easy to implement, but the same information could be cached by many processes, with much waste of space. Such redundancy can be avoided by having one system-wide cache on the client, with the extra complications this implies.

Caching in a distributed file system has definite similarities with demand paged virtual memory, and with distributed shared memory.

There is a problem keeping cached copies of a shared file consistent with the original, and with each other. There are a number of approaches to this.

Write-Through Any write to cached data is also written to the server. Write-through is very reliable, but it implies heavy overheads. It exploits the cache only for reading. The client cache manager must query the server before providing information from the cache, to check that it is up to date. Such a check could be made at fixed intervals, or on every access. But it only requires two short messages—it saves the transfer of large volumes of data.

Delayed-Write A write to cached data is not passed on to the server immediately. It is done at fixed intervals, or only when data is about to be ejected from the cache. This means that there are times when the server is not up to date.

Write-on-Close Caching could be implemented so that writes are only visible to other processes when a file is closed. In this case, if two processes

are writing, then the last one to close overwrites anything written by the previous one.

Centralised application of read/write interlock Many processes can be reading cached data at the same time. But only one at a time can have permission to write, and all other caches must be invalidated while it is doing so. Like all centralised solutions, it does not scale well to large systems.

There would seem to be a better chance of avoiding cache inconsistencies if the granularity of caching is kept as small as possible.

Caching can be summarised by saying that it reduces the amount of traffic on the network, as well as the load on the server, at the expense of the local machine. Overall performance can be expected to improve. The major drawback is the problem of cache consistency. Also it is not viable on small memory, diskless machines.

16.3 Replication

Multiple copies of the same file may be kept on different servers, to increase reliability, and to distribute the workload over the system. This is not just caching, but replicating resources in their entirety, and permanently.

Replication can be done at the user level. The user keeps copies of files on different servers, and is responsible for knowing where they are, and for updating them. The various copies could all be mounted at different places in the user's directory tree. More commonly, only one copy, the primary copy, is mounted. Then if it becomes unavailable for any reason, the user manually mounts another copy.

It is far more common for replication to be transparent to the user, implemented by system processes known as replica managers. Each of these maintains a physical copy of some or all files. They periodically swap updates among themselves.

Reading replicated files

Replication of read only files is trivial, but it does ensure availability when the primary server is down. If requests are processed in parallel by all of the replica servers, then it is even fault tolerant.

Reading from replicated files is very straightforward. The client can communicate with just one of the replica managers, as if it were the only one. Another possibility is that the client may communicate with many, or all, of the replica managers. In such a case it would compare the results, and if there were differences, it could use the version supplied by the majority of servers.

Writing replicated files

Once writable files are replicated, there are questions of consistency, if some are updated, and others not. Various mechanisms have been developed for handling this situation.

Read one/write all

A client can read from any copy, but it must write to all replicas. This cannot be done if even one machine is down. It is possible for such replication to be totally synchronous. In such a case the client blocks until updates are written to all copies. The problem is the very long response times. This will be prohibitive for most purposes. Write all replication can also be asynchronous.

Available copies replication

This copes with some replica managers being out of action. Writes are done on all managers that are available. There must be some way of ensuring that the other copies are updated, when they eventually do become available.

Quorum based replication

With a quorum based scheme, clients must get permission from a certain number of servers before reading or writing a replicated file. This number, or quorum as it is called, could be different for reads or writes. For example, more than one could be required for a read, but one or two less than the total could be required for writing.

Primary copy replication

With this scheme, all requests go to one primary server, and writes are later propagated to the others. Replica managers update each other by exchanging what are known as gossip messages, containing the most recent updates. When a gossip message comes in, the receiver merges it with its own data. One of these secondary servers can take over if the primary fails. If the primary crashes before updating all of the secondaries, it has a log to check when it recovers. Of course the primary server, and its log, constitute single points of failure.

Network partitions

Sometimes a fault causes a network to be divided into two parts, with some clients and servers on one side, and some on the other. Both halves may be able to continue to function. There is no problem with reads in either partition.

Pessimistic schemes, such as quorum consensus, limit availability during such a breakdown. Updates are allowed in the partition with the majority of replicas, not in the other one.

The optimistic approach, such as available copies replication, allows updates in both partitions. All clients have full access to files during the break.

Presumably the fault will eventually be repaired, and the system must be able to detect any inconsistencies at that point, and remove them. Version numbers or timestamps can be used at repair time to identify servers with stale data, and update them.

16.4 DCE distributed file service

The OSF Distributed Computing Environment, which was introduced in Section 13.7, has its own distributed file system. This Unix compatible system is aimed at large networks, with thousands of clients, spread over a wide geographical area. It implements one global namespace. A file can be moved from one location to another transparently—it has the same name everywhere. So in effect the user is presented with one, large, worldwide file system.

We will take a brief look at some aspects of the DFS.

Directory service

A main goal of DCE is to make all resources available to all processes. The number and location of these resources is constantly changing. So the system has to know where they all are. This is the function of the directory service, which is replicated and distributed. It contains a hierarchical set of names, and their corresponding attributes, including location.

In DCE, the global network is segmented into groups of resources, or cells. There are three services provided for managing this namespace.

Cell Directory Service It manages resources in a particular DCE cell. It can be replicated within the cell.

Global Directory Service This manages names outside the local cell. Effectively it links together the CDS from different cells.

Global Directory Agent This is the bridge between CDS and the outside world. It uses either GDS or DNS.

Files

As we have seen, a number of different file system types have been developed for use with Unix, such as Ext2, UFS, etc. DCE has introduced its own file system, called Episode. This provides the following features.

- Enhanced security, using access control lists.
- Provision for larger files.
- Replication with read only replicas, for availability.

- Logging. Each entry in the log stores the old and new value of the data. This leads to faster recovery after a crash, and so greater availability.

- POSIX 1003.1 compliant. A programmer uses the standard POSIX system calls.

Then there is a wide area part that pulls all of the local machines together. Every DCE node is either a file server or a file client, or both. They communicate using DCE RPC. As it expects to work over wide area networks, authentication and security is very important. It uses a mechanism known as Kerberos, which we will examine in the next chapter.

Caching

The DFS uses a stateful protocol, and makes much use of caching, to achieve high performance and availability. The server and the clients cooperate to achieve cache consistency.

Token manager

Each server has a token manager which keeps track of what clients are doing, and synchronises their access to files. When a server gives out data, the token manager also issues a token, which specifies the validity of the accompanying data, and permissible operations on it. It may invalidate this data later, by sending an invalidate token.

As the server is stateful, it keeps track of which files each client has open, and whether for reading or writing. It acknowledges a request to open a file by sending back an open token, which specifies the open mode of the file.

Data tokens are sent with requested blocks of a file. A server can issue more than one read token for the same data at the same time. But it guarantees that there will only be one valid write token in existence for any particular file block at any time. Such data tokens have an expiry time, typically 2 minutes. When the token expires, the client must apply to have it renewed.

The token manager also acts as a lock manager, issuing lock tokens over ranges of bytes in a file.

Cache manager

The main addition to the client kernel is the DFS cache manager. Read or write operations are sent to the cache manager, which checks if it has the file, and the necessary token. If so, it may proceed without contacting the server. Otherwise it must do an RPC to the server, asking for a token and data. The normal transfer unit is 64K. If some other process wants the same data for writing, the server sends a request to the first one, asking for the token back. The first client must return the token as soon as convenient.

16.5 Sun network file system

This is the most common distributed file system. As it is used with Linux, we shall examine it in some detail. While it was originally designed as part of SunOS, the operating system for Sun workstations, the definitions of the protocols are in the public domain. This has led to its widespread adoption, so that it has become a *de facto* standard. It can be, and has been, implemented on top of a range of different hardware and operating systems.

The essence of NFS is that an arbitrary collection of clients and servers can share file systems. Any particular machine can be a client, or a server, or both. A server exports directories, while a client imports them, and inserts them at some point in its own directory tree.

Semantics

NFS tries to look like a Unix file system as much as possible, and does not attempt to improve on it. It only maintains one copy of a file, and the most recent update is the version visible to the system. Any replication or caching is extra, not part of NFS. As several clients can import the same directory, sharing is implicit in the system. This sharing is controlled by the Unix access permission mechanism on the server, but there are a number of slight differences between NFS and Unix semantics.

- Unix only checks permissions on open(); NFS checks them on each access, as it is stateless. So NFS will see changes in permissions since a file was opened; Unix will not.

- When deleting a file held open by many users, Unix marks it for deletion, and the last close() deletes it. NFS has no concept of an open file, so it will delete it immediately. The next access by another user will return an error.

- Unix provides read or write locks on a file. NFS clients on different machines cannot use their local Unix kernel to do this. Nor does the server maintain state information between requests. Clients can use the network lock manager, but these locks are not part of NFS, and are advisory only.

Transparency

NFS provides a certain amount of, though not total, transparency.

Access Access to local or remote files is identical.

Location The actual importing of a directory is not transparent; the client must know about the remote machine. But after that all operations are fully location independent.

Migration If a server moves a directory, then it must be re-mounted.

Replication This is not provided by NFS. If directories are replicated, then it is obvious to the client, and each replica must be imported separately.

Concurrency NFS does not provide any concurrency control. If required, then locks can be used. But as NFS itself is stateless, such locking has to be implemented by a separate stateful server.

Failure If the server to which the client is connected should fail, the client cannot access any files on that server.

Performance Due to the use of a network, it cannot be as good as a local system. But if both the server and the client cache data, then performance can be quite acceptable.

Scaling NFS has scaled well so far. But to scale to even larger distributed systems, it will have to improve in the area of replication.

Protocols

There are two phases in setting up and using NFS. The first involves establishing the connection between the client and server, and inserting the remote files into the local directory structure. This has only to be done once, but it is essential. The mechanism for implementing this connection is known as the mount protocol, and is dealt with in the next section.

Then, when the remote files have been integrated into the local file system, all subsequent searches, reads, or writes, are implemented by the NFS daemons themselves.

These daemons are background processes, running on both server and client. They handle the work involved in moving data back and forth between the client and the server. They communicate with each other by means of synchronous remote procedure calls: the client blocks until the server replies. We have seen the RPC protocol in Chapter 14, so we will just take its use for granted here. The NFS daemons will be dealt with in Section 16.7.

These remote procedures define the set of requests the client can make on the server. They are all stateless, so there is no concept, at this level, of opening or closing a file. The client must give full information about the file with each request. Otherwise, the set of remote procedures provided are very similar to the standard Unix system services for files. These NFS protocols will be dealt with in Sections 16.8 and 16.9.

16.6 The mount protocol

The mount protocol is used to establish the initial connection between the client and the server. This is an extension of the standard Unix mount() service to distributed systems. Instead of joining together file systems on two disks attached to the same machine, it joins together file systems from different machines. But the end result is the same seamless tree structured file system.

Mounting remote directories

Before any file accesses can be made, a client must first of all import or mount a remote directory onto some point in its own directory tree. The contents of the local directory on which it is mounted, or any of its subdirectories, are no longer visible. They are not deleted, they just cannot be seen or accessed while the remote file system is mounted.

Cascading mounts are permitted—a file system can be mounted on top of a directory which is itself remotely mounted. Figure 16.3 shows very simple directory structures on a client, and two different servers.

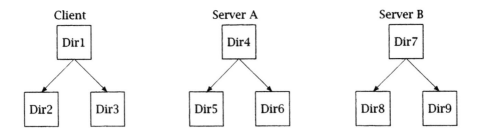

Figure 16.3: A client and two servers

If the client mounts Dir4 from Server A onto its local Dir3, the local file system on the client now looks like Figure 16.4.

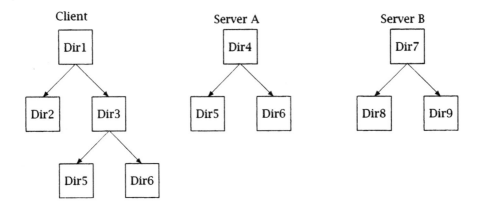

Figure 16.4: File system after mounting Dir4

Note that the original contents of Dir3 are not now visible. If the client then mounts Dir7 from Server B onto Dir5, we get the situation shown in Figure 16.5. The original contents of Dir5 are now not visible. While the directories and files are spread over three different machines, to the client they appear as one logical file system.

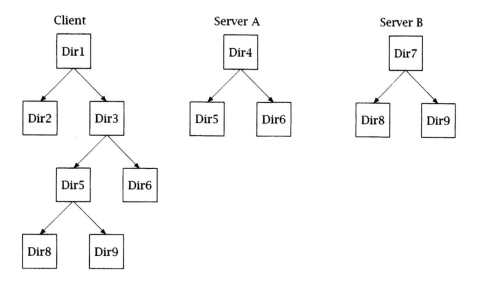

Figure 16.5: File system after mounting Dir7

Server

The mount service runs as a user level process on each server machine. It is RPC program number 100005. The file /etc/exports lists the file systems available for mounting remotely, and who can mount them.

The mount daemon mountd reads this file, and from it creates a list of which directories can be exported, and machines to which they can be exported, with the appropriate access permissions, read only or read/write. The showmount command lists these mount points.

When a request comes from a client to mount a file system, it goes to mountd, which checks that this client has permission to mount the particular file system.

The mountd server returns a file handle, which is globally unique. An NFS handle combines the file system id, along with the inode number of the directory, and the inode generation number. This generation number is incremented every time the inode is reused. This prevents a client using an old handle to access a reused inode, and hence a file it has no rights to. This file handle is the start point for all other NFS applications.

File handles are opaque to the client; it never looks inside at the contents, which only make sense to the server. A file handle is still valid after a server crash and reboot.

The mountd server keeps a list of all the file handles it has issued, so that it can inform clients if it is going down.

Client

Remote file systems are usually mounted at boot time. The procedure is almost identical to the local mount described in Section 10.5. The `file_system_type` corresponding to NFS is found, and the relevant `read_super()` is called. This asks `rpcbind` on the server for the port number of the mount daemon. It then asks the mount daemon to mount the specified file system. If this is a valid request, the mount daemon returns a handle for that file system. Figure 16.6 shows the sequence of messages.

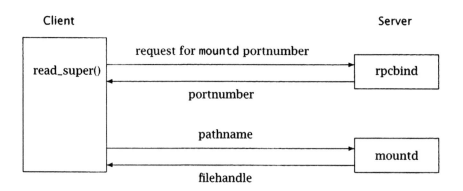

Figure 16.6: Mounting a remote file system

All of the other operations described in Section 10.5 are then carried out.

Information needed for future access to the newly mounted file system, such as name, IP and port number of the server, as well as the file handle, are saved in the `struct nfs_sb_info` of the `super_block`, see Figure 16.7, from `<linux/nfs_fs_sb.h>`.

```
struct nfs_sb_info{
        struct nfs_server s_server;
        struct nfs_fh     s_root;
};
```

Figure 16.7: NFS specific super block information

Options

A hard mount is when the user process is suspended until the request is fulfilled. If the server crashes, the client will keep trying to contact it. This is used for long-term processes. A soft mount returns failure after a small number of retries. If the server crashes, it tries the maximum number of times, and then returns an error.

There is also an automounter, which mounts a remote file system when it is referenced for the first time. See the manual page for `autofs`. It runs as

a user level process on each client machine. It maintains a table of potential mount points, with one or more servers listed for each, in /etc/auto.master. It probes all of these, and the first to respond is mounted, using the normal mount() function. The file system is unmounted when it has been unused for a specified time, typically 5 minutes.

It is possible to replicate in this way. If a file system is replicated on many servers, all of them can be put into the automount table. It is likely that a different one will be first to reply each time. But because a server has to respond to the automounter, at least you are sure that the one you are using is alive.

The umount() service carries out all the tasks done on a stand-alone system, as described in Section 10.5. After this, the original contents of the parent directory are again visible. But it also lets the server know that this directory has been unmounted.

The mount protocols

The mount daemon on the server provides a number of remote procedures, which are briefly described here.

MNT

This maps a pathname, an ASCII string describing a directory on the server, to a file handle. The server adds an entry to its mount list, to say that the particular client has mounted this directory, and returns the file handle.

DUMP

This returns a list of remotely mounted file systems. Each entry in the list is a <client name, directory> pair.

UMNT

Given the pathname of a mounted directory, it removes it from the mount list. Any use of the file handle after this is invalid, and will result in a 'stale file handle' error.

UMNTALL

This removes all entries in the mount list which belong to the calling client.

EXPORT

This returns a list of all file systems which are available for export, and specifies which clients are allowed to mount them.

16.7 The NFS daemons

There are two background processes, or daemons, which run NFS, one on the server, the other on the client machine.

Server daemon

The server daemon is nfsd, RPC program number 100003. It is usually multi-threaded, to increase the degree of concurrency of the server. If the underlying operating system does not support threads, nfsd forks a number of child processes. The server receives datagrams on port 2049. This is hardcoded into the client and server code in most applications, such as Linux, not mapped by rpcbind. When a request arrives, it is sent to an available nfsd daemon thread. This verifies the sender, then forwards the request to the local file system. When the local file system responds, nfsd sends a reply to the client. It is then ready to handle the next request.

Client daemon

The NFS client daemon is nfsiod. There is only one client for all processes on the same machine, with a shared cache. But it can be multi-threaded; a parameter to nfsiod is the number of threads. This is typically 7.

The whole procedure, for a write(), is illustrated in Figure 16.8.

Client   Server

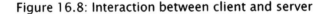

data

write() ⇄ nfsiod ═══════════════════► nfsd ⇄ write()
                  ◄───────────────────
acknowledgement

Figure 16.8: Interaction between client and server

On a client machine, the system calls, and all of the high-level processing, are identical for local and remote files. The local kernel determines whether a file is local or remote at open(). If it is a local file, then it is handled by its own particular file system code. If the file is in a remotely mounted directory, the NFS open() function is called, which acquires an NFS filehandle from the server. This is stored in the nfs_inode_info field of the inode, see Figure 16.9 from <linux/nfs_fs_i.h>.

- read_cache_jiffies is the time when data corresponding to this inode was cached for reading.

- read_cache_mtime is the value in the mtime of the inode when caching began.

- attrtimeo defines for how long the cached attributes are valid.

```
nfs_inode_info{
        struct nfs_fh fhandle;
        unsigned long read_cache_jiffies;
        unsigned long read_cache_mtime;
        unsigned long attrtimeo;
};
```

Figure 16.9: NFS specific inode information

Also, the i_op field of the inode points to NFS functions which, when
called, pass the request to the NFS client software: see Figure 16.10.

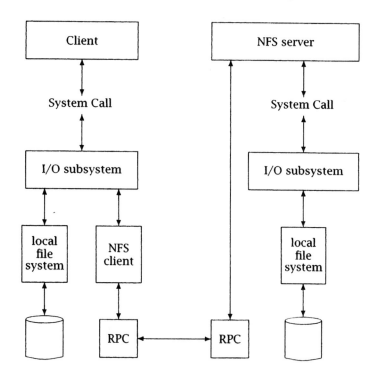

Figure 16.10: Handling local and remote file systems

Normally all NFS reading and writing is synchronous to the local process,
which sleeps in the meantime. But performance can be improved by doing
asynchronous read ahead and write behind. In this way a client writes to a
local buffer, and returns immediately. The nfsiod daemon updates the server
in the background.

User authentication information such as uid, gid, etc. is sent with each
request. It is supplied automatically by the RPC mechanism. Any process can
send requests to the server, so a user could build a client of their own.

Each RPC is given a unique transaction id by the client. The server returns
it, so the client can match replies with requests.

16.8 NFS protocols

Linux uses Version 2 of NFS. The procedures provided can be grouped into five classes: those which create and remove subdirectories, those which create and remove directory entries, those which lookup directory contents, those which deal with attributes of files, and finally those dealing with reading and writing. Functionally, these procedures are almost identical to the Unix system services for manipulating files.

Subdirectories

There are two procedures for creating and removing subdirectories.

MKDIR

Given a file handle for a directory, and a directory name, it will create a subdirectory with that name, if it does not already exist. It returns a handle to the new directory.

RMDIR

Given a file handle for a directory, and the name of a subdirectory in it, this procedure will remove the subdirectory.

Manipulate directory entries

There are five procedures which manipulate the entries in a directory.

CREATE

Given a file handle for a directory, and a filename, it will create a file with that name, in the specified directory, if it does not already exist. It returns a handle to the file.

LINK

Given a file handle for an object, and the location in the file system where a link is to be created (specified by a file handle for a directory, and a name for the link), it will create a hard link, and return a handle to it.

SYMLINK

Given a file handle for a directory, a filename, and a string containing the symbolic link data, it will create a new symbolic link, with that name. It returns a file handle to the entry.

RENAME

Given a file handle for a directory, as well as old and new names for an object in that directory, this procedure will rename it.

REMOVE

Given a file handle for a directory, and the name of a file in it, this procedure will remove it. As NFS is stateless, this can actually remove a file held open by the same, or another, client. Any further attempts to access it will return a 'stale file handle' error.

Lookup directory contents

Pathnames are parsed by the client, step by step, each part involving a separate RPC, which returns a file handle for the current part of the pathname. This handle is then used in the next RPC. To improve efficiency here, a cache of name to file handle mappings is maintained by the client.

LOOKUP

Given a file handle corresponding to a directory, and a filename, it will search the directory for a file of that name. If found, it returns a handle for that file. It has to be called once for each component of a pathname.

READLINK

When given a file handle corresponding to a symbolic link, this procedure returns the ASCII string corresponding to the link, i.e. the absolute pathname.

READDIR

Given a file handle for a directory, this returns a linked list of directory entries. Each entry contains a name, a file identifier or inode number, and a cookie. These can be used in subsequent calls to READDIR, to obtain further entries. The cookie specifies to the server where the last read finished. There is also a flag returned which indicates when the end of the directory has been reached.

File attributes

There are three procedures which deal with file attributes.

GETATTR

This procedure returns the attributes associated with the object corresponding to the supplied file handle. The information is cached by the client daemon in the inode. The `attrtimeo` field in the `struct nfs_inode_info` determines

when these cached attributes become invalid. For files, this is normally 3 seconds; for directories (which tend to change less frequently) it is 30 seconds. This procedure is only called when the attributes are stale, to refresh them.

SETATTR

This sets the specified attributes for the object corresponding to the supplied file handle.

PATHCONF

Given a file handle for a file or directory, it returns information about a configurable limit, or the presence of an option, associated with that file or directory. An example would be the maximum length of a pathname component, or whether the server is case sensitive with regard to names.

Read and write

These are the procedures that do the actual work.

READ

This procedure is passed a `struct` containing three parameters: a file handle, an offset, and a byte count. It returns the appropriate data. Note that the offset has to be set each time, it is not remembered.

WRITE

This procedure is passed a `struct` containing four parameters: a file handle, an offset, and a byte count, as for READ. Then there is the data to be written.

16.9 NFS version 3

An extended version of NFS was issued in 1994. It has a number of new procedures.

MKNOD

Given a file handle for a directory, a filename, and an indication of the type of special file, e.g. character special, block special, named pipe, it will create an entry for that type in the specified directory. It returns a file handle.

ACCESS

This procedure checks if the user has the specified access to the file corresponding to the supplied file handle.

READDIR

With Version 2 of this procedure, the cookie specified where to begin the next read. If the contents of the directory changed in the meantime, this cookie would be invalid. Version 3 now returns a cookie verifier, the value of which is changed each time the contents of the directory changes. It is possible for the client to detect such changes, and begin reading the directory again.

READDIRPLUS

This procedure is similar to READDIR, but it returns full information about each entry, including a file handle for each. It is provided for efficient implementation of `ls -l`.

FSSTAT

Given a file handle for a mount point, it returns usage statistics about the file system this handle represents, e.g. free space, free inodes, etc.

FSINFO

Given a file handle for a mount point, it returns non-volatile file system state information, such as the number of inodes, as well as general information about the NFS implementation on the server, such as the maximum size of a read or write.

WRITE

This procedure has been extended to include asynchronous writing. There is also a commit request to go with this. There is one extra parameter, the `stable` flag. If this is set to FILE_SYNC, then the server must write the data to disk before returning. This is synchronous writing, which can be slow.

If the flag is set to UNSTABLE, then the server may return after writing none, some, or all of the data to disk. This is asynchronous writing. But it does let the client know, by returning a result value. If this is FILE_SYNC, then all of the data has been written to disk. If the value returned is UNSTABLE, then at least some of the data had not been written when the reply was sent.

It also returns a cookie, which the client can use to check whether the server has rebooted, and lost state, since the last write. This cookie value changes each time the server reboots.

COMMIT

This procedure is sent a file handle, an offset within the file, and a byte count. It flushes that range of bytes to disk. The server acknowledges a commit by specifying just what has been written, so that the client can determine if any writes are missing.

16.10   Caching with NFS

To achieve an acceptable level of performance, caching on both the server and
client machines is essential. But this introduces consistency problems. A stale
cache may be read. An updated cache may not be written back.

Server caching

The server reads ahead from the disk into its memory cache, to avoid the
overhead of repeated reads from a disk for the same file. When write requests
come in over the network, it makes the changes in memory; it may or may not
write them to disk immediately. But it will eventually flush its cache, typically
every 30 seconds.

To handle non-idempotent operations, such as write, the server maintains
a duplicate request cache. This caches all requests, along with the transaction
id. It checks this cache when a request comes in. If there is a copy of the
request already in the cache, it returns the previous reply. Such a request may
result from a lost acknowledgement. It needs to keep all requests for the most
recent few seconds.

Client caching

On the client, caching is managed by the nfsiod daemon. This transfers data
to and from the server in blocks of 8K. It always reads ahead one block. It does
delayed writing; only when the entire 8K is full is it written to the server.

Cached pages are dirty if the i_mtime and read_cache_mtime fields of
the inode do not have the same values. Such pages are flushed at intervals,
typically 30 seconds. This timeout is triggered if the read_cache_jiffies
field of the nfs_inode_info is more than 30 seconds behind the current time.
So the server is always less than 30 seconds out of date. However nfsiod
writes back directory blocks as soon as they have been modified.

Clients cannot determine whether a file is shared or not. So there is not
absolute consistency between all clients caching the same file. One possible
solution is to send the time the file was last modified with each block from the
server. This is the value stored in the i_mtime field of the server inode. Any
locally cached blocks with an older timestamp are then invalidated.

On read access, the client need only ask the server for the last modification
time, using GETATTR. It then knows whether its cache is stale or not. If the
client has checked in the last few seconds, it takes a chance. But clock skew
between client and server could make this of doubtful value.

16.11   File locking with NFS

Because NFS is stateless, it cannot implement locking itself. This is done using
two other servers.

Lock manager

First of all, there is the lock manager, lockd. This is RPC program number 100021, and can use either TCP or UDP. The lock manager runs on all machines, both clients and servers. At user level, locking a range of bytes is done in the usual way, using fcntl(). But the NFS client redirects the request to the local lockd, which forwards it to lockd on the server.

The network lock manager provides four functions.

TEST

This checks whether the specified lock is available to the client or not.

LOCK

This is the standard request to establish a lock on a range of bytes in a file. If the lock cannot be granted immediately, the reply will indicate this. But the server will remember the request, and as soon as it becomes possible to grant the lock, it will do so, and notify the client lock manager.

CANCEL

The client lock manager can order the server to cancel an outstanding request for a lock.

UNLOCK

This routine removes the specified lock.

All of these functions are synchronous. There are also asynchronous functions which achieve the same results. With these, the client does not block waiting for a reply; there is no reply. When it is ready, the server makes an RPC to the client. This is known as 'call back'.

The lockd daemon makes no attempt to detect deadlocks. It only implements advisory locking.

Status manager

If the lock manager on the server were to crash, then it would lose all state; when it recovers, it could give out conflicting locks. To prevent this, there is a second daemon, statd, RPC program number 100024, which can use either TCP or UDP. This runs on both clients and servers, and monitors their status, when requested.

So the actual procedure is more complicated than described in the previous subsection. As well as requesting a lock from lockd, the NFS client also informs its local statd, which creates a file corresponding to the server name in the directory /etc/sm. It also informs statd on the server machine, which creates

a file corresponding to the client name, on its machine. The NFS client does not reply to the local requesting process until both lockd and statd have replied.

The statd daemon really only has any effect when it comes up again after a crash. The server daemon reads its /etc/sm directory, and notifies lockd on all client sites that are recorded as holding locks on that server. Such a client promptly resubmits requests for previously granted locks. If the client lockd cannot reinstall a lock after the server restarts (for example, some other process acquires it), it sends the client process a SIGLOST signal.

When a client comes up again after a crash, its statd daemon reads the names of any servers it was dealing with, from /etc/sm. It then notifies the server statd daemon that it has crashed, and restarted. This passes the notification on to the server lockd, which cancels all locks held by that client.

16.12 Summary

1. A distributed file system allows a file on one machine appear as if it actually existed on another machine. It consists of a file server, and a client. A user makes normal system calls, which are translated to remote calls to a server.

   Such a distributed file system can provide stateful or stateless service. It should also be transparent to a user—it should look just like a conventional file system.

   It must be possible to identify each file in the system, in a way that is location independent. A typical solution is to allow remote directories to be mounted as part of a local directory tree.

2. Caching of files on the client is used to reduce network traffic, and improve performance. The major drawback with it is the problem of cache consistency.

3. Multiple copies of the same file may be kept on different servers, to increase reliability, and to distribute the workload over the system. With writable files, such replication introduces problems of transparency and consistency. Various mechanisms have been developed, such as read one/write all, available copies, quorum based, and primary copy replication.

   If a fault partitions a network, both parts may be able to function. Inconsistencies must be resolved at repair time.

4. OSF DCE has its own distributed file system, designed for large networks. It provides directory services, to manage the global namespace. The file system uses a stateful protocol, and Kerberos style authentication. It relies heavily on client caching, and ensures cache consistency by using tokens, issued by the server. These can be revoked, and also have expiry times.

5. The Sun network file system is the most commonly used distributed file system in the Unix environment. It attempts to emulate Unix semantics, but there are some slight differences. It provides a certain amount of, though not total, transparency.

6. The connection between client and server is set up using the mount protocol, which inserts a remote directory into a local directory tree. After that, reads and writes are implemented by the NFS protocols themselves.

7. The file server daemon is called nfsd. The client daemon is nfsiod. Both can be multi-threaded.

8. The NFS protocols deal with subdirectories, lookup and manipulate directory contents, and handle attributes of files, as well as reading and writing files.

9. Version 3 of NFS has introduced an asynchronous WRITE procedure, as well as a COMMIT procedure.

10. The client relies heavily on caching, to reduce the overhead of network communication. Because clients cannot determine whether a file is shared or not, there can be discrepancies.

11. There is also a network lock manager, lockd, which is not strictly part of NFS. It uses the status monitor, statd, to synchronise client and server state after a crash.

16.13 Discussion questions

1. It would be possible to introduce a third element into a distributed file system, namely a directory server, which would keep track of which files are where. Discuss the advantages and disadvantages of this.

2. Discuss the advantages and the disadvantages of stateful versus stateless servers.

3. How could migration transparency be implemented in a distributed file system?

4. If two clients have the same file cached, using write through caching, how can they interfere with each other? What solutions are available for this problem?

5. Discuss the advantages and disadvantages of client caching on a per process basis, or on a system-wide basis.

6. Caching in a distributed file system has definite similarities with demand paged virtual memory. Discuss.

7. With available copies, or quorum based, replication, an unavailable server will not be written to, and so becomes inconsistent. How can this inconsistency be remedied?

8. With NFS, could a client mount the same remote directory at two different points in its own directory tree? Why would it want to do this?

9. An NFS client must give full information about the file at each request, as the server is stateless. In Unix, this information is provided once, at open(). How then can it be said to emulate Unix semantics?

10. In what circumstances would a hard mount be advisable, rather than a soft
    mount?

11. Can NFS use the directory lookup cache provided by the virtual file system,
    or does it have to maintain its own cache?

12. NFS uses 'cookie verifiers' to assure the client that a directory has not
    changed since a previous request. But it is a stateless protocol. Why the
    need for these verifiers then?

13. When a user process does a read(), an NFS client checks whether its cache
    is stable or not, by calling GETATTR on the server. This returns the last
    modification time of the file, which can be compared to the timestamp on
    the cached version. As the client is making an RPC anyway, would it not
    be just as well for it to do a READ?

Fault tolerance and security **17**

In this final chapter we consider how computer systems, including distributed systems, deal with threats to their correct functioning. Such threats can come from two sources. All computer systems will develop faults at some time or another. But there may also be deliberate attempts to cause the system to malfunction, and this is the area of security.

17.1 Fault tolerance

A fault is a malfunction, the cause of an error. It can be a hardware or a software fault. It has to be expected that even the best system will suffer a fault from time to time. What is important is how well a system can deal with faults when they occur.

Types of fault

A fault can be transient, intermittent, or permanent.

- A transient fault occurs once only. It is usually a hardware fault, such as a random cosmic ray flipping a bit in memory. There is not much that can be done about identifying the fault, and repairing it, as it does not occur again. The emphasis is on detecting it, and recovering from it.

- An intermittent fault occurs again and again, at unpredictable intervals. It is the most difficult type of fault to diagnose, as you never know when it will occur again. It can be a failing hardware component, or a bug in software.

- A permanent fault is just that—something is broken, and must be replaced. This can be a hardware component, or a piece of code which is not doing what it is supposed to do.

Detecting faults

The first requirement for a fault tolerant system is that it be able to detect a fault. This should be done as soon as possible, as the longer it goes undetected, the more errors will be caused, reducing the chance of identifying the underlying fault.

The general approach to this is to use redundancy. Data faults can be detected by using information redundancy, such as check-bits or checksums. They can indicate that a data item has been corrupted. A step up from this is to use error correcting codes. There is a greater overhead involved here, but they make it possible to recreate the correct value.

Another possibility is to use time redundancy, by repeating the operation. For example, a file can be read twice, and the two readings compared. If they do not match exactly, we know that an error has occurred. This more than doubles the time involved. Sometimes it is possible to use physical redundancy, by installing extra equipment, e.g. duplicate processing on two different CPUs.

Recovering from faults

When a fault tolerant system detects a fault, it either fails gracefully, or masks it. Graceful failure means that it informs the user, notifies any other processes it is communicating with, closes all I/O streams it has open, returns memory, and stops the process. Masking a fault would include retrying an operation on a different CPU, attempting to contact a different server on a network, using a different software routine, or using an alternative source for data. At the very least, faults should be confined to the process in which they occur. They must not spread to other processes or to the operating system itself.

17.2 Faults in file systems

The user of a file system must be confident that the files will still be there when they are required. Disks do fail, particularly floppies. The following are some common faults.

- Bad Read. One or more sectors cannot be read. At best, the user loses part of a file. At worst, a whole directory, or the inode table, can be lost.

- Bad Write. Information is written to the wrong sector. Chains of pointers can be corrupted. One file can be linked into another, or even worse, into the free list, resulting in chaos.

- When a system uses a disk buffer cache, a power failure can leave the disk in an inconsistent state.

- Viruses can cause corruption, or partial or even total loss of data.

- There will always be faults attributable to humans, intentional or not.

Security features

In designing safeguards against these faults, the following factors have to be balanced:

- What is the mean time between failure (MTBF) for the hardware? In other words, what are the odds against the system crashing?

- What is the operational cost of making backup copies? If it only requires a click on an icon, or can be done automatically, then why not do it? But in some systems it may mean shutting the computer down.

- What is the cost of loss of information? The loss of the latest version of a student program is very different from the loss of banking information.

One hundred per cent protection requires that everything be recorded in duplicate, or even in triplicate. This involves two or three similar drives, all writing in unison. Reads are also duplicated, and compared.

Another security feature is read after write, sometimes called verify. This involves a heavy time overhead.

Backups

Generally some degree of loss can be tolerated, and the policy adopted is regular backups. One approach to this is to do a total backup at fixed intervals. The entire file system is copied to tape, or to another disk. This may imply significant down-time. If done on a daily basis, then some time during the night is best. If done on a weekly basis, then the weekend is typically chosen.

Because the foregoing system copies everything, and many files are unchanged over long periods, a scheme of incremental backups has been developed. This works on a time cycle, which may be a week, a month, or more. Such a cycle starts with a total backup. Then at each successive period, only those files that have changed since the last backup are saved. This can take place in parallel with normal processing, the only restrictions being that a user cannot write to a file while it is being backed up, and the system cannot back up a file while it is open for write. The file is marked to indicate the time of backup.

Recovery

Recovery from a crash is easy when using a total backup. The disk is reformatted or replaced, and the backup tape is copied to the disk. We then have a copy of the file system as it was a day, a week, or a month ago.

When using the incremental system, the procedure is more complicated. First the most recent incremental tape is loaded, and all files and directories on it are copied to the disk. At this stage we have a partial file system, containing all of the files created or changed since the previous backup, and all directories referring to these files.

The next most recent incremental tape is then loaded. This is first scanned for directories. Any directory on this tape that has already been restored is ignored, as the version on disk is more recent. If a directory is not on the disk, then it is restored.

The next step is to scan that tape for files. For each file, if it is already on the disk, then it is ignored, as the copy on disk is more recent. If it is not on the disk, but is referenced in a directory on the disk, this means that it was unchanged between backups, this version on tape is the most recent version, so it is restored. If it is not on the disk, and is not referenced in any directory on the disk, this means that it has been deleted between backups, so it can be ignored.

This whole procedure is repeated for every partial tape, back to the total backup. Such rebuilding can proceed in parallel with the normal use of the system, if required.

17.3 Faults in distributed systems

Distributed systems involve a number of machines, and a communications infrastructure which can be spread over quite a wide area. Hence by their nature such systems are more prone to faults than stand-alone machines. But these same characteristics can be used to ensure that the system as a whole can survive faults. With a multiplicity of machines, a distributed system can be designed so that faulty or non-functioning elements of the system, whether processors, disk storage, or communications, can be replaced by other, fully functioning elements.

Failure

A distributed system may fail in a range of possible ways, so all of these must be known. A particular machine may fail, a particular link in the network may fail, or a message may be lost. It is certainly not easy to decide which of these has actually happened.

Different failures manifest themselves in different ways. Silent failures are when the system does not respond any more. In general it is not possible to distinguish between slow response due to overloading, or a server being down. The common approach is to use timeouts and retransmission. A so-called Byzantine failure is worse. In this case the server appears to be working, but it is in fact supplying false or garbled responses.

A system must first of all be able to detect failure. This can be done by each machine broadcasting 'I am up' messages at fixed intervals. If such a message is not received within a particular time span, then it can be assumed that machine is down. In such a case, all the other machines in the distributed system must be notified. It may be necessary to reconfigure logical rings, or elect a new coordinator.